AMERICAN
POPULAR CULTURE

Reference Sources in the Humanities Series

James Rettig, Series Editor

AMERICAN POPULAR CULTURE

A Guide to the Reference Literature

Frank W. Hoffmann

1995
Libraries Unlimited, Inc.
Englewood, Colorado

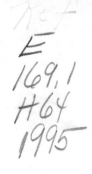

LIBRARIES UNLIMITED, INC.
P.O. Box 6633
Englewood, CO 80155-6633
1-800-237-6124

Library of Congress Cataloging-in-Publication Data

Hoffmann, Frank W., 1949-
   American popular culture : a guide to the reference literature /
Frank W. Hoffmann.
   xvi, 286 p. 17x25 cm.
   Includes bibliographical references and index.
   ISBN 1-56308-142-3
   1. Popular culture--United States--Bibliography. 2. Reference
books--Popular culture--Bibliography. I. Title.
Z1361.C6H64 1995
[E169.1]
016.973--dc20   94-29794
                                                   CIP

Contents

Chapter 11—Special Collections *(continued)*

Chapter 12—Societies and Associations 197

Chapter 13—Journals *(continued)*

Introduction

Defining the Popular Culture Field

Any attempt at formulating a meaningful definition of popular culture is fraught with pitfalls. This is caused in part by the interdisciplinary nature of the field; the majority of its components have long possessed their own identity. In addition, the intellectual bias of many within the formal educational establishment has retarded the development of the genre. Its relationship to mass production constructs as well as its sheer pervasiveness in the public mind would seem to go far in explaining its cool reception among academics and cultural elitists.

As more and more scholars have come to recognize popular culture as a barometer, mirror, and monument of the world around them,[1] the genre has been accorded increasingly greater prominence—through publications, course offerings, collections in libraries and so forth—in those settings involving learning and information exchange. Therefore, scholars and educators have expended a correspondingly greater effort to delineate the popular culture field to maximize its utility.

Ray Browne, founder of the Popular Culture Association and—until his retirement in 1992—curator of the leading archive devoted to popular culture materials, has set forth perhaps the most succinct definition of the field: "...all the experiences in life shared by people in common, generally, though not necessarily, disseminated by the mass media."[2] He has further clarified this statement by suggesting the popular culture is "all those elements of life which are not narrowly intellectual or creatively elitist," including the spoken and printed word, sounds, pictures, objects, and artifacts.

In short, popular culture—standing clearly apart from elitist elements, encompasses *popular, mass,* and *folk* components. Figure 1 highlights the key areas of popular culture as well as their relationship with popular culture as a whole.

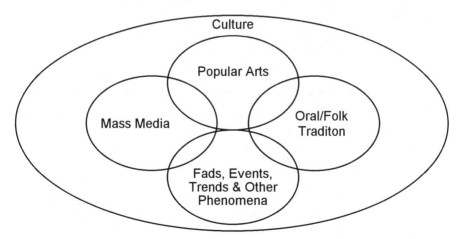

In the sense that popular culture might be viewed as "unofficial culture," or "the culture of the non-elite," it has existed ever since the beginnings of civilization itself. However, the bulk of information available to us regarding the values and interests of ordinary people before the Modern Era (a period ushered in by a complex mix of socioeconomic developments such as the Renaissance, the Industrial Revolution, and the rise of democratic forms of government) was disseminated by means of the oral tradition. Generally, these ordinary folk were denied access to the small but growing information base. The literate elite rarely considered the activities of the lower classes worthy of space in their corpus of writings. Accordingly, the popular culture legacy from the pre-Modern Era has been relatively small.

The rise of the mass media—beginning with the invention of the printing press (generally attributed in the Western world to Gutenberg in the mid-fifteenth century), and followed by successive waves of new communications media such as high-circulation newspapers and magazines, the telephone, the phonograph, radio, television, the cinema and computers—rendered it possible to disseminate increasingly greater amounts of information, including popular materials. Hence, the inevitability of its growing use by educators, librarians, and other members of the cultural elite as a means of providing a more complete picture of our society, both past and present.

Libraries and Popular Culture Resources

In a recent article for *USA Today*, Patricia Schuman, then president of the American Library Association, addressed the dire straits facing "all types and sizes of libraries across the country" and other problems and potential repercussions for the public at large:

> ...what [the library], its contents, and the people who run it represent is one of the most fundamental rights we have as American citizens; the right to information, knowledge, and all the benefits that this knowledge and information deliver—the right to know. The spotlight must be turned on this right because we are in serious danger of losing it; this is crucial to an informed, just, and equitable society; without it, we are far too vulnerable to the power of those who would like to abridge the right to make our own decisions...[3]

While there are many socioeconomic forces behind this dilemma, a significant degree of responsibility would appear to lie with librarians themselves. Their collection development policies and service priorities have played a role in rendering libraries irrelevant to many individuals. Don Roberts was an early voice calling for material in libraries to reflect the needs and interest of their users—and potential users—for them to remain a vital force in contemporary society. In an article appearing in *Library Journal* over a generation ago, he cited the failure of the profession to display much sensitivity to the acquisition—and use—of popular culture materials:

> We have a negative commitment to the popular culture of our society, even though this culture (especially in the music industry) is of the highest is has been for many, many generations. The shocking, repetitious print equivalent stuff pouring out of the publishing houses is reviewed, purchased,

and processed toward oblivion on the shelves regardless, while the Number One recorded literature is not even considered! And so we continue to run the vestiges of a defunct Western humanism and post-Renaissance classicism (typified in a way by the Caldecott/Newbery awards and book selection mystiques) on the hapless, cynical library dropout taxpayers and their children.[4]

Other librarians and educators have echoed Roberts' call to action, including Gordon Stevenson, Wayne Wiegand, Carlos Haen, B. Lee Cooper, E. K. Dortmund, William Schurk, Haynes McMullen, and Jay Dailey. These pioneers—as well as a new wave of disciples over the past decade—have noted the beneficial aspects of using popular culture materials within a library, such as

1. Aesthetic enjoyment. Involvement with the popular arts can play a significant role in the fostering of lifelong leisure habits.

2. Increased social awareness. Various popular culture phenomena have played a role in heightening our collective social responsibilities and ethical values to a degree not generally characteristic of rank-and-file organizations and institutions.

3. A more comprehensive approach to formal education. The incorporation of all levels of social and cultural expression—the *popular*, the *mass*, and *folk*—into a structured learning context provides a dimension vital to the fullest understanding of a given event, concept, movement, and so forth.

4. Its appeal to students and patrons. The relevance of popular culture concepts and materials to our everyday lives renders them indispensable as a means of heightening motivation and involvement in both learning and the information dissemination process.

The widespread use of popular culture resources within a library setting, however, brings a number of problems. In the area of selection and acquisitions, these problems include:

1. An overwhelming abundance of materials to choose from. Video and audio tapes, genre paperbacks, comic books, trading cards, compact discs, etc.—retail shelves are spilling over with the faddish fruits of our throwaway, capitalistic economy.

2. The general lack of knowledge of these materials on the part of librarians.

3. The limited number of review sources, the majority of which are non-library in orientation.

4. The biases—as manifested on a number of levels: format, cultural elitism, intellectual freedom, and so forth—of both librarians and their clientele regarding these resources.

5. the rapidity with which popular culture materials go out-of-print (a situation owing less to their intrinsic value than to a highly competitive marketplace).

6. The limited avenues of distribution—at lease from a librarian's perspective, given their predilection for using jobbers for acquisitions—for popular culture materials.

The fields of maintenance and technical processing are also beset by considerable dilemmas in the implementation of popular culture materials, including

1. The lack of durability characterizing their physical construction.

2. The high degree of appeal characterizing these materials (which intensifies the likelihood of theft, mutilation, and so forth).

3. The varying physical character—shape, size, etc.—of these materials (which complicates the process of storage and arrangement).

4. The lack of focus shown by widely employed subject-heading schemes in dealing with popular culture resources.

Popular Culture Coverage by the Reference Literature

Despite the multiplicity of problems posed by popular culture artifacts themselves, there exists a significant number of reference sources—developed along traditional lines such as dictionaries, handbooks, etc.—which do a more than adequate job of covering the fields falling under the popular culture umbrella. While many libraries may have, in fact, resisted the wholesale incorporation of popular culture formats such as comic books, feature films on video, and popular music recordings, they nevertheless tend to carry information resources devoted to these—and other—primary sources materials; e.g., comic book price guides, movie handbooks, cinema and music biographies, discographies, etc. Even those reference tools of a less traditional nature (e.g., companion volumes and concordances to relatively obscure—at least to librarians and educators—genre fiction works) which were once relegated to specialty retail outlets, are now available in libraries to an increasingly greater degree.

The resources comprising *American Popular Culture: A Guide to the Reference Literature* have been culled from essentially the same sources a searcher might employ in accessing more mainstream topics. Catalogs and union lists of library holdings supplied a large number of titles for preview as well as assisted in bibliographic control. While some established guides to the reference literature (e.g., Eugene Sheehy's *Guide to Reference Books*, the Walford set) offered poor coverage, other tools provided a wealth of valuable entries, most notably regularly updated retrospective guides to the literature (e.g., *American Reference Books Annual*), commercial bibliographies (e.g., *Books in Print, Cumulative Book Index*), periodical indexes, and current review journals (encompassing professional, trade, scholarly, and mass circulation titles).[5] Libraries of all types presently include these lead-in tools in their respective collections as well as some of the information sources documenting popular culture found within this work.

It appears likely, in time, that an increasingly greater number of popular culture materials will become available through American library collections. Until that void is more adequately filled, however, this work will serve to assist librarians, scholars, educators, students, and other enthusiasts in identifying those sources that delineate various popular culture topics with the greatest degree of thoroughness, authoritativeness, timeliness, and accuracy. Resources have not been limited by format; automation (on-line and laser optical databases, microcomputer software) and audiovisual titles complement print materials in cases where the previously noted criteria are met and efficient (i.e., random) access to their respective contents is possible.

How to Use the Work

The reference sources in this compilation have been chosen not only according to traditional evaluative criteria (e.g., quality, subject coverage, timeliness), but also for their availability via libraries and purchase (through jobbers, publishers, and retailers). The book's entries provide sufficient bibliographical data to enable the user to readily locate a particular source in both library and commercial catalogs.

The main text of *American Popular Culture* is arranged alphabetically by broad subject or genre heading. More specialized topics are also organized alphabetically within these headings, and further subdivided by last name of author. This multifaceted layout can be readily discerned by means of browsing through the table of contents. The text includes many cross-references to assist in accessing the appropriate heading. Author/title and subject indexes provide additional approaches to the location of desired citations.

The compiler attempted to include not only titles of high quality, but also those of relatively recent vintage. The cut-off date for inclusions was mid-1993. In a few cases, the compiler was unable to obtain a first-hand copy of titles cited in this book. However, due to the widely recognized value of these works, the compiler relied on the critical evaluations in the review literature and, in rare instances, the assessments of colleagues.

Abbreviations

adv.	advertising
bibl.	bibliography
comp.	compiler
discog.	discography
ed.	edition
filmog.	filmography
illus.	illustrations
LC	Library of Congress number
n.d.	no date
p.	pages
pap.	paperback
vol.	volume
vols.	volumes

Notes

1. Marshall Fishwick. *Popular Culture and the Expanding Consciousness*, edited by Ray Browne. New York: Wiley, 1973. p. 40.

2. Ray Browne, ed. *Popular Culture and the Expanding Consciousness*. New York: Wiley, 1973. p. 6.

3. Patricia Glass Schuman. "Vanishing Act: The Collapse of America's Libraries," *USA Today*. 121:2566 (July 1992) 11.

4. Don Roberts. "Listen, Miss, Mrs., Mr. Librarian," *Library Journal* (November 15, 1970) 30.

Note that networking with collectors and other popular culture enthusiasts—including some academics—has been invaluable in fleshing out many of the subgenre categories.

Chapter 1

General References

Collecting—General

Handbooks

1. Bernardo, Karen, comp. **The Vestal Press Resource Catalogue.** Vestal, NY: Vestal, 1993. 77p. Illus., pap. ISBN 1-87511-11-8.

Vestal Press has enjoyed a well-deserved reputation as a leading resource for collectors and hobbyists in the special-interest areas of mechanical music, pianos and player pianos, reed organs, carousels, slot machines, jukeboxes, theater pipe organs, picture postcard histories, radios, phonographs and recordings, and movie memorabilia. Following years of requests for resources as well as information about organizations and the repair, location, etc., of collectibles, the company decided to publish its own guidebook. Although not complete and loosely organized (it has no table of contents to clarify its classified arrangement), the work provides a fascinating array of practical information, including, publisher catalogs, record ads, annotated bibliographies, listings of manufacturers of collectibles, listings of schools and organizations involved with the aforementioned fields. A concise index arranged by interest areas assists in accessing the text. An order form for cited books is also included.

Collecting—Cards, Non-Sports

Handbooks

2. Benjamin, Christopher, and Dennis W. Eckes. **The Sport Americana Price Guide to the Non-Sports Cards.** Part Two. 3rd ed. Cleveland, OH: Edgewater, 1988. Illus., adv.

This tool is billed as the definitive guide to all popular non-sports American tobacco and bubblegum cards. Illustrations and prices for wrappers are also included. The artifacts covered all fall within the 1961-1987 period.

Collecting—Foods and Eating Habits

Encyclopedias

3. Bowers, Q. David. **The Moxie Encyclopedia.** Vestal, NY: Vestal, 1985. 760p. Illus., pap. LC 85-5325. ISBN 0-911572-43-0.

Although now sold primarily in the New England area, this soft drink enjoyed a national prominence on a par with that of Coca-Cola earlier in the century. All facets of the company—its history, the sales gimmicks it employed, and its cultural impact—are covered.

1

Handbooks

4.   Goldstein, Shelly. **Goldstein's Coca-Cola Collectibles ID & PG.** 128p. Illus., pap. ISBN 0-89145-462-4. Available from A.M.R. (206-659-6434) and Jukebox Collector (515-265-8324).

Printed entirely on enamel stock in full color, the work wins kudos for overall attractiveness. The assortment of Coca-Cola collectibles included here (plates, calendars, signs, bottles, toys, etc.), although not complete, is representative of the company's output.

5.   Petretti, Alan. **Petretti's Coca-Cola Collectibles Price Guide.** 6th ed. Radnor, PA: Chilton, 1991. 408p. Illus. ISBN 0-87069-627-0. Available from A.M.R. (206-689-6434) and Jukebox Collector (515-265-8324).

The tool includes an exhaustive collection of photos (numbering in the thousands) and descriptions of the advertising and production material used by the Coca-Cola Company and its many bottlers. The current value of these items is noted.

6.   Vehling, Bill, and Michael Hunt. **Pepsi-Cola Collectibles (with Prices).** Gas City, IN: L-W Promotions, n.d. 48p. Illus., pap.

An informative, albeit downsized, equivalent of the Wilson guide to Coke collectibles. Although Pepsi has always lagged behind the Atlanta-based giant with respect to the licensing of promotional merchandise, a wide variety of materials can nevertheless be identified (e.g., trays, playing cards, letterheads, records, tin signs).

7.   Walters, Jeff. **Classic Soda Machines.** 220p. Illus., pap. Available from A.M.R. (206-659-6434) and Jukebox Collector (515-265-8324).

Billed as "the most comprehensive reference book and price guide of soda machines ever published," the book features over 180 of the most collectible models, including Coca-Cola, Dr. Pepper, Pepsi-Cola, Royal Crown, and 7-Up. Over 160 pages include full-color illustrations.

8.   Wilson, Al, and Helen Wilson. **The Coca-Cola Book.** Atglen, PA: Schiffer, 1994. 256p. Illus., pap. LC 93-87056.

The book documents the huge variety of sales devices, licensed toys, advertising gimmicks, and related items created by the Coca-Cola Company. It provides practical information on the buying and selling of these materials. The first-rate illustrations—most in color—are useful for identification purposes.

Collecting—Musical Instruments

Encyclopedias

9.   Bowers, Q. David. **Encyclopedia of Automatic Musical Instruments.** Vestal, NY: Vestal, 1972. 1008p. Illus. ISBN 0-911572-08-2.

Winner of the ALA Reference Book Award for 1972, the book covers thousands of types and models of music boxes, player pianos, orchestrions, band organs, fair organs, reproducing pianos, and all other variations of automatic music machines produced in the United States and Europe over the years. Histories of builders and inventors in the mechanical music field are also included in this comprehensive source. The text is profusely illustrated with photographs and advertisements. In short, an invaluable guide to the purchase, sale, and maintenance of these instruments.

Collecting—Phonographs and Recordings

Bibliographies, Discographies, etc.

10. Dethlefson, Ronald, and Ray Wile. **Edison Disc Artists and Records, 1919-1929.** Bakersfield, CA: Ronald Dethlefson, n.d. 104p. Illus. Perfect-bound. Available from publisher (805-872-1530).

A compilation of all Edison Diamond Discs, LPs and 78s, this tool lists hundreds of Edison disc records by title, artist, and catalog number. It also traces the music and recording technology of the 1910s and 1920s. The illustrations (numbering more than fifty) have been taken from original catalogs and in-house publications. A 68-page portfolio of catalog reproductions and disc liner notes is also included.

11. Fagan, Ted, and William R. Moran. **Encyclopedic Discography of Victor Records, Volumes I and II.** 2 vols. Westport, CT: Greenwood, 1991. 393p.; 702p. ISBN 0-313-23003-X; 0-313-25320-X.

These two volumes, based on the original recording ledgers of the company—and augmented by extensive research in rare Victor publications, catalogs, bulletins, and correspondence with collectors, archivists, and others—represent the only systematic cataloging of these rare recordings attempted to date. Volume I, subtitled "The Pre-Matrix Series," covers the Consolidated Talking Machine Company, Eldridge R. Johnson, and the Victor Talking Machine Company, January 12, 1900 to April 23, 1903. It includes a special appendix, "The Victor Talking Machine Company," by B. L. Aldridge. Volume II, subtitled "The Matrix Series," covers the period from April 1903 to 1907, when the Matrix Numbering System had reached number 4999.

Handbooks

12. Adams, Frank. **Jukeboxes 1900-1992, Volume I.** Arlington, WA: A.M.R., n.d. 182p. Illus. Spiral-bound with plastic covers. ISBN 1-56642-000-8. Available from Jukebox Collector (515-265-8324).

The book concentrates on the multitude of manufacturers who produced jukeboxes other than the widely covered big four: Wurlitzer, Seeburg, Rock-ola, and Rowe-AMI. Coverage includes Edison and several other phonographs of the era; coin-operated cylinder machines such as the Autophone and Kalamazoo; Link, Ristaucrat, Mills, Evans, Aireon, Filben, and others— more than ninety models and thirty-five companies in all. Illustrations—some in color—with informative captions and a price guide augment the text.

13. Ayliffe, Jerry. **An American Premium Guide to Jukeboxes and Slot Machines.** 3rd ed. Florence, AL: Books Americana, 1992. 350p. Illus. ISBN 0-89689-082-1. pa.

The volume provides identification data and price valuations for such jukebox manufacturers as Wurlitzer, Seeburg, Rock-ola, AMI, Mills, Fey, Caille, Jennings, Pace, Watling, Northwestern, Columbus, Advance, Leebold, and Master. It also covers gum balls, arcade, and trade stimulators.

14.   Botts, Rick. **A Complete Identification Guide to the Wurlitzer Jukebox.** Des Moines, IA: Jukebox Collector Magazine, 1992. 114p. Illus., pap. ISBN 0-912789-01-8. Available from A.M.R. Publishing (206-659-6434).

   The Wurlitzer jukeboxes from 1934-1984 are covered. The book's chronological arrangement and full-page illustrations render it easy to identify any particular model. The company directly cooperated in the project, providing both photos and reference data.

15.   Docks, Les. **American Premium Record Guide, 1900-1965; Identification and Value Guide to 78s, 45s, and LPs.** 4th ed. Florence, AL: Books Americana, 1993. 460p. Illus., pap.

   The book not only covers all record formats, but spans virtually all popular music genres, including jazz, big band swing, the blues, rhythm and blues, country and western, rock 'n' roll, and rockabilly. Arranged by artist (over 7,500 in all), the entries provide discographic information and price valuations geared to the collecting world. The text is interspersed with 1,500 photos of record labels to assist in identification.

16.   Lynch, Vincent. **American Jukebox—The Classic Years.** San Francisco: Chronicle, 1990. 120p. Illus., pap. ISBN 0-87701-7220; 0-87701-678-X pap. Available from A.M.R. (206-659-6434) and Jukebox Collector (515-265-8324).

   Nearly 100 full-color reproductions show vintage jukeboxes and advertising from the "classic era" between 1937-1948. The volume covers wall boxes, table models, and speakers in addition to floor versions. An appendix lists detailed information about each jukebox.

17.   Pearce, Chris. **Vintage Jukeboxes.** Arlington, WA: A.M.R.; Secaucus, NJ: Book Sales, 1988. 128p. Illus. ISBN 1-55521-323-5. Available from Jukebox Collector (515-265-8324).

   Focusing on the "Big Four" companies, the book traces the golden years during the 1940s and 1950s. A rich lode of information on the technical achievements, the design wars, and the marketing strategies of Wurlitzer, Rock-ola, AMI, and Seeburg. The full-color illustrations consist of display photos and advertisements of the machines.

Collecting—Mass Media—Radios

Handbooks

18.   Breed, Robert F. **Collecting Transistor Novelty Radio: A Value Guide.** Gas City, IN: L-W Promotions, n.d. 226p. Illus., pap. ISBN 0-89145-446-2.

   The work is essentially a collection of 525 photographs of radios in all shapes and sizes, divided into eleven categories. Price valuations have been provided for all models cited in the text.

Collecting—Mass Media—Television

Handbooks

19.   Hake, Ted. **Hake's Guide to TV Collectibles.** Radnor, PA: Chilton, 1990. 200p. Illus., pap. LC: 90-70399. ISBN 0-87069-571-1. Available from the publisher (800-345-1214).

This is a pictorial guide to more than 1,500 collectibles (e.g., lunch boxes, clothing, books, magazines, trading cards) related to nearly 200 of America's favorite television programs. It includes large dollops of television history in addition to price valuations. Hake, allegedly the nation's leading authority on television memorabilia, has provided the largest listing of these collectibles within one source.

Collecting—Sports and Recreation

Handbooks

20. Beckett, James. **The Sport Americana Football, Hockey, Basketball, and Boxing Card Price Guide.** 6th ed. Cleveland, OH: Edgewater, 1989. Unpaged. Illus., adv.

Advertised as the most comprehensive price guide and checklist ever issued on non-baseball sports cards, the work follows the format established by the author's *The Sport Americana Price Guide to Baseball Collectibles.* Entries are arranged by sport and subdivided first by brand name (in alphabetical order) and then chronologically by year of issue.

Collecting—Sports and Recreation—Baseball

Handbooks

21. Baker, Mark Allen. **Sports Collectors Digest Baseball Autograph Handbook: A Comprehensive Guide to Authentication and Valuation of Hall of Fame Autographs.** 2nd ed. Iola, WI: Krause, 1991. Unpaged. LC 89-83584. ISBN 0-87341-169-2.

Despite its misleading subtitle, the book provides general information spanning the entire baseball scene. It primarily provides pricing insights (e.g., discerning authentic autographs from counterfeits), essential collecting information, such as how to acquire autographs, and approaches to organizing, storing, and displaying collections.

22. Beckett, James. **The Sport Americana Baseball Card Price Guide.** Cleveland, OH: Edgewater, 1979-. Illus., adv., annual. Number 14, 1992 ed.: 816p.; ISBN 0-937424-51-X. Number 15, 1993 ed.: 1120p. ISBN 0-937424-65-X.

Widely recognized as the number one price guide among baseball card collectors and dealers, the work provides far more than price valuations (three levels: mint, very good-excellent, fair-good) for virtually all cards issued in the U.S. Also included are sections on "How to Collect," "Obtaining Cards," "Preserving Cards," "Hobby Nomenclature," "Determining Value," "Scarce Series," "Grading Your Cards," "Condition Guide," "Selling Your Cards," and "Additional Reading."

Arranged alphabetically by brand name, and subdivided chronologically by year of issue, entries include an illustration of a typical card in the series, a paragraph of background information about the series, and price valuations for individual cards (in numerical order) and the complete set in question.

The breadth of card companies included is astounding, ranging from majors such as Topps and Fleer to short runs by the likes of the American Tract Society, Granny Goose Foods, Pittsburgh's KDKA, and Morrell Meats. Prices are based upon input from dealers and collectors. The 100-odd ads included (many full page in size) represent a gold mine of buying and selling data.

23.   Beckett, James. **The Sport Americana Price Guide to Baseball Collectibles.** 2d ed. Cleveland, OH: Edgewater, 1988. Illus., adv.

Intended as a complement to the author's annual, *The Sport Americana Baseball Card Price Guide,* the work provides a comprehensive listing of box cards, coins, labels, Canadian cards, stamps, stickers, pins, and other baseball memorabilia. Individual entries, arranged in alphabetical order by name of category, include background information, checklist data, and price values per item.

24.   Florence, Gene. **Florence's Standard Baseball Card Price Guide.** 5th ed. Paducah, KY: Collector Books, 1992. 576p. Illus., pap. ISBN 0-89145-508-6.

Arranged alphabetically by card manufacturer, the tool's 60,000-plus entries include the early 1992 issues. Price breakdowns are given for "mint," "extra fine," and "very good" condition. Both front and back views of noteworthy cards are shown in a color section. This is a very useful source, but it lacks the authoritativeness and comprehensiveness of the Beckett series of price guides.

25.   Fritsch, Jeff, and Dennis W. Eckes. **The Sport Americana Baseball Card Team Checklist.** No. 6. Cleveland, OH: Edgewater, 1992. 320p. Illus., adv. ISBN 0-937424-60-9.

Billed as the most complete baseball and team checklist available, the book should prove invaluable to the collector specializing in an individual team. The respective big league players are organized under the team—or teams—for which they played. The card companies represented include Topps, Bowman, Donruss, Fleer, Score, Play Ball, Goudey, and Upper Deck (all issues up through the 1990 season).

26.   Kurowski, Jeff, ed. **Sports Collectors Digest Baseball Card Price Guide.** 7th ed. Iola, WI: Krause, 1993. 784p. Illus., adv., pap. ISBN 0-87341-233-8, BP07.

Despite a format that roughly approximates that of the Beckett guide, collectors and researchers may find it useful to compare the coverage of both, given omissions in each. For example, under "A," only Kurowski included Affiliated Food Rangers, Ames 20/20 Club, and Ault Foods, whereas the 1990 Beckett guide had exclusivity in listing the American Tract Society. The SCD volume is superior in its inclusion of a thorough survey of "Baseball Card History," a clearly delineated section on how to use the main text (which encompasses the following subheadings: Arrangement; Identifications; Photographs; Dating; Numbering; Names; Grading; Valuations; Sets; Errors/Variations; Counterfeits/Reprints; Unlisted Cards; Collectors Issues; New Issues), and a twenty-page exclusive entitled, "Minor League Teams Set Price Guide: 1940-1989." As with the Beckett guide, the dozens of ads included here provide a wealth of entry points for the interested collector.

27.   Remark, John F., and Nathan M. Bisk. **Martin-Smith's Official 1948-1989/90 Baseball Card Alphabetical Cross-Reference Guide.** Tampa, FL: Martin-Smith, 1989. 623p. Pap. ISBN 0-88128-368-1.

The book includes every major league baseball player from 1948 through 1989 to have been depicted on a baseball card. Players have been arranged alphabetically by last name; the work is further subdivided chronologically by season. Card numbers for each brand are given in each entry. All rookie cards—a popular component of the hobby—are listed in alphabetical order by name as well as by year in the back of the volume. This tool effectively complements the various baseball card price guides on the market.

28.   Smalling, Jack, and Dennis W. Eckes. **The Sport Americana Baseball Address List.** No. 7. Cleveland, OH: Edgewater, 1992. 160p. Illus., adv. ISBN 0-937424-61-7.

Touted by its publisher as the definitive guide for autograph hunters, the work provides addresses—or information for cases in which the player is deceased—of virtually all major league baseball players past and present. Despite its limited application, the book should prove useful to autograph seekers. A word of warning: Inquiries sent to the listed addresses carry no guarantee of receipt of an autograph or, if sent, of its authenticity.

Indexes

29.   Beckett, James. **The Sport Americana Alphabetical Baseball Card Checklist.** 4th ed. Cleveland, OH: Edgewater, 1990. Illus., adv.

An alphabetical listing, by player last name, of virtually all cards (Major and Minor Leagues) through the 1990 sets. It functions as a valuable cross-reference to standard price guide volumes.

Collecting—Sports and Recreation—Basketball

Handbooks

30.   Beckett, James. **The Sport Americana Basketball Card Price Guide & Alphabetical Checklist.** No. 3. Cleveland, Ohio: Edgewater, 1993. Unpaged. Illus., adv., pap. ISBN 0-937424-70-6.

The work covers the cards devoted to the major professional league in North America, the National Basketball Association, as originally compiled in *The Sport Americana Football, Hockey, Basketball, and Boxing Card Price Guide.* Arranged alphabetically by card company brand name and subdivided chronologically by year of issue, coverage spans the 1948 through the 1992/93 season.

Collecting—Sports and Recreation—Football

Handbooks

31.   Beckett, James. **The Sport Americana Football Card Price Guide.** No. 10. Cleveland, Ohio: Edgewater, 1993. Unpaged. Illus., adv., pap. ISBN 0-937424-68-4.

The tool has pulled the football section (including the NFL, the old All American Conference, and other professional leagues) out of *The Sport Americana Football, Hockey, Basketball, and Boxing Card Price Guide.* Arranged alphabetically by card company brand name and subdivided chronologically by year of issue, coverage ranges from 1948 through the 1992/93 season. Although not a keeper for most libraries, its portable configuration renders it ideal for handy reference at card shows, flea markets, and retail outlets.

Collecting—Sports and Recreation—Hockey

Handbooks

32.   Beckett, James. **The Sport Americana Hockey Card Price Guide.** No. 3. Cleveland, Ohio: Edgewater, 1993. Unpaged. Illus., adv., pap. ISBN 0-937424-69-2.

This source follows the format present in other *Sport Americana* titles, with coverage from 1948 through the 1992/93 season.

Collecting—Sports and Recreation—Pinball Machines

Handbooks

33. Flower, Gary, and Bill Kurtz. **Pinball: The Lure of the Silver Bell.** Secaucus, NJ: Book Sales, 1988. 128p. Illus. ISBN 1-55521-322-7.

The book surveys the history of pinball from its beginnings in the 1930s to today's complex microelectronics. It includes a comprehensive list of all pinball machines manufactured in the United States from 1939 onward. The attractive layouts are enhanced by enamel stock.

34. Bueschel, Richard. **Pinball 1: An Illustrated Historical Guide to Pinball Machines, Volume 1.** Wheat Ridge, CO: Coin Slot Books, 1988. 256p. Illus,. pap. ISBN 0-86667-047-5.

The first 135 pages cover the early period 1775 through 1931. The balance of the volume focuses on the various yearly models from 1932 to the present day. A four-page price guide to pinball machines is included as a separate insert.

Collecting—Toys

Handbooks

35. DeWein, Sibyl, and Joan Ashabraner. **The Collectors Encyclopedia of Barbie Dolls and Collectibles.** Paducah, KY: Collector Books; distr. New York: Crown, 1977. 305p. Illus., index. ISBN 0-89145-052-1.

The perfect tool for Barbie doll collectors (of which there are legions!). Other dolls belonging to the Barbie line—Ken, Midge, Cara, Scooter, Skipper, Todd, etc.—are covered as well. Entries include yearly model numbers and modifications made in outfits, hair styles, type of hands, makeup, coloring, etc. The illustrations are photographs of the dolls themselves; they serve to assist collectors in identifying the features unique to a given doll model.

36. Jaramillo, Alex. **Cracker Jack Prizes.** New York: Abbeville, 1990. 96p. illus. ISBN 1-55859-000-5.

The chronologically arranged work covers the firm from the perspective of the prizes found in each box. All of the glossy, heavy-duty pages include color pictures. The book includes an introductory essay, "The History, Appeal, and Prizes of Cracker Jack," followed by succinct surveys of each decade beginning in 1910.

Ecology *(See: Social Phenomena—The Ecology Movement, p. 232)*

Economics and Merchandising

Encyclopedias

37.   Hoffmann, Frank, and William Bailey. **The Encyclopedia of Fads: Fashion and Merchandising.** Binghamton, NY: Haworth, 1993. Illus., index, bibl. ISBN 56204-376-7; 1-56023-031-2 pap.

The work presents concise profiles (one to five pages per entry) of about 120 fads related to the business and fashion sectors in the United States since colonial times. The entries are arranged alphabetically; an index facilitates access through the inclusion of terms not necessarily used for entry headings. The black-and-white illustrations, reproduced from Library of Congress masters, enhance the overall appeal of the volume.

Handbooks

38.   **World's Greatest Brands: An International Review by Interbrand.** New York: Wiley, 1992. 260p. illus., index. ISBN 0-471-57283-7.

The work surveys 300 of the most successful brands (e.g., Coca-Cola, IBM, McDonald's). Although the term "brand" is clearly delineated (i.e., "a trademark which, through careful management, skillful promotion and wide use comes in the minds of consumers to embrace a particular and appealing set of values and attributes, both tangible and intangible"), the specific criteria for inclusion are rather vague. This listing is divided into two major sections: brands known worldwide (the primary authority here appears to be results of an International Survey of the World's Leading Brands) and those more generally known on a national level. The international section is arranged by industry, and the national section by nation; a brand name index facilitates access.

Feminism *(See: Social Phenomena—Feminism, pp. 190, 232)*

Folklore/Mythology

Atlases/Gazetteers/Travel Books

39.   Harpur, James, and Jennifer Westwood. **The Atlas of Legendary Places.** New York: Weidenfeld & Nicolson, 1989. 240p. Illus., maps, index. LC: 89-9110. ISBN 1-55584-335-2.

The thirty-seven sites included in this work are arranged under subjectively named chapters, such as "Eternal Realms" (e.g., Atlantis), "Sacred Wonders" (e.g., Machu Picchu), and "Timeless Landscapes" (e.g., the Himalayas). Each entry is several pages in length, the text being punctuated by maps, illustrations, quotations, and references —(albeit incomplete) —to other works on the topic. Supplementary features include a gazetteer (offering more precise geographical details) and a subject index.

Bibliographies

40. Clements, William M., and Frances M. Malpezzi, comps. **Native American Folk-lore, 1879-1979: An Annotated Bibliography.** Athens, OH: Swallow/Ohio University, 1984. 247p. Index. LC 83-6672. ISBN 0-8040-0831-0.

Limited to English language works about groups located north of Mexico, the bibliography includes adult books and journal articles dealing with "oral narratives, songs, chants, prayers, formulas, orations, proverbs, riddles, word play, music, dances, games, and ceremonials" (pp. xiii-xiv). The 5,450 entries feature short descriptive annotations arranged by culture area (following introductory essays for each) and subdivided by tribe. The subject and author/ editor/translator indexes feature competent coverage and cross-referencing.

41. Jones, Steven Swann. **Folklore and Literature in the United States: An Annotated Bibliography of Studies of Folklore in American Literature.** New York: Garland, 1984. 262p. Index. (Garland Folklore Bibliographies, Volume 5; Garland Reference Library of the Humanities, Volume 392.) LC 82-49182. ISBN 0-8240-9186-8.

The work lives up to its stated purpose of examining "the influence of folklore upon American literature." The studies, covering the 1920s through 1980, are arranged by author and feature descriptive, evaluative annotations.

Directories

42. Bartis, Peter T., and Barbara C. Fertig. **Folklife Sourcebook: A Directory of Folklife Resources in the United States and Canada.** Washington, D.C.: American Folklife Center, Library of Congress, 1986. 152p. (Publications of the American Folklife Center, No. 14.) LC 85-600334. ISBN 0-8444-0521-3.

Maintained through surveys conducted by the American Folklife Center, the directory lists serials dealing with this field and federal agencies, state folk cultural programs, societies, institutions, and foundations either maintaining archives or administering folklife programming. The latter portion of the tool lists higher education programs in folklore and folklife, recording companies, and directories to specific topics or networks.

Encyclopedias

43. Cohen, Daniel. **The Encyclopedia of Monsters.** New York: Dorset, 1990. 287p. ISBN 0-88029-442-6.

The phenomena described here (100 in all, with cinematic and literary creations excluded) have been organized into eight categories: humanoids, land monsters, monster birds and bats, phantoms, river and lake monsters, sea monsters, visitors from outer space, and weird creatures in folklore. Each entry describes the creature's background, the evolution of its legend, its behavior and physical characteristics, sightings and their locations, controversies surrounding the sightings, and organized efforts to find it.

44. Guiley, Rosemary Ellen. **The Encyclopedia of Ghosts and Spirits.** New York: Facts on File, 1992. 384p. Illus., index. LC 91-37427. ISBN 0-8160-2140-6.

The source is notable in that the author makes an effort to balance the viewpoints of both believers and skeptics in covering virtually all notable apparitions originating from both the mass media and oral traditions of Western culture. With the exception of occasional errors of a minor nature, the text maintains a consistently high level of accuracy.

45. Guiley, Rosemary Ellen. **The Encyclopedia of Witches and Witchcraft.** New York: Facts on File, 1989. 421p. Illus., index, bibl. LC 89-11776. ISBN 0-6160-1793-X.

This encyclopedia treats a potentially controversial subject in a no-nonsense, factual manner. The more than 400 entries, —arranged in alphabetical order, —cover animals, beliefs, events, legends, myths, rituals, people, places, and other aspects of witchcraft throughout history. A selective bibliography (limited to works of high quality) and a detailed index help render the work the finest available on this subject.

46. Cotterell, Arthur. **The Macmillan Illustrated Encyclopedia of Myths & Legends.** New York: Macmillan, 1989. 260p. Illus., index, bibl. LC 89-8282. ISBN 0-02-580181-3.

The text is divided into three main sections: cultural areas (eighteen in all, from Egypt to Oceana), characters and concepts (alphabetically listed heroes and deities, from Achilles to Zeus, followed by related myths), and a micropedia (over 1,000 concise entries, in alphabetical order, representing names, places, themes, etc., of secondary importance). A selective bibliography and competent index enhance the tool's utility.

47. Potter, Carole. **Knock on Wood: An Encyclopedia of Talismans, Charms, Superstitions & Symbols.** New York: Beaufort, 1983. 263p. Illus., bibl. LC 82-24440. ISBN 0-8253-0144-0.

This wide-ranging source covers the history of talismans, charms, superstitions, and symbols, as well as comparatively recent concepts (e.g., Uncle Sam, Mother's Day). The more than 400 entries are arranged alphabetically, with extensive cross-references.

48. Rovin, Jeff. **The Encyclopedia of Monsters.** New York: Facts on File, 1989. 390p. Illus., index. LC 89-30417. ISBN 0-8160-1824-3.

A nice complement to the Cohen book, Rovin opens with a concise survey of monsters since the appearance of written records. Defining them as characters unexplained by science who function primarily to frighten human beings, he refers to a variety of sources, including motion pictures, television, literature, comic books, mythology, folklore, religion, toys, computer games, and trading cards. Each entry includes the monster's name, nickname, species, gender, dimensions, features, and history, along with a picture.

Handbooks

49. Bierhorst, John. **The Mythology of North America.** New York: Morrow, 1985. 259p. LC 85-281. ISBN 0-688-04145-0.

This survey of North American Indian mythology identifies eleven clearly delineated regions, focusing on the similarities and differences between them.

50. Coffin, Tristram Potter, and Henning Cohen, eds. **The Folklore of American Holidays.** 2d ed. Detroit: Gale Research, 1991. ISBN 0-8103-7602-4.

The book offers a kaleidoscopic look at the beliefs, myths, pageantry, games, celebrations, etc., behind the major (i.e., nonlocalized) holidays of the United States and Canada.

51. Emrich, Duncan. **Folklore on the American Land.** Boston: Little, Brown, 1988. 707p. General & song indexes, bibl. LC 72-161865. ISBN 0-316-23721-3.

Emrich provides a breezy survey of American folklore, encompassing childhood rhymes and ditties, folk tales, street cries and epithets, legends and tales, folk songs and ballads, folk beliefs, and superstitions.

52. Monaghan, Patricia. **The Book of Goddesses & Heroines.** Rev. ed. St. Paul, MN: Llewellyn, c1981, 1990. 421p. Illus., alternative name & association indexes, bibl. LC 89-77418. ISBN 0-87542-573-9.

The work concentrates on goddesses from myth rather than historical women. The nearly 1,500 entries are arranged in alphabetical order; access is enhanced by both an alternative name (including minor figures) and association index.

Geographical Phenomena

Handbooks

53. Brandon, Jim. **Weird America: A Guide to Places of Mystery in the United States.** New York: E. P. Dutton, 1978. 257p. Illus. LC 77-11641. ISBN 0-525-47491-9.

The tool delineates scientific and pseudo-scientific oddities, such as UFOs and archeological finds. Arranged by state and subdivided by area or city, the listing was intended to be used for planning a sightseeing itinerary. Despite its incomplete listing of reported phenomena, the frequent lack of adequate documentation, and the fact that many oddities wouldn't attract any interest at present (e.g., peaches falling out of the sky in Shreveport in 1961), enough interesting entries are present to render the work useful for enthusiasts.

54. Keylin, Arleen, and Gene Brown, eds. **Disasters from the Pages of "The New York Times."** New York: Arno, 1976. 315p. Illus. LC 75-43948. ISBN 0-405-06681-3.

The work covers more than 140 disasters as reported in the nation's leading newspaper, from the great Chicago fire of October 8-9, 1871, to the crash of a jet plane at Kennedy Airport on June 24, 1975, which claimed 113 lives. The entries are presented in chronological order, with front-page stories photoreproduced along with continuations from the inside pages. Types of disasters presented here include earthquakes, tidal waves, fires, floods, hurricanes, avalanches, crashes, blizzards, and explosions.

Humor

Biographies

55. Smith, Ronald Lande. **The Stars of Stand-Up Comedy: A Biographical Encyclopedia.** New York: Garland, 1986. 227p. Illus. (Garland Reference Library of the Humanities, Vol. 564.) LC 84-48408. ISBN 0-8240-8803-2.

Arranged alphabetically, each of the 101 comic or comic team entries includes one or more pictures; birth date and place; a listing of records, television appearances, videos, and films; book biographies and autobiographies; and a short discussion of the comic's background, philosophy, and type of humor. The highly readable sections—ranging from vintage humorists, such as Groucho Marx and Smith and Dale, up through more recent figures, such as Richard Pryor and Eddie Murphy—provide a fascinating look at American history and mores. Counterculture performers (e.g., Lenny Bruce, Tom Lehrer) are presented along with more mainstream fare (e.g., Bob Hope and Steve Allen).

56. Smith, Ronald Lande. **Who's Who in Comedy: Comedians, Comics, and Clowns from Vaudeville to Today's Stand-Ups.** New York: Facts on File, 1992. 512p. Illus., index. LC 92-42881. ISBN 0-8160-2338-7.

The approximately 450 alphabetically arranged entries cover close to 100 years of humorists. The entries include given name, date of birth (and, where applicable, death), biographical and career data, and critical analysis. The three appendixes are devoted to nickname and character name, catch phrase, and categorical (impressionists, dialect, television, etc.).

Dictionaries

57. Smith, Ronald Lande. **The Comedy Quote Dictionary.** New York: Doubleday, 1992. 288p. Index. LC 91-31396. ISBN 0-385-41691-1.
   The quotes, arranged by subject and indexed by source, have been culled from all walks of life. Given the lack of up-to-date tools covering this area, it should prove useful to libraries of all types.

Directories

58. Ellenbogen, Glenn C., ed. **The Directory of Humor Magazines and Humor Organizations in America (and Canada).** 2nd ed. New York: Wry Bred, 1989. 186p. Index. ISBN 0-9606190-7-0.
   The alphabetically arranged entries (with organizations and newsletters, newspapers, periodicals, etc., integrated into one listing) include the following information (where applicable): founder, address, format, name of edition, phone number, date founded, a description of the contents, frequency, circulation rate, physical dimension, and a representative sample or excerpt. There are two useful appendixes: Magazines in America and Canada Rank Ordered by Circulation and Writers Markets for Humorous Articles in American and Canadian Humor Magazines.

Language

Dictionaries

59. Ammer, Christine. **Have a Nice Day—No Problem!: A Dictionary of Clichés.** New York: E. P. Dutton, 1992. 448p. Index. ISBN 0-525-93394-8.
   The tool includes approximately 3,000 familiar expressions. Entries cover basic meanings, historical derivation, and notation as to whether the cliché remains widely used or is losing popularity. Examples of use span popular literature—both contemporary and all-but-forgotten titles—and classics such as the Bible and Shakespeare's dramatic works. Overall, entries are more thorough than those in comparable titles; i.e., Eric Partridge's Dictionary of Clichés (5th ed., New York: Routledge, 1978) and Brewer's Dictionary of Phrase & Fable (14th ed., New York: HarperCollins, 1989).

60. Cassidy, Frederic G., and Joan H. Hill, eds. **Dictionary of American Regional English. Vol. I: A-C; Vol. II: D-H.** Cambridge, MA: Belknap\Harvard University, 1985; 1991. 903p.; 980p. LC 84-29025. ISBN 0-674-20511-1; 0-674-20512-X.
   Part of a projected five-volume set dedicated to systematically recording the regional variations of English spoken across the United States, each entry provides definitions, part of speech, variant spellings, pronunciation, alternative forms, usage labels, and cross-references. Unique features include unusual meanings for common terms, regional colloquialisms, words found only among particular social or ethnic groups, dated quotations illustrating the word's

evolution, and computer-generated maps indicating the geographical distribution of a word's usage.

61.   Chapman, Robert L, ed. **New Dictionary of American Slang.** New York: Harper & Row, 1986. 485p. LC 86-45086. ISBN 0-06-181157-2.

Building on Wentworth and Flexner's Dictionary of American Slang (2nd ed., New York: Thomas Y. Crowell, 1975), Chapman surveys the full range of American history. Terms from recent decades relating to the counterculture, minorities, the information revolution, the yuppie ethic, etc., are included along with taboo and other marginal words not found in general dictionaries. The entries give pronunciation, word-class and dating notation, definitions, illustrative phrases, and cross-references.

62.   Chapman, Robert, ed. **Thesaurus of American Slang.** New York: Harper & Row, 1989. 489p. LC 89-45029. ISBN 0-06-016140-X.

A unique slang compilation, it provides dictionary-like features, such as definitions and parts of speech, and then lists a word's slang synonyms (the main portion of the entry) and cites related terms.

63.   Costello, Robert B., ed. **American Expression: A Thesaurus of Effective and Colorful Speech.** Jess Stein, consulting ed. New York: McGraw-Hill, 1981. 172p. (A Sachem/Norback Book.) Index. LC 81-6030. ISBN 0-07-047137-1.

The tool—a phrase list in classified arrangement, with an index to the subject headings—offers colorful American expressions that might be of use to linguists or other specialists studying regionalisms, slang, or popular culture, as well as to authors seeking a more forceful style of writing.

64.   Spears, Richard A. **NTC's American Idioms Dictionary.** Lincolnwood, IL: National Textbook, 1987. 463p. LC 86-63996. ISBN 0-8442-5450-9.

Entries provide the full form of the idiom, followed by variant and shorter versions, as well as one or more definitions and examples of usage. There is a lengthy introduction on how to use the source and further access is made possible via the 100-page phrase finder index.

65.   Urdang, Laurence, ed. director, and Nancy LaRoche, ed.-in-chief. **Picturesque Expressions: A Thematic Dictionary.** Detroit: Gale Research, 1980. 408p. index. LC 80-22705. ISBN 0-8103-1122-4.

The work comprises more than 3,000 idiomatic entries arranged by thematic categories. Each entry includes a historical etymology as well as a quote illustrating the derivation of the term. Cross-references are frequently utilized at the subject and entry levels.

Handbooks

66.   Dickson, Paul. **The Dickson Word Treasury.** New York: John Wiley, 1992. 372p. Illus., index, bibl., pap. LC 91-25819. ISBN 0-471-55168-6.

Drawn from scholarly publications, vintage trade catalogs, specialized dictionaries, interviews with dictionary editors, and communication with an array of people, the work is organized into fifty-seven categories (e.g., acronyms, alimentary words, neologisms).

67.   Dickson, Paul. **Slang! The Topic-by-Topic Dictionary for Contemporary American Lingoes.** New York: Simon & Schuster, 1990. 295p. Index, bibl., pap. LC 89-49628. ISBN 0-671-67251-7.

The tool has arranged 3,900 terms under twenty-four subject categories (e.g., auctioneering, yuppie slang). The entries focus on definitions; etymologies receive minimal attention.

68.   Keyes, Ralph. **"Nice Guys Finish Seventh": False Phrases, Spurious Sayings, and Familiar Misquotations.** New York: HarperCollins, 1992. 188p. Author and key-word indexes, bibl. LC 92-52539. ISBN 0-06-270020-0.

Keyes employs a scholarly approach, explaining each expression (both in and out of context), discussing its source, and comparing its content with related quotes.

69.   Miner, Margaret, and Hugh Rawson, eds. **A Dictionary of Quotations from Shakespeare: A Topical Guide to Over 3,000 Great Passages from the Plays, Sonnets, and Narrative Poems.** New York: E. P. Dutton, 1992. 368p. ISBN 0-525-93451-0.

The Shakespeare passages are arranged by 400 categories (e.g., democracy, mass media, Star Wars) possessing contemporary significance. Approximately half of the quotations have annotations, providing information regarding meaning and context.

70.   Rawson, Hugh. **Wicked Words.** New York: Crown, 1989. 435p. LC 89-672. ISBN 0-517-57334-2.

The work provides definitions and historical surveys of over 1,000 acerbic words and phrases (e.g., insults, curses).

71.   Sommer, Elyse, and Mike Sommer, eds. **Similes Dictionary: A Collection of More Than 16,000 Comparison Phrases.** Detroit: Gale Research, 1988. 950p. LC 87-36109. ISBN 0-8103-4361-4.

The figurative expressions are arranged in 558 thematic categories (e.g., anger, ability, happiness, intelligence). A large number of cross-references and an alphabetical list of the similes have been appended to each group.

72.   Tuleja, Tad. **Quirky Quotations.** New York: Crown, 1992. 224p. LC 92-2501. ISBN 0-517-58560-X.

The source focuses on less well known quotations, with each entry including a paragraph of trivia. The classified arrangement includes 16 chapters of diversified topics (e.g., bloopers). The lack of an index undercuts its utility as a reference tool to some degree.

Chapter 2

Mass Media

(See also: Humor, pp. 12, 224; Social Phenomena—Minorities, pp. 189, 233)

General

Bibliographies

73.   Friedman, Leslie J. **Sex Role Stereotyping in the Mass Media: An Annotated Bibliography.** New York: Garland, 1977. 324p. Author and subject indexes. LC 76-52685. ISBN 0-8240-9865-X.

The more than 1,000 works (including books, journal articles, speeches, reports, U.S. documents, filmstrips, statistical studies, and sound recordings) have been organized into ten categories: mass media, advertising, broadcast media, film, print media, popular culture, media images of minority women, media images of men, children's media, and the impact of media stereotypes on occupational choices.

74.   Soukup, Paul A., comp. **Christian Communication: A Bibliographical Survey.** Westport, CT: Greenwood, 1989. 400p. (Bibliographies and Indexes in Religious Studies, no. 14.) Name, title, and subject indexes. LC 89-12076. ISBN 0-313-25673-X.

The work provides a selective cross section of the literature, including "only those items deemed relevant and substantial." It opens with a bibliographic essay (Chapter 1) that provides an overview of the history and primary concerns of Christian communication, and Chapter 2 lists general resources (i.e., periodicals, bibliographies, directories, and catalogs). The heart of the book (Chapters 3-9) is composed of 1,311 sources arranged by various subcategories: communication theory history, rhetoric, interpersonal communication, mass communication, intercultural communication, and other media (e.g., music, dance). The appended evaluative, informative annotations are perfectly tailored for research and collection development. Extensive cross-references highlight those items applicable to more than one category.

Dictionaries

75.   Diamant, Lincoln, ed. **The Broadcast Communications Dictionary.** 3rd ed. Westport, CT: Greenwood, 1989. 255p. LC 88-25093. ISBN 0-313-26502-X.

The more than 6,000 terms included here have been drawn from the fields of radio and television programming and production; network and local station operations; broadcast equipment and engineering; cable television technology; satellite communications technology; audio and videotape production; advertising; media usage; communications research; and defense, government, trade, and allied groups. The tool also includes many helpful special features(e.g., italicizing terms when used to define other entries, definitions often directing the user to similar or related terms).

Directories

76.   Bowker, R.R., Staff, ed. **AV Market Place: The Complete Business Directory.** New York: R. R. Bowker. Annual. 1994 ed.: 1146p. ISBN 0-835203419-3.

Scrupulously updated each year, this tool is without peer in its field of coverage. The first section categorizes some 1,500 AV products and services, followed by a company directory (about 6,000 firms in all) noting names of contacts, availability of catalogs, etc. Other sections cover associations, film and television commissions, awards and festivals, a calendar of meetings and conventions, lists of periodicals and reference books, and an industry yellow pages.

77.   Pollack, Martin, ed. **National Black Media Directory.** Ft. Lauderdale, FL: Alliance Publishers, 1989. 135p. Spiralbound. ISBN 0-936836-16-4.

Billed as the leading source of black American print and electronic media information, the directory lists magazines, newspapers, and radio and television stations providing information and programming important to the black community. It is arranged by state; the table of contents notes corresponding pagination for each state.

Guides to the Literature

78.   Cates, Jo A. **Journalism: A Guide to the Reference Literature.** Englewood, CO: Libraries Unlimited, 1990. 214p. (Reference Sources in the Humanities.) LC 89-78335. ISBN 0-87287-716-7.

The tool focuses on both print and broadcast journalism in North America. The 728 annotated entries cover traditional reference books, libraries, associations, wire services, and government bodies. Unusual for a bibliographic guide, the annotations display both grace and wit.

Handbooks

79.   Franks, Don, comp. **Tony, Grammy, Emmy, Country: A Broadway, Television and Records Awards Reference.** Jefferson, NC: McFarland, 1986. 202p. Index. LC 85-43577. ISBN 0-89950-204-0.

Arranged by award and subdivided first by year and then by category, the listing encompasses theater's Tony Awards (1947-1984), the recording industry's Grammy Awards (1959-1984), the Country Music Association Awards (1967-1984), and television's Emmy Awards (1948-1983). The index covers names of performers, television shows, plays, song titles, and organizations in one integrated listing. One might quibble with the compiler's choices (e.g., the Emmys but not the Golden Globe Awards or the Peabodys) as well as the fact that this information can be obtained from other sources; still, the book remains useful within its established guidelines.

Book Publishing

Handbooks

80.   Joyce, Donald Franklin. **Black Book Publishers in the United States: A Historical Dictionary of the Presses, 1817-1990.** New York: Greenwood, 1991. 225p. Index, bibl. LC 91-10528. ISBN 0-313-26783-9.

Each of the profiles of forty-six black-owned publishing companies includes information regarding their respective histories, publications, lists of libraries holding them, bibliographies containing sources on the companies, addresses, and names of officers.

Comic Books/Comic Strips/Cartooning

Bibliographies

81. Gifford, Denis. **American Comic Strip Collections, 1884-1939: The Evolutionary Era.** Boston: G. K. Hall, 1990. 218p. Title and name indexes. ISBN 0-8161-7270-6.

Gifford focuses upon reprints of newspaper comic strips in comic book form, a key stage in the evolution of the latter format. Each entry includes (where applicable) item number, title, subtitle, publication date, length of run, number of last issue, original price, page count, size, publishing house and address, editorial staff, artist (if not a collaborative effort), syndicate, contents of book, and author commentary (most notably addressing the book's significance). The latter, combined with editorials reprinted from the original sources, constitute the high point of the tool. On the other hand, the absence of a character index somewhat diminishes its value.

Biographies

82. Goulart, Ron. **The Great Comic Book Artists, Volume 2.** New York: St. Martin's Press, 1989. 112p. Illus., pap. LC 86-3711. ISBN 0-312-01768-5.

The alphabetically arranged entries include one page each for the artist bio and black-and-white reprinted art. The subjective choices for inclusion reflect a pronounced American, corporate publisher bias; this, and the blurry comic book reproductions, render the title a cut below Goulart's usual high standard.

Encyclopedias

83. Goulart, Ron, ed. **The Encyclopedia of American Comics.** New York: Facts on File, 1990. LC 90-2974. ISBN 0-8160-1852-9; 0-8160-2582-7 pap.

The 650 alphabetically arranged entries cover comic strips, comic books, and their creators, dating from the appearance of the Katzenjammer Kids in 1897 to the present. The entries devoted to the strips address their history, development, content, and distribution, whereas those concerned with artists trace their careers and assess the respective contribution of each.

84. Horn, Maurice, ed. **The World Encyclopedia of Cartoons.** 2 Vols. Detroit: Gale Research, 1980. 787p. Illus.

This represents a definitive work on comic art encompassing comic books, comic strips, political cartooning, and film animation. The alphabetically arranged entries include artists, titles of works, characters, etc., from an international perspective; they are well written and feature perceptive analysis. The supplementary material includes five appendixes (Pulitzer Prize Winners, Sigma Delta Chi Award Winners, Academy Award Winners, Cartoons in Japan, Animation in Japan), a Glossary, a Select Bibliography, Notes on the Contributors, five indexes (Proper Name, Subject, Illustrators, Geographical, Contributors), and a special section, Richard E. Marschall's "A History of *Puck, Judge,* and *Life,*" comprising eighty-seven pages. Those desiring greater depth or more up-to-date material would be advised to search out more specialized titles.

85. Rovin, Jeff. **The Encyclopedia of Super Villains.** New York: Facts on File, 1987. 416p. Illus., index. LC 87-8831. ISBN 0-8160-1356-X.

A complement to *The Encyclopedia of Superheroes* (see entry 86), the work lists—in alphabetical order by popular name or title—super-powered villains culled from literature, folklore, television, cinema, toys, advertisements, religion, and comic books. The entries include the villain's real name (where known); the source of the character's first appearance; any accomplices or henchmen; a brief biography explaining the origins of the villain's powers and evil ways; a quote typifying the character; and relevant ties with other characters, or with the writers and artists.

86. Rovin, Jeff. **The Encyclopedia of Superheroes.** New York: Facts on File, 1985. 443p. Illus., index. LC 85-10329. ISBN 0-8160-1168-0.

Drawn from all quarters of the popular culture realm (albeit primarily from comic books), the 1,300 bios included in the book are arranged alphabetically by popular name. Each entry gives (where possible) the chronology of appearances, companions, occupation, costume, tools and weapons, special powers, media presence, and representative quotations. Six appendixes supplement the main text, providing information about superhero teams, obscure or borderline superheroes from the genre's golden age, foreign superheroes, minor superheroes, and the characters found in the comic book, *Dial "H" for Hero.* One minor drawback is the failure of the index to cite the alter-ego names of these figures.

Handbooks

87. Overstreet, Robert M. **The Official Overstreet Comic Book Price Guide.** New York: House of Collectibles, 1971-, v. 1-. Roughly 700p. annual. Illus., adv. Marketed to the collectors market by Overstreet Publications, Cleveland, Tennessee.

Long recognized as the authoritative pricing source for comic book aficionados, the tool offers a comprehensive overview of the genre. Sections regularly carried in the annual editions include: Grading Comic Books, Storage of Comic Books, Investor's Data (including Market Updates, The Top 50 Titles, The 50 Most Valuable Books), The First Wave of Comic Books 1933-1943 (Key Books Listed and Ranked), Comics With Little If Any Value, Collecting Foreign Comics and American Reprints, Proper Handling of Comic Books, How to Sell Your Comics, Comic Book Mail Order Services, Comic Book Conventions, Comic Book Clubs, The History of Comics Fandom, How to Select Fanzines, Fan Publications of Interest, Collecting Strips, Collecting Original Art, Directory of Comic and Nostalgia Shops, Directory of Advertisers (for each edition), and special features (generally historical surveys of the genre's key artists, companies, and characters).

The bulk of each edition is the price guide proper, arranged alphabetically by comic book title, with bibliographic data and three-tiered valuations (Good, Fine, Mint) for numerically designated issues. All known American comic book publications are included. Illustrations consist of front covers of representative titles—three black-and-white, postage stamp-sized reproductions per page, in addition to several color inserts (usually ads)—and function as a highly informative component of the tool, aiding both in identification and historical research. The ads, many of them full page, are astounding in their diversity, providing access to supplies and memorabilia associated with the genre as well as comic books themselves.

88. Overstreet, Robert M., and Gary M. Carter. **The Overstreet Comic Book Grading Guide.** New York: Avon, 1992. 303p. Illus., pap. LC 91-92479. ISBN 0-380-76910-7.

The book, assembled by comic book industry giant Robert Overstreet, is centered on teaching the reader how to grade and value any title. It includes a 100-point grading system, a newly introduced 10-point whiteness level system, hundreds of detailed illustrations (highlighted by a sixteen-page color section), a checklist for recognizing and evaluating defects, and an extensive glossary of terms. Individual chapters also include background information on many other related topics, such as "Why Is Grading So Important?," "The Evolution of Comic Book Grading," "How to Describe Comic Book Condition," "Diagram of a Comic Book," "Restoration Notes by Susan Cicconi," "Comic Book Restoration by Mark Wilson," and "A Word About Mail Order." A "Cross Index of Comic Book Covers" helps the reader locate the examples relating to the grading of comic books. This is a genuinely well researched and informative source that no other grading guide has equaled.

Indexes

89. Satin, Allan D. **A Doonesbury Index: An Index to the Syndicated Daily Newspaper Strip "Doonesbury" by G. B. Trudeau, 1970-1983.** Metuchen, NJ: Scarecrow Press, 1985. 269p. Bibl. LC 85-2037. ISBN 0-8108-1800-0.

Besides offering alphabetical access to the subjects and characters of the Doonesbury strip, the tool also indexes other notable political editorial cartoons and important people, themes, concepts, and issues from the seventies.

Films

Almanacs

(See also: Science Fiction, pp. 74, 206, 228)

90. Gertner, Richard, ed. **International Motion Picture Almanac, 1984.** 55th ed. New York: Quigley, 1984. 663p. ISBN 0-900610-30-1.

The major section, "Who's Who," provides data on approximately 4,000 individuals (actors, executives, writers, etc.) active in films and television, including name, real name (where different), occupation, date and place of birth, education, thumbnail bios, and credits. The next largest section, "Feature Pictures," gives the title, length in minutes, studio, date of release, and featured players of movies released since 1955. The almanac also includes directories of film festivals, services, talent agencies, publicists, equipment and supplies, production companies, theater circuits, etc.

Bibliographies/Filmographies/Videographies

91. Altomara, Rita Ecke. **Hollywood on the Palisades: A Filmography of Silent Features Made in Fort Lee, New Jersey, 1903-1927.** New York: Garland, 1983. 226p. Illus., name and title indexes. (Garland Reference Library of the Humanities, Vol. 368.) LC 82-21004. ISBN 0-8240-9225-2.

The work includes a brief introduction, which surveys the origins of filmmaking in the town, and three primary listings: "Stellar Attractions" (films starring established actors), "Early Auteurs" (notable directors working there early in their careers), and "Supporting Features" (more obscure productions). Although credits are sometimes sketchy, many unique titles cited here are not recorded in other sources.

92.   Campbell, Craig W. **Reel America and World War I: A Comprehensive Filmography and History of Motion Pictures in the United States, 1914-1929.** Jefferson, NC: McFarland, 1985. xi, 303p. Illus., index. ISBN 0-89950-087-0.

Following a historical survey of the era (approximately one-half of the book), the filmography entries are arranged by type of film (e.g., short war-related films) and subdivided by year and month of release. They include title, producing/releasing company, number of reels, directors, stars and other key cast members, miscellaneous additional data, and encapsulated summaries.

93.   Friedwald, Will, and Jerry Beck. **The Warner Brothers Cartoons.** Metuchen, NJ: Scarecrow, 1981. 271p. Index. LC 80-27839. ISBN 0-8108-1396-3.

This represents a complete filmography of the more than 850 shorts (produced between 1930 and 1969) in the studio's "Looney Tunes" and "Merry Melodies" series. The entries include titles, release dates, directors, writers, credited design and background people, and terse plot summaries. Also included are an introduction, which gives a historical outline of the studio and key personnel (e.g., voice and music credits), and a "Cast of Characters" (about twenty-five of the main stars, such as Bugs Bunny and Daffy Duck).

94.   Gray, John, comp. **Blacks in Film and Television: A Pan-African Bibliography of Films, Filmmakers, and Performers.** New York: Greenwood, 1990. xi, 496p. Artist, title, subject, and author indexes. ISBN 0-3131-27486-X.

The listing covers six main areas: Cultural History and the Arts; African Film; Black Film in the Diaspora: Europe, the Caribbean and Latin America; Black Film in the Diaspora: United States; Blacks in American Television and Video; and The Black Performer. Each area is subdivided by country, and materials are listed by format: books, articles, news articles, etc. The two appendixes cover reference works and film resources.

95.   Hayes, R. M. **3-D Movies: A History and Filmography of Stereoscopic Anema.** Jefferson, NC: McFarland, 1989. 414p. Illus. LC 89-42720. ISBN 0-89950-407-8.

An authoritative and well-researched work, featuring a wealth of attractive illustrations. The first six chapters survey the genre from 1855 peepshows to television showings in the 1980s. A 250-page filmography follows, giving credits, technical details, and critical commentary for more than 200 movies. The book concludes with a directory that lists and describes currently available processes and firms supplying 3-D services. The book's prime deficiency is its lack of footnotes or a bibliography.

96.   Lenburg, Jeff. **The Encyclopedia of Animated Cartoon Series.** Westport, CT: Arlington House Publishers, 1981. 190p. Illus., index. LC 81-4477. ISBN 0-87000-441-7.

This is an exhaustive filmography of every cartoon series (not single cartoon releases or animated features) produced for theater and television, from 1909 through 1980. The entries are arranged in three categories—silent, theatrical sound, and television—and subdivided alphabetically. The data provided for each series include names of animators, producers, studios, animation techniques, and social setting, followed by a listing of titles for each year of a series' run.

97.   Lentz, Harris M., comp. **Science Fiction, Horror & Fantasy Film and Television Credits Supplement: Through 1987.** Jefferson, NC: McFarland, 1989. 924p. Index, bibl. LC 88-42646. ISBN 0-89950-364-0.

The work updates the two-volume compilation published in 1984 in addition to adding information from 1983-1987. Credits cover actors and actresses, directors, producers, screenwriters, cinematographers, special effects technicians, make-up artists, and art directors. A new sixty-six-page section provides alternative titles for both film and television entries, and two subgenres—mystery and spy—have been added.

98.   Ottoson, Robert L. **American International Pictures: A Filmography.** New York: Garland, 1985. 425p. Illus., index. (Garland Reference Library of the Humanities, Vol. 492.) LC 83-49335. ISBN 0-8240-8976-6.

This catalog of AIP productions includes only U.S. copyrighted works; foreign features purchased and sold directly to television have been excluded. Arrangement is by decade, subdivided alphabetically by title within each year. Entries include title, date, running time, cast, production credits, a plot synopsis, and a terse critique. The title and personal name index assists in providing access to the main text.

99.   Ottoson, Robert. **A Reference Guide to the American Film Noir: 1940-1958.** Metuchen, NJ: Scarecrow, 1981. 285p. Illus., index, bibl. LC 80-23176. ISBN 0-8108-1363-7.

The filmography incorporates 215 films with descriptive annotations (e.g., plot synopses, discussion of film noir characteristics) ranging from 300 to 450 words. An appendix lists forty-five more films with "thematic similarities" to the genre.

100.   Sigoloff, Marc. **The Films of the Seventies: A Filmography of American and Canadian Films 1970-1979.** Jefferson, NC: McFarland, 1984. 424p. Index. LC 83-42887. ISBN 0-89950-095-1.

The almost 1,000 alphabetically arranged entries include cast lists, credits, plot synopses, and information regarding box office performance and critical reception. Films considered by Sigoloff to be "out of the mainstream" (and, therefore, irrelevant to his attempt to provide an overview of the decade through its films) have been omitted; e.g., exploitation films, sex-oriented movies, low-budget independent films, animation features, documentaries.

101.   Welch, Jeffrey Egan. **Literature and Film: An Annotated Bibliography, 1909-1977.** New York: Garland, 1981. 315p. Index. (Garland Reference Library of the Humanities, Vol. 241.) LC 80-8509. ISBN 0-8240-9478-6.

The listing covers notable monographs and articles published in North America and Great Britain between 1909 and 1977 that are concerned with the relationship between films and works of literature. The 1,102 entries (not counting 133 dissertations produced from 1939 onwards, which appear in a separate listing) are arranged chronologically by year and subdivided by author's name. An alphabetical list of fiction writers and the films derived from their work functions as a subject index and provides titles of both the works and the films; the names of the director, scenarist, and producer; and the film's year of release.

102.   Wescott, Steven D. **A Comprehensive Bibliography of Music for Film and Television.** Detroit: Information Coordinators, 1985. 432p. Index. (Detroit Studies in Music Bibliography, No. 54.) LC 85-27184. ISBN 0-89990-027-5.

The work is concerned with music's role as a dramatic element in film and television. The 6,340 citations have been organized into three main categories: "History" (dealing with surveys and critiques), "Composer," and "Themes" (aesthetics, special topics, and research).

103.   Writers' Program of the Work Projects Administration in the City of New York, 1935-1940, with the Museum of Modern Art, New York, comps. **The Film Index: A Bibliography. Volume 1: The Film as Art.** New York: Museum of Modern Art Film Library, 1941. Reprinted, Millwood, NY: Kraus International, 1988. 723p. Illus., index. LC 87-35288. ISBN 0-527-29329-6.

Long overdue for reprinting, this insightful volume—part of a three-volume set—analyzes journal articles, monographs, and ephemeras relating to films and motion picture production from its infancy through 1936. Many materials outside the entertainment sphere have been included, thereby rendering the subject-title index unique with respect to its interdisciplinary inclusions. It is divided by a wide array of subjects—each of which has been painstakingly delineated.

104. Writers' Program of the Work Projects Administration in the City of New York, 1935-1940, with the Museum of Modern Art, New York, comps. **The Film Index: A Bibliography. Volume 2: The Film as Industry.** White Plains, NY: Kraus International, 1985. 587p. LC 41-8716. ISBN 0-527-29334-2.

Projected for publication in the early 1940s, the material languished in the archives of the Museum of Modern Art for over four decades. The material has been arranged under nine major headings (Advertising and Publicity, Associations and Organizations, Distribution, Exhibition, Finance, History, Jurisprudence, Labor Relations, and Production) and subdivided alphabetically by author, or title for anonymous works. The annotations provide full descriptions of each item's contents.

Biographies

105. Dixon, Wheeler W. **The "B" Directors: A Biographical Directory.** Metuchen, NJ: Scarecrow, 1985. 594p. Index, bibl., filmog. LC 85-14321. ISBN 0-8108-1835-3.

The work consists of more than 350 biographical profiles of directors who have made low-budget features at one time or another during their careers. The title index represents something of a problem in that less than one-third of the titles noted in the filmographies appended to each entry—the so-called "major" films—are included.

106. Drew, William M. **Speaking of Silents: First Ladies of the Screen.** Introduction by Kevin Brownlow. Vestal, NY: Vestal, 1989. 256p. Illus. ISBN 0-911572-81-3; 0-911572-74-0 pap.

Ten of the most glamorous women of the silent screen were interviewed in their later years by Drew. They were Madge Bellamy, Eleanor Boardman, Leatrice Joy, Laura La Plante, May McAvoy, Patsy Ruth Miller, Colleen Moore, Esther Ralston, Blanche Sweet, and Lois Wilson. The interviews provide a close-up look at silent-era filmmaking as well as personal insights.

107. Ellrod, J. G. **Hollywood Greats of the Golden Years: The Late 1920s Through the 1950s.** Jefferson, NC: McFarland, 1989. 222p. Illus., index. LC 89-42713. ISBN 0-89950-371-3.

The eighty-one alphabetically arranged biographical entries cover major stars who were deceased by 1989, including Joan Crawford, Henry Fonda, and Marilyn Monroe.

108. Fischer, Dennis. **Horror Film Directors, 1931-1990.** Jefferson, NC: McFarland, 1991. 877p. Illus., title index, bibl. LC 91-52510. ISBN 0-89950-609-7.

This scholarly volume defines the horror film genre, explains the role of the director, and profiles the field's notable directors. The major portion of the text is divided into two alphabetically arranged sections: I. The Major Directors, and II. The Hopeless and the Hopeful: Promising Directors, Obscurities, and Horror Hacks. The supplementary material includes the introductory survey article, "A Brief History of Horror Films," the appendix, "Classic Horror Films by Non-Horror Directors" (a running commentary covering these directors in no particular order), and the title index.

109. Lloyd, Ann, and Graham Fuller, eds. **The Illustrated Who's Who of the Cinema.** New York: Macmillan, 1983. 480p. Illus. LC 83-790. ISBN 0-02-923450-6.

The work includes almost 2,500 biographies (with more than 1,500 photos) of leading actors, supporting and character actors, directors, animators, camera operators, choreographers, composers, critics, dancers, set and costume designers, lyricists, producers, screenwriters, stunt personnel, etc.—in short, all notable contributors to the art form. The alphabetically arranged entries include dates of birth and death, professional status, location of birth, a career sketch (with critical assessment), and a listing of the films with which the entrant was involved.

110. Morsberger, Robert E., Stephen O. Lesser, and Randall Clark, eds. **American Screenwriters.** Detroit: Gale Research, 1984. 382p. Illus., index. (Dictionary of Literary Biography, Vol. 26.) LC 83-25414. ISBN 0-8103-0917-3.

The source consists of biographical profiles of sixty-five notable screenwriters, including some directors (e.g., Billy Wilder), television writers (e.g., Rod Serling), and novelists (e.g., James Agee).

111. Neibaur, James L. **Tough Guy: The American Movie Macho.** Jefferson, NC: McFarland, 1989. 224p. Illus., index, bibl., filmog. LC 88-27309. ISBN 0-89950-382-9.

Following a introductory survey of silent film tough guys, the work provides lengthy analytical studies of a small group of actors selected for their originality, popularity, and influence. Among those included are Humphrey Bogart, John Wayne, and James Dean. Although the focus is on their respective macho roles, general career outlines are also provided for each.

112. Pitts, Michael R. **Horror Film Stars.** Jefferson, NC: McFarland, 1981. 324p. Illus., index, bibl. LC 80-11241. ISBN 0-89950-003-X; 0-89950-004-8 pap.

The text consists of biographical essays of both "stars" of the genre (e.g., Bela Lugosi) and "players," who generally gave only a portion of their career over to horror titles. The lion's share of the text is devoted to the fifteen actors accorded star status.

113. Quinlan, David. **Quinlan's Illustrated Directory of Film Stars.** New York: Hippocrene, 1986. 460p. Illus., bibl. ISBN 0-87052-346-5.

The work contains biographical data, filmographies, and photographs for more than 1,600 film stars. A large number of individuals from the first edition have been shifted to the companion volume, *The Illustrated Encyclopedia of Movie Character Actors* (New York: Hippocrene, 1986) in order to make room for some 300 performers new to this edition. Coverage includes British and major foreign-language stars as well as Hollywood personnel. Each entry includes vital statistics (e.g., real name, birthdate), a thumbnail bio, a two-by-two-inch photo, and a list of film appearances (or non-acting roles, e.g., directing), including unreleased films and television movies. Despite the tendency toward subjective commentary and randomized trivia, much useful information can be located here.

114. Rainey, Buck. **Saddle Aces of the Cinema.** San Diego, CA: A.S. Barnes; London: Tantivy, 1980. 307p. Illus., index, filmog. LC 78-75328. ISBN 0-498-02341-9.

The lives and careers of fifteen cowboy film stars, whose working days generally straddled the silent and sound eras, are covered here. The subjects include Gene Autry, Hoot Gibson, and Tom Mix.

115. Rainey, Buck. **Sweethearts of the Sage.** Jefferson, NC: McFarland, 1992. 652p. Filmog. LC 91-52639. ISBN 0-89950-565-1.

The work is composed of biographies of 258 actresses appearing in Westerns. Many of the stars included here did not work exclusively in this genre; however, their work in horse operas is highlighted in these somewhat sketchy, albeit informative, profiles.

116.   Segrave, Kerry, and Linda Martin. **The Post-Feminist Hollywood Actress: Biographies and Filmographies of Stars Born after 1939.** Jefferson, NC: McFarland, 1990. 313p. Index, bibl., filmog. LC 90-42755. ISBN 0-89950-387-X.

These fifty biographical profiles include personal milestones as well as quotations relevant to the feminist movement. The appendixes provide statistics regarding gender representation; e.g., percentage of films with one gender in a major role.

117.   Singer, Michael, comp. and ed. **Film Directors: A Complete Guide.** 3rd ed. Beverly Hills, CA: Lone Eagle, 1985. 436p. Illus., index, filmog. ISBN 0-943728-15-0.

The source covers around 1,400 living film directors (arranged alphabetically). Its entries include basic biographical data (e.g., agent's name, address, and phone number) as well as a chronological listing of feature film and telefeature titles (with release year, nation of origin, etc.).

118.   Truitt, Evelyn Mack. **Who Was Who on Screen.** Illus. ed. New York: R. R. Bowker, 1984. 438p. Illus., bibl., filmog. ISBN 0-8352-1906-2; 0-8352-1867-8 pap.

Covering some 3,100 American, British, French, and German actors who died between 1905 and 1982 (the stars, bit players, and even animal performers), the entries include concise biographical profiles and complete film credits. This condensed version of the third edition of the title (New York: R. R. Bowker, 1983) is marred by a number of errors and omissions; nevertheless, it remains a useful source for data relating to the silver screen.

Catalogs/Union Lists

119.   Brady, Anna. **Union List of Film Periodicals: Holdings of Selected American Collections.** Westport, CT: Greenwood, 1984. 316p. Title change and geographical indexes. LC 83-22585. ISBN 0-313-23702-6.

The listing, including more than 1,000 film-related periodicals arranged alphabetically by title, distinguishes between open and closed publications, title variations, and complete, partial, or broken runs. The main text is supplemented by sections explaining how to use the tool and how to identifying participating libraries and their respective National Union Catalog codes.

120.   Gartenberg, Jon, with others, eds. **The Film Catalog: A List of Holdings in the Museum of Modern Art.** Boston: G. K. Hall, 1985. 443p. Illus., index, filmog. ISBN 0-8161-0443-3.

MOMA's computer-generated catalog includes about 5,500 titles, ranging from fiction and documentary to television commercials and home movies. Alphabetically arranged by title (except when more appropriate to employ type, such as newsreel, or descriptive title, such as "screen test" designations), the entries cite title, alternate title, date, country, classification, producer or production company, director, and museum film number. The producer and director index assists greatly in accessing the catalog. The appended filmography is arranged in chronological order.

121.   Matzek, Richard A., comp. **Directory of Archival Collections on the History of Film in the United States.** For the Audiovisual Committee, Resources and Technical Services Division, Association of College and Research Libraries On-Line Audiovisual

Catalogers. Chicago: Resources and Technical Services Division, American Library Association, 1983. [46p.] pap.

The monograph delineates fifty-six U.S. archival collections concerned with movie history. Arranged by state and institution, it provides information on services, restrictions, and times open to the public. An appendix indicates the location of archival resources relating to twenty-four studios.

122. Sleeman, Phillip J., Bernard Queenan, and Francelia Butler. **200 Selected Film Classics for Children of All Ages: Where to Obtain Them and How to Use Them.** Springfield, IL: Charles C. Thomas, 1984. 296p. Illus., index. LC 83-4988. ISBN 0-398-04869-X.

This compilation covers films—available in English and the 16mm format—derived from books of high literary quality that concentrate on "extending the life experiences of children and adults." The alphabetically arranged listing is supplemented by programming tips, a discussion of film rentals, a film care and projection guide, a directory of film companies and distributors, and an author index.

Dictionaries

123. Konigsberg, Ira. **The Complete Film Dictionary.** New York: New American Library, 1987. 420p. Illus. LC 87-5747. ISBN 0-453-00564-0; 0-452-00980-4 pap.

The tool's more than 3,500 entries address all elements of the film industry, including technology, production, film making, distribution, economics, history, and criticism. The text is enhanced by line drawings and motion-picture stills.

124. Singleton, Ralph S. **Filmmaker's Dictionary.** Beverly Hills, CA: Lone Eagle, 1986. 188p. LC 86-15303. ISBN 0-943728-08-8.

The source defines the 1,500 technical terms, slang, and expressions most "widely-used" within the film and television industry. The definitions are first rate, and many other useful features can be found (for example, words defined elsewhere in the dictionary are placed in caps); however, Konigsberg's *The Complete Film Dictionary* (see entry 123) provides more exhaustive coverage of the field.

125. Slide, Anthony. **The American Film Industry: A Historical Dictionary.** Westport, CT: Greenwood, 1986. 431p. Index, bibl. LC 85-27260. ISBN 0-313-24693-9.

This thorough and lucidly written work contains more than 600 entries delineating producing and releasing companies, technological innovations, film series, genres, organizations, and technical terms.

126. Thomas, Nicholas, ed. **International Dictionary of Films and Filmmakers. [Volume] 1: Films.** 2nd ed. Chicago: St. James Press, 1990. 1105p. Bibl. ISBN 1-55862-037-0.

127. Thomas, Nicholas, ed. **International Dictionary of Films and Filmmakers. Volume 2: Directors.** 2nd ed. Chicago: St. James Press, 1991. 958p. Bibl., filmog. LC 90-64265. ISBN 1-55862-038-9.

Volume 1 covers 650-odd films (arranged alphabetically by title). The entries are divided into three parts: production details, a bibliography of published editions of the script and commentaries in periodicals and books, and a critical essay.

Volume 2 is composed of 480 alphabetically arranged director entries that focus on the primary themes exhibited by each's output.

Directories

128.   Singer, Michael, comp. and ed. **Michael Singer's Film Directors: A Complete Guide.** 9th ed. Lone Eagle, 1992. 560p. Illus., index. ISBN 0-943728-46-O.

The tool includes more than 2,500 directors, noting nationalities, birthdates, films, and business addresses both for the directors and their agents.

Encyclopedias

129.   Bogle, Donald. **Blacks in American Film and Television: An Encyclopedia.** Hamden, CT: Garland, 1988. 510p. Illus., index, bibl. (Garland Reference Library of the Humanities, v. 604.) LC 87-29241. ISBN 0-8240-8715-1.

The directory is a competent survey of blacks in these two media. It is divided into three major sections: "Movies," "Television," and "Profiles" (of key writers, producers, actors, etc.)—all alphabetically arranged (the first two categories by program title). The supplementary materials include a five-page "Introduction" to the role of blacks in the cinema and television. Not every black-oriented film has been included—rather, the focus is upon mainstream American titles which have become a part of our national shared experience. The television section includes titles with general credits for black personnel. The bios section is very selective, including only major entertainment figures. The black-and-white photos, taken from the author's archive as well as the Paramount, Warner Brothers, Columbia, and United Artists holdings, enhance the text's attractiveness.

130.   Brown, Gene, and Harry M. Geduld, eds. **The New York "Times" Encyclopedia of Film.** 13 Vols. New York: Times Books, 1984. Illus., index (v. 13). LC 81-3607. ISBN 0-8129-1059-1.

Volumes 1-12 provide chronologically arranged reprints of news stories, feature articles, interviews, and promotional pieces that originally appeared in the newspaper between 1896-1979. Additional access to the material is provided by the key word index, which refers the user to the running heads (month and year) within the unpaged text. This fascinating chronicle of film history rises above its unattractive format (derived from the original publication's 35mm film records).

131.   Buscombe, Edward, ed. **The BFI Companion to the Western.** New York: Atheneum, 1988. 432p. ISBN 0-689-11962-3.

The work consists of a historical essay surveying the genre from the silent era to the late 1980s, followed by about 800 entries devoted to notable themes, characters, weapons, locations, and individuals (actors, directors, scriptwriters, etc.) relating to the genre.

132.   Hardy, Phil, ed. **The Encyclopedia of Horror Movies.** New York: Harper & Row, 1986. 408p. Illus., bibl. LC 86-45718. ISBN 0-06-0550503.

The work encompasses 1,300 entries—arranged chronologically, and subdivided alphabetically within each year by film title—which provide 100 to 1,000 words addressing each film's interest or historical importance in the development of the genre. Included are credits (director, producer, studio, etc.) a brief plot synopsis, and a critical commentary. The valuable supplementary material includes an introductory essay, "The Horror Film in Perspective," and three appendixes (All-Time Horror Rental Champs, Critics' Top Ten, Horror Oscars). The index comprises exclusively title entries; the inclusion of all personal names cited in the text would have been worthwhile. Nevertheless, the tool represents a useful starting point for enthusiasts of this genre.

133.   Holland, Ted. **B Western Actors Encyclopedia: Facts, Photos and Filmographies for More Than 250 Familiar Faces.** Jefferson, NC: McFarland, 1989. 493p. Illus. LC 88-42566. ISBN 0-89950-30603.

The source is composed of four sections: heroes (approximately ninety stars, such as Gene Autry and Tim McCoy), sidekicks (some sixty partners and "saddle pals" like Gabby Hayes), cowgirls (more than sixty leading ladies requiring the assistance of the hero), and the "bad guys." The preface and introductory essays opening each chapter attempt to delineate the genre and its component parts.

134.   Langman, Larry, and Edward Borg. **Encyclopedia of American War Films.** New York: Garland, 1989. 696p. Illus., index, bibl. (Garland Reference Library of the Humanities, v. 873.) LC 89-1491. ISBN 0-8240-7540-4.

This is a compilation of about 3,000 films (i.e., features, documentaries, short subjects, serials, animation) concerned with war. Each entry cites studio, release date, director, screenwriter, and notable credits, and discusses the film's overall significance as well. The appendixes list biographical films by subject, Academy Award-winning films dealing with war, and wars treated on film.

135.   Lieberman, Susan, and Frances Cable, comps. **Memorable Film Characters: An Index to Roles and Performers, 1915-1983.** Westport, CT: Greenwood, 1984. 291p. Indexes. (Bibliographies and Indexes in the Performing Arts, No. 1.) LC 84-10844. ISBN 0-313-23977-0.

This compilation covers more than 1,500 movie characters chosen on the basis of the compilers' own insights, award-nominated film listings, and feedback from a questionnaire sent to film buffs. Each entry provides the name of the character, a description of that character, title and date of the film, and name of the actor. Actor and film indexes considerably enhance the work.

136.   Milne, Tom, and Paul Willemen. **The Encyclopedia of Horror Movies.** edited by Phil Hardy. New York: Harper & Row, 1986. 408p. Illus., bibl., pap. LC 86-45716. ISBN 0-06-096146-5.

The tool includes plot synopses, critiques, and other information on approximately 1,300 horror feature films originating in Europe, Japan, Mexico, and the United States between 1896 and 1985. The entries, chronologically arranged and written by five movie journalists, range from 100 to 1,000 words in length, and often include a photograph. Four useful appendixes are also present: a listing of the most profitable horror films with respect to rental revenue, the top ten horror films chosen by nine critics, those winning Oscars, and a selective bibliography. The work rivals Walt Lee's *A Reference Guide to Fantastic Films* (Los Angeles: Chelsea-Lee, 3 Vols., 1974) and Don Willis's *Horror and Science Fiction Films* (Metuchen, NJ: Scarecrow, 3 Vols., 1973, 1983, 1985) as the definitive source in the genre. Weaknesses include the absence of those films made only for videocassette, biographical information on horror film directors, a more extensive bibliography, information regarding availability on video, and data on special effects.

137.   Siegel, Scott, and Barbara Siegel. **The Encyclopedia of Hollywood.** New York: Facts on File, 1990. xi, 499p. Illus. LC 89-11799. ISBN 0-8160-1792-1.

The book succeeds as an up-to-date reference aid providing general background information about the genres, technical concepts, and major personalities (actors, directors, cinematographers, moguls, etc.) composing Hollywood films. However, it doesn't improve upon the standard for Hollywood coverage set by such titles as Halliwell's *Filmgoer's and Video Viewer's Companion* (see entry 164), Lyon's *International Directory of Films and Filmmakers* (see entries 177-178), *The Illustrated Who's Who of the Cinema* (edited by

Ann Lloyd and Graham Fuller) and *The World Encyclopedia of the Film* (edited by Tim Cawkwell and John Smith). The choices of entries for inclusion (e.g., Caroll Baker and Alexis Smith)—and omission (e.g., blacklisting/censorship, Sydney Greenstreet)—are sometimes questionable, as is probably true of any compact source of this nature. The absence of introductory essays, sidebars, appendixes, chronological charts, etc., and brevity of the entries have limited the likelihood of deriving a coherent overview of the historical development of the cinema; nevertheless, points are succinctly made and reveal a degree of accuracy and perception not always present in such popularly written works.

138. Stanley, John. **Revenge of the Creature Features Movie Guide: An A to Z Encyclopedia to the Cinema of the Fantastic.** 3rd ed. Pacific, CA: Creatures at Large, 1988. 420p. Illus. LC 87-91426. ISBN 0-940064-05-7; 0-940064-04-9 pap.
Stanley cites about 4,000 films (including made-for-television and videocassette originals) that feature "extrahuman forces"; i.e., nonhuman monsters, psychological terror, psychic phenomena, supernatural forces, mythological creatures, and fantasies. The entries, many of which are hard to find in other sources, include director and major cast credits, plot synopses, and critiques.

139. Weldon, Michael, with others. **The Psychotronic Encyclopedia of Film.** New York: Ballantine Books/Random House, 1983. 815p. Illus., index, bibl., pap. LC 82-90841. ISBN 0-345-30381-4.
The tool covers more than 3,000 "psychotronic" films (i.e., the cross-fertilization of weird horror movies and electronic gadget-filled science fiction flicks). The title entries include a plot synopsis, credits, and a commentary.

Guides to the Literature

140. Armour, Robert A. **Film: A Reference Guide.** Westport, CT: Greenwood, 1980. xxiv, 251p. Indexes, bibl. (American Popular Culture.) LC 79-6566. ISBN 0-313-22241-X.
Following an introductory essay surveying the evolution of the film medium and its impact on society, the text is divided into eleven thematic chapters: History of Film, Film Production, Film Criticism, Film Criticism by Genre, Film and Related Arts, Film and Society, Major Actors, Major Directors and Other Production Personnel, Major Films, International Influence on American Film, and Reference Works and Periodicals. Two appendixes are also included: (1) a selective chronology of American films and events; and (2) research collections of colleges and universities; major research centers; and archives, public libraries, studios, and miscellaneous holdings. Access is enhanced by the presence of subject and name indexes.

141. Fisher, Kim N. **On the Screen: A Film, Television, and Video Research Guide.** Littleton, CO: Libraries Unlimited, 1986. 209p. Indexes. (Reference Sources in the Humanities Series.) LC 86-20965. ISBN 0-87287-448-6.
The work focuses on English-language materials dealing with film, television, and video published between the 1960s and 1985. Arranged alphabetically by subject categories (e.g., Ohio), the entries include author, title, imprint, pagination, LC number, ISBN (or ISSN), and evaluative annotations. Further information sources include the listing of on-line databases, "Research Centers and Archives," and "Societies and Associations." Access is enhanced by the presence of author-title and subject indexes.

142. Limbacher, James L. **Sexuality in World Cinema.** 2 Vols. Metuchen, NJ: Scarecrow, 1983. Index, bibl., filmog. LC 83-3019. ISBN 0-8108-1609-1.

The annotated listing of more than 13,000 films is supplemented by sections that give (1) notes on the history of censorship, pornography, and obscenity in relation to motion pictures; (2) a glossary of sex and media terms, including slang; and (3) an index to films by twenty-six classified fields, each of which is preceded by a concise historical outline.

143.   Pitts, Michael R. **Western Movies: A TV and Video Guide to 4,200 Genre Films.** Jefferson, NC: McFarland, 1986. 623p. Index, bibl. LC 85-3105. ISBN 0-89950-195-8.

The broadly defined appellation of "western" here denotes feature films (forty-plus minutes of four reels) from both television and the screen; musicals, dramas, and television pilots are also included. The entries, arranged alphabetically, provide title variations, casts, director, scriptwriter, running time, release company, year, plot, and a concise critique. The work's utility is enhanced by a 100-page index of people involved with these fields, a listing of video dealers, and two trivia lists: one of performers and their real names, and the other matching cowboys and their horses.

144.   Parish, James Robert, and Michael R. Pitts. **The Great Gangster Pictures II.** Metuchen, NJ: Scarecrow, 1987. 397p. Illus. LC 86-28002. ISBN 0-8108-1961-9.

Defining the genre as having "thematic ties in some ways with the underworld or organized crime," the authors include feature films (both theatrical and television releases) and serials ranging from the silent era to the present. The broad criteria result in some strange inclusions; for example, *Reefer Madness* and *The Great Muppet Caper*. Each entry includes release date, length, production personnel, cast, a plot summary, critical comments (often drawing from published reviews), and an evaluation of the film's aesthetic and philosophical message in the context of the genre. The more than 400 entries are arranged alphabetically by film title, with cross-references from alternative titles. Although no index has been provided, the positive features (an engaging, informative text and evocative photos) more than offset this weakness.

Handbooks

145.   Adams, Les, and Buck Rainey. **Shoot-Em-Ups: The Complete Reference Guide to Westerns of the Sound Era.** Metuchen, NJ: Scarecrow, 1985. 633p. Illus., index. LC 78-656. ISBN 0-8108-1848-5.

A reprint of the 1978 work published by Arlington House, the source organizes the 3,000 films by year, thereby allowing for the study of trends, contrasting values, and variations in the making and naming of westerns. The absence of name or subject indexes, however, will diminish its value for trivia buffs.

146.   Allan, Elkan, ed. **A Guide to World Cinema; Covering 7,200 Films of 1950-84, Including Capsule Reviews and Stills from the Programmes of the National Film Theatre, London.** London: British Film Institute/Whittet Books; distr. by Gale Research, 1985. 682p. Illus., index. I: 0-905483-33-2.

International in scope, the tool includes all films shown at the British Film Institute during the thirty-five-year period. Despite the small print and reproductions of movie stills, the commentaries—ranging from scholarly to chatty in approach—for each title offer a vast quantity of raw data for researchers.

147.   Anderson, Craig W. **Science Fiction Films of the Seventies.** Jefferson, NC: McFarland, 1985. 261p. Index. LC 83-42898. ISBN 0-89950-086-2.

These fifty titles represent a sampling of the decade's science fiction offerings, which, in fact, blend into the horror, supernatural, and comedy genres (e.g., Woody Allen's

Sleeper and Mel Brooks' *Young Frankenstein*). Arranged in chronological order, the entries provide cast and credits, plot summaries, and critical analysis.

148.   Andrew, Geoff. **The Film Handbook.** Boston: G. K. Hall, 1990, c1989. 362p. Index, bibl., glossary. (Handbook of the Performing Arts.) LC 89-77760. ISBN 0-8161-9093-3 pap.
    The work focuses on major directors. The entries, arranged alphabetically by name, include biographical data, critiques (and a complete filmography) of the given director's output, and bibliographical listings.

149.   Aros, Andrew A. **A Title Guide to the Talkies, 1975 through 1984.** Metuchen, NJ: Scarecrow, 1986. 347p. Name index. LC 85-27682. ISBN 0-8108-1868-X.
    The book updates Richard B. Dimmitt's *A Title Guide to the Talkies* (Metuchen, NJ: Scarecrow, 1965), which listed 16,000 features from October 1927 through December 1963. Aros incorporated another 3,429 titles in his *A Title Guide to the Talkies, 1964 Through 1974* (Metuchen, NJ: Scarecrow, 1976), in addition to the 3,891 entries in this volume. The primary aim of each volume has been to facilitate the identification of novels, plays, poems, and short stories upon which Hollywood films are based.

150.   Benson, Michael. **Vintage Science Fiction Films, 1896-1949.** Jefferson, NC: McFarland, 1985. 219p. Illus., index, bibl., filmog. LC 83-42889. ISBN 0-89950-085-4.
    The bulk of the text is divided into three sections: "Silents," "Sound 1929-1949," and "Serials 1915-1949." Within each category, essays are followed by chronologically arranged film title entries that include plot synopses and information on the actors, directors, studios, producers, make-up artists, and technological developments.

151.   Bowers, Q. David. **Nickelodeon Theatres and Their Music.** Vestal, NY: Vestal, 1986. 214p. Illus. LC 86-5594 ISBN 0-011582-50-3; 0-911572-49-X pap.
    The seminal era of American movies—1900-1915—is portrayed via early movie house pictures, portraits of silent-film stars, and illustrations of the player pianos and organs used to accompany the shows.

152.   Bowser, Eileen. See: **History of the American Cinema.**

153.   Cadden, Tom Scott. **What a Bunch of Characters! An Entertaining Guide to Who Played What in the Movies.** Englewood Cliffs, NJ: Prentice-Hall, 1984. 326p. Index, bibl. LC 84-3272. ISBN 0-13-951914-9; 0-13-951906-8 pap.
    The work cites the key roles played by fifty leading actors and actresses of American film (e.g., Bogart, Davis, Garbo, Redford). Arranged by name, the entries include film credits and brief plot synopses; the index encompasses 2,600 features.

154.   Corey, Melinda, and George Ochoa. **A Cast of Thousands: A Compendium of Who Played What In Film.** 3 Vols. New York: Facts on File, 1992. 2,544p. ISBN 0-8160-2429-4.
    Although lacking the comprehensive coverage provided by Jay Nash and Stanley Ross' *Motion Picture Guide* (Evanston, IL: CineBooks, 1987, 12 vols.), this useful source lists actors and actresses and their roles for 10,000 films from 1912 to 1991.

155.   Drew, Bernard A. **Motion Picture Series and Sequels: A Reference Guide.** Hamden, CT: Garland, 1990. 412p. (Garland Reference Library of the Humanities, v. 1186.) Index., bibl. LC 90-3321. ISBN 0-8240-4248-4.

The tool covers more than 900 series and sequels going back to 1899. The entries include studio, year of release, director, major cast, alternate titles (when appropriate), plot synopsis, and citations to literary (and other) sources. The title index enhances the reader's access to the text.

156.   Dixon, Wheeler, ed. **Producers Releasing Corporation: A Comprehensive Filmography and History.** Jefferson, NC: McFarland, 1986. 166p. Illus., index, bibl., filmog. LC 84-43242. ISBN 0-89950-179-6.

This survey of PRC, one of Hollywood's "B" movie studios, includes a chronology, a brief history of the studio, a survey of PRC westerns, biographical profiles of key PRC personnel, filmographies of notable PRC directors, an explanation of "B" movie structure, 1944 industry statistics, and a comprehensive film checklist.

157.   Dye, David. **Child and Youth Actors: Filmographies of Their Entire Careers, 1915-1985.** Jefferson, NC: McFarland, 1988. 310p. Illus., index. LC 87-46441. ISBN 0-89950-247-4.

Dye includes child and teenage actors who have appeared in at least two movies, television films or series, or stage productions, between 1914 and 1985. The alphabetically arranged (by actor name) entries provide vital statistics, a chronological list of media performances, information about these roles, and (where applicable) information about the adult career. Includes a film title index.

158.   Emmens, Carol A. **Short Stories on Film.** Littleton, CO: Libraries Unlimited, 1978. 345p. Indexes. LC 78-13488. ISBN 0-87287-146-0.

The source covers more than 1,300 films released from 1920 to 1976 that are based upon short stories. The entries are arranged alphabetically by author and subdivided alphabetically by story titles. Entries include film title, a source material note, technical information, production credits, cast credits, and an annotation. Short story and film title indexes and a directory of distributors are also provided.

159.   Enser, A. G. S. **Filmed Books and Plays: A List of Books and Plays from Which Films Have Been Made, 1928-86.** Rev. ed. Brockfield, VT: Gower, 1987. 770p. Indexes. LC 87-157. ISBN 0-566-03564-2.

This edition updates and enlarges the previous editions (1928-1974; 1975-1983). The alphabetically arranged title index (which includes a change from original book title) identifies the film's producer/distributor and the date, author, title, and publisher of the book from which the film is derived. The author index notes, by writer, the works that have been filmed.

160.   Erickson, Hal. **Syndicated Television: The First Forty Years, 1947-1987.** Jefferson, NC: McFarland, 1989. 418p. Index. LC 89-42583, ISBN 0-89950-410-8.

The source lists—by decade, subdivided by genre (e.g., adventure/mystery)—the programs that are or were in first run syndication. It supplements the data provided by Tim Brooks and Earle Marsh's *Complete Directory to Prime Time Network TV Shows 1946-Present* (4th ed., New York: Ballantine, 1988; now available in a 5th edition, 1992).

161.   Garland, Brock. **War Movies.** New York: Facts on File, 1987. 230p. Illus., index, bibl. LC 87-9052. ISBN 0-8160-1206-7.

The work surveys over 450 films depicting war (or having elements in common with it); this is far from a comprehensive listing. However, the choices represent the best of the genre and the entries are highly informative (including descriptive analysis, a star rating denoting the relative quality of each movie, company name, year of release, director, major cast members, color or black-and-white). In addition, a thirteen-page introduction surveys the history of the genre, and the eighty-five black-and-white photos enhance the appeal of the text.

162.   Gehring, Wes D., ed. **Handbook of American Film Genres.** Westport, CT: Greenwood, 1988. 405p. Index, filmog. LC 87-31784. ISBN 0-313-24715-3.
       Unequaled in its expansiveness as a film criticism source, the tool covers nineteen film genres—including action-adventure, five comedy, three "fantastic," two "songs and soaps" genres, the social problem film, biography, and the art film—each featuring essays by a noted scholar. These essays encompass four parts: a historical and analytical overview, a bibliographical summary of the genre's key literature, a checklist of these texts, and a filmography of the genre's major productions.

163.   Halliwell, Leslie. **Halliwell's Film Guide.** New York: HarperCollins. Annual. Illus., pap. LC 89-54159.
       This source offers thumbnail sketches of some 18,000 English-language films and television movies arranged alphabetically by title. Each entry includes country of origin; year of release; running time; black-and-white or color; production credits; alternate titles; a synopsis; critical evaluation and quotation from reviews; writer, director, photography, music, and other credits; additional notes; Academy Awards and nominations; and video information.

164.   Halliwell, Leslie. **Halliwell's Filmgoer's and Video Viewer's Companion.** 9th ed. New York: HarperCollins, 1990. 786p. Illus. LC 89-45916. ISBN 0-06-096392-1 pap.
       The tool provides biographical data for actors, directors, writers, bit players, cinematographers, etc., in addition to topics relating to film and video history.

165.   Haun, Harry. **The Movie Quote Book.** New York: Lippincott & Crowell, 1980. 415p. Filmog. LC 80-7865. ISBN 0-690-02000-7.
       The quotations are arranged thematically (e.g., love), with the context provided for each; i.e., the speaker, the message of the quote, the name of the film, and the screenwriter.

166.   Hayes, R. M. **Trick Cinematography: The Oscar Special-Effects Movies.** Jefferson, NC: McFarland, 1986. 370p. Illus., index. LC 84-43219. ISBN 0-89950-157-5.
       Hayes cites all personnel involved with films nominated for an Academy Award in the special effects, scientific, or technical categories. Each entry includes an analysis of the technical effects employed as well as a listing of the key actors, producers, directors, editors, secondary and "bit" characters, stuntmen, costume designers, script supervisor's assistants, matte artists, camera operators, and any other contributors to the film.

167.   Hiatt, Sky. **Picture This!: A Guide to Over 300 Environmentally, Socially, and Politically Relevant Films and Videos.** New York: Noble, 1992. 389p. Index. LC 91-50642. ISBN 1-879360-05-5 pap.
       The film entries consist of one-page critiques of more than 300 topics, such as war, poverty.

168.   Hilger, Michael. **The American Indian in Film.** Metuchen, NJ: Scarecrow, 1986. 196p. Actor name and topical index, bibl. LC 86-10061. ISBN 0-8108-1905-8.
       Hilger covers motion pictures concerned, to a notable degree, with native Americans (i.e., they have major characters who are native Americans or plots that involve native Americans). The text is organized into four main parts: silent films, early sound films, films of the 1950s and 1960s, and films of the 1970s and 1980s. Within these headings,

the title entries are arranged chronologically and include cataloging data, a plot synopsis, and excerpts of film reviews.

169. Hirschhorn, Clive. **The Hollywood Music.** New York: Crown, 1981. Illus., index. LC 81-3122. ISBN 0-517-54044-4.
    The work includes 1,344 films arranged chronologically (from Jolson's *The Jazz Singer* [1927] to Diamond's *The Jazz Singer* [1980]) with each year making up a chapter. Borderline musicals are delineated in three appendixes: fringe musicals, miscellaneous musicals, and documentaries.

170. **History of the American Cinema.** Musser, Charles. **Volume 1: The Emergence of Cinema: The American Screen to 1907.** Bowser, Eileen. **Volume 2: The Transformation of Cinema.** Koszarska, Richard. **Volume 3: An Evening's Entertainment. The Age of the Silent Feature Picture, 1915-1928.** New York: Scribner's, 1990. xvii, 613p.; xii, 337p.; xi, 395p. Illus., indexes, bibl. ISBN 0-684-18413-3; 0-684-18414-1; 0-684-18415-X.
    Part of a projected ten-volume set, the text is composed of substantive articles concentrating on feature films, documentaries, and avant-garde/experimental/ art films. These contributions tend to focus on the following perspectives: technology, social and economic conditions, and style and aesthetics. Includes both general and film title indexes.

171. Kael, Pauline. **Taking It All In.** New York: Holt, Rinehart and Winston, 1984. 527p. Index. (A William Abrahams Book, v. 7.) LC 83-8445. ISBN 0-03-069362-4; 0-03-069361-6 pap.
    This compilation of 150 *New Yorker* film reviews, published between June 8, 1980, and June 13, 1983, is the seventh in a series spanning more than two decades. Kael has long been considered one of the leading movie reviewers around; her work is insightful and provocative in approach.

172. Kinnard, Roy. **Fifty Years of Serial Thrills.** Metuchen, NJ: Scarecrow, 1983. 210p. Illus., index. LC 83-13950. ISBN 0-8108-1644-X.
    Studio by studio, Kinnard provides a history of each company and analyzes its output within each section. His introduction attempts to delineate the socio-economic forces behind the rise and fall of the serial as well as its influence on more recent adventure epics.

173. Koszarska, Richard. See: **History of the American Cinema.**

174. Langman, Larry. **A Guide to American Screenwriters: The Sound Era, 1929-1982.** 2 Vols. New York: Garland, 1984. (Garland Reference Library of the Humanities, Vol. 501.) LC 84-48018. ISBN 0-8240-8927-8.
    This set provides the name of the screenwriter and a chronological listing of U.S. credits in volume 1; volume 2 gives access by title. Excluded from coverage are short subjects, less-than-feature-length cartoons, made-for-television movies, works failing to identify a screenwriter, and porn trade titles.

175. Langman, Larry. **Writers on the American Screen: A Guide to Film Adaptations of American and Foreign Literary Works.** New York: Garland, 1986. 329p. Index, bibl. (Garland Reference Library of the Humanities, Vol. 658.) LC 85-28991. ISBN 0-8240-9844-7.

Covering poems, short stories, plays, and novels, the entries—arranged alphabetically by writer's name, followed by titles of writings, and then film titles—cite year of the film's release and releasing studio. Includes a title index.

176. Lee, Walt. **Reference Guide to Fantastic Films: Science Fiction, Fantasy & Horror.** 3 Vols. Los Angeles: Chelsea-Lee, 1974. 742p. Pap. LC 72-88775. ISBN 0-913974-04-8.

This is an extremely useful, albeit dated, title listing of credits on 40,000 fantasy films up through 1972. Concise descriptions explain why each movie has been included.

177. Lyon, Christopher, and Susan Doll, eds. **The International Directory of Films and Filmmakers: Volume I: Films.** Chicago: St. James Press, 1984. 536p. Bibl. LC 83-24616. ISBN 0-912289-04-X.

178. Lyon, Christopher, and Susan Doll, eds. **The International Directory of Films and Filmmakers: Volume II: Directors/ Filmmakers.** Chicago: St. James Press, 1984. 611p. Bibl., filmog. LC 83-24616. ISBN 0-912289-05-8.

Volume 1 covers approximately 600 of the "most widely studied films"; entries include credits, production dates and locations, cost, and an analysis of the film's legacy. Over 450 notable directors are profiled and critiqued in Volume 2.

179. Magill, Frank N., ed. **Magill's Survey of Cinema: English Language Films: First Series.** 4 Vols. Englewood Cliffs, NJ: Salem, 1980. 1989p. Indexes (vol. 4). LC: 80-52131. I: 0-89356-225-4.

The tool includes more than 500 English-language films and cites for each release date, credits, running time, its overall significance, and critical commentaries on the major contributors. Volume 4 includes performer, director, screenwriter, editor, and cinematographer indexes.

180. Maltin, Leonard. **The Disney Films.** Updated ed. New York: Crown, 1984. 343p. Illus., index. LC 84-12667. ISBN 0-517-55407-0.

The bulk of the work looks at the feature films (arranged chronologically) released during Walt Disney's tenure. The balance of the volume consists of critical surveys entitled "Without Walt," "Disney Shorts," "Disney TV," and "Disneyana."

181. McCarty, John. **The Modern Horror Film: 50 Contemporary Classics.** New York: Carol Publishing Group, 1990. 256p. Illus. ISBN 0-8065-1164-8.

The tool covers fifty titles from the horror genre dating from the 1959-1989 period. Each entry addresses the film's background, significance, cast, and other key personnel (producer, director, writer, composer, etc.).

182. **The Motion Picture Guide. 1989 Annual: The Films of 1988.** Evanston, IL: CineBooks; distr. by R. R. Bowker, 1989. 665p. Illus., index. LC 85-71145. ISBN 0-933997-20-5.

Divided into two sections, U.S. releases and international releases, the source categorizes films by genre, identifies works receiving the highest rating (five stars), notes films likely to appeal to parents and those involved with youth, and provides a complete alphabetical listing of these titles as well as where to obtain them.

183.   Mula, James J., Daniel Curran, and Jeffrey H. Wallenfeldt, eds. **Spies and Sleuths: Mystery, Spy and Suspense Films on Videocassette.** Evanston, IL: CineBooks, 1988. 211p. Indexes. LC 88-71573. ISBN 0-933997-18-3.

Covering the genre from *The Cat and the Canary* (1927) to *Black Widow* (1987), the title entries indicate year of release, running time. studio name, alternative title, principal cast and their respective roles, production credits, MPAA rating, parental recommendation, and a rating of up to five stars and gives a summary and critique of each film's plot. Series and source author indexes have been included.

184.   Musser, Charles. See: **History of the American Cinema.**

185.   Nash, Jay Robert, and Stanley Ralph Ross. **The Motion Picture Guide, 1927-1984, A-B.** Chicago: Cinebooks, 1985. 324p. Illus., index. LC 85-71145. ISBN 0-933997-01-9.

Part of a projected twelve-volume set, Nash and Ross will cover more than 25,000 English-language and important foreign language films released theatrically. The entries offer author ratings (zero to five stars), year of release, running time, production/releasing company, cast list, production credits, film classification (e.g., musical), analysis of the film, note on availability in videocassette, parental recommendation and MPAA rating. The appendix includes an awards list. Accessibility is enhanced by a proper name index.

186.   Neibaur, James L. **Movie Comedians: The Complete Guide.** Jefferson, NC: McFarland, 1986. 247p. Illus., index, bibl., filmog. LC 84-43204. ISBN 0-89950-163-X.

This breezily written tool includes an essay discussing all film comedians predating Charlie Chaplin, sixteen entries devoted to major stars, and broad chapters (e.g., 1930s-1940s) covering such "minor" figures as Dudley Moore.

187.   Novak, Ralph, and Peter Travers, eds. **People Magazine Guide to Movies on Video.** New York: Collier/Macmillan, 1987. 464p. Index. LC 87-9420. ISBN 0-02-029862-5.

This is a compilation of movie reviews appearing in *People Weekly* between 1977 and 1986. The entries, arranged alphabetically by film title, include MPAA rating, date of release, and videotape distributor (where applicable). The reviews are straightforward—long on plot synopsis and short on philosophical discussion—yet insightful. The source also offers a couple of interesting special sections: "Children's Movies" (covering films—usually available on video—that date back as far as *Snow White,* 1937) and the "Best and Worst Movies" for the Action/Adventure, Children's, Comedies, Dramas, Foreign, Musicals, Mystery/Suspense, and Science Fiction/Horror genres. Includes a title index.

188.   Nowlan, Robert A., and Gwendolyn Wright Nowlan. **Cinema Sequels and Remakes, 1903-1987.** Jefferson, NC: McFarland, 1989. 954p. Illus., index. LC 88-42640. ISBN 0-89950-314-4.

Devoted to "all films, silent or sound, from the genres of drama, action-adventure, romance, comedy or thriller" (p. xii) that have had at least one English-language sound remake or sequel, the entries—arranged alphabetically by the primary film—give production data, plot summaries, a comparison of remakes or sequels, and the identification of other media on which a film was based (where relevant).

189.   Nowlan, Robert A., and Gwendolyn Wright Nowlan. **Movie Characters of Leading Performers of the Sound Era.** Chicago: American Library Association, 1990. 396p. LC 88-37686. ISBN 0-8389-0480-7 pap.

The 400-odd entries, organized alphabetically by performer name, give a concise bio; key roles acted with character name and description, film title, date issued, studio, and directors; and character names, film titles, and dates for other roles played.

190. Okuda, Red, with Edward Watz. **The Columbia Comedy Shorts: Two-Reel Hollywood Film Comedies, 1933-1958.** Jefferson, NC: McFarland, 1986. 262p. Illus., index, bibl., filmog. LC 84-43241. ISBN 0-89950-181-8.

A survey of an art form (sixteen to twenty minutes in length) that was highly visible from the 1930s through the mid-1950s, the work consists of a profile of Columbia Pictures (a leading proponent of the genre); a look at the technical features of production; an analysis and listing of the 526 titles produced in Hollywood by series; and concise sketches of leading directors, writers, and performers.

191. Parish, James Robert, and George H. Hill. **Black Action Films: Plots, Critiques, Casts and Credits.** Jefferson, NC: McFarland, 1989. 385p. Illus., index. LC 89-42871. ISBN 0-89950-456-6.

The rationale provided by the authors for this source is the significance of black action films in articulating the black community's feelings and in providing work opportunities for African American talent. The text comprises 235 films from the 1950s through the 1980s (theatrical and television movies available in the video format). Arranged alphabetically by title, the entries include basic production data as well as a discussion of the critical and political reactions to the films.

192. Parish, James Robert, and Michael R. Pitts. **The Great Detective Pictures.** Metuchen, NJ: Scarecrow, 1990. 616p. Illus., bibl. LC 90-8551. ISBN 0-8108-2286-5.

A typical volume in the authors' Great Pictures series, it covers around 350 feature films, serials, and made-for-television movies. Entries (arranged alphabetically by title) provide year released, running time, production credits, name of production company, cast credits, a plot summary, and a critique.

193. Parish, James Robert, and Michael R. Pitts. **The Great Science Fiction Pictures.** Metuchen, NJ: Scarecrow, 1977. 309p. Illus., bibl. ISBN 0-8108-1029-8.

194. Parish, James Robert, and Michael R. Pitts. **The Great Science Fiction Pictures II.** Metuchen, NJ: Scarecrow, 1990. 489p. Illus., bibl. LC 89-24058. ISBN 0-8108-2247-4.

Together the volumes treat 800-odd films and radio and television programs. Both are liberally illustrated with black-and-white movie stills and include chronological lists of films covered.

195. Parish, James Robert, and Michael R. Pitts. **The Great Spy Pictures II.** Metuchen, NJ: Scarecrow, 1986. 432p. Illus., bibl. LC 86-11900. ISBN 0-8108-1913-9.

This updated compilation includes "all pictures which feature spying, espionage, or foreign intrigue," in addition to many spoofs, satires, serials, minor films, and B movies of the spy genre, including science fiction and westerns incorporating any of the aforementioned elements. The alphabetically arranged entries each include name of studio, release date, running time, cast and production credits, a plot synopsis, succinct evaluative commentary, and listings for spy/adventure programs on radio and television, spy novels, and relevant book series.

196. Pickard, Roy. **Who Played Who on the Screen.** New York: Hippocrene, 1989. 351p. Illus. ISBN 0-87052-789-4.

Originally published as *Who Played Who in the Movies* (1988), this updated and expanded edition includes about 800 real persons and fictional characters portrayed in film. Each entry includes a discussion of the subject relative to his or her film portrait along with a chronological listing of these films, actor playing the role, name of film in its country of origin, name of director, and year of release.

197. **Rating the Movies for Home Video, TV, and Cable.** by the editors of Consumer Guide. 576p. Illus., pap.

The work includes summaries and ratings for over 3,700 films. The entries—arranged alphabetically by title, include a discussion of talent and directors, running time, MPAA rating, year of release, etc. The objective, reliable ratings (four-star scheme) represent a strength. The prime weakness is the limited number of titles (e.g., cult films are generally ignored) composing the text.

198. Robertson, Patrick. **The Guinness Book of Almost Everything You Didn't Need to Know About the Movies.** Enfield, England: Guinness; distr. by Sterling, 1986. 144p. Illus. ISBN 0-85112-481-X.

The brief entries provide trivia about movie personalities, their work and private lives, film curiosities, anecdotes, eccentricities, etc. The patented Guinness flavor can be discerned throughout: lists of stars serving prison terms, stars having enjoyed the longest careers, and so on, in addition to insults, blunders, and anachronisms not caught by film editors. Containing material generally missing from standard reference tools, the book's appeal is enhanced by heavy use of boldface type (which optimizes skimming text) and frequent halftone illustrations.

199. Robertson, Patrick. **Movie Facts and Feats.** New York: Sterling, 1980. 288p. Illus., indexes, filmog. (A Guinness Record Book.) LC 80-52340. ISBN 0-8069-0204-3.

The tool incorporates a diversified array of subjects, in a classified arrangement, including historical data, industry statistics, credits, out-takes, and film treatments of Buffalo Bill, Cinderella, soccer, etc. Accessibility is enhanced by name, subject, and title indexes.

200. Rothwell, Kenneth S., and Annabelle Henkin Melzer. **Shakespeare on Screen: An International Filmography and Videography.** New York: Neal-Schuman, 1990. 404p. Indexes, bibl. LC 90-31509. ISBN 1-55570-049-7.

This source delineates 750 films and videos released since 1899. A list of documentaries about Shakespeare is also included. Accessibility to the text is enhanced by three indexes: play, series, and genre; year of production or release; and name (actors, production staff, authors, critics, editors).

201. Sandahl, Linda J. **Rock Films: A Viewer's Guide to Three Decades of Musicals, Concerts, Documentaries, and Soundtracks, 1955-1986.** New York: Facts on File, 1987. 239p. Illus., indexes. LC 86-24347. ISBN 0-8160-1281-4; 0-8160-1576-7 pap.

The work is organized into three sections: musicals (films in which rock is performed on-screen within the context of a story), concerts and documentaries, and soundtracks. The entries note release date, cast, and rock songs and performers. There is one notable drawback: films utilizing only one rock song (e.g., *High School Confidential,* which features Jerry Lee Lewis performing the title track) have been excluded. The text can be accessed by name, film title, and songs performed indexes.

202. Selby, Spencer. **Dark City: The Film Noir.** Jefferson, NC: McFarland, 1984. 255p. Index, filmog. LC 83-19984. ISBN 0-89950-103-6.

This insightful volume evades defining the genre, but rather focuses upon the tone or mood characterizing the examples included here. Part 1 analyzes twenty-five of the more definitive film noir productions, whereas the second portion lists about 500 additional titles belonging to this genre.

203.   Shull, Michael S., and David E. Wilt. **Doing Their Bit: Wartime American Animated Short Films, 1939-1945.** Jefferson, NC: McFarland, 1987. 198p. Illus., indexes, bibl., filmog. LC 85-43589. ISBN 0-89950-218-0.
        This tool surveys 271 war-related cartoons released between 1939-1945. A sixty-eight-page introduction discusses pre-1960 cartoons as a barometer of cultural attitudes. The six appendixes include data regarding the proportional representation of war-related cartoons, the frequency of various war-related subjects, and a selected list of World War I era cartoons. Accessibility is enhanced by cartoon character and primary/secondary war-related topics indexes.

204.   Singer, Michael, comp. and ed. **Michael Singer's Film Directors: A Complete Guide.** 7th ed. Beverly Hills, CA: Lone Eagle, 1989. 544p. Indexes. ISBN 0-943728-27-4.
        The text includes sections on "Living Directors" and "Notable Directors of the Past," as well as six interviews (Irvin Kerschen, Harry Hook, Mira Nair, Richard Donner, Keenen Ivory Wayans, and George Sidney). Film title (separate living and dead directors subsections), foreign-based director, directors guild, agent and manager, and directory advertiser indexes complement the main body of the work.

205.   Skorman, Richard, with Gail Bradney and Tony Etz. **Off-Hollywood Movies: A Film Lover's Guide.** New York: Harmony Books/Crown, 1989. 370p. Illus., indexes. LC 88-2093. ISBN 0-517-56863-2 pap.
        The source covers 445 off-Hollywood movies; i.e., art films playing at repertoire and revival theaters, film societies, film festivals, and first-run art houses. Also included are a section criticizing dubbing of foreign films and looking at concerns relating to off-Hollywood movies and an appendix entitled "Renting and Purchasing Videos through the Mail." Access to the text is enhanced by director, actor, country, and cinematographer indexes.

206.   Skretvedt, Randy, and Jordan R. Young, eds. **The Nostalgia Entertainment Sourcebook: The Complete Resource Guide to Classic Movies, Vintage Music, Old Time Radio & Theatre.** Buena Park, CA: Moonstone, 1991. 160p. Hardcover and pap. eds. ISBN 0-940410-25-7; 0-940410-24-9 pap.
        The work includes 1,133 sources of classic movies on video, old-time radio shows on tape, fan clubs for vintage entertainers, movie posters, 78 r.p.m. records, big band radio stations, jazz festivals, film festivals, libraries, museums, etc.

207.   Slide, Anthony. **Silent Portraits: Stars of the Silent Screen in Historic Photographs.** Vestal, NY: Vestal, 1989. 280p. Illus. ISBN 0-911572-78-3.
        Living proof that a picture can be worth a thousand words, this tool represents a panoramic compilation of portraits depicting more than 500 personalities, complemented by biographical captions.

208.   Stacy, Jan, and Ryder Syvertsen. **The Great Book of Movie Monsters.** Chicago: Contemporary Books, 1983. 352p. Illus., indexes. LC 83-7748. ISBN 0-8092-5525-1.
        The work's 300-odd entries, arranged alphabetically by name of monster, indicate how each monster was created, its size and weight, occupation, dietary preferences, methods of communication, friends/ and enemies, intelligence, accomplishments, and "What to Do If You Meet." Supplementary material includes monster, movie, director, and studio indexes.

209. Stacy, Jan, and Ryder Syvertsen. **The Great Book of Movie Villains: A Guide to the Screen's Meanies, Tough Guys, and Bullies.** Chicago: Contemporary Books, 1984. 256p. Illus., indexes. LC 84-14254. ISBN 0-8092-5351-8 pap.

This volume covers over 250 cinematic villains. The entries, arranged alphabetically by name, are each designed to look like a dossier, including film data, a description of a villain and his or her powers, occupation, intelligence, friends, enemies, and evil deeds. The text is complemented by actor, movie, director, and studio indexes.

210. Warren, Bill. **Keep Watching the Skies: American Science Fiction Movies of the Fifties. Volume II: 1958-1962.** Jefferson, NC: McFarland, 1986. 839p. Illus., index, bibl. LC 81-19324. ISBN 0-89950-170-2.

Warren covers 155 films in lengthy essays (up to 6,000 words) that provide plot summaries, insights as to how the film was made, an evaluation of the acting, excerpts from review sources, and his own commentary on matters such as durability and emotional impact. The appendixes include an alphabetical listing (by film title) of credits and casts in addition to a chronological film outline (by release date).

211. Willis, Donald C. **Horror and Science Fiction Films III.** Metuchen, NJ: Scarecrow, 1984. 335p. LC 84-13885. ISBN 0-8108-1723-3.

Updating the earlier volumes in the series (the first covered 4,400 films released through 1971, the second 2,350 through 1981), this installment adds 760 titles through December 1983. Its strengths include informative annotations and the citing of reviews from a diversified array of sources.

212. Zucker, Harvey Marc, and Lawrence J. Babich, comps. **Sports Films: A Complete Reference.** Jefferson, NC: McFarland, 1987. Illus., indexes, bibl. LC 86-21090. ISBN 0-89950-227-X.

The tool covers over 2,000 sports films produced between 1896 and 1984, generally confined to spectator sports in twelve categories, including baseball, basketball, football, wheels, horses and other animals, soccer, rugby, cricket, and hurling. Information about athletes who have appeared in films and athletes portrayed in films is also provided. Proper name and title indexes optimize access to the text.

Indexes

213. **Film Literature Index.** 1973-. Quarterly, with annual cumulations. Albany, NY: Film and Television Documentation Center, SUNY at Albany.

The work provides access to over 300 periodicals (some on a selective basis) devoted to the international film literature. The articles are entered under author name, over 1,000 subject headings, and various proper names (e.g., screenwriters, performers, directors, cinematographers, professional societies, festivals, awards). Book reviews are found under both author and subject listings. The volumes include television coverage in a separate section.

214. Goble, Alan, ed. **The International Film Index, 1895-1990.** Vol. 1: **Film Titles.** Vol. 2: **Directors' Filmography and Indexes.** New York: K. G. Saur, 1991. 1800p. Index, bibl. ISBN 0-86291-623-2.

The tool incorporates 182,456 films (features, shorts, television movies, animation, documentaries, serials, and silent-era material) by 24,688 directors from around the world. It is perfect for identifying obscure items, alternative titles, or a director's complete output.

215. Hanson, Patricia King, and Stephen L. Hanson, eds. **Film Review Index. Volume 1: 1882-1949.** Phoenix, AZ: Oryx, 1986. 397p. Indexes, bibl. LC 85-43369. ISBN 0-89774-153-6.

216. Hanson, Patricia King, and Stephen L. Hanson, eds. **Film Review Index. Volume 2: 1950-1985.** Phoenix, AZ: Oryx, 1987. 416p. Indexes, bibl. LC 85-43369. ISBN 0-89774-331-8.

The set cites reviews and discussions of more than 5,000 movies (2,000-plus in volume 1), arranged by title. Books as well as popular and technical journals are covered. Both volumes include director, year of production, and country of origin indexes.

217. Harrison, P. S. **Harrison's Reports and Film Reviews.** Vols. 1-5: **1919-1934.** Vols. 7-14: **1938-1962.** Vol. 15: **Index.** Hollywood, CA: Hollywood Film Archive, 1992. 10,800p. Edited by D. Richard Baer. Index. ISBN 0-913616-10-9.

This is a complete reprint of *Harrison's Reports and Film Reviews,* which offered aesthetic analysis of individual titles in addition to sociological and technical commentaries of the industry. It is particularly noteworthy for the direct, insightful opinions of Harrison.

218. Moulds, Michael, ed. **International Index to Film Periodicals 1985: An Annotated Guide.** London: International Federation of Film Archives; distr. by St. James Press, 1972-. Annual. Indexes. ISBN 0-906973-13-9 (1986 ed.).

The work categorizes the film literature from over eighty-five periodicals. It is organized into sections on topical headings (subdivided alphabetically), separate films, and biographies. Author and director indexes have been included.

219. Slide, Anthony, ed. **Selected Film Criticism 1951-1960.** Metuchen, NJ: Scarecrow, 1985. 186p. Index. (Selected Film Criticism, No. 7.) LC 81-23344. ISBN 0-8108-1763-2.

Slide has pulled together views from scholarly and mass circulation journals for 137 features in this compilation.

220. Willis, Donald, ed. **"Variety's" Complete Science Fiction Reviews.** New York: Garland, 1985. 479p. Illus., index. LC 85-25257. ISBN 0-8240-6263-9; 0-8240-8712-7 pap.

The source has compiled more than 1,000 science fiction reviews appearing in *Variety* from 1907 through 1984. The entries, arranged chronologically and photoreproduced from the original pages, include the film's country of origin, production and cast credits, rating, and running time. The reviews blend a plot synopsis, a modicum of critical analysis, and reference to each film's money-making potential. The title index enhances the utility of the tool.

Journalism

Bibliographies

221. Slide, Anthony, ed. **International Film, Radio, and Television Journals.** Westport, CT: Greenwood, 1985. 428p. Index, bibl. (Historical Guides to the World's Periodicals and Newspapers.) LC 84-8929. ISBN 0-313-23759-X.

This is an annotated listing (arranged alphabetically) of media titles, noting for each key articles; sources, where indexed; availability of back runs in paper or microforms; library holdings; and publishing history and data. The appendixes include bibliographic essays on fan club publications, fan magazines, in-house journals, and national film periodicals of foreign countries. They also include journals arranged by country of origin and main text entries arranged by selected topics.

222. Sloan, William David, comp. **American Journalism History: An Annotated Bibliography.** Westport, CT: Greenwood, 1989. 344p. (Bibliographies and Indexes in Mass Media and Communications, No. 1.) Index. LC 88-35800. ISBN 0-313-26350-7.

The compilation includes 2,657 entries (books and articles from more than 100 magazines), arranged in chronological order. Despite its gaps (e.g., spare coverage of "The Press and the Age of Reform, 1900-1917"), much material unavailable elsewhere has been included. Accessibility is enhanced by the author-subject index.

Biographies

223. Downs, Robert B., and Jane B. Downs. **Journalists of the United States.** Jefferson, NC: McFarland, 1991. 400p. Index, bibl. LC 91-52634. ISBN 0-89950-549-X.

The work provides biographical outlines of almost 600 print and broadcast journalists from the 1600s to the present. The entries, strongest in coverage of the eighteenth- and nineteenth-century figures, range from several paragraphs to two pages. The introduction includes concise essays on selected topics, such as censorships and women journalists. This represents a worthy supplement to the *Encyclopedia of Twentieth Century Journalists* (1986) and the narrow selection of entries on newspaper and magazine journalists within the *Dictionary of Literary Biography* (Documentary Series, Vol. 8. Detroit: Gale Research, 1991).

224. Krantz, Les, ed. **American Photographers: An Illustrated Who's Who.** New York: Facts on File, 1989. 352p. Illus., index. LC 89-1435. ISBN 0-8160-1419-1.

This attractive tool profiles the lives and output of over 1,000 photographers, ranging from those in the advertising and fashion industries to leading photojournalists. Over one-third of the photos illustrating their work, which have been carefully reproduced on high-quality paper stock, are in color.

225. McKerns, Joseph, ed. **Biographical Dictionary of American Journalism.** Westport, CT: Greenwood, 1989. 820p. Indexes. bibl. LC 88-25098. ISBN 0-313-23818-9.

The volume's 500 biographical essays cover American journalists born after 1690, with a particular emphasis on nationwide celebrity. The format employed matches that of the *Dictionary of American Biography.* Accessibility is enhanced by means of general, media, professional field, and Pulitzer Prize indexes.

226. Riley, Sam G., ed. **American Magazine Journalists, 1850-1900.** Detroit: Gale Research, 1989. 387p. Illus., index, bibl. (Dictionary of Literary Biography, v. 79.) ISBN 0-8103-4557-9.

Following a well-written foreword, which surveys magazine publishing trends to the political and socio-economic climate of the period, the work's entries closely adhere to the format followed by the *Dictionary of Literary Biography* series.

227. Riley, Sam G., ed. **American Magazine Journalists, 1900-1960: First Series.** Detroit: Gale Research, 1990. 401p. Illus., index, bibl. (Dictionary of Literary Biography, v. 91.) LC 89-48356. ISBN 0-8103-4571-4.

Riley includes comprehensive biographical profiles of thirty-seven publishers and editors of American magazines between 1900 and 1960.

Directories

228. Bjoerner, Susan, comp. and ed. **Newspapers Online.** Needham Heights, MA: BiblioData, 1987-. Annual (semi-annual updates). Index.

International in scope, the source lists over 150 newspapers available on-line. Entries note vendors, filename(s), date beginning on-line service, gap between publication and appearance in the on-line format, a description of the paper and its geographical area, inclusions and exclusions (e.g., includes obituaries), and numbers for searching assistance.

Indexes

229. Gatten, Jeffrey N., comp. **The Rolling Stone Index: Twenty-Five Years of Popular Culture, 1967-1991.** Ann Arbor, MI: Popular Culture Ink, 1992. 550p. Indexes. ISBN 1-56075-030-8.

An invaluable tool for both students and researchers, this book is devoted to perhaps the leading arbiter of American popular culture during the last quarter century. The individual sections (the overall arrangement consists of separate author, title, and subject indexes) provide efficient access to nearly 12,000 feature articles; more than 8,000 letters to the editor; almost 2,700 reviews of books, concerts, and films; and more than 9,800 record reviews. It provides in-depth indexing to over 36,500 names mentioned in the "Random Notes" column and includes a section that discusses the personalities that have graced the magazine's front cover.

230. Lane, Susan, and Elizabeth Hasten. **The 1992-1993 Guide to Newspaper Syndication.** Newspaper Syndication Specialists, 1992. 184p. Index, bibl. LC 91-066481. ISBN 0-9615800-4-6 pap.

The work provides background information about more than 250 syndicates. The focus is upon helping feature writers and cartoonists get their submissions accepted. Sections include executive interviews, a listing of best-selling and recently added features and cartoons, a directory of the 100 largest newspapers, and guidelines for submissions.

Radio

(See also: Mass Media—Films, pp. 174, 198, 224)

Bibliographies

231. Green, Thomas Allen. **Radio: A Reference Guide.** Westport, CT: Greenwood, 1989. 172p. (American Popular Culture series.) Index. LC 88-24647. ISBN 0-313-222-76-2.

A useful bibliographic compilation of more than 500 sources covering radio and radio programming, the work includes chapters on radio history, networks, music, drama, comedy and variety, news, sports, women in the medium, advertising, religious broadcasting, and armed forces radio, and providing a listing of organizations, collections, journals, and indexes. Each chapter includes a comprehensive introductory essay followed by a selective bibliography. An integrated index lists pertinent names, titles, and subjects.

232. Pringle, Peter K., and Helen H. Clinton. **Radio and Television: A Selected, Annotated Bibliography. Supplement Two: 1982-1986.** Metuchen, NJ: Scarecrow, 1989. 237p. Bibl. LC 88-23968. ISBN 0-8108-2158-3.

With this third volume, the series now covers 1920-1986 (the 1978 edition spanned 1926-1976 and the 1982 edition, 1977-1981). The text is organized into six main parts: broadcasting, radio, television, cable television, new technologies, and home video. The annotated entries, encompassing almost 1,000 books, pamphlets, and reports, are complemented by a separate listing of periodicals relevant to the six areas. Author and title indexes optimize the utility of the title.

Biographies

233. Slide, Anthony. **Great Radio Personalities.** 128p. Illus. ISBN 0-911572-72-4 pap.

The book's format consists of black-and-white portraits of leading Golden Age entertainers (e.g., Abbott and Costello, Jack Benny, George Burns and Gracie Allen, Bob Hope, Baby Snooks) complemented by copious biographical captions.

Dictionaries

234. Hurst, Walter E., and Donn Delson. **Delson's Dictionary of Radio & Record Industry Terms.** Thousand Oaks, CA: Bradson, 1980. 111p. LC 80-24486. ISBN 0-9603574-2-4 pap.

The concise definitions presented here span the fields of marketing, broadcasting, contracts, copyrights, music genres, and production.

Encyclopedias

235. Douglas, Alan S. **Radio Manufacturers of the 1920s. Volume I: A-C Dayton to J. B. Ferguson, Inc.; Volume II: Freed-Eisemann to Preiss; Volume III: RCA to Zenith.** Vestal, NY: Vestal, 1988; 1989; 1991. 256p.; 272p.; 292p. Illus. LC 87-31088. I: 0-911572-68-6 pap.; 0-911572-83-X/0-911572-77-5 pap.; 0-911572-93-7/ 0-911572-94-5 pap.

The series offers an outline history for each of the major radio firms of the 1920s. The focus is on company principals and their factories, biographical information on radio pioneers, and figures reporting the financial ups and downs of a then-volatile industry. Included are over 650 illustrations (many are reproductions of ads) of the more notable models.

236. Dunning, John. **Tune in Yesterday: The Ultimate Encyclopedia of Old-Time Radio, 1925-1976.** Englewood Cliffs, NJ: Prentice-Hall, 1976. 703p. Illus., index. LC 76-28369. ISBN 0-13-932616-2.

Arranged alphabetically by program title, the entries cite sponsors, writers, typical plots, cast and format changes, opening and closing dates, and thumbnail sketches of the major performers.

237. Terrace, Vincent. **Radio's Golden Years: The Encyclopedia of Radio Programs, 1930-1960.** San Diego: A. S. Barnes; London: Tantivy, 1981. 308p. Illus., index. LC 79-87791. ISBN 0-498-02393-1.

The alphabetically arranged entries for 1,500 nationally broadcast network and syndicated entertainment programs include story line data, cast lists, announcer and music credits, sponsors, program openings, network and syndication information, and length and date of broadcasts. The name index provides greater accessibility to the text.

Handbooks

238. Barabas, Suzanne, and Gabor Barabas. **Gunsmoke: A Complete History and Analysis of the Legendary Broadcast Series.** Jefferson, NC: McFarland, 1990. 836p. Illus., index, bibl. ISBN 0-89950-418-3.

The work covers the twenty-nine years in which the program ran on radio and television. It includes a history of the series, punctuated by accounts of the real Dodge City, discussions of the rise of the Western as genre literature and drama, and interviews with guest performers. Episode-by-episode accounts, along with a listing of the guest cast and writers, constitutes the core of the work. Appendixes include selected quotations from various shows and data regarding directors, producers, awards, writers, time slots for the broadcast, and principal performer credits.

239. Bunis, Marty, and Sue Bunis. **The Collector's Guide to Antique Radios.** 2nd ed. Paducah, KY: Collector Books, 1992. 208p. Illus., pap. ISBN 0-89145-498-5. Also available from Jukebox Collector (515-265-8324).

Arranged alphabetically by brand name, the tool provides background information for approximately 5,000 models.

240. Collins, Philip. **Radios Redux: Listening In Style.** San Francisco: Chronicle Books, 1992. 120p. Illus. pap. ISBN 0-8118-0099-7; 0-8118-0086-5 pap. Also available from AMR Publishing and Jukebox Collector.

The companion volume to *Radios: The Golden Age* (see entry 241) showcases over eighty vintage models—from the glass and chrome "Radio Glo" of the 1930s to the sporty plastic "Midgetronic" of the 1950s—in striking color photographs.

241. Collins, Philip. **Radios: The Golden Age.** San Francisco: Chronicle Books, 1987. 119p. Illus., index (checklist), bibl. ISBN 0-87701-477-9; 0-87701-419-1 pap. Also available from AMR.

This is a full-color chronicle of the handsomest and most desired radios of the late 1920s through the early 1940s, featuring 110 photos by Robert Patterson. It covers traditional wood models to later flamboyant experiments in mass production and innovative design (often in plastic).

242. Greenfield, Thomas Allen. **Radio: A Reference Guide.** New York: Greenwood, 1989. xiii, 172p. Index. LC 88-24647. ISBN 0-313-22276-2.

Following a historical survey of the formative years of the medium, the text is divided into seven bibliographic essays: Radio Networks and Station Histories, Radio Drama, Radio News, Radio Music, Radio Comedy and Variety, Radio Sport, and Short Waves: Miscellaneous Subjects; more than 500 sources in all are cited.

243. Johnson, David, and Betty Johnson. **Guide to Old Radios: Pointers, Pictures & Process.** Radnor, PA: Chilton, 1989. 192p. Illus. ISBN 0-87069-518-5; 0-87069-5814 pap. Also available from AMR and Jukebox Collector.

The book covers a wide range of topics—determining the age of a radio, understanding how it operates, evaluating the best methods to preserve it, and deciding how much it is worth. A price guide has been included for over 3,300 separate models.

244. Pitts, Michael R. **Radio Soundtracks: A Reference Guide.** 2nd ed. Metuchen, NJ: Scarecrow, 1986. 337p. Index. LC 85-30409. ISBN 0-8108-1875-2.

The source is organized into five parts: "Radio Programs Available on Tape Recordings" (arranged by program name); "Radio Specials on Tape Recordings"; "Radio Programs Available on Long Playing Records"; "Performers' Radio Appearances on Long Playing Records"; and "Compilation Record Albums," composed of radio material. An appendix entitled "Tape and Record Sources" is also included.

Television

(See also: Mass Media—Films, pp. 174, 198, 224; Mass Media—Radio, pp. 176, 199, 225; Popular Literature—Science Fiction, pp. 180, 206, 228)

Bibliographies

245. Cooper, Thomas W., with others. **Television & Ethics: A Bibliography.** Boston: G. K. Hall, 1988. 203p. Indexes. LC 88-7206. ISBN 0-8161-8966-8.

Rather than focusing on how ethics influence plotting and character development in programming, the tool is primarily concerned with the impact of television upon the viewer along with the ethical implications of such power. The main bibliographic section, encompassing 105 pages, is subdivided by areas such, as film, public relations, publishing, and other fields of communication, as well as the teaching of media ethics. Less relevant fields—including the business, legal, medical, scientific, and governmental professions— are also included. Short annotations are included for nearly 500 entries, primarily to clarify the content of the more ambiguous titles. Covering the period from classical Greece to 1987, the compilation includes the significant research, dialogues, and case studies within the industry. The program and subject-author indexes enhance accessibility to the text.

246. Hill, George H., and Sylvia Saverson Hill. **Blacks on Television: A Selectively Annotated Bibliography.** Metuchen, NJ: Scarecrow, 1985. 223p. Index. LC 84-23639 ISBN 0-8108-1774-8.

The listing is composed of 2,834 monographs, theses, dissertations, and periodical articles concerning the contribution of blacks to American television between 1939 and 1984. Arranged by format, the articles are subdivided under forty topical headings; annotations have been employed only for book-length entries. The appendixes cite television and cable stations owned by African Americans and black Emmy winners.

247. Signorielli, Nancy, comp. and ed. **Role Portrayal and Stereotyping on Television: An Annotated Bibliography of Studies Relating to Women, Minorities, Aging, Sexual Behavior, Health, and Handicaps.** Westport, CT: Greenwood, 1985. 214p. Indexes, bibl. (Bibliographies and Indexes in Sociology, No. 5.) LC 85-9823. ISBN 0-313-24855-9.

The volume's 423 entries are organized into five parts: "Women and Sex-Roles," "Racial and Ethnic Minorities," "Aging and Age-Roles," "Sexual Behavior and Orientation," and "Health and Handicaps" (each arranged alphabetically by author). The entries, consisting largely of research published in journals, books, and federal documents, describe sampling techniques and findings (where relevant). Author and subject indexes are also included.

Catalogs

248. Black, Sharon, and Elizabeth Sue Moersh, eds. **Index to the Annenberg Television Script Archive: Volume 1, 1976-1977.** Phoenix, AZ: Oryx, 1990. 206p. Indexes. LC 89-16199. ISBN 0-89774-553-1.

The work encompasses 2,477 archived prime-time television scripts aired on the major networks during the 1976-1977 period. Entries are organized alphabetically by title; each includes draft date, script date, date aired, subject covered, famous people as characters, time, adaptation source, author, title, pagination, and notes. Other strong points include a lucidly written introduction (explaining access strategies), author and subject indexes, and the striking typography and layout design.

249. Rouse, Sarah, and Katharine Loughney, comps. **3 Decades of Television: A Catalog of Television Programs Acquired by the Library of Congress, 1949-1979.** Washington, D.C.: Motion Picture, Broadcasting, and Recorded Sound Division, Library of Congress, 1989. 688p. Illus., index. LC 86-20098. ISBN 0-8444-0544-2.

This tool represents a compilation of 1,400-odd television programs acquired by the Library of Congress that were commercially released between 1949 and 1979. Arranged alphabetically by title, the entries cite copyright, production company and date, telecast data, condition of copy, shelf number, cast, credits, synopses, and format and content/genre descriptors. The text is supplemented by a genre or format index.

Dictionaries

250. Ensign, Lynne Naylor, and Robin Eileen Knapton. **The Complete Dictionary of Television and Film.** Briarcliff Manor, NY: Stein and Day, 1985. 256p. LC 83-42634. ISBN 0-8128-2922-0.

The terminology (general, technical, jargon, and slang) of the television and film industries is covered in more than 3,000 entries, arranged alphabetically and spanning both older and contemporary words and phrases.

251. Miller, Carolyn Handler. **Illustrated T.V. Dictionary.** New York: Harvey House, 1980. 135p. Illus. LC 78-73761, ISBN 0-8178-6220-X.

Following a concise introductory survey of television history and technology, Miller brings together technical and common usage terms as well as key performers, developers, innovators, and programs in a work geared to the uniformed layperson.

252. Slide, Anthony. **The Television Industry: A Historical Dictionary.** New York: Greenwood, 1991. ix, 374p. Illus. ISBN 0-313-25634-9.

International in scope, Slide provides a historical focus on terms relating to networks, organizations, distributors, producers, technical terms, and other aspects of the medium.

Encyclopedias

253. Brown, Les. **Les Brown's Encyclopedia of Television.** 3rd ed. Detroit: Gale Research, 1992. 723p. ISBN 0-8103-8871-5. Available in paperback from Visible Ink Press.

This volume is now a reference staple, spanning influential people, programs, and events with respect to the medium as well as to less pronounced issues of a technical, financial, and governmental nature.

254.   Terrace, Vincent. **Encyclopedia of Television: Series, Pilots, and Specials.** 3 Vols. New York: Zoetrope, 1985-1986. Illus., index. ISBN 0-918432-69-3.

The entries, alphabetically arranged by title, include cast and credits, story lines, running times, dates, and networks. The first two volumes cover the periods 1937-1973 and 1974-1984, respectively. Volume 3, the index, covers producers, directors, performers, and writers with a full credit list, and the item number in the text for each work.

Guides to the Literature

255.   Cassata, Mary, and Thomas Skill. **Television: A Guide to the Literature.** Phoenix, AZ: Oryx, 1985. 148p. Indexes. LC 83-43236. ISBN 0-89774-140-4.

The work consists of three expanded bibliographic essays that originally appeared in *Choice* (vol. 19, 1982), on test patterns (overview of the field, historical development, reference sources); the environment (processes and effects of television, news, politics); and directions (the industry, criticism, collected works). The text is complemented by author, title, and subject indexes.

Handbooks

256.   Brooks, Tim, and Earle Marsh. **The Complete Directory to Prime Time TV Stars, 1946-Present.** 4th ed. New York: Ballantine, 1988. 1086p. Index, pap. LC 87-91863. ISBN 0-345-32681-4.

Winner of the American Book Award, the fourth edition includes not only new programs on the big three networks but also the Fox output and over 350 syndicated series that have achieved national distribution. The work opens with a historical overview of the medium—including technical, corporate, and programming developments. The heart of the book "is an alphabetical listing of every regular series ever carried on commercial [networks] during prime time, network series carried in the early evening and late night hours, and top syndicated programs that were aired primarily in the evening hours." Each entry lists dates of the first and last broadcast; days, times, and networks on which the series was broadcast; regular cast members and guests; and a brief description of the program. The appendixes include complete prime-time network schedules from the 1946-1947 season through 1987-1988, a list of Emmy Award winners, the top 100 series of the period covered, and hit theme songs.

257.   Castleman, Harry, and Walter J. Podrazik. **Harry and Wally's Favorite TV Shows.** New York: Prentice-Hall, 1989. 628p. Index. ISBN 0-13-933250-2.

The book includes over 2,100 programs arranged alphabetically by title. The shows are rated on a zero-to-four-star scale; additional data includes original air date, number of episodes, producer, and stars. Applicable entries refer the user to a home video section. Both "contemporary" material and reruns are covered; prime-time comedy and drama series receive greater attention than variety, game, and talk shows. Soap operas and children's programs are omitted altogether. A performer index provides greater access to the contents.

258. Einstein, Daniel. **Special Edition: A Guide to Network Television Documentary Series and Special News Reports, 1955-1979.** Metuchen, NJ: Scarecrow, 1987. 1051p. Indexes. LC 86-6599. ISBN 0-8108-1898-1.

The source is divided into three parts: (1) "Network Television Documentary Series Programming: 1955-1979," arranged alphabetically by series title; (2) "Documentary Programming Produced by David L. Wolper," productions arranged in chronological order; and (3) "Network Television News Specials and Special Reports, 1955-1979," arranged chronologically by year, month, and day. The entries (covering 7,000 individual programs and over 120 series of programs) include program title, a brief annotation, date, and subjects covered. The text is complemented by personality and personnel indexes.

259. Erickson, Hal. **Syndicated Television: The First Forty Years, 1947-1987.** Jefferson, NC: McFarland, 1989. 418p. Index. LC 89-42583. ISBN 0-89950-410-8.

The source is arranged chronologically by decade; within each decade, first-run syndication programs are included under genre subheadings ("adventure/mystery" to "women's programs"). The writing combines the best elements of subjective analysis and informative asides a la trivia fact books. It is every bit the equal of the long-standing pacesetter in the field, *The Complete Directory to Prime Time TV Stars 1946-Present,* by Tim Brooks and Earle Marsh (see entry 256).

260. Gianakos, Larry James. **Television Drama Series Programming: A Comprehensive Chronicle, 1982-1984.** Metuchen, NJ: Scarecrow, 1987. 838p. index. LC 85-30428. ISBN 0-8108-1876-0.

The source extends the author's *Television Drama Series Programming: A Comprehensive Chronicle, 1947/59-1980/82.* (Metuchen, NJ: Scarecrow, 1988) Each series is listed by date and time within the respective networks; data cited includes chief actors and a chronologically arranged episode checklist. A cumulative title listing to television series has also been included.

261. Maltin, Leonard, and others, eds. **Leonard Maltin's TV Movies.** See: Mass Media—Films—Handbooks

262. Marill, Alvin H. **Movies Made for Television: The Telefeature and the Mini-Series, 1964-1979.** Westport, CT: Arlington House Publishers, 1980. 399p. Illus., indexes. LC 80-22924. ISBN 0-87000-451-4.

Marill provides a chronological listing of more than 1,000 made-for television films in addition to including a separate section for the mini-series (i.e., films spanning more than two evenings). Each entry cites premiere date, running time, production credits, cast, and plot outline. Accessibility is enhanced by film title, actor, and director indexes.

263. McNeil, Alex. **Total Television: A Comprehensive Guide to Programming from 1948 to 1980.** New York: Penguin, 1980. 1087p. Index. pap. ISBN 0-14-004911-8.

The book's coverage of over 3,400 network and syndicated series is organized into five sections: a listing, in alphabetical order, of all primetime and daytime series from fall 1948 to March 1980; a season-by-season listing of special programs and broadcasts; primetime fall schedules for the three leading networks in chart form, 1948-1979; an edited listing of Emmy and Peabody Award winners; and the Nielsen top-rated series for each season. An appendix notes programming for the first two months of 1980.

264. Parish, James Robert, and Vincent Terrace. **The Complete Actors' Television Credits, 1948-1988.** 2 Vols. 2nd ed. Metuchen, NJ: Scarecrow, 1989-1990. Illus. ISBN 0-8108-2204-0 (v. 1); 0-8108-2258-X (v. 2).

Arranged by actor (volume 1) and actress (volume 2) name, the work's entries incorporate all entertainment programs broadcast on network and cable television in addition to those produced for syndication.

265. Rose, Brian G., ed. Robert S. Alley, advisory ed. **TV Genres: A Handbook and Reference Guide.** Westport, CT: Greenwood, 1985. ix, 453p. Index, bibl., videography. ISBN 0-313-23724-7.

Specialists have explored the essential features of nineteen formats or styles of television programming (e.g., game shows, sitcoms, westerns). Each chapter includes a historical survey, an analysis of themes and issues, a bibliographic essay, and a videography.

266. Shapiro, Mitchell E. **Television Network Prime-Time Programming, 1948-1988.** Jefferson, NC: McFarland, 1989. 743p. Index. LC 89-45006. ISBN 0-89950-412-4.

Arranged by night of the week (beginning with Sunday; each day constitutes a chapter), the book presents information regarding the programming of the pioneering national networks: ABC, CBS, NBC, Dumont, and Fox. For each week, the designated evening includes a month-by-month scheduling grid followed by a listing of all programming moves. The listing gives date, time, title of series; its length in minutes; type-of-program designation; and notation of specific moves made by network—e.g., debut, cancellation, moved; time slot to which or from which the program was moved, where applicable. Each chapter concludes with a year-by-year summary of key programming moves on the designated weeknight.

267. Spignesi, Stephen. **Mayberry, My Hometown: The Ultimate Guidebook to America's Favorite TV Small Town.** Ann Arbor, MI: Popular Culture, Ink, 1991. 300p. Illus., pap. ISBN 1-56075-023-5.

Spignesi's book represents the best of all worlds for a reference tool: not only is it notable for its accuracy, its broad array of cross-references, and its conscientious attention to detail, it's also a fascinating cornucopia of information culled from The Andy Griffith Show and two spin-off series, *Gomer Pyle, U.S.M.C.,* and *Mayberry, R.F.D.,* which can be read from beginning to end like a work of fiction. The work is divided into the following sections: Part I—"The Mayberry Pocket Almanac: A Handy Guide to Mayberry People, Places & Things" (including floor plans, time slots and Nielsen Rankings by season, character frequency charts, etc.); Part II—"The Mayberry Encyclopedia: From 'A1A' to 'Zone Detection System'"; Part III—"Going Home to Mayberry: A Look at the 'Return'"; Part IV—"Mayberry Confidential: Some of Our Favorite Mayberryites Speak Their Minds"; Part V—"Mayberry Fandom: 'A Rendezvous With Destiny'"; and Part VI—"The Subconscious Prober Primer: A Topical Index to the Encyclopedia." Additional essays interspersed throughout the text (e.g., Richard Kelly's "Staying Alive in Mayberry," which delineates the universal qualities of the Mayberry cosmos, and "A Mayberry Miscellany," an alphabetical listing of additional information about the program. The prime flaw consists of overly brief plot synopses that might have been listed in a separate section in chronological order by broadcast date rather than by obscure program titles in Part II.

268. Steinberg, Cobbett. **TV Facts.** New York: Facts on File, 1985. xi, 478p. Index. ISBN 0-87196-312-4.

Steinberg presents a wealth of statistical and narrative information on U.S. television between 1950-1985. The tool is divided into six chapters covering programs, viewers, ratings, advertisers, awards, and networks and stations.

269. Trimble, Bo. **The Star Trek Concordance.** New York: Ballantine Books, 1976. 256p. Illus., pap. LC 76-9778. ISBN 0-345-25137-7-695.

As much a good browse as a reference book, the contents include a time line of the episodes of the original television series, a listing of episodes in alphabetical order, fan art depicting the show's characters, plot summaries (arranged chronologically) for both the 1960s series and the animated spinoff, and a lexicon describing nearly all features contained within the episodes.

270. West, Richard. **Television Westerns: Major and Minor Series, 1946-1978.** Jefferson, NC: McFarland, 1987. 155p. Illus., index. LC 87-42525. ISBN 0-89950-252-0.

The book covers over 130 television western series that premiered between 1946 and 1978. The chronologically arranged entries range in length from two paragraphs to several pages for the most popular series (e.g., *Bonanza, Gunsmoke, Rawhide*). They offer a menu of miscellaneous facts (dates and networks of original airing, performers, theme music, etc.), gossip, and subjective commentary. A valuable part of the work, the appendixes list actors and names of characters they played; Emmy Award winners; ratings winners; titles under which shows played when rerun in syndication; and original network air times.

271. Woolery, George W. **Animated TV Specials: the Complete Directory to the First Twenty-Five Years, 1962-1987.** Metuchen, NJ: Scarecrow, 1989. 542p. Illus., name (4) and subject (2) indexes. LC 89-5856. ISBN 0-8108-2198-2.

This is an alphabetically arranged title listing of animated programs presented as television specials, ranging from classics (e.g., the longest-running show, *Rudolph the Red-Nosed Reindeer*) to toy-promoting hack work (e.g., *He-Man*). Films first released in theaters are excluded. The entries include premiere date, producer, director, writer, company and distributor, principal characters and voices, a plot synopsis, and supplementary data, such as awards won and names of songs. The appendixes provide the following data: longest-running specials, programs employing stop-motion puppetry, holiday and topical shows, and series. Minor flaws in an otherwise solid work include the lack of distinction between top-notch productions and hack jobs and the need for further appendixes (e.g., stories or background behind the creation of major successes, Nielsen ratings for top specials).

272. Woolery, George W. **Children's Television: The First Thirty-Five Years, 1946-1981. Part II: Live, Film, and Tape Series.** Metuchen, NJ: Scarecrow, 1985. 788p. Indexes. LC 82-5841. ISBN 0-8108-1651-2.

Woolery covers more than 600 nationally televised children's series (arranged alphabetically by title). The main listing is complemented by an introductory survey of children's television; a chronology; and lists of awards, longest-running series, and series based on other media (e.g., literature, film). The text is complemented by name, subject, and first-run indexes.

273. Woolley, Lynn, Robert W. Malsbary, and Robert G. Strange. **Warner Bros. Television: Every Show of the Fifties and Sixties Episode-by-Episode.** Jefferson, NC: McFarland, 1985. 296p. Illus., index. LC 84-43217. ISBN 0-89950-144-3.

The book lists all Warner Brothers series alphabetically by title, followed by a chronological listing of aired episodes (each of which is annotated). Biographical sketches of performers are also included. Although rather superficial in approach, first-rate entertainment value can be found here. A name index has been included.

Indexes

274.   Prouty, Howard H., ed. **Variety Television Reviews, 1923-1988.** 15 Vols. New York: Garland, 1989-1991. indexes. ISBN 0-8240-2587-3 (vol. 1).

The source reprints all *Variety* television reviews in chronological order by issue date. Accessibility is enhanced by title, subject, name, local programming, and international programming indexes.

Theater *(See: Performing Arts—Theatrical Arts, p. 178; Theatre, p. 226)*

Video

Bibliographies/Discographies/Videographies, etc.

275.   **Video Yesteryear** (catalog). Sandy Hook, CT: Video Yesteryear. Annual. 250+p. Updated with irregular supplements. Available free upon request (800-243-0987).

The source lists more than 1,200 vintage titles available on the VHS tape format. The program material includes classic films from the silent and pre-World War II eras, cult films, television shows, compilations of animation and other special interest subjects, and so on. The annotations appended to each entry (in addition to black-and-white stills for the majority of titles) are highly informative.

Catalogs/Union Lists

276.   Prelinger, Richard, and Celeste R. Hoffnar, eds. **Footage: North American Film and Video Sources.** New York: Prelinger, 1989-. Annual. 1989 edition: 795p. Indexes, pap. LC 88-90769.

The source covers 1,635 collections in institutions, organizations, and corporations across North America. The geographically arranged entries (the fifty states, Puerto Rico, and the Virgin Islands listed alphabetically, followed by the Canadian provinces, Mexico, the British Virgin Islands, and Cuba) each include source and collection name, address, chief officials, services, collection descriptions, cataloging, access, and rights. Its value is greatly enhanced by the inclusion of essays on film and video research, stock footage, copyright and other legal activities, and the preservation of film and video material. Collection name, television series, and subject indexes have also been provided.

Handbooks

277.   American Film & Video Association. **AFVA Evaluations.** Highsmith: American Film & Video Association. Annual. Illus., index. 1991 edition: 340p.; ISBN 0-917846-07-9.

This guide delineates over 1,200 educational and nontheatrical audiovisual titles submitted for the 1991 AFVA Festival competition. The entries cover uses, commentary, synopsis, subject, and distributors for each title.

278.   Boyle, Deirdre. **Video Classics: A Guide to Video Art and Documentary Tapes.** Phoenix: Oryx, 1986. 160p. Illus., indexes, pap. LC 83-43239. ISBN 0-89774-102-1.

Boyle, a leading writer on the video medium, focuses on eighty independent video productions of the 1970s and 1980s notable for their quality as well as their controversial subject matter. Although lacking comprehensive title inclusion, the book does an admirable job of introducing the reader to video art and documentary work. Accessibility is enhanced by titles, artist/producer, and subject indexes.

Chapter 3

Performing Arts

(See also: Mass Media—Films, pp. 174, 198, 224; Radio, pp. 176, 199, 225; Television, pp. 177, 200, 226)

General

Bibliographies

279.   Cohen-Stratyner, Barbara Naomi, ed. **Performing Arts Resources. Volume Twelve: Topical Bibliographies of the American Theatre.** New York: Theatre Library Association, 1987. 195p. Bibl. LC 75-646287. ISBN 0-932610-09-0.
Continuing in the mode of prior volumes in this series on theater history, the twelfth installment consists of the following essays: "Preliminary Checklist of Early Printed Children's Plays in English, 1780-1855," by Jonathan Levy and Martha Mahard; "Actresses of All Work: Nineteenth-Century Sources on Women in Nineteenth-Century American Theatre," by Noreen C. Barnes and Laurie J. Wolf; "A Checklist of American Civil War Drama: Beginnings to 1900," by Rosemary L. Cullen; "Female Impersonation on the American Stage, 1860 to 1927; A Selected Bibliography of Performed Materials, and a Review of Literature," by Geraldine Maschio; and "Workers on Stage: An Annotated Bibliography of Labor Plays of the 1930s," by Colette A. Hyman.

279a. **Harvard University Library.** c/o Jeanne T. Newlin, Curator, Theatre Collection, Cambridge, MA 02138.
This is alleged to be one of the largest existing collections of playbills, programs, prints, photographs, promptbooks, and other materials relating to the performing arts; the resources on the English-speaking stage of the eighteenth and nineteenth centuries are unequaled. It also includes resources on ballet and modern dance, the circus, magic, minstrel shows, cinema, and pantomime.

Chapter 4

Politics

(See also: Minorities, pp. 66-68, 133-41, 201, 233-34)

General

Dictionaries

280.   Raymond, Walter J. **Dictionary of Politics: Selected American and Foreign Political and Legal Terms.** 6th ed., rev. Lawrenceville, VA: Brunswick, 1978. 956p. Illus., maps, bibl. LC 78-50189. ISBN 0-931494-00-1.

Despite some unevenness of coverage, this remains a useful compilation of political terms. The appendixes include forty-six documents (e.g., the U.S. Constitution) referred to by the entries in the text.

Handbooks

281.   Gallup, George H. **The Gallup Poll: Public Opinion 1972-1977.** 2 Vols. Wilmington, DE: Scholarly Resources, 1978. Index. LC 77-25755. ISBN 0-8420-2129-9.

This compilation extends the coverage of Gallup Poll surveys beyond that provided by the three-volume set published by Random House in 1972, *The Gallup Poll: Public Opinion 1935-1971*. The polls—arranged chronologically and consisting of the questions and response data—focus on the primary issues of interest during the 1972-1977 period (e.g., abortion, the Vietnam War). The main text is complemented by an explanation of statistical sampling methods employed and a chronicle of notable events from this time frame (in order to bring out, in greater relief, the relationship between these developments and public opinion). A subject index has also been included.

Chapter 5

Popular History

General

Almanacs

282. Biracree, Tom, and Nancy Biracree. **Almanac of the American People.** New York: Facts on File, 1988. 336p. LC 88-3882. ISBN 0-8160-1821-9; 0-8160-2329-8 pap.

Based on material gathered from government publications, magazine surveys, and data collected by business and professional organizations, the tool provides a diversified look at contemporary life in the United States. Covered topics include education, leisure activities, consumer trends, and housing statistics.

Atlases

283. Beck, Warren A., and Ynez D. Haase. **Historical Atlas of the American West.** Norman, OK: University of Oklahoma, 1989. xiii, 156p. Illus., maps, index, bibl. ISBN 0-8061-2193-9.

The source employs maps to delineate 78 topics related to the 17 western states. Coverage includes such concepts as European settlement and notable events.

Catalogs/Union Lists

284. Makower, Joel, ed. **The American History Sourcebook.** Prentice-Hall, 1989. 548p. Illus., index, pap.

The work provides the locations—along with visiting times and descriptions of the collections—of more than 3,000 museums, libraries, archives, photo collections, historical societies, and other sources for U.S. history, politics, and culture. A subject index enhances accessibility to the text.

Dictionaries

285. Buenker, John D., and Edward R. Kantowicz, eds. **Historical Dictionary of the Progressive Era, 1890-1920.** New York: Greenwood, 1988. ix, 599p. Indexes, bibl. ISBN 0-313-2430903.

The work's more than 800 entries touch upon the key people, events, organizations, legislation, and concepts comprising the Progressive Era. The lucid writing (contributed by a number of U.S. scholars) emphasizes dates and other factual information as well as assessments of historical impact. The text is supplemented by chronology, name, title, and subject indexes.

286.   Cole, Sylvia, and Abraham H. Lass. **The Facts on File Dictionary of Twentieth Century Allusions. From Abbott and Costello to Ziegfield Girls.** New York: Facts on File, 1991. xi, 292p. Index. ISBN 0-8160-1915-0.

The tool defines more than 900 twentieth-century allusions. The introduction considers an allusion to be "a reference transformed through use into a metaphor, into a word or phrase that stands for something." Both origins and current usage of terms are provided.

Directories

287.   Smith, Allen. **Directory of Oral History Collections.** Phoenix: Oryx, 1988. 141p. ISBN 0-89774-322-9.

The work documents "collections of oral history materials, whether large or small, public or private, which provide adequate cataloging and indexing and allow access to qualified researchers." The collections listed might be small portions of a larger library, in a special library, autonomous collections, or the collections of a private individual willing to share with researchers. Entries include name and address, collection size, nature of holdings, service goal, hours or considerations of access, catalog or location aids, and additional comments. Completeness of data is based upon responses from questionnaires sent to entities cited in prime library and oral history directories. The entries are arranged by state, and subdivided by city and collection title. Accessibility is enhanced by subject and interviewee indexes.

Handbooks

288.   Boardman, Barrington. **Flappers, Bootleggers, "Typhoid Mary" & The Bomb: An Anecdotal History of the United States from 1923-1945.** Introduction by Isaac Asimov. New York: HarperCollins, 1989. 320p. Reprint of 1988 ed. Pap. LC 88-45642. ISBN 0-06-091581-1.

The work includes hundreds of trivial but telling facts, for example,, forgotten headlines, biographical footnotes of the famous, ordinary people who left a mark, false prophecies and big lies, and famous last words.

289.   Trager, James. **The People's Chronology: A Year-by-Year Record of Human Events from Prehistory to the Present.** Rev. ed. New York: Holt, 1992. 1102p. Illus., index. ISBN 0-8050-1786-0.

This monumental volume has been said to include more factual material than any of its competitors. The more than 30,000 events (from three million B.C. through 1990) are organized by topical headings.

Chapter 6

Popular Literature

(See also: Social Phenomena—Minorities, pp. 133-41, 189-90, 201, 233-34)

General

Guides to the Literature

290.   Rosenberg, Betty. **Genreflecting: A Guide to Reading Interests in Genre Fiction.** 3rd ed. Littleton, CO: Libraries Unlimited, 1986. 345p. Indexes. LC 91-28074. ISBN 0-87287-930-5.

The tool is organized into six sections—westerns, thrillers, romances, science fiction, fantasy, and supernatural/horror—that each feature a discussion of themes, notable authors, anthologies, bibliographies, criticism, films, magazines, publishers, reviews, associations, conferences, and awards. Accessibility is enhanced by indexes of genre authors, genre themes, and secondary materials.

Handbooks

291.   Inge, M. Thomas, ed. **Handbook of American Popular Literature.** Westport, CT: Greenwood, 1988. x, 408p. Index, bibl. LC 87-32294. ISBN 0-313-25405-2.

The work comprises fifteen essays (five original and ten revised and updated since first appearing in the author's *Handbook of Popular Culture,* published in 1982). The topics covered are Best Sellers, Big Little Books, Children's Literature, Comic Books, Detective and Mystery Novels, Fantasy, Gothic Novels, Historical Fiction, Popular History and Biography, Pulp and Dime Novels, Romantic Fiction, Science Fiction, Verse and Popular Poetry, Western Fiction, and Young Adult Fiction. The essays, written by subject scholars, include a historical survey, critical writings, key reference works, and existing research collections.

The Beat Movement

Bibliographies

292.   Milewski, Robert J. **Jack Kerouac: An Annotated Bibliography of Secondary Sources, 1944-1979.** With the assistance of John Z. Guzlowski and Linda Calendrillo. Metuchen, NJ: Scarecrow, 1981. 225p. Index. (The Scarecrow Author Bibliographies, No. 52.) LC 80-24477. ISBN 0-8108-1378-5.

Devoted to Kerouac's life and output, the source is composed of three parts: reviews of his primary works, arranged by individual title; general reviews and articles; and creative works (music and literature) influenced by him. The appendixes include a chronological listing of Kerouac's primary novels and articles, a historical outline of his life, and various documents, such as his will and Viking Press inferoffice memos regarding *On the Road.*

Guides to the Literature

293.   Goodman, Michael B., with Lemuel B. Coley. **William S. Burroughs: A Reference Guide.** New York: Garland, 1990. 270p. Index. (Garland Reference Library of the Humanities, v. 635.) LC 89-26026. ISBN 0-8240-8642-2.

Updating Goodman's earlier work, *William S. Burroughs: An Annotated Bibliography of His Work,* this guide is arranged into ten parts, including a compilation of Burroughs's own writing (with reviews of his books cited), journal articles and book essays, interviews and biographical material, collections of letters and manuscripts, a miscellaneous section covering Burroughs's other activities (e.g., public readings, appearances, art shows, films, videos, dramatic adaptations, recordings, merchandising), and a listing of previous bibliographies on the author. The book also provides a chronology of his life.

Best Sellers

Bibliographies

294.   Scharnhorst, Gary, and Jack Bales. **Horatio Alger, Jr.: An Annotated Bibliography of Comment and Criticism.** Introduction by Herbert R. Mayes. Metuchen, NJ: Scarecrow, 1981. 179p. Index. (The Scarecrow Author Bibliographies, No. 54.) LC 80-25960. ISBN 0-8108-1387-4.

This represents an expanded version of Scharnhorst's critique, *Horatio Alger, Jr.* (Twayne). It consists of a biobibliographical essay (twenty-six pages in length), followed by an annotated bibliography of almost 700 items arranged by type of material (e.g., reviews, introductions, obituaries) and subdivided chronologically.

Guides to the Literature

295.   Hinckley, Karen, and Barbara Hinckley. **American Best Sellers: A Reader's Guide to Popular Fiction.** Bloomington, IN: Indiana University, 1989. 260p. Index. LC 88-45754. ISBN 0-253-32728-8.

The first chapter lists the 468 best-selling titles from 1965 to 1985, also providing plot synopses and biographical data for each volume's author (216 in all). The balance of the volume categorizes the titles by topic and genre, and explores types of literary characters, major patterns, trends, and themes.

Children's Series

Bibliographies

296.   Jones, Dolores B., comp. **Bibliography of the Little Golden Books.** Westport, CT: Greenwood, 1987. 172p. Indexes, bibl. (Bibliographies and Indexes in American Literature, No. 7.) LC 86-27090. ISBN 0-313-25025-1.

Following an introduction regarding the origins of Little Golden Books (the creators, marketing strategies, series spin-offs, analysis of their literary value, etc.), the book provides an alphabetically arranged "list of all the Little Golden Book titles issued by Simon & Schuster (later Golden Press and Western) from the series inception in 1942 through 1985." It is complemented by a series list arranged in alphabetical order and appended by concise annotations. Name and format indexes have also been included.

Handbooks

297.   Roman, Susan. **Sequences: An Annotated Guide to Children's Fiction in Series.** Chicago: American Library Association, 1985. 134p. Indexes. LC 84-24447. ISBN 0-8389-0428-9.

The work represents a selective compilation of children's book sequences (exhibiting the evolution of character and plot through each title with closely related stories) and sequels (same characters with stories often exhibiting only artificial unity). Arranged alphabetically by author, the entries are appended by annotations describing the series and its merits, as well as noting a broad reading or interest level. Accessibility is enhanced by the inclusion of title, main character, and series indexes.

Gothic Fiction *(See: Horror Fiction, pp. 64, 228)*

Historical Fiction

Bibliographies

298.   Gerhardstein, Virginia Brokaw. **Dickinson's American Historical Fiction.** 5th ed. Metuchen, NJ: Scarecrow, 1986. 352p. Indexes. LC 85-27656. ISBN 0-8108-1867-1.

This classic tool organizes 3,048 novels published between 1917 and 1984 (in addition to a number of older standard works) into the following time frames: colonial times through the American Revolution, the young nation (1783-1860), the Civil War, frontier expansion, 1877-1917, World War I, the 1920s and 1930s, World War II, the tense years (1945-1959), and the turbulent years (1960-1977). Also included is a listing of individual, family, social, economic, biographical and autobiographical, and other chronicles spanning longer periods of time. Author-title and subject indexes optimize accessibility to the text.

299.   Menendez, Albert J. **Civil War Novels: An Annotated Bibliography.** New York: Garland, 1986. 174p. Indexes. (Garland Reference Library of the Humanities, Vol. 700.) LC 86-18379. ISBN 0-8240-9933-8.

An update of the author's 1957 work, *Fiction Fights the Civil War,* it includes over 1,000 entries (alphabetically arranged by author). The annotations vary from a single line to a paragraph in length; some are evaluative in nature. Subject and title indexes have also been provided.

Horror Fiction

(See also: Science Fiction, pp. 74, 180, 206, 228)

Bibliographies

300.   Carter, Margaret L., ed. **The Vampire in Literature: A Critical Bibliography.**
Ann Arbor, MI: UMI, 1989. 135p. (Studies in Speculative Fiction, no. 21.) LC 89-31932.
ISBN 0-8357-1998-7.
   The work concentrates on both the fiction and nonfiction prose in which the vampire
motif can be found. The diversified listing includes Marilyn Ross's *Dark Shadows* series,
Woody Allen's *Count Dracula,* Gogol's *Viy,* and such contemporary science fiction
writers as Robert Silverberg.

301.   Fisher, Benjamin Franklin. **The Gothic's Gothic: Study Aids to the Tradition of
the Tale of Terror.** New York: Garland, 1988. 485p. Indexes. (Garland Reference Library
of the Humanities, Vol. 567.) LC 88-18059. ISBN 0-8240-8784-4.
   This compilation of 2,614 citations (some with concise commentaries) covers
primary and secondary sources alluding to Gothicism; the formats include books, articles,
theses, and the graphic arts. It is organized into two portions: authors (more than 100
British, American, and Canadian writers arranged in alphabetical order), and subjects (e.g.,
orientalism, vampires). Accessibility is enhanced by author, artist, subject, title, and critic
indexes.

302.   Frank, Frederick S. **Gothic Fiction: A Master List of Twentieth Century Criticism
and Research.** Westport, CT: Meckler, 1988. 193p. Indexes. (Meckler's Bibliographies on
Science Fiction, Fantasy, and Horror, 3.) LC 87-24705. ISBN 0-88736-218-4.
   This exhaustive compilation is organized by chapters and includes primary and
secondary bibliographic and other reference works; literary histories, theories, and genre
studies; American Gothic fiction; French Gothic fiction; German Gothic fiction; Gothic
themes (e.g., the evil eye); the Wandering Jew and the "double figure;" Werewolfery and
Vampirism; and the Gothic film. Critic and author-artist indexes have also been provided.

303.   Frank, Frederick S. **Guide to the Gothic: An Annotated Bibliography of Criticism.** Metuchen, NJ: Scarecrow, 1984. 421p. Indexes. ISBN 0-8108-1669-5.
   The work includes approximately 2,500 citations organized by topical headings
(e.g., nationalities, subgenres). Accessibility has been optimized by critic and author
indexes.

304.   Joshi, S. T. **H. P. Lovecraft and Lovecraft Criticism: An Annotated Bibliography.**
Kent, OH: Kent State University, 1981. 473p. Indexes. (The Serif Series: Bibliographies and
Checklists, No. 38.) LC 80-84662. ISBN 0-87338-248-X.
   The text of this exhaustive volume is divided into three sections: works by Lovecraft
in English (i.e., books, periodical articles, edited works, and apocrypha); works by
Lovecraft translated into other languages; and works about Lovecraft (news items, encyclopedias, books, pamphlets. periodical articles, theses, and unpublished papers). Concise
annotations are provided for the more important critical works. Also included are indexes
of Lovecraft titles, other author titles, names, periodicals, and foreign languages.

Biographies

305. Bleiler, E. F., ed. **Supernatural Fiction Writers: Fantasy and Horror.** 2 Vols. (1169p.) New York: Scribner, 1985. Index, bibl. ISBN 0-684-17808-7.

This two-volume work covers almost fifty American and European authors of supernatural fiction (Apuleius to Roger Zelasny). The essays incorporate biographical and critical information; primary and secondary references are appended to them.

Encyclopedias

306. Spignesi, Stephen. **The Shape Under the Sheet: The Complete Stephen King Encyclopedia.** Ann Arbor, MI: Popular Culture, Ink, 1990. 800p. Illus., index. ISBN 1-56075-018-9.

George Beahm, author of *The Stephen King Companion,* offers the following assessment of the work: "A cornucopia for King fans with something for everyone, [this title] is It: The Final Word on people, places, and things King." Spignesi's book includes the following features: (1) an 18,000-entry, 400,000-word concordance to every novel and short story written by King through 1990, including unpublished manuscripts; (2) a first line index to all of the novels and short stories; (3) an insider's look at the author through exclusive interviews with family, friends, and contemporaries; (4) a biography section featuring previously unpublished photos from King's childhood; (5) data—often unavailable elsewhere—about King's poetry and the film adaptations and audio versions of his works; (6) a section covering *Castle Rock,* the Stephen King newsletter; and (7) an overview—somewhat tongue-in-cheek—of death, torture, and other forms of violence in the author's writings entitled "How King Kills."

Guides to the Literature

307. Barron, Neil, ed. **Horror Literature: A Reader's Guide.** Hamden, CT: Garland, 1990. 596p. Index, bibl. (Garland Reference Library of the Humanities, v. 1220.) LC 89-27454. ISBN 0-8240-4347-2.

The work spans Gothic romance, early modern and contemporary horror fiction, criticism, films, art, library collections, periodicals, etc. Despite the fact that close to one-half of the text duplicates Barron's *Fantasy Literature* (see entry 379), it is an exceptionally well conceived and executed research tool.

308. Frank, Frederick S. **Through the Pale Door: A Guide to and Through the American Gothic.** Westport, CT: Greenwood, 1990. 338p. (Bibliographies and Indexes in American Literature, no. 11.) LC 90-31733. ISBN 0-313-25900-3.

This selective listing of 509 annotated entries spans from the late eighteenth century to contemporary writers. In the introduction Frank explains that the entries "summarize the energy and depth of the American Gothic vision" and "attest to the unity of mood and theme that marks the American Gothic movement." Categorically speaking, he is referring to traditional Gothic novels; Gothic plays; tales of spiritualism, vampirism, and lycanthropy; nickel and dime Gothics; and Gothic short stories. Each entry features an alphabetical listing of books by the author in question with key critical materials cited and Gothic qualities discussed.

309. Tymn, Marshall B., ed. **Horror Literature: A Core Collection and Reference Guide.** New York: R. R. Bowker, 1981. 559p. Index. LC 81-6176. ISBN 0-8352-1341-2; 0-8352-1405-2 pap.

An exhaustive survey of the horror literature, most of the book's chapters are each prefaced by a historical essay: Frederick Frank's "The Gothic Romance: 1762-1820," Benjamin Fisher's "The Residual Gothic Impulse: 1824-1873," Jack Sullivan's "Psychological, Antiquarian, and Cosmic Horror: 1872-1919," Gary Crawford's "The Modern Masters: 1920-1980," Robert Weinberg's "The Horror Pulps: 1933-1940," and Steve Eng's "Supernatural Verse in English." Its value is considerably enhanced by Mike Ashley's "Reference Sources," which surveys scholarly work in the field.

Handbooks

310. Beahm, George, ed. **The Stephen King Companion.** Kansas City, MO: Andrews and McMeel, 1989. 363p. Illus. LC 89-17811. ISBN 0-8362-7978-6.
    A solid introduction to King and his artistic legacy, the volume is organized into three parts: (1) a profile based on a *Playboy* interview, the transcripts of his *Banned Books Week* lecture, and the commentaries of a number of observers; (2) an examination of his cultural impact, which includes the input of fans and critics; and (3) synopses of his works. The text is complemented by sidebars providing trivia and focused observations and an appendix including a price guide to collectibles; and a guide to resources; and lists of King's books in print; works about King and his output, and films, videos, and audiocassettes.

311. Shreffler, Philip A. **The H. P. Lovecraft Companion.** Westport, CT: Greenwood, 1977. 198p. Illus., index, bibl. LC 76-52605. ISBN 0-8371-9482-2.
    In examining Lovecraft's stories and their influence, this tool dates and abstracts sixty-two works, identifies real-life counterparts for elements of his fictional landscape, documents the characters and stories where they appear, and delineates his gods and monsters.

Indexes

312. Jaffery, Sheldon R., and Fred Cook. **The Collector's Index to Weird Tales.** Bowling Green, OH: Bowling Green State University Popular Press, 1985. 162p. Illus. LC 85-71020. ISBN 0-87972-283-5; 0-87972-284-3 pap.
    This four-part index delineates the contents of *Weird Tales*, reputed to be the only mass market magazine publishing horror and supernatural fiction during most of its existence (1923-1954). The first section chronologically arranges the contents of each issue, and the remaining indexes list (in alphabetical order) the authors and their stories, the poets and their poems, and the artists and the issues featuring their cover art.

Minority Writers

(See also: Social Phenomena, pp. 133-41, 189-90, 233-34)

Bibliographies

313. Jacobson, Angeline, comp. **Contemporary Native American Literature: A Selected & Partially Annotated Bibliography.** Metuchen, NJ: Scarecrow, 1977. 262p. Index. LC 77-5614. ISBN 0-8108-1031-X.
    Although the work covers autobiography, biography, fiction, humor, myths, legends, and "spiritual expression," over 80 percent of the 2,024 titles cited here are poems

published in periodicals between 1960 and 1976. Despite its uneven treatment of the Native American literature, however, the tool helps in addressing a long-neglected area.

Minority Writers—African Americans

Biographies

314. Metzger, Linda, senior ed. **Black Writers: A Selection of Sketches from Contemporary Authors.** Detroit: Gale Research, 1989. xxiv, 619p. ISBN 0-8103-2772-4.

The work is composed of more than 400 concise entries providing biographical and aesthetic insights on black writers, including black novelists, poets, short-story writers, dramatists, and journalists from the twentieth century. Foreign writers who have written in English or been translated into that language and nonfiction writers notable from a social or political standpoint (e.g., Malcolm X) have also been included.

315. Roses, Lorraine Elena, and Ruth Elizabeth Randolph. **Harlem Renaissance and Beyond: Literary Biographies of 100 Black Women Writers 1900-1945.** Boston: G. K. Hall, 1990. 413p. Bibl. LC 89-38731. ISBN 0-8161-8926-0.

Featuring one-to two-page biographical sketches, the source covers 100 African American women novelists, short-story writers, playwrights, poets, essayists, critics, historians, journalists, and editors.

Minority Writers—Hispanic Cultures

Bibliographies

316. Lomeli, Francisco A., and Donaldo W. Urioste. **Chicano Perspectives in Literature: A Critical and Annotated Bibliography.** Albuquerque, NM: Pajarito, 1976. 120p. Illus., indexes. pap. LC 76-56073.

The entries are organized into the following sections: poetry, novel, short fiction, theater, anthology, literary criticism, oral tradition in print, journal, and literatura chicasesca. A glossary defines technical terminology and literary concepts. Author, title, and name indexes have also been provided.

Biographies

317. Kanellos, Nicolas, ed. **Biographical Dictionary of Hispanic Literature in the United States: The Literature of Puerto Ricans, Cuban Americans, and Other Hispanic Writers.** Westport, CT: Greenwood, 1989. 374p. Index, bibl. LC 88-37288. ISBN 0-313-24465-0.

The volume features fifty Hispanic writers (excluding Mexican-Americans), arranged alphabetically. Each entry includes a biographical survey, an analysis of primary themes, a critical review, and bibliography of materials by and about the writer. An author-title index enhances accessibility to the text.

Handbooks

318.   Martinez, Julio A., and Francisco A. Lomeli, eds. **Chicano Literature: A Reference Guide.** Westport, CT: Greenwood, 1985. 492p. Bibl. LC 83-22583. ISBN 0-313-23691-7.

The work is split between thirty biographical/critical articles about literary figures and ten surveys of literary genres and topics (e.g., Chicano philosophy).

Minority Writers—Jewish Americans

Bibliographies

319.   Cronin, Gloria L., and others. **Jewish American Fiction Writers: An Annotated Bibliography.** Garland, 1991. 1250p. (Reference Library of the Humanities, v. 972.) Bibl. LC 91-20634. ISBN 0-8240-1619-X.

This is a compilation of secondary source material devoted to sixty-two Jewish American fiction writers and their respective output, including book-length criticism, critical articles and chapters, interviews, biographical sources, bibliographies, and dissertations. Although many key authors (e.g., Scholem Asch, Leon Uris, Herman Wouk) have been included, those major figures already covered by Garland in depth in individual works (e.g., Saul Bellow, Bernard Malamud, Isaac Bashevis Singer) have been omitted. The work is "superior in coverage and content" to its closest competitor, *Twentieth-Century American Jewish Fiction Writers* (Detroit: Gale Research, 1984).

Mystery/Detective/Crime/Espionage Fiction

Bibliographies

320.   Albert, Walter. **Detective and Mystery Fiction: An International Bibliography of Secondary Sources.** Madison, IN: Brownstone, 1985. 781p. Index. ISBN 0-941028-02-X.

The volume's 3,167 entries—numbered consecutively throughout—are organized into four parts: (1) bibliographies, dictionaries, encyclopedias, and checklists; (2) general reference works; (3) dime novels, juvenile series, and pulps; and (4) books and articles devoted to individual mystery writers.

321.   Barzun, Jacques, and Wendell Hertig Taylor. **A Catalogue of Crime: Being a Reader's Guide to the Literature of Mystery, Detection, and Related Genres.** Rev. and enl. ed. New York: Harper & Row, 1989. 952p. Index. LC 88-45884. ISBN 0-06-010263-2.

The tool consists of 5,045 entries spread over five chapters covering novels; short stories and collections; studies and history of the genre; true crime, espionage, and cryptography; and the literature of Sherlock Holmes. The annotated entries within each section are arranged alphabetically by author and subdivided by title. An author-title index has also been included.

322. Cook, Michael L., and Stephen T. Miller. **Mystery, Detective, and Espionage Fiction: A Checklist of Fiction in U.S. Pulp Magazines, 1915-1974.** 2 vols. New York: Garland, 1988. (Fiction in the Pulp Magazines, Vol. 1; Garland Reference Library of the Humanities, Vol. 838.) LC 88-7190. ISBN 0-8240-7539-0.

Volume 1 lists approximately 200 pulps alphabetically by title, followed by a chronological list of contents and a summary of publication data. Volume 2 lists stories alphabetically by author.

323. Hubin, Allen J. **Crime Fiction 1749-1980: A Comprehensive Bibliography.** New York: Garland, 1984. 712p. Index. LC 82-48772. ISBN 0-8240-9219-8.

Encompassing mystery, detective, suspense, thriller, Gothic, police, and spy novels, the 60,000 titles (listed alphabetically under the authors) are limited to English-language books published through 1980.

324. Hubin, Allen J. **1981-1985 Supplement to Crime Fiction, 1749-1980**. New York: Garland, 1988. 260p. Indexes. (Garland Reference Library of the Humanities, Vol. 766.) LC 87-23637. ISBN 0-8240-7596-X.

Duplicating the format of the parent volume (see entry 323), this supplement contributes 6,900 new book titles, provides additional data on 4,300 previously listed materials, notes 440 new series, and includes 3,200 film titles. Title, setting, series, movie title, screenwriter, and director indexes have also been provided.

325. Johnson, Timothy W., and Julia Johnson, eds. Robert Mitchell and others, associate eds. **Crime Fiction Criticism: An Annotated Bibliography.** New York: Garland, 1981. 423p. Index. (Garland Reference Library of the Humanities, Vol. 233.) LC 80-8497. ISBN 0-8240-9490-5.

The work is arranged in two parts: (1) reference sources, books, dissertations, and articles and portions of monographs; and (2) individual authors. It is notable for a substantial amount of fanzine material. A critic index enhances access to the text.

326. Kramer, John E., and John E. Kramer. **College Mystery Novels: An Annotated Bibliography, Including a Guide to Professorial Series-Character Sleuths.** New York: Garland, 1983. 356p. Index. (Garland Reference Library of the Humanities, Vol. 360.) LC 82-48291. ISBN 0-8240-9237-6.

The genre treated here is defined by the authors as any "full length work of mystery or suspense fiction which is set in an institution of higher education and/or has as a principal character a student, a faculty member, or an administrator at a college or university." The book is divided into two parts: "Professional Series-Character Sleuths," which includes fifty-one essays, each concerning a detective from a mystery series, appended by a listing of series titles; and "Free-Standing College Mystery Novels," which cited 632 titles appended by annotations (often including plot summaries and author data).

327. Skene-Melvin, David, and Ann Skene-Melvin, comps. **Crime, Detective, Espionage, Mystery, and Thriller Fiction and Film: A Comprehensive Bibliography of Critical Writing through 1979.** Westport, CT: Greenwood, 1980. 367p. Indexes. LC 80-1194. ISBN 0-313-22062-X.

The bibliography, arranged alphabetically by author, includes many impressive critics (e.g., T. S. Eliot, Thomas Mann, George Orwell, G. K. Chesterton). The exhaustive subject index includes titles of works; authors; fictional characters; individual films; actors (e.g., Basil Rathbone); film directors; magazines; publishers; and general topics, such as the crime fiction of various nations, films, television, short stories, comics, women, hero, dime novels, pulps, spies, etc. A title index has also been provided.

328.   Townsend, Guy M., ed. John J. McAleer and others, associate eds. **Rex Stout: An Annotated Primary and Secondary Bibliography.** New York: Garland, 1980. 199p. Index. (Garland Reference Library of the Humanities, Vol. 239.) LC 80-8507. ISBN 0-8240-9479-4.

The work covers novels, short stories, anthologies, articles, reviews, and poetry by Stout, in addition to critiques and biographical materials (e.g., interviews). Most entries include annotations or plot summaries. A title index enhances access to the text.

Biographies

329.   Bruccoli, Matthew J., and Richard Layman, eds. **Dictionary of Literary Biography Documentary Series: An Illustrated Chronicle. Vol. Six: Hardboiled Mystery Writers: Raymond Chandler, Dashiell Hammett, Ross Macdonald.** Detroit: Gale Research, 1989. 383p. Illus., index. LC 82-1105. ISBN 0-8103-2781-3.

The resources compiled here include photographs, manuscript facsimiles, letters, notebook and diary entries, interviews, and contemporary critiques that chronicle the lives and output of these authors.

330.   Reilly, John M., ed. **Twentieth-Century Crime and Mystery Writers.** 2nd ed. New York: St. Martin's Press, 1985. 1094p. Title index, bibl. LC 84-40813. ISBN 0-312-82418-1.

Covering 640 English-language writers, each entry includes tabular biographical data, a signed critical essay, information on manuscript collections and works on the author, and the author's commentary on his or her output. Also included are appendixes devoted to key nineteenth-century and foreign-language authors.

Encyclopedias

331.   Begg, Paul, and others. **The Jack the Ripper A to Z.** North Pomfret, VT: Headline; distr., Trafalgar Square, 1992. 523p. Illus., index. ISBN 0-7472-0424-1; 0-7472-3676-3 pap.

The tool incorporates every person, setting, object, etc., related to the Ripper case. Despite its British focus, the subject has long since become international in scope and appeal. No set of authors could be more qualified for the task at hand—Begg wrote *Jack the Ripper: The Uncensored Facts* (Parkwest, 1992); Martin Fido, *The Crime, Detection, and Death of Jack the Ripper;* and Skinner, *The Ripper Legacy.*

332.   Cook, Michael L. **Mystery, Detective, and Espionage Magazines.** Westport, CT: Greenwood, 1983. 795p. Index, bibl. (Historical Guides to the World's Periodicals and Newspapers.) LC 82-20977. ISBN 0-313-23310-1.

This encyclopedic survey of dime novels, pulps, and digests published in the United States, Canada, and Great Britain between 1882 and 1982, provides concise entries describing contents, publication history, title changes (where applicable), volume and issue data, publisher, editor, pricing, pagination, and current status. The appendixes include a listing of periodicals by category, a listing of notable writers in the "Golden Age," and a chronology based on the initial appearance of each title.

Guides to the Literature

333.   Barnes, Melvyn. **Murder in Print: A Guide to Two Centuries of Crime Fiction.**
London: Barn Owl Books; distr., Spoon River, 1987, c1986. 244p. Index. ISBN 0-
9509057-4-7.
The book surveys almost 500 titles by 260 writers, including both "milestones" of
crime fiction and gems that feature extraordinary writing or have incorporated a new
technique, style, etc.

334.   Breen, Jon L. **Novel Verdicts: A Guide to Courtroom Fiction.** Metuchen, NJ:
Scarecrow, 1984. 266p. Indexes, bibl. LC 84-14110. ISBN 0-8108-1741-1.
The tool provides annotations to 421 novels and short stories with a notable degree
of courtroom activity. Most titles treated here are by either American or British authors.
General, type-of-offense, and location-of-trial indexes have also been provided.

335.   East, Andy. **The Cold War File.** Metuchen, NJ: Scarecrow, 1983. 362p. Index, bibl.
LC 83-7584. ISBN 0-8108-1641-5.
The source covers seventy-seven spy series dating primarily from the 1960s.
Arranged alphabetically by author, each entry gives biographical data, discusses the traits
characterizing the featured agent, identifies the major titles within the series, notes mass
media tie-ins, and assesses the popularity and availability of the series. Appendix 1 lists
titles in series running beyond 1969; appendix 2 cites titles issued by different publishers
later than 1969. Access to the text is enhanced by an index of secret agents.

336.   McCormick, Donald, and Katy Fletcher. **Spy Fiction: A Connoisseur's Guide.**
New York: Facts on File, 1990. 346p. Index, bibl. ISBN 0-8160-2098-1. 1st edition titled,
Who's Who in Spy Fiction (Elm Tree Books, 1977).
The book consists of two main parts: (1) a listing, in alphabetical order, of over 225
authors (largely American and British) that provides biographical and bibliographical
information; and (2) a collection of eight essays, including "A Brief History of American
Spy Fiction," and "Crossfertilization: The Relationship between Writers and the World-
wide."

337.   Pronzini, Bill, and Marcia Muller. **1001 Midnights: The Aficionado's Guide to
Mystery and Detective Fiction.** New York: Arbor House, 1986. 879p. Bibl. LC 85-30817.
ISBN 0-87795-622-7.
The tool's stated goal is to provide "aficionados, students, and collectors, as well
as casual and new readers, with a reference guide to one thousand and one individual titles;
to additional works by their authors; and to books of a similar type (whodunit, thriller,
police procedural, etc.) by other writers. Every major author in the field, beginning with
Edgar Allan Poe, and every major work up to and including books published in 1985 are
covered" (p. 1). In achieving its purpose, the book's comprehensive coverage overcomes
such weaknesses as a pronounced negative tone in the reviews and the lack of indexes.

Handbooks

338.   Bullard, Scott R., and Michael Leo Collins. **Who's Who in Sherlock Holmes.** New
York: Taplinger, 1980. 251p. LC 79-66638. ISBN 0-8008-8281-4; 0-8008-8282-2 pap.
Essentially an index to proper names, places, and objects appearing in the four
Holmes novels and fifty-six short stories, the tool also provides a citation to William
Baring-Gould's *The Annotated Sherlock Holmes* (New York: Potter/Crown, 1967) in each

entry. Although not as comprehensive as Jack Tracy's *The Encyclopedia Sherlockiana* (New York: Doubleday, 1977) it is an extremely informative source.

339.   Conquest, John. **Trouble Is Their Business: Private Eyes in Fiction, Film, and Television, 1927-1988.** New York: Garland, 1990. liii, 497p. Index. (Garland Reference Library of the Humanities, Vol. 1151.) ISBN 0-8240-5947-6.

This volume provides background information on the authors and characters (arranged alphabetically) of the private eye literature. It also includes separate sections on film, television, and radio, in addition to an appendix organizing sleuths by location of practice. A title index has also been provided.

340.   Keating, H. R. F. **Crime & Mystery: The 100 Best Books.** New York: Carroll & Graf, 1987. 219p. Index. LC 87-17377. ISBN 0-88184-345-8.

Each of the subjectively chosen titles (including works by Christie, Doyle, Sayers, and Queen, as well as more obscure writers like John Franklin Bardin) includes a scintillating two-page critique.

341.   Knudson, Richard L. **The Whole Spy Catalogue: An Espionage Lover's Guide.** New York: St. Martin's Press, 1986. 182p. Illus. LC 86-15443. ISBN 0-312-87069-8 pap.

Utilizing a fireside-type approach, Knudson includes the following chapters: (1) "The Second-Oldest Profession," a historical survey of espionage; (2) an alphabetical listing of the leading English-language spy novelists, including a reference to their characters and a bibliography of their output; (3) a delineation of the most notable sleuths appearing in films and television; (4) "The Gadgetry of Spying," which looks at electronic bugs, weapons, etc.; (5) cryptography; and (6) coverage of renowned contemporary spies from real life. The book also includes a concise glossary.

342.   Mackler, Tasha. **Murder by Category: A Subject Guide to Mystery Fiction.** Metuchen, NJ: Scarecrow, 1992. 470p. Index, bibl. ISBN 0-8108-2463-9.

The source organizes 1,800-odd mystery titles by topical category with each entry including bibliographic data, a descriptive annotation, and, where applicable, series notations and cross-references to related categories. An author index has also been included.

343.   Magill, Frank N., ed. **Critical Survey of Mystery and Detective Fiction.** 4 Vols. Englewood Cliffs, NJ: Salem, 1988. Index. LC 88-28566. ISBN 0-89356-486-9.

The work covers more than 280 authors from the nineteenth century to the late 1980s. Authors represented include those whose reputation is based largely on mystery writing (e.g., Christie), pioneering contributors, such as Poe, and those best known for their output in other areas (e.g., Twain). The alphabetically arranged entries include a concise biography, pseudonyms, plot types, and major series characters.

344.   Menendez, Albert J. **The Subject Is Murder: A Selective Subject Guide to Mystery Fiction.** 2 Vols. New York: Garland, 1986-1990. Indexes. (Garland Reference Library of the Humanities, Vol. 627.) ISBN 0-8240-8655-4 (v. 1); 0-8240-2580-6 (v. 2).

The tool places material published from the 1920s up through 1989 in twenty-nine subject categories (e.g., medicine, the sea, libraries). Each section is prefaced by a brief essay. Access is enhanced by author and title indexes.

345.   Nichols, Victoria, and Susan Thompson. **Silk Stalkings: When Women Write of Murder. A Survey of Series Characters Created by Women Authors.** Berkeley, CA: Black Lizard/Creative Arts, 1988. 522p. LC 88-10491. ISBN 0-88739-096-X pap.

The authors have compiled more than 600 fictional characters and classified them in the main section of the work according to occupation: private eyes, lawyers, bankers, authors, aristocrats, etc. Each character receives a page or more of commentary, whereas the author is allotted a paragraph or less. A section of tabular data arranged by author follows; series characters are listed here, along with book titles and dates of publication. Three appendixes add to the tool's usefulness: (1) a chronological listing of series characters citing dates of first and last appearances along with the author and total number of books in which the character appeared; (2) a pseudonym cross-listing; and (3) the linking of series characters to authors.

346. Olderr, Steven. **Mystery Index: Subjects, Settings, and Sleuths of 10,000 Titles.** Chicago: American Library Association, 1987. 492p. Indexes. LC 87-1294. ISBN 0-8389-0461-0.

The tool is probably best employed by utilizing the indexes, which provide references to the main entry section. The entries include the author, birth and death dates, title(s), and primary character and order of his or her appearance in a series. Title, subject-and-setting, and character indexes have also been provided.

Indexes

347. Contento, William, with Martin H. Greenberg. **Index to Crime and Mystery Anthologies.** Boston: G. K. Hall, 1990. 736p. ISBN 0-8161-8629-4.

The source indexes more than 1,000 anthologies published between 1875 and 1990 from five perspectives: book authors, book titles, story authors, story titles, and book contents (the last section listing anthologies by editor).

Romance

Bibliographies

348. Kay, Mary June. **The Romantic Spirit: A Romance Bibliography of Authors and Titles.** San Antonio, TX: MJK Enterprises, 1983, c1982. 565p. Index. ISBN 0-9610996-1-5 pap.

349. Kay, Mary June. **The Romantic Spirit: A Romance Bibliography of Authors and Titles.** 1983-1984 update. San Antonio, TX: MJK Enterprises, 1984. 287p. Index. ISBN 0-9610996-1-5 pap.

The two works combined include approximately 5,000 author/pseudonym entries, which include an alphabetical list of titles, the romance line to which any of the titles belong, and a symbol designating relevant subgenres per title. A second section groups titles together by romance line and lists them in numerical order; each title and line provides a reference to the appropriate author/pseudonym entries. Both volumes include an author/pseudonym index.

Biographies

350. Henderson, Lesley, ed. D. L. Kirkpatrick, consulting ed. **Twentieth-Century Romance and Historical Writers.** 2nd ed. Chicago: St. James Press, 1990. 856p. Index, bibl. ISBN 0-912289-97-X. 1st ed. titled **Twentieth-Century Romance and Gothic Writers** (St. James Press, 1982).

This biobibliography of 530 writers (a rather diffuse listing including the likes of Zane Gray, James Michener, and Barbara Cartland) includes author comments and critical essays focusing on each's style and legacy within the genre. A title index has also been provided.

Guides to the Literature

351. Fallon, Eileen. **Words of Love: A Complete Guide to Romance Fiction.** New York: Garland, 1984. 386p. Bibl. (Garland Reference Library of the Humanities, Vol. 382.) LC 82-49132. ISBN 0-8240-9204-X.

The tool is organized into the following topical sections: the history of romance, the contemporary romance boom, a delineation of romance subgenres, publications, organizations of interest to romance writers, and historically important and present-day authors (the more than 200 concise sketches within these two biographical segments stand in contrast to the longer essay format employed elsewhere in the text). Also included are listings of pseudonyms and authors arranged according to subgenre.

352. Ramsdell, Kristin. **Happily Ever After: A Guide to Reading Interests in Romance Fiction.** Littleton, CO: Libraries Unlimited, 1987. 302p. Indexes. LC 87-22588. ISBN 0-87287-479-6.

The source is organized around a diverse array of romance categories. Each includes definitions, historical background, elements of appeal, methodologies for advising readers, and focused bibliographies (partially annotated). Author-name-title and subject indexes have also been provided.

Handbooks

353. Falk, Kathryn, Melinda Helfer, and Kathe Robin, comps. **Romance Reader's Handbook.** Brooklyn Heights, NY: Romantic Times, 1989. 351p. Illus., bibl., spiral-bound. ISBN 0-940338-25-4.

The majority of the pages are devoted to an alphabetically arranged listing of over 2,000 pseudonyms for romance writers. Although two comparable works of recent vintage offer broader retrospective coverage (i.e., Eileen Fallon's *Words of Love* and Mary June Kay's *The Romantic Spirit*), this tool provides more current information not readily available elsewhere. It also includes a roster of "Bookstores That Care," author address, and a "Source Section" (i.e., pointers on getting published, directories of agents and publishers, ads for book search services).

Science and Fantasy Fiction

Atlases

354. Post, J. B. **An Atlas of Fantasy.** New York: Souvenir, 1979, c1973. Rev. ed. Introduction by Lester del Rey. Illus., index. ISBN 0285-624245.

Long a map librarian at the Free Library of Philadelphia, Post has combined a background knowledge of fantasy and science fiction with the training and access to facilities to locate (and obtain) copies of the rare maps that compose this work. The book includes a selective array of maps—in classified order—charting imaginary realms. Among the lands present are Eden, Hell, the world of Sherlock Holmes, Treasure Island, the lands depicted in fiction by Edgar Rice Burroughs and J. R. R. Tolkien, Pooh's Turf,

George S. Chappell's whimsical Alimentary Canal, and Allestone, created from stories by Thomas Williams Malkin, who died at the age of six. Shortfalls do exist. The compiler freely admits to an "infinite" number of omissions; e.g., Neverland, Graustark, Akenfield, the Ponderosa Ranch, and the village from the television show *The Prisoner*. In addition, the black-and-white illustrations are often virtually impossible to read (owing largely to the poor condition of the source map). On the other hand, Post's annotations—which complement each map—represent a strength, providing an accurate historical and literary context. An artist index has also been provided.

Bibliographies

355.   Bleiler, Everett Franklin, with the assistance of Richard J. Bleiler. **Science-Fiction, the Early Years.** Kent, OH: Kent State University Press, 1990. 998p. Indexes. ISBN 0-87338-416-4.

   Novels, novellas, short stories, and plays—over 3000 entries alphabetically arranged by author—from the infancy of science fiction to the rise of genre periodicals in 1930 compose this source. Access is enhanced by author, title, and motif indexes.

356.   Brown, Charles N., and William G. Contento. **Science Fiction, Fantasy & Horror: A Comprehensive Bibliography of Books and Short Fiction Published in the English Language.** Oakland, CA: Locus. Annual. 1991 ed.: ISBN 0-9616629-9-9.

   This annual publication provides author, title, and broad subject access to books, reprints, and shorter works appearing in anthologies, collections, and magazine issues for 1987. The appendixes include a survey of book and magazine publishing trends, developments in the cinema, a necrology, a bibliographic essay, a roster of publishers' addresses, and a list of awards presented the previous year.

357.   Clareson, Thomas D., comp. **Science Fiction in America, 1870s-1930s: An Annotated Bibliography of Primary Sources.** Westport, CT: Greenwood, 1984. 305p. Indexes. (Bibliographies and Indexes in American Literature, No. 1.) LC 84-8934. ISBN 0-313-23169-9.

   The 838 entries provide standard bibliographical data and annotations composed of plot summaries and critical analyses. The insights—from a leading scholar in the field—constitute a major strength of the tool. Author and short-title indexes have also been provided.

358.   Cottrill, Tim, Martin H. Greenberg, and Charles G. Waugh. **Science Fiction and Fantasy Series and Sequels: A Bibliography. Volume 1: Books.** New York: Garland, 1986. 398p. Indexes, bibl. (Garland Reference Library of the Humanities, Vol. 611.) LC 85-45121. ISBN 0-8240-8671-6.

   The source lists approximately 6,300 book titles from 1,200 series. Arranged alphabetically by author (except any series with many authors, which are arranged by series name), the entries include series title headings for book titles, publisher, and publication date. Access is enhanced by sequence and book title indexes.

359.   Glut, Donald F. **The Frankenstein Catalog.** Jefferson, NC: McFarland, 1984. 525p. Illus., indexes. LC 81-6026. ISBN 0-89950-029-3.

   Considered the definitive bibliography of Frankensteiniana, the 2,666 annotated entries cover all editions of the original novel, critical writings, film and stage adaptations, poetry, animated cartoons, radic and television series and specials, comic books and strips, spoken word recordings, and sheet music. Name and title indexes have also been included.

360. Hammond, J. R. **Herbert George Wells: An Annotated Bibliography of His Works.** New York: Garland, 1977. 257p. Index. (Garland Reference Library of the Humanities, Vol. 84.) LC 76-52667. ISBN 0-8240-9889-7.

The bibliography is divided into eight chronologically arranged segments: (1) sixty-one novels, romances, and short story collections, in addition to four volumes of collected essays; (2) a listing of forty-seven nonfiction books and forty-three pamphlets by Wells published between 1892 and 1945; (3) an annotated listing of titles from The Atlantic Edition and thirteen other collected editions of his works; (4) a description of five posthumously published works; (5) a discussion of three volumes of collected letters; (6) a listing of thirty-nine books by others that contain a preface by Wells; (7) a listing of fifty-three books containing a contribution by Wells; and (8) a list giving the page in which 111 of his illustrations appear. The five appendixes include: (1) a list of books and pamphlets by Wells published between 1892 and 1945 in chronological order; (2) reference to unreprinted writings; (3) a chronological listing (1909-1976) of critical, biographical, and bibliographical studies on Wells; (4) orientation to the University of Illinois Wells Archive and the Bromley Central Library; and (5) an outline of the aims and activities of the H. G. Wells Society. A title index enhances access to the text.

361. Jaffery, Sheldon. **Future and Fantastic Worlds: A Bibliographical Retrospective of DAW Books (1972-1987).** Mercer Island, WA: Starmont House, 1987. 297p. Indexes, bibl. (Starmont Reference Guide, No. 4.) LC 87-9901. ISBN 1-55742-003-3; 1-55742-002-5 pap.

DAW produced paperback science fiction/fantasy novels and short-story anthologies during the post-World War II era. The text consists of a numerical listing, utilizing the collector's number, of the DAW monographs. Each entry includes bibliographic data, publishing history (where applicable), cover artist, original price, plot summary, and occasional added notes of interest. Author-title, artist-title, and title indexes have also been provided.

362. Justice, Keith L. **Science Fiction, Fantasy, and Horror Reference: An Annotated Bibliography of Works About Literature and Film.** Jefferson, NC: McFarland, 1989. 226p. Indexes. LC 89-2841. ISBN 0-89950-406-X.

The 304 titles are organized by the following topics: general history and criticism; author studies; general bibliographies; author bibliographies; biographies, autobiographies, letters, and interviews; encyclopedias, dictionaries, indexes, and checklists; television, film, and radio; comics, art, and illustration; and anthologies, collections, and annotated editions. The annotations provide a critical focus useful to librarians, scholars, enthusiasts, and others. The appendixes are devoted to series publications and a core materials listing. Access is enhanced by title and author/editor indexes.

363. King, Betty. **Women of the Future: The Female Main Character in Science Fiction.** Metuchen, NJ: Scarecrow, 1984. 273p. Index, bibl. LC 83-20130. ISBN 0-8108-1664-4.

King has included novels and anthologized stories that possess strong central female characters and are in print or readily available from libraries. The material is organized by two analytical indexes; i.e., "Physical and Mental/Emotional Characteristics of Characters" (occupation, ethnic backgrounds, etc.) and "Story Particulars" (settings of time, place, society, etc.).

364. Lynn, Ruth Nadelman. **Fantasy Literature for Children and Young Adults: An Annotated Bibliography.** 3rd ed. New York: R. R. Bowker, 1989. Indexes. ISBN 0-8352-2347-7.

The source includes 3,300 fantasy novels and anthologies appropriate for grades 3-12. Part 1 covers English-language titles published in the United States between 1900 and 1988. Organized into ten categories, inclusion here was based on recommendations from at least two sources. Part 2—"Research Guide"—includes critical books, articles, dissertations, interviews, and biographical information. Author/illustrator, title, and subject indexes have also been provided.

365. Newman, John, and Michael Unsworth. **Future War Novels: An Annotated Bibliography of Works in English Published since 1946.** Phoenix, AZ: Oryx, 1984. 101p. Indexes, bibl. LC 83-43245. ISBN 0-89774-103-X.

The 191 novels included here are organized into the following time frames: 1946-1949, 1950-1959, 1960-1969, 1970-1979, and 1980-1983. The annotations address locale, characterization, plot, military details, and literary worth. Access is enhanced by author and title indexes.

366. Peplow, Michael W., and Robert S. Bravard. **Samuel R. Delany: A Primary and Secondary Bibliography, 1962-1979.** Boston: G. K. Hall, 1980. 178p. Indexes, bibl. (Masters of Science Fiction and Fantasy.) LC 80-20108. ISBN 0-8161-8054-7.

The bibliography is arranged by the following formats (all portions arranged chronologically): fiction, nonfiction, juvenilia, unpublished speeches and nonfiction, and 274 critical studies of Delany (many from fanzines). The tool also includes a discussion of the two most notable collections of Delanyana and a biographical profile. Indexes to works by Delany and works about Delany have also been provided.

367. Schlobin, Roger C. **Urania's Daughters: A Checklist of Women Science-Fiction Writers, 1692-1982.** Mercer Island, WA: Starmont House, 1983. 79p. Index, bibl. (Starmont Reference Guide, No. 1.) LC 83-2467. ISBN 0-916732-57-6; 0-916732-56-8 pap.

Essentially a checklist of approximately 830 novels and anthologies (usually first editions) written by women that were published between 1692 and 1982, the entries are arranged alphabetically by authors' real names, and subdivided by titles. A preliminary compilation of pseudonyms, variant names, and joint authors, in addition to a title index, are also included.

368. Tymn, Marshall B., and Mike Ashley. **Science Fiction, Fantasy, and Fiction Magazines.** Westport, CT: Greenwood, 1985. 970p. Index, bibl. ISBN 0-313-21221-X.

This guide includes sections on English-language magazines, associational English-language anthologies, academic periodicals and major fanzines, and non-English-language magazines. The individual magazine profiles cover publication history and supplementary information sources, such as indexes, reprints, and library locations.

369. Tymn, Marshall B., Roger C. Schlobin, L. W. Currey, comps. and eds. **A Research Guide to Science Fiction Studies: An Annotated Checklist of Primary and Secondary Sources for Fantasy and Science Fiction.** With a bibliography of doctoral dissertations by Douglas Justus. New York: Garland, 1977. 165p. Indexes, bibl. LC 76-52682. ISBN 0-8240-9886-2.

The 404 entries cited here include general surveys, histories, genre studies, works on individual authors, bibliographies, and periodicals. Author and title indexes and a listing of roughly 400 doctoral dissertations (without annotations) have also been provided.

Biographies

370.   Bleiler, E. F., ed. **Supernatural Fiction Writers: Fantasy and Horror.** 2 Vols. New York: Scribner's, 1985. (1169p.) Index, bibl. LC 84-27588. ISBN 0-684-17808-7.

The source includes biobibliographical essays on 148 authors of note within the fantasy and horror genres. The entries are arranged in chronological and geographical categories, and further divided alphabetically by author name.

371.   Cowart, David, and Thomas L. Wymer, eds. **Twentieth-Century American Science-Fiction Writers.** 2 Vols. Detroit: Gale Research, 1981. Illus., index. (Dictionary of Literary Biography, Vol. 8; A Bruccoli Clark Book.) LC 81-4182. ISBN 0-8103-0918-1.

This tool covers ninety-one American science fiction authors that achieved success between 1900 and 1970. The entries (ranging from several to twenty-one pages in length) contain biographical data, a list of the author's work, a critical analysis of that output, and a selected bibliography of books and articles about the author.

372.   Gunn, James, ed. **The New Encyclopedia of Science Fiction.** New York: Viking, 1988. 524p. Illus. LC 87-40637. ISBN 0-670-81041-X.

The source incorporates 529 essays on writers and illustrators as well as 346 on the mass media and assorted topics (e.g., lost worlds, time travel). Entries vary in length from a few descriptive sentences to exhaustive surveys that critique the subject under consideration.

373.   Smith, Curtis C. **Twentieth-Century Science Fiction Writers.** Chicago: St. James Press, 1986. 933p. Bibl. ISBN 0-912289-27-9.

Over 600 authors are covered here, including mainstream writers like Mark Twain and Sinclair Lewis. The signed contributions—all at least 1,000 words long—provide biographical information, critical analysis, and complete listings of the writer's output.

Catalogs/Union Lists

374.   Lewis, Arthur O. **Utopian Literature in the Pennsylvania State University Libraries: A Selected Bibliography.** University Park, PA: Pennsylvania State University Libraries, 1984. Illus., index. (Bibliographical Series, No. 9) pap.

This represents a catalog of 550 utopian works held by Penn State's Pattee Library. The entries—ranging from Plato to contemporary writers—are arranged alphabetically and feature descriptive and critical annotations.

Dictionaries

375.   Manguel, Alberto, and Gianni Guadalupi. **The Dictionary of Imaginary Places.** San Diego, CA: Harcourt Brace Jovanovich, 1987. 454p. Illus., maps, index. LC: 86-26063. ISBN 0-15-626054-9.

This is an expanded edition of a work first published in 1900. More than 1,200 fantasy worlds are described here; the illustrations and maps add significantly to the dictionary's appeal. The scope includes a blend of the familiar (e.g., Lewis Carroll, J. R. R. Tolkien) and the unexpected (e.g., Francois Rabelais, Richard Wagner, and Gustave Flaubert).

Encyclopedias

376. Ash, Brian, ed. **The Visual Encyclopedia of Science Fiction.** New York: Harmony/Crown, 1977. 352p. Illus., indexes, bibl. ISBN 0-517-53174-7; 0-517-53175-5 pap.

This represents a seminal work likely to appeal to the uninitiated as well as hard-core fans. The text is organized into four major sections: a chronological listing of key developments in science fiction since the early nineteenth century (e.g., an important author's first publication, the appearance and cessation of a magazine); the exploration of notable themes (lost and parallel worlds, cities and cultures); a philosophical analysis of the genre; and a look at the contributions by fandom, science fiction art, cinema, television, magazines, comics, commentators, and fringe cults. Author and title indexes have also been provided.

377. Tuck, Donald H., comp. **The Encyclopedia of Science Fiction and Fantasy through 1968. Volume 1: Who's Who and Works, A-L. Volume 2: Who's Who and Works, M-Z.** Chicago: Advent, 1974; 1978. 530p. Index. LC 73-91828. ISBN 0-911682-22-8.

The set provides biobibliographical information on notable writers, anthologists, editors, and artists. With the exception of Ash's *Visual Encyclopedia of Science Fiction* (see entry 376), this may be the most comprehensive tool of its kind. Access is enhanced by a title index.

Guides to the Literature

378. Barron, Neil, ed. **Anatomy of Wonder: A Critical Guide to Science Fiction.** 3rd ed. New York: R. R. Bowker, 1987. 874p. Index. LC 87-9305. ISBN 0-8352-2312-4.

This has been an indispensable work for librarians since the appearance of the first edition in the mid-1970s. The 2,650 annotated titles are organized under three main headings: English-language science fiction (subdivided by date with a separate section for children's and young adult literature), foreign-language science fiction (arranged by nation), and research aids (i.e., reference works; histories and criticisms; biographical studies; television shows, films, and illustrations; magazines; and important library and private collections).

379. Barron, Neil, ed. **Fantasy Literature: A Reader's Guide.** Hamden, CT: Garland, 1990. 586p. (Garland Reference Library of the Humanities, v. 874.) LC 89-23693. ISBN 0-8240-3148-2.

Following the formula established by his *Anatomy of Wonder* (see entry 378), Barron covers fantasy literature from Homer's *Odyssey* to 1988. The selective bibliographic entries include annotations that summarize contents and cite best editions; key works are starred.

380. Fletcher, Marilyn P., comp. and ed., and James L. Thorson, consulting ed. **Reader's Guide to Twentieth-Century Fiction.** Chicago: American Library Association, 1989. 673p. Index, bibl. LC 88-7815. ISBN 0-8389-0504-8.

Although its scope (Anglo-American science fiction as well as several Eastern bloc authors available in English translation) falls short of Barron's *Anatomy of Wonder* (see entry 378), Fletcher's author entries are far more exhaustive, including biographical profiles, plot summaries, and analyses of themes and styles. The appendixes include lists of science fiction periodicals and Hugo and Nebula award winners. A title index has also been provided. Despite the presence of some typos, this remains a useful tool.

381. Gallagher, Edward J. **The Annotated Guide to Fantastic Adventures.** Mercer Island, WA: Starmont House, 1985. 170p. Indexes, bibl. (Starmont Reference Guides, No. 2.) LC 84-16228. ISBN 0-916732-71-1; 0-916732-70-3 pap.

This is a chronological listing of the stories appearing in *Fantastic Adventures,* a magazine published between May 1939 and March 1953 that focused on fantasy and marginal forms of science fiction rather than the hard-core variety typified by the contents of *Amazing Stories.* In addition to an introductory history of the publication, six appendixes are included: a list of issues (with dates and cover artists); a list of departments (by issue); a list of biographies in the magazine, arranged by name; a list of illustrators (cover and interior); seventeen story "motifs"; and a list of editorial personnel. Access is enhanced by author and title indexes.

382. Green, Scott E. **Contemporary Science Fiction, Fantasy, Horror Poetry: A Resource Guide and Biographical Directory.** Westport, CT: Greenwood, 1989. 216p. Index. LC 89-16966. ISBN 0-313-26324-8.

Following an introductory survey of science fiction poetry in the United States, the source covers American verse published in magazines (commercial and small press), single-author collections, and anthologies. It also includes a directory of poets, thumbnail biographies, and lists of publications and awards.

383. Tymn, Marshall B., ed. **The Science Fiction Reference Book: A Comprehensive Handbook and Guide to the History, Literature, Scholarship, and Related Activities of the Science Fiction and Fantasy Fields.** Mercer Island, WA: Starmont House, 1981. 536p. Index, bibl. LC 80-28888. ISBN 0-916732-42-5; 0-916732-24-X pap.

The source closely parallels the coverage provided in Barron's *Anatomy of Wonder* (see entry 378). Although the latter is generally more thorough in its treatment of the literature, Tymn's book is superior on a number of fronts; for example, it includes a forty-four-page survey of science fiction fandom and fanzines and an eighty-six-page discourse on writing awards.

384. Tymn, Marshall B., and Mike Ashley, eds. **Science Fiction, Fantasy, and Weird Fiction Magazines.** Westport, CT: Greenwood, 1985. xxx, 970p. (Historical Guides to the World's Periodicals and Newspapers.) Index, bibl. LC 84-11523. ISBN 0-313-21221-X.

The tool covers the magazines of this field from 1882 into the 1980s, with a special emphasis on the golden age of pulps (1926 to early 1950s). The main text is divided into four parts: an alphabetically arranged listing of 279 U.S. and British Commonwealth titles devoted to science fiction, fantasy, and weird fiction; English-language anthologies; selected fanzines and academic journals devoted to the field; and 178 foreign-language titles. Also included are Thomas Clareson's survey of the science fiction/fantasy genre and two appendixes (an index to cover artists and a chronological listing of magazine founding dates).

385. Waggoner, Diana. **The Hills of Faraway: A Guide to Fantasy.** New York: Atheneum Publishers, 1978. 326p. Illus., index, bibl. LC 76-900. ISBN 0-689-10846-X.

Waggoner's 996-item bibliography (arranged alphabetically by author and subdivided by a chronological listing of works) is prefaced by two chapters concerned with literary definition and followed by four appendixes ("A Timeline of Fantasy, 1858-1975"; "Some Fantasy Award Winners"; the reproduction of twenty-one fantasy illustrations from periodicals and juvenile books; and a classification of fantasy subgenres). Although confusing in places, the source nevertheless contains many fascinating insights.

Handbooks

386. Antczak, Janice. **Science Fiction: The Mythos of a New Romance.** New York: Neal-Schuman, 1985. 233p. Illus., index, bibl. (Diversity and Direction in Children's Literature Series, 2.) LC 84-14726. ISBN 0-918212-43-X pap.

An offshoot of the author's doctoral dissertation, "The Mythos of a New Romance: A Critical Analysis of Science Fiction for Children as Informed by the Literary Theory of Northrup Frye," the book analyzes children's science fiction as romance and as it is related to mythology and legend. The chapters include: "Science Fiction: The Story of a Modern Quest," "The Growth and Development of a Genre," "Symbols in Science Fiction," "The Hero," "The Hero's Adventures," "Beauties, Beasts, Comrades, and Traitors: The Minor Characters," "Worlds Apart: Romantic Settings," "New Directions/New Maturity," and "A New Romance." Also provided are lists of works noted in each chapter.

387. Brians, Paul. **Nuclear Holocausts: Atomic War in Fiction, 1895-1984.** Kent, OH: Kent State University, 1987. 398p. Index, bibl. LC 86-10685. ISBN 0-87338-335-4.

Following an exhaustive introduction to the subject, the annotated bibliography, which includes English-language novels, short stories, and plays, is arranged alphabetically within five sections: "The History of the Holocaust," "The Causes of Nuclear War," "The Short-Term Effects of Nuclear War," "The Long-Term Consequences of Nucleur War," and "Avoiding the Holocaust." More than a mere bibliography, the work effectively delineates the literary output—with much attention paid to overall context—of this genre.

388. Burgess, Michael. **A Guide to Science Fiction & Fantasy in the Library of Congress Classification Scheme.** San Bernardino, CA: Borgo, 1984. 86p. Index. (The Borgo Reference Library, Vol. 8.) LC 80-11418. ISBN 0-89370-807-0; 0-89370-907-7 spiralbound.

Due to the fragmentation of related science fiction and fantasy genres as well as particular topics, Burgess has provided a pathfinder to the Library of Congress classification scheme, LC subject headings, and Anglo-American Cataloguing Rules (second edition). Accordingly, the tool lists 460 topical and form subject headings; main entry headings for 2,700 authors (and, where present, LC classification numbers for their works and those about them); similar headings for forty-four artists and sixteen films; and 320 classification numbers, along with twenty categories from literature tables, relevant to science fiction and fantasy literature.

389. Gammell, Leon L. **The Annotated Guide to "Startling Stories."** Mercer Island, WA: Starmont House, 1986. 90p. (Starmont Reference Guide, No. 3.) LC 86-6012. ISBN 0-930261-50-X pap.

This source offers chronologically arranged plot summaries and critiques of novels and brief synopses of short stories that appeared in the magazine *Startling Stories* from January 1939 to Fall 1955.

390. Garber, Eric, and Lyn Paleo. **Uranian Worlds: A Guide to Alternative Sexuality in Science Fiction, Fantasy, and Horror.** 2nd ed. Boston: G. K. Hall, 1990. 286p. Index. LC 90-37434. ISBN 0-8161-1832-X.

Prefaced by an informative historical overview and introductions by Samuel Delaney and Joanna Russ, the annotated bibliography (alphabetically arranged by author) includes plot summaries, a code denoting form of homosexuality and prominence of the theme for each entry, and biographical notes. Appendixes provide a selected filmography and videography and an alphabetically arranged list of book titles. A chronological index has also been provided.

391. Holdstock, Robert, and Malcolm Edwards. **Alien Landscapes.** New York: Mayflower Books, 1979. 116p. Illus. LC 79-13431. ISBN 0-8317-0285-0.

Utilizing the work of contemporary illustrators (collectively known as Young Artists), the book explores ten alien worlds created by the following science fiction novelists: Arthur C. Clarke (Rama), Anne McCaffrey (Pern), James Blish (Okie Cities), Hal Clement (Mesklin), Harry Harrison (Eros), Frank Herbert (Arrakis from *Dune*), Larry Niven (Ringworld), Isaac Asimov (Trantor from the *Foundation Trilogy*), Brian Aldiss (Hothouse), and H. G. Wells (End of the World). A Galactic Time Chart and an introductory essay providing historical background on the literary depiction of other worlds provide a greater sense of unity to the volume.

392. Jakubowski, Maxim, and Malcolm Edwards. **The SF Book of Lists.** New York: Berkley Publishing, 1983. 384p. ISBN 0-425-06187-6.

Despite the lack of indexing, this entertaining volume contains many informative lists: e.g., "The Years of Futures Past" (a chronology of the best science fiction), "Great Aliens of Science Fiction," "John Sladek's List of Seven Great Unexplained Mysteries of Our Times," collaborators, pseudonyms, milestones in bad science fiction, and books that have become movies.

393. Lord, Glenn, ed. and comp. **The Last Celt: A Bio-Bibliography of Robert Ervin Howard.** New York: Berkley Publishing, 1977, c1976. 415p. Illus., indexes, bibl. ISBN 0-425-03630-8 pap.

The work has four main parts: the autobiography, containing four autobiographical essays and a letter written by Howard; the biography, with five essays about Howard; the bibliography, organized into eighteen subsections (books, fiction, verse, articles, letters, translations, unpublished fiction/verse/articles, books and articles about Howard, and two indexes); and miscellanea, including photographs of Howard and the covers of the magazines in which his stories appeared. Series and short story/verse/letter indexes have also been provided.

394. Mallett, Daryl F., and Robert Reginald. **Reginald's Science Fiction and Fantasy Awards: A Comprehensive Guide to the Awards and Their Winners.** 2nd ed. San Bernardino, CA: Borgo, 1991. 248p. Indexes. (Literary Guides, No. 1.) LC 90-15074. ISBN 0-89370-826-7; 0-89370-926-3 pap.

The tool documents the winners of 126 separate awards (including films, illustrators, and periodicals, as well as books) in three sections (each arranged alphabetically by award, then chronologically by year granted): English-language awards (including British Commonwealth prizes), foreign-language awards, and nongenre awards occasionally given to science fiction or fantasy writers. Each award is introduced by a brief history. Access is enhanced by author and award indexes.

395. Naha, Ed. **The Science Fictionary: An A-Z Guide to the World of SF Authors, Films, & TV Shows.** New York: Wideview; distr., PEI Books/Harper & Row, 1980. 388p. LC 80-16748. ISBN 0-87223-629-3 pap.

The source describes 999 films, 192 television shows, and 204 authors in three alphabetically arranged sections. A final segment lists science fiction awards, periodicals, and themes.

396. Pringle, David. **Modern Fantasy: The Hundred Best Novels: An English-Language Selection, 1946-1987.** New York: Peter Bedrick; distr., HarperCollins, 1989. 284p. Index. LC 89-33072. ISBN 0-87226-328-2; 0-87226-219-7 pap.

This is a subjective, albeit intriguing, listing strongly biased in favor of new wave, experimental, and surrealistic authors. The two-page entries include a plot summary, author data, publication history, and a commentary by Pringle. The author index enhances access to the listing.

397. **Science Fiction & Fantasy Book Review Annual.** Westport, CT: Meckler, 1988-. Annual. Indexes. ISSN: 1040-192X.

Each volume includes some 600 signed reviews arranged alphabetically by author in three parts: fiction, young adult fiction, and nonfiction. These sections are prefaced by author profiles, surveys of publishing trends, and lists of award winners. Title and contributor indexes have also been provided.

398. Brown, Charles N., and William G. Contento, eds. **Science Fiction, Fantasy & Horror.** Oakland, CA: Locus; distr. by Meckler Corp., 1986-. Annual. ISSN 0898-4077.

Conceived as a supplement to Contento's *Index to Science Fiction Anthologies and Collections* (see entry 400), the work organizes books and stories published in the United States and Great Britain into seven categories: books by author and title; new publications in all formats, by author; subjects/formats, by author; short stories, by author and title; and contents lists for anthologies and separate periodical issues. The appendixes include statistical summaries of publishing in this genre, selected readings, awards, necrology, and a directory of publishers.

399. Wolfe, Gary K. **Critical Terms for Science Fiction and Fantasy: A Glossary and Guide to Scholarship.** Westport, CT: Greenwood, 1986. 162p. Index, bibl. LC 86-3138. ISBN 0-313-22981-3.

The work contains a 26-page introductory essay ("Fantastic Literature and Literary Discourse") followed by a glossary of almost 500 critical terms and concepts. The definitions frequently refer to notable authors and critics. An index of primary authors has also been included.

Indexes

400. Contento, William. **Index to Science Fiction Anthologies and Collections.** Boston: G. K. Hall, 1978. 608p. Index, bibl. (A Reference Publication in Science Fiction.) LC 78-155. ISBN 0-8161-8092-X.

Contento covers English-language anthologies and collections through June 1977. The source is divided into four parts: a checklist of books, an author index, a story index, and listings of book contents. Regarding the 12,000 stories cited, Contento has noted anthology locations and all original sources, along with volume, date, and page references to magazines.

401. Fletcher, Marilyn P. **Science Fiction Story Index, 1950-1979.** 2nd ed. Chicago: American Library Association, 1981. 610p. Indexes. LC 80-28685. I: 0-8389-0320-7 pap.

This tool cites the short stories and novellas within 953 English-language anthologies. The stories are arranged alphabetically in two sections—the author and title indexes.

402. Hall, H. W., ed. **Science Fiction and Fantasy Reference Index, 1878-1985: An International Author and Subject Index to History and Criticism.** 2 Vols. Detroit: Gale Research, 1987. (1460p.) LC 87-173. ISBN 0-8103-2129-7.

This index—volume 1 arranged by author, volume 2 by subject—covers over 19,000 books, articles, audiovisual resources, and news reports. The "Thesaurus of Science Fiction and Fantasy Indexing Terms" assists in the location of appropriate subject headings.

403.   Hall, H. W., ed. **Science Fiction Book Review Index, 1923-1973.** Detroit: Gale Research, 1975. 438p. Index, bibl. ISBN 0-8103-1054-6.

The tool represents a complete record of all books reviewed in science fiction magazines during the 1923-1973 period as well as a record of all science fiction and fantasy books and books of interest to enthusiasts of the genre reviewed in non-science fiction magazines from 1970 to 1973. The main section is arranged alphabetically by author, with books listed alphabetically by title under each author's name. Data for each entry includes author, title, pseudonym, joint authors and editors, place of publication, publisher, date of publication, number of pages, and LC card number. The appendixes include a bibliography listing science fiction magazines from 1923 through 1973; a title checklist of the general, library, and amateur magazines covered by the index; a list of major science fiction indexes; and an editor index to science fiction magazines. A book title index enhances access to the text. It has been compiled at Texas A & M's Evans Library, where a definitive collection of science fiction periodicals is housed.

404.   Hall, H. W., ed. **Science Fiction Book Review Index, 1974-1979.** Detroit: Gale Research, 1981. 391p. Index. LC 81-1490. ISBN 0-8103-1107-0.

The source cites reviews of about 6,200 novels and short story anthologies culled from 250 periodicals from 1974 through 1979. The review citations have been organized by book or story author. A book title index has also been provided.

405.   Hall, H. W., and Geraldine L. Hutchins, eds. **Science Fiction and Fantasy Book Review Index, 1980-1984: An Index to More Than 13,800 Book Reviews Appearing in Over 70 Science Fiction, Fantasy, and General Periodicals from 1980-1984.** Detroit: Gale Research, 1985. 761p. LC 85-25219. ISBN 0-8103-1646-3.

In addition to the book review index (arranged in two sections by author and title), the source incorporates a five-year cumulation of "Science Fiction and Fantasy Research Index," which provides nearly 16,000 author and subject access points to books, articles, and essays of history and criticism (including films, television programs, and graphic arts). The source continues Hall's 1974-1979 compilation (see entry 404).

406.   Hall, H. W., and Jan Swanbeck, comps. **Science Fiction and Fantasy Research Index. Volume 10.** San Bernardino, CA: Borgo, 1994. 80p. ISBN 0-8095-6803-9.

This irregularly issued series (roughly every two or three years) provides author and subject access to monographs, articles, and essays of a scholarly nature.

407.   Justice, Keith L., comp. **Science Fiction Master Index of Names.** Jefferson, NC: McFarland, 1986. 394p. Index. LC 85-42533. ISBN 0-89950-183-4.

The tool indexes approximately 18,000 names (actual, mytho-historical, and biblical people are included rather than fictional characters) from 122 monographs of history and criticism within the area of science fiction, fantasy, weird, and supernatural literature. In addition to including pseudonyms and names not related to science fiction, it functions as an index to unindexed works.

408.   Parnell, Frank H., with Mike Ashley, comps. **Monthly Terrors: An Index to the Weird Fantasy Magazines Published in the United States and Great Britain.** Westport, CT: Greenwood, 1985. 602p. Indexes, bibl. LC 84-19225. ISBN 0-313-23989-4.

The source covers 168 weird fantasy periodicals from the United States, England, and Canada that appeared between 1919-1983. The contents include an issue index organized alphabetically by magazine title (followed by a chronological listing of each issue's material); an author index, with biographical data and a listing of appropriate contributions; artist, editor, and series indexes; a historical overview of the genre; and geographical and chronological listings of the magazines.

Westerns

Bibliographies

409.   Drew, Bernard A., with Martin H. Greenberg and Charles G. Waugh. **Western Series and Sequels: A Reference Guide.** New York: Garland, 1986. 173p. Illus., title index. (Garland Bibliographies on Series and Sequels; Garland Reference Library of the Humanities, Vol. 625.) LC 85-45132. ISBN 0-8240-8657-0.
        The 375 entries reflect a broad interpretation of the Western genre, with the inclusion of series set in the Canadian west, the French and Indian wars, and the Civil War.

Women Writers

Bibliographies

410.   Grimes, Janet, and Diva Daims. **Novels in English by Women, 1891-1920: A Preliminary Checklist.** With the editorial assistance of Doris Robinson, New York: Garland, 1981. 805p. Index. (Garland Reference Library of the Humanities, Vol. 202.) LC 79-7911. ISBN 0-8240-9522-7.
        The tool contains more than 15,000 U.S. and British novels written by over 5,000 women authors between 1891 and 1920. The work was compiled from the bibliographic entries in *Publishers' Weekly* and *Bookseller* during that period. Each item includes author name, nationality, birth and death dates (if available), titles and title notes, pen names, publishing data, and sources for verification and citation. A title index has also been provided.

Handbooks

411.   Baechler, Lea, and A. Walton Litz, eds. **Modern American Women Writers.** New York: Scribner's, 1991. 583p. LC 90-52917. ISBN 0-684-19057-5.
        The book is composed of forty-one American women writers published since 1870, including Emily Dickinson and Alice Walker. With essays (ranging from eight to twenty-two pages) emphasizing the social and historical background of these authors, it represents a more in-depth and up-to-date source than Mainero's *American Women Writers.*

412.   Mainiero, Lina, ed. **American Women Writers: A Critical Reference Guide from Colonial Times to the Present.** New York: Ungar, 1979-1982. 4 Vols. LC 82-40286. ISBN 0-8044-3150-7.
        The work covers more than 1,000 American women authors of literary, popular, and juvenile fiction and nonfiction, spanning the colonial era to the present. Each entry includes concise biographical data, a biocritical essay noting an author's significance and overall literary contribution, major works, themes, and writing style, and a listing of works by and about her.

Chapter 7

Popular Music

General

Bibliographies/Discographies

413.   Cooper, B. Lee, and Wayne S. Haney. **Response Recordings: An Answer Song Discography 1950-1990.** Metuchen, NJ: Scarecrow, 1990. 272p. Indexes, bibl. LC 90-8728. ISBN 0-8108-2342-X.

   Response recordings—whereby an artist reacts to prior releases by other performers—are listed (alphabetically by song title generating the response) and analyzed in this source. Although not complete, it will undoubtedly remain the standard in this field for many years. Song title and performing artist indexes have also been included.

414.   Lynch, Richard Chigley, comp. **Broadway on Records.** Westport, CT: Greenwood, 1987. 347p. Indexes, disc. LC 87-11822. ISBN 0-313-25523-7.

   The listing spans 469 Broadway and off-Broadway musicals from 1931 to 1986. The entries, arranged alphabetically by title, include opening dates, theater, record label and number, composer, lyricist, musical director, cast, songs, cast members performing each song, and recording format. Access is enhanced by performer and technical personnel indexes.

415.   Lynch, Richard Chigley, comp. **TV and Studio Cast Musicals on Record: A Discography of Television Musicals and Stage Recordings.** Westport, CT: Greenwood, 1990. 330p. Indexes, disc. (Discographies, No. 38.) LC 90-40205. ISBN 0-313-27324-3.

   Employing essentially the same format as that of *Broadway on Records* (see entry 414), the 657 entries—arranged alphabetically by title—incorporate almost 6,500 song titles, covering the period 1874-1988. Performer and technical personnel indexes have also been included.

416.   Morgereth, Timothy A. **Bing Crosby: A Discography, Radio Program List and Filmography.** Jefferson, NC: McFarland, 1987. 554p. Illus., index. LC 85-43582. ISBN 0-89950-210-5.

   The 2,395 entries are divided into three sections: recordings (chronologically arranged), radio broadcasts, and feature films. The utility of the tool extends far beyond Crosby's life and career; much can be learned about popular music disseminated by the mass media during the Depression and World War II era and about many of Crosby's show-business contemporaries.

417.   O'Brien, Ed, and Scott P. Sayers. **Sinatra: The Man and His Music . . . The Recording Artistry of Frances Albert Sinatra 1939-1992.** Austin, TX: TSD, 1992. pap.

   Termed "the most comprehensive Sinatra discography yet" by Howard Reich, reviewer for the Chicago *Tribune,* the book includes (1) recording dates, master numbers, arrangers, conductors, and locations for every Sinatra recording session, plus best source for locating each respective song; (2) a complete listing of Sinatra's recordings, in alphabetical order by song title, with cross references; (3) a complete listing of unissued Sinatra tracks; (4) recording information on all Sinatra V-Disc sessions; (5) session information for songs recorded for movies as well as a complete listing of his songs used on movie soundtracks; (6) chart history (with reference to *Billboard* and *Cash Box*) of all albums and singles; (7) rare photographs from concerts and recording states; (8) unused cover art for Sinatra projects; and (9) Sinatra Grammy nominations and awards.

418.   Hart, Jane Poirier, ed. **Spectrum: Your Guide to Today's Music**. Chatsworth, CA: Schwann, 1988-. Quarterly. Approximately 400p. Pap.

Long the *Books in Print* equivalent for sound recordings, the serial is one of a family of publications that have descended from the Schwann record catalog. It offers "terse citations of rock/pop, jazz, musicals, gospel/religious, New Age, spoken and miscellaneous, children's, and international (ethnic and pop) recordings as well as videos and related categories." The entries include title of release, label and number, and formats available.

419.   Tudor, Dean. **Popular Music: An Annotated Guide to Recordings**. Littleton, CO: Libraries Unlimited, 1983. 647p. Index, bibl. LC 83-18749. ISBN 0-87287-395-1.

The work supplements the four-volume series, "American Popular Music on Elpee," organizing long playing recordings under the following music categories: "Black," "Folk," "Jazz," "Mainstream," "Popular Religious," and "Rock." Criteria for inclusion here are a recording's impact, influence, and importance.

Biographies

420.   Birosik, Patti Jean. **The New Age Music Guide: Profiles and Recordings of 500 Top New Age Musicians**. New York: Macmillan, 1989. 218p. LC 89-9928. ISBN 0-02-041640-7 pap.

The source is divided into fourteen subgenres (e.g., environmental sounds, electronic/computer music, jazz-fusion); each of the 500 entries includes the artist's name, cites album titles (and label), and provides a description of his or her output.

421.   Hardy, Phil, and Dave Laing. **The Faber Companion to 20th-Century Popular Music**. Winchester, MA: Faber and Faber, 1990. 875p. ISBN 0-571-13837-3.

Although the 2,000-odd entries cover key artists as far back as the turn of the century (e.g., Billy Murray), they reveal a decidedly contemporary rock-pop emphasis. Notable album releases are discussed within the biocritical profiles.

422.   White, Mark. **"You Must Remember This...": Popular Songwriters 1900-1980**. New York: Scribner's, 1985. 304p. Indexes, bibl. LC 85-1974. ISBN 0-684-18433-8.

The tool profiles 130 popular song writers from the twentieth century, most of them Americans. Song title, composer and lyricist, performer, and show and film indexes have also been included.

Directories

423.   Levine, Michael. **The Music Address Book: How to Reach Anyone Who's Anyone in Music**. New York: Harper & Row, 1989. 231p. Index. LC 89-45102. ISBN 0-06-096383-2 pap.

The source provides the business office or correspondence addresses for over 3,000 artists, managers, record labels, and fan clubs in the popular music field. Practical advice for those considering a career in the business is also offered—e.g., how to copyright music, lyrics, and sound recordings; "Avoiding Ripoffs;" a glossary of terms.

Encyclopedias

424.   Clarke, Donald, ed. **The Penguin Encyclopedia of Popular Music.** New York: Viking Penguin, 1989. 1378p. Index. ISBN 0-670-80349-9.

The 3,000-odd entries cover artists, songwriters, producers, record companies, musical trends, etc., from the 1930s through the 1980s. An appendix identifies distributors specializing in hard-to-find records.

425.   Rehrig, William H. **The Heritage Encyclopedia of Band Music: Composers and Their Music.** Edited by Paul E. Bierley. 2 Vols. New York: Integrity, 1991. 1065p. Index, bibl. LC 91-73637. ISBN 0-918048-08-7.

The work covers all composers whose music has been adapted for concert band, including Schubert, Sousa, Walton, Bernstein, such popular music tunesmiths as Neil Diamond, and film composers like Jerry Goldsmith. Supplementary materials include a preface by Alfred Reed and nine appendixes (i.e., history of American band music, publishing practices, publishers' addresses, band journals, foreign band music, marches, sources and repositories, American band research, and the Robert Hoe Jr. LP series). A title index has also been included.

Guides to the Literature

426.   Elliker, Calvin. **Stephen Collins Foster: A Guide to Research.** New York: Garland, 1988. 197p. Index, bibl. (Garland Composer Resource Manuals, Vol. 10; Garland Reference Library of the Humanities, Vol. 782.) LC 87-35853. ISBN 0-8240-6640-5.

Attempting "to serve the research needs of both the general public and scholarly community," as well as to correct a number of the misconceptions about Foster, the book lists his works, materials about him, an iconography, realia or personal effects, his surviving letters, memorials (by state), dramatic and literary tributes, and musical tributes. Insightful comments accompany most entries.

Handbooks

427.   Bronson, Fred. **The Billboard Book of Number One Hits.** Rev. ed. New York: Billboard, 1988. 712p. Illus., indexes. LC 88-14707. ISBN 0-8230-7545-1.

The book looks at all recordings reaching number one on the *Billboard* pop singles charts, from "Rock Around the Clock" (1955) to "Together Forever" (June 18, 1988). Each song entry notes artist, label, writer, producer, date reached number one and top five songs at that time, length of time on chart, a photo, and text discussing artist's career and the song's history, with quotations by artist and associates. Lists of most number one hits by writer, producer, label, and artists are also included. Artist and title indexes enhance access to the text.

428.   Cohen-Stratyner, Barbara, ed. **Popular Music, 1900-1919: An Annotated Guide to American Popular Songs.** Detroit: Gale Research, 1988. 656p. Indexes. LC 88-21191. ISBN 0-8103-2595-0.

The alphabetically arranged song entries encompass a wide range of media—recordings, television, films, musicals, etc. Lyricists, composers, original publishers, and (at the editor's discretion) references to performances and performers. The tool also functions as a social history, touching upon many events and personalities from that era. Author, performer, and chronological indexes have also been provided.

429.   Cooper, B. Lee. **The Popular Music Handbook: A Resource Guide for Teachers, Librarians, and Media Specialists.** Littleton, CO: Libraries Unlimited, 1984. 415p. Index, bibl., discog. LC 84-19448. ISBN 0-87287-393-5.

This source organizes popular music recordings and print resources under topics relevant to teaching and research; e.g., ecology, civil rights, drugs. Within each topic, such subheadings as "teaching strategies" and teaching units will assist less knowledgeable educators and students during the planning and information-gathering process.

430.   Cooper, B. Lee. **A Resource Guide to Themes in Contemporary American Song Lyrics, 1950-1985.** Westport, CT: Greenwood, 1986. 458p. Index, bibl., discog. LC 85-21933. ISBN 0-313-24516-9.

The tool explores the literary themes present in popular music recordings (generally 45 r.p.m. singles) for the better part of four decades. The text is divided into the following broad headings (which are, in turn, subdivided into more specific themes, events, fads, etc.): Characters and Personalities; Communications Media; Death; Education; Marriage, Family Life, and Divorce; Military Conflicts; Occupations, Materialism, and Workplaces; Personal Relationships, Love and Sexuality; Political Protest and Social Criticism; Poverty and Unemployment; Race Relations; Religion; Transportation Systems; Urban Life; and Youth Culture.

431.   Dichter, Harry, and Elliott Shapiro. **Handbook of Early American Sheet Music 1768-1889.** New York: Dover, 1977. 287p. Illus., index, bibl. LC 77-70454. ISBN 0-486-23364-2.

This reprint of a 1941 Bowker publication is organized into three parts: (I) a classified arrangement of songs (e.g., Presidential Songs, Temperance Items); (II) a directory of early American music publishers; and (III) a listing of lithographers and artists involved with American sheet music prior to 1870. Supplementary material discusses "Early Copyrights," "First Editions," "Famous American Musical Firsts," and "Broadsides and Periodicals."

432.   Ganzl, Kurt, and Andrew Lamb. **Ganzl's Book of the Musical Theatre.** New York: Schirmer Books/Macmillan, 1989. 1373p. Illus., indexes, discog. LC 88-18588. ISBN 0-02-871941-7.

The work provides synopses and information on characters and stage and film productions of 198 musical theater (operetta, comic opera, musical comedy, and contemporary musicals) pieces. The entries are arranged by nation and subdivided chronologically (spanning the late 1700s through 1987). Author, title, composer, lyricist, and song title indexes have also been provided.

433.   Gilbert, Bob, and Gary Theroux. **The Top Ten, 1956-Present.** New York: Fireside, 1982. 302p. Illus. LC 82-10478. ISBN 0-671-43215-X pap.

The book provides a close-up look at the ten top hits for the years 1956 through 1980. Listings are based on an analysis of national trade chart activity, major market radio air play, industry sales figures, and music licensing tally reports, resulting in a distinct MOR bias and some curious omissions—the McGuire Sisters' "Sugartime," 1958; Jimmy Gilmore & the Fireballs' "Sugar Shack," 1963; and Marvin Gaye's "I Heard It Through the Grapevine," 1968-1969; all considered, by industrywide concensus, to be the top hits of their respective years of release. The arrangement is chronological, with each section (i.e., year) comprising two pages of music news notes, including a listing of the forty biggest hit singles and ten most successful LPs, followed by a one-page story about each of the ten top songs (in ascending order) generally accompanied by a photo of the artist in question. In the absence of an index, the "contents" provides an itemized listing of all entries.

434. Iwaschkin, Roman. **Popular Music: A Reference Guide.** New York: Garland, 1986. 658p. Index., bibl. (Garland Reference Library of the Humanities, Vol. 642.) LC 85-45140. ISBN 0-8240-8680-5.

The 5,000 bibliographic entries are divided into the following parts: music (e.g., folk, country, Cajun, black, jazz, stage and screen); biographies; education; music business; songs and recordings; literary works; and periodicals.

435. Jacobs, Dick. **Who Wrote That Song?** White Hall, VA: Betterway, 1988. 415p. Illus., index. LC 88-19351. ISBN 1-55870-108-7; 1-55870-100-1 pap.

The tool incorporates more than 12,000 American songs titles (in alphabetical order) written between the 1850s and 1980s. The entries include composer, lyricist, artist who introduced or popularized it, other performers who recorded or popularized it, and Broadway show or film including it; unlike *Popular Music,* however, albums containing it are not noted. Supplementary sections include "The Songwriters" and "The Award Winners" (Academy, Grammy, and Songwriter Hall of Fame awards). *The Great Song Thesaurus* (see entry 436) offers more comprehensive coverage.

436. Lax, Roger, and Frederick Smith. **The Great Song Thesaurus.** 2nd ed. New York: Oxford University, 1989. 774p. LC 88-31267. ISBN 0-19-505408-3.

The volume is composed of the following sections: search access by lyric key lines; a listing of over 11,000 important songs by period or year from the Elizabethan era to 1986, along with a commentary; award winners by year for both film and theater; themes, trade marks, and signatures; elegant plagiarisms; song titles (alphabetical); British song titles (chronological); lyricists and composers; American and British theater, film, radio, and television; and a thesaurus of song titles by subject, key word, and category. The coverage here is considerably more thorough than is the case with Jacobs' *Who Wrote That Song?* (see entry 435).

437. Osborne, Jerry. **The Official Price Guide to Records.** 9th ed. New York: House of Collectibles, 1990. ix, 971p. Illus. ISBN: 0-876-37819-X.

Syndicated music columnist and radio show host Osborne has been compiling record price guides since the early 1970s. His early offerings—published on his private press, O'Sullivan-Woodside—tended to focus on specific genres (e.g., rhythm and blues, country and western, film soundtracks, mainstream poprock) and formats (LPs and singles). His House of Collectibles series has attempted to incorporate all styles into one A-Z artist listing. Although each successive edition includes more recent releases, serious collectors may regret the omission of countless acts included in previous editions (particularly artists who haven't released a charting single, EP, or LP—e.g., Bohemian Vendetta, H. P. Lovecraft, Cafe Jacques, Troll, World of Oz) as well as less specific data within the entries. For instance, individual song/album title entries, subdivided under artist, have been replaced by label designations and year of release ranges (e.g., Imperial: 67-70). The main entry section is enhanced by the presence of numerous cross-references. Many additional sidebars have been included; e.g., "Bootlegs and Counterfeits," "Promotional Issues," "Record Types Defined," "Guidelines for Pricing Records Not Found in This Edition," "What to Expect When Selling Your Records to a Dealer."

438. Osborne, Jerry, Perry Cox, and Joe Lindsay. **The Official Price Guide to Memorabilia of Elvis Presley and The Beatles.** New York: House of Collectibles, 1990. Illus., index. ISBN 0-876-37080-6.

Although Osborne has treated each of these artists in a separate volume, this book claims to be the first to bring them together. It is either a rip-off (given the truncation necessary to conjure up a new title) or a good deal, depending upon your point of view (and prior purchases). Nevertheless, its wide-ranging entries, accurate market valuations, and more than 200 photos (along with an eight-page color insert) make for a strong reference source.

439. Pollock, Bruce, ed. **Popular Music: An Annotated Guide to American Popular Songs. Volume 9: 1980-1984.** Detroit: Gale Research, 1986. 336p. Indexes. LC 64-23761. ISBN 0-8103-0848-7.

The source provides an alphabetically arranged listing of popular songs introduced between 1980 and 1984. The entries cite the composer and lyricist, publisher, date of publication, how the song initially reached the public, and whether it won (or was nominated for) any awards. Lyricist/composer, medium, and chronological indexes have also been provided.

440. Pollock, Bruce, ed. **Popular Music: An Annotated Guide to American Popular Songs. Volume 10: 1985.** Detroit: Gale Research, 1986. 161p. Indexes. ISBN 1-8103-0849-5.

Although shifting to one-year coverage, the tenth volume continues the format employed by prior editions. A publisher listing has been added that includes addresses and performing rights affiliations. Access is enhanced by lyricist/composer, medium, and chronological indexes.

441. Pollock, Bruce, ed. **Popular Music: An Annotated Guide to American Popular Songs, Including Introductory Essay, Lyricists and Composers Index, Important Performances Index, Awards Index, and List of Publishers. Volume 11: 1986.** Detroit: Gale Research, 1987. 171p. Indexes. LC 85-653754. ISBN 0-8103-1809-1.

This is a continuation of Pollock's long-running series. The important-performances index incorporates the media sections included in prior volumes. Lyricist/composer, awards, and chronological indexes have also been provided.

442. Pollock, Bruce, ed. **Popular Music: An Annotated Guide to American Popular Songs. Volume 13: 1988.** Detroit: Gale Research, 1989. 157p. Indexes. LC 85-653754. ISBN 0-8103-4645-0.

This supplement adds another 500 titles to the series. Access is optimized by lyricist/composer, important-performances, and chronological indexes.

443. Shapiro, Nat, and Bruce Pollock, eds. **Popular Music, 1920-1979: An Annotated Index of Over 18,000 American Popular Songs.** 3 Vols. Rev. cumulation. Detroit: Gale Research, 1985. Indexes. LC 85-6749. ISBN 0-8103-0847-9.

This work represents a cumulation of eight volumes (each covering a period of five or ten years). The entries (arranged alphabetically by song title) generally include title and alternate titles, country of origin (for non-U.S. songs), lyricists and composers, publisher and copyright date, information on song's origins, and performance history (e.g., stage shows and films utilizing it, key performers, citations to record label names). Lyricist/composer, important-performances, and awards indexes have also been provided. The source has been continued by Bruce Pollock (see entries 439-442).

444. Soderbergh, Peter A. **Dr. Records' Original 78 RPM Pocket Price Guide.** Lombard, IL: Wallace-Homestead, 1987. 203p. Illus., index, pap. ISBN 0-87069-493-6.

The work is divided into two main sections: Part One—Popular Records 1917-50, and Part Two—Classical Records 1900-40. The entries are lean; they provide song title (arranged alphabetically under artist) with the label and number, date of release, and price value. The price figures are supposed to represent averages that will differ according to location, condition, etc. Soderbergh does not make it clear how his values are determined; however, they appear to be authoritative. The listing is further enhanced by six informative sidebars: "To Sell or Not to Sell"; "Collecting 78s (Getting Started)"; "High-Value Jazz 78s"; "Did You Know?" (trivia); "Quo Vadis, 78s?"; "It's Easy to Remember, but . . ." (recent deaths of key artists). The glossary of record label abbreviations and index to recording artists also optimize the tool's effectiveness.

445. Suskin, Steven. **Berlin, Kern, Rodgers, Hart, and Hammerstein: A Complete Song Catalogue.** Jefferson, NC: McFarland, 1990. 312p. Index. LC 89-43632. ISBN 0-89950-471-X.

The source lists all copyrighted songs and productions (in alphabetical order) by these composers. An introductory chapter, "A Few Words About the Songwriters," provides biographical information and discusses some of their work.

446. Tyler, Don. **Hit Parade: An Encyclopedia of the Top Songs of the Jazz, Depression, Swing, and Sing Eras.** New York: Quill/William Morrow, 1985. 257p. Indexes. LC 85-12375. ISBN 0-688-06149-4 pap.

The entries are arranged alphabetically by song title within each of the four stylistically defined chapters. They identify the composer and lyricist in addition to telling how the song was introduced, the performer with whom it was associated, and whether or not there have been any revivals. Song title and proper name indexes have also been provided.

447. Whitburn, Joel. **The Billboard Book of Top 40 Albums.** New York: Billboard, 1987. 330p. Illus., index. LC 87-24982. ISBN 0-8230-7513-3.

The tool provides the chart history of each album ascending to *Billboard's* top 40 positions since the appearance of this particular chart in 1955. The entries note date, position, and weeks in the top 40, artist biographies, singles from the album making the singles top ten, and label. Separate sections designate top soundtracks, original cast productions, television shows, label compilations, concerts and festivals, Christmas releases, etc.

448. Whitburn, Joel. **Billboard #1s 1950-1991.** Menomonee Falls, WI: Record Research, 1992. 336p. Pap.

This volume provides a week-by-week listing of every number-one single and album from *Billboard's* pop, rhythm and blues, country, and adult contemporary charts.

449. Whitburn, Joel. **Billboard Hot 100 Charts—The Sixties, 1960-1969.** Menomonee Falls, WI: Record Research, 1991. Illus., index.

450. Whitburn, Joel. **Billboard Hot 100 Charts—The Seventies, 1970-1979.** Menomonee Falls, WI: Record Research, 1991. Illus., index.

451. Whitburn, Joel. **Billboard Hot 100 Charts—The Eighties, 1980-1989.** Menomonee Falls, WI: Record Research, 1991. Illus., index.

452. Whitburn, Joel. **Billboard Pop Charts, 1955-1959.** Menomonee Falls, WI: Record Research, 1992. Illus., index.

Each of these volumes reproduces the week-by-week "Hot 100" charts for the designated time span, in black and white, at about 70 percent of their original size when published in *Billboard* magazine. The accessibility of the charts is enhanced by an alphabetically arranged title section that includes the artist, its debut date, and its peak on the charts. The 1950s volume—which in large part predates the "Hot 100" chart, includes the multiple pop singles charts ("Best Sellers in Stores," "Most Played in Juke Boxes," and "Most Played by Jockeys")—that *Billboard* published weekly between 1955-1958. Otherwise, its format is virtually identical to the other volumes.

453. Whitburn, Joel. **Billboard's Top 10 Charts, 1958-1988.** Menomonee Falls, WI: Record Research, 1990. 600p. Index. pap.
The work includes some 1,550 Top 10 charts, arranged in chronological order, derived from the "Hot 100" listing. Access is enhanced by a song title index.

454. Whitburn, Joel. **Bubbling Under the Hot 100, 1959-1985.** Menomonee Falls, WI: Record Research, 1992. 384p.
The book documents those singles recordings charting from position number 101 on down. Each entry notes the date of first chart appearance, peak chart position, total weeks charted, and label and record number, as well as the average dealer asking price for a near-mint-condition copy. Those songs (more than 6,000) that ultimately made the *Billboard* "Hot 100" are included in a separate section in which each entry cites peak "Hot 100" position, debut "Bubbling Under" date, and week-by-week positions for the latter chart. In addition to the "Artist" and "'Hot 100' Bound" sections, a "Song Title" Index refers to the artist's name, peak chart position, and year of chart debut for the "Artist" portion of the book. In keeping with the thoroughness typifying a Whitburn tool, a wide array of fact-filled extras can be found: e.g., artist bios and title notes indicating (1) flip sides of "Hot 100" hits, "answer" songs, "imitation" songs, etc.; (2) records crossing over to or from R&B, country, or adult contemporary charts; and (3) re-releases, recharted "Hot 100" singles, or specialized types of records.

455. Whitburn, Joel. **Music & Video Yearbooks 1987/1988/1989/1990/1991; Music Yearbooks 1983/1984/1985/1986.** Menomonee Falls, WI: Record Research, various page lengths. Illus., pap.
These volumes cover each year in music, based on *Billboard's* singles, albums, and videocassette (beginning with the 1987 edition) charts.

456. Whitburn, Joel. **Pop Singles Annual 1955-1990.** Menomonee Falls, WI: Record Research, 1991. 736p. Illus. hardcover and paperback editions.
This source provides a year-by-year ranking of nearly 20,000 charting singles from the "Hot 100." The rankings are based upon Whitburn's own formula for incorporating chart performance data: first, highest position achieved, and second, number of weeks on the chart. Some may quibble with this system; but then, it could be argued that the charts themselves will always represent an imperfect means of assessing the relative popularity of any given recording.

457. Whitburn, Joel. **Top Pop Singles 1955-1990.** Menomonee Falls, WI: Record Research, 1991. 848p. Illus. hardcover and paperback editions.
The tool includes nearly 20,000 singles—every "Hot 100" hit—arranged by artist. Each entry includes peak chart position, chart peak date and chart debut date, total weeks charted, and label and record number. There are also many special features; e.g., artist bios, record notes, Record Industry Association of America (RIAA) platinum and gold

record certifications, top artist and record achievements, all-time artist and record rankings, and a chronological listing of all number-one songs.

458.   White, Adam. **The Billboard Book of Gold & Platinum Records.** New York: Billboard Books/Watson-Guptill, 1990. 308p. Illus. LC 89-18566. ISBN 0-8230-7547-8.

White includes all singles and albums awarded gold and platinum status since the Recording Industry Association of America established uniform measures (500,000 copies for gold; one million for platinum) in 1958. Each artist entry indicates month and year of release, level and date of certification, *Billboard* chart peak, and label.

Indexes

459.   Havlice, Patricia. **Popular Song Index.** Metuchen, NJ: Scarecrow, 1975. 933p. Index, bibl. LC 75-9896. ISBN 0-8108-0820-X.

The parent volume in this highly regarded series, it indexes 32,000-odd songs from 3,101 book anthologies published between 1940 and 1972. The text provided a listing of books indexed, followed by song title entries (alphabetically arranged), which include the first line of the song and first line of the chorus. A composer and lyricist index has also been included.

460.   Havlice, Patricia. **Popular Song Index. First Supplement.** Metuchen, NJ: Scarecrow, 1978. Index, bibl. LC 77-25219. ISBN 0-8108-1099-9.

Following the format established in Havlice's parent volume (see entry 459), it covers the 1972-1975 period. Access is enhanced by the composer and lyricist index.

461.   Havlice, Patricia. **Popular Song Index. Second Supplement.** Metuchen, NJ: Scarecrow, 1984. 530p. Index, bibl. LC 83-7692. ISBN 0-8108-1642-3.

This update covers 156 books largely published from 1974 through 1981, with a few reaching back as far as the 1950s. Like the parent volume (see entry 459), it includes a composer and lyricist index.

462.   Havlice, Patricia. **Popular Song Index. Third Supplement.** Metuchen, NJ: Scarecrow, 1989. 875p. Index. ISBN 0-8108-2202-4.

The tool indexes song collections published during the 1979-1987 period. Following the format established in prior editions, the songs are accessed by title and first line (the song's first line and choruses' first line are differentiated). Full information is provided under title entries. As in the past, many of the 181 collections (referred to in entries by number) have a traditional song bias. For more contemporary tastes, a competing title, *Find That Tune* (1989), would prove more useful. A composer and lyricist index has also been provided.

463.   **Popular Music Periodicals Index.** Metuchen, NJ: Scarecrow, 1973-. Annual.

Perhaps the leading tool for accessing popular music periodicals (with coverage ranging from fifty-five to sixty-five titles), it is organized alphabetically by author and subject. Despite a time lag of approximately one year from the appearance of these periodicals and the publication of this title, it should prove useful to libraries of all types.

The Blues/Rhythm and Blues/Black Contemporary

Bibliographies/Discographies

464.   Gribin, Anthony, and Matthew M. Schiff. **Doo-Wop: The Forgotten Third of Rock 'n Roll.** Iola, WI: Krause Publications, 1992. 616p. Illus., pap.

Called the most complete and detailed history of the doo-wop genre ever compiled, the book features a listing (arranged alphabetically by artist) of more than 25,000 songs complete with available discographical data. Additional features include (1) the 500 best doo-wop songs ever recorded; (2) the technology of the doo-wop era; (3) the evolution of doo-wop music; (4) the lyrics of doo-wop music; (5) the idiosyncrasies of the genre; and (6) the naming of doo-wop groups. This is an unrivaled compendium of information about the style, pulling together material from a vast array of sources.

465.   Hart, Mary L., Brenda M. Eagles, and Lisa N. Howorth. **The Blues: A Bibliographic Guide.** New York: Garland, 1989. 636p. Indexes, bibl., discog., filmog. (Music Research and Information Guides, vol. 7; Garland Reference Library of the Humanities, vol. 565.) LC 89-34943. ISBN 0-8240-8506-X.

Incorporating a wide variety of materials (monographs, dissertations, liner notes, journals, etc.), the book is organized into the following sections: "Blues Biographies," "Blues on Film," "Blues in American Literature," and "Blues Research." Author and title indexes have also been provided.

Encyclopedias

466.   Herzhaft, Gerard. **Encyclopedia of the Blues.** Translated by Brigitte DeBord. Fayetteville: University of Arkansas, 1992. 513p. Illus., index, bibl., discog.

These alphabetically arranged biographical sketches of African American blues artists, written by a French discographer and music historian, feature a wealth of perceptive insights. Useful supplementary sections include "Blues Standards" (pp. 435-78), an annotated review of individual tunes, and "Blues Artists and Their Instruments" (pp. 479-93). However, such weaknesses Herzhaft's bias against white blues practitioners (Eric Clapton, Stevie Ray Vaughan, and others are relegated to second-class status and many deserving artists are ignored altogether) and rock performers in general (including a host of black performers like Otis Redding) diminish the book's value to some degree.

467.   Warner, Jay. **The Billboard Book of American Singing Groups: A History, 1940-1990.** New York: Billboard/Watson-Guptill, 1992. 542p. Illus., discog.

Although this work includes many pop or rock acts reaching as far back as the Andrews Sisters and up through the Bangles in the late 1980s, the substantial portion is devoted to rhythm and blues (or doo-wop) groups; formation details, career developments, and discographical data (including both A- and B-sides, record labels and catalog numbers, release dates, etc.). Despite its comprehensiveness, there are some flaws: no bibliography (to assist readers in identifying biographical and record-related information), no index, and the absence of some notable aggregates (e.g., The Rascals, The Commodores, and The Reflections).

Handbooks

468. Oliver, Paul, ed. **The Blackwell Guide to Blues Records.** Cambridge, MA: Basil Blackwell, 1989. 347p. Discog. LC 89-17734. ISBN 0-631-16516-9.

Oliver's historical survey of the blues is followed by eleven chapters, each delineating a particular style or time frame of the blues (e.g., "Piano Blues and Boogie-Woogie," "Rhythm and Blues," "Soul Blues and Modern Trends"). The contributors of the various segments each cite ten "essential" recordings, as well as thirty more "basic" albums; a healthy number of these titles are no longer in print in the United States.

469. Taft, Michael. **Blues Lyric Poetry: A Concordance.** 3 Vols. New York: Garland, 1984. Index, bibl., discog. LC 83-48630. ISBN 0-8240-9236-8.

The source employs a KWIC concordance format in covering more than 2,000 blues lyrics recorded between 1920 and 1942. A word frequency list is also included.

Country and Western

Bibliographies/Discographies

470. Ginell, Gary, comp. **The Decca Hillbilly Discography, 1927-1945.** Westport, CT: Greenwood, 1989. 402p. Illus., indexes, bibl. (Discographies, No. 35.) LC 89-17186. ISBN 0-313-26053-2.

This work covers over seventeen hundred 78 r.p.m. discs from the Decca numerical series 5000, 17000, and 45000. Although the main portion of the text consists of a numerical arrangement, access is also provided by release date, composer credits, and record location. Artist and title indexes have also been provided.

471. Smith, John L., comp. **The Johnny Cash Discography.** Westport, CT: Greenwood, 1985. 203p. Indexes, bibl. (Discographies, No. 13.) LC 84-19799. ISBN 0-313-24654-8.

The tool incorporates more than 500 Cash recording sessions from late 1954 (his earliest) through April 1984. The chronologically arranged entries include dates, session location, session numbers, personnel listing, and songs recorded. Access is enhanced by indexes of song titles, U.S. releases, European releases, bootleg releases, and songs from ABC television series.

Biographies

472. Vaughan, Andrew. **Who's Who in New Country Music.** New York: St. Martin's Press, 1990. 128p. Illus. LC 89-27126. ISBN 0-312-03953-0.

Although the casual writing style and the omission of data (with a couple of exceptions) after 1988 diminish the book's value to some extent, it remains a useful source of information on country performers.

Encyclopedias

473. Dellar, Fred, and others. **The Harmony Illustrated Encyclopedia of Country Music.** Rev. ed. New York: Harmony/ Crown, 1986. 208p. Illus. LC 86-18423. ISBN 0-517-56502-1; 0-517-56503-X pap.

Considered a classic within the field since its appearance in 1977, the updated edition includes fifty new biographies; the 400-odd remaining entries have been revised to account for developments over that ten-year period. The entries note birthplaces, birthdates, awards, chart positions of selected songs, career highlights, and notable albums and include a publicity or album cover picture or both. An appendix provides nonbiographical material (e.g., articles covering the Austin and Nashville scenes and the Country Music Association) and brief entries devoted to minor performers. The new edition represents a step backwards in that the discography is now "selective," many illustrations are recycled, and updated entries have added little new information. Nevertheless, it remains a valuable tool, especially given its reasonable cost.

474. Stambler, Irwin, and Grelun Landon. **The Encyclopedia of Folk, Country & Western Music.** 2nd ed. New York: St. Martin's Press. 1984. 902p. Illus., bibl. ISBN 0-312-248199 pap.
　　The information about these 600-odd artists has been culled from both personnel (questionnaires and interviews) and secondary sources (the literature and promotional releases). A substantial listing of awards given by relevant music associations has also been included.

Handbooks

475. Dellar, Fred, and Richard Wootton. **The Country Music Book of Lists.** New York: Times Books; distr., Harper & Row, 1984. 175p. Illus. LC 84-40110. ISBN 0-8129-6339-3 pap.
　　This potpourri of data ranges from completely trivial to more serious reference data. Examples of the lists include Country Music Hall of Fame members appended by thumbnail biographies, Fan clubs (with addresses), and Country Music Association and Music City News award winners.

476. Whitburn, Joel. **Joel Whitburn's Top Country Singles, 1944-1988.** Menomonee Falls, WI: Record Research, 1989. 535p. ISBN 0-89820-070-9.
　　Compiled from the *Billboard* magazine country singles charts, the work is divided into three sections: (1) the artist listing (in alphabetical order), including concise biographical sketches followed by each artist's charting song; (2) the alphabetically arranged song title listing, which includes the artist who recorded the song as well as its date of entry onto the charts; and (3) a series of appendixes (e.g., the Top 200 artists in this genre, top achievements, and top hits by the decades' top labels).

Folk/Ethnic

Bibliographies/Discographies

477. Feintuch, Burt. **Kentucky Folkmusic: An Annotated Bibliography.** Lexington: University Press of Kentucky, 1985. 105p. Indexes, bibl., discog. LC 85-6225. ISBN 0-8131-1556-6.
　　This rather exclusive listing (i.e., any performers disseminated through the mass media have been omitted from the text) includes 709 monographs and periodical articles dealing with Kentucky-related "Community-based music performed and perpetuated for largely noncommercial reasons." The entries are arranged alphabetically under the following headings: collections and anthologies; fieldworkers, collectors, and scholars; singers, musicians, and other performers; text-centered studies; studies of history, context, and

style; festivals; dance; and discographies, checklists, and other specialized reference tools. Author, subject, and periodicals-cited indexes have also been included.

478.   Miller, Terry E. **Folk Music in America: A Reference Guide.** New York: Garland, 1986. 424p. Index., bibl. (Garland Reference Library of the Humanities, Vol. 496.) LC 84-48014. ISBN 0-8240-8935-9.

This exhaustive compilation of academic monographs, articles, dissertations, and encyclopedic essays are organized under such sections as "General Resources," "Music of American Indians and Eskimos," "Anglo-American Folksongs and Ballads," "Later Developments" (bluegrass, country and western, protest music from the 1960s), instruments and instrumental music (banjo, dulcimers, fiddle, guitar), folk hymnody, singing school and shape-note tradition, and black and various folk music traditions.

479.   Stoneburner, Bryan C., comp. **Hawaiian Music: An Annotated Bibliography.** Westport, CT: Greenwood, 1986. 100p. Index. (Music Reference Collection, No. 10.) LC 86-9914. ISBN 0-313-25340-4.

The 564 entries include books, anthologies, pamphlets, dissertations, periodical articles, unpublished papers, and record reviews covering the Hawaiian genre, musicians, native instruments, and music life. Supplementary sections include a "Glossary of Hawaiian Terms" and a listing of journals along with their respective locations.

Biographies

480.   Hood, Phil, ed. **Artists of American Folk Music: The Legends of Traditional Folk, the Stars of the Sixties, the Virtuosi of New Acoustic Music.** New York: William Morrow, 1986. 159p. Illus., index. LC 85-63796. ISBN 0-688-05916-3.

The book includes thirty-one biographical sketches or interviews ranging from Leadbelly and Woody Guthrie in the 1930s to leaders of the folk revival into late 1950s and early 1960s. The folk genre as a whole is surveyed in an introduction and epilogue.

Jazz

Bibliographies/Discographies

481.   Carner, Gary, ed. **Jazz Performers: An Annotated Bibliography of Biographical Materials.** Westport, CT: Greenwood, 1990. 364p. Indexes, bibl. (Music Reference Collection, No. 26.) LC 90-31765. ISBN 0-313-26250-0.

The bibliography is composed of nearly 3,000 biographical citations (arranged alphabetically by musician and subdivided by author) on over 800 jazz acts. The compilation—including books, articles from scholarly journals, dissertations, etc.—reveals few primary materials. A supplementary bibliography places 1,024 sources under five headings: collections, general, histories and textbooks, illustrated, and reference. Author and subject indexes have also been included.

482.   Connor, D. Russell. **Benny Goodman: Listen to His Legacy.** Metuchen, NJ: Institute of Jazz Studies/Scarecrow, 1988. 357p. Index, discog. (Studies in Jazz, No. 6.) LC 87-32069. ISBN 0-8108-2095-1.

This is a chronicle of Goodman's recording sessions from his earliest in 1926 to a concert recording in 1986 days before his death. The entries note date and location of each session, musicians, works recorded, labels and numbers of releases, critical notes, and relevant biographical details. "Air checks" (noncommercial recordings made from broadcasts, films, or concerts) have also been included.

483.   Cuscuna, Michael, and Michel Ruppli, comps. **The Blue Note Label: A Discography.** Westport, CT: Greenwood, 1988. 510p. Illus., index. (Discographies, No. 29.) LC 88-162. ISBN 0-313-22018-2.

The sessions for this pioneering independent label are arranged in alphabetical order, and cite personnel, recording locations and dates, and master and issue numbers. Also included are single numerical listings, album numerical listings, compact disc numerical listings, and cassette numerical listings. Access is enhanced by an artist index.

484.   Gray, John, comp. **Fire Music: A Bibliography of the New Jazz, 1959-1990.** Westport, CT: Greenwood, 1991. 515p. Indexes, bibl. (Music Reference Collection, No. 31.) LC 91-20601. ISBN 0-313-27892-X.

Following the "New Jazz Chronology," the bibliography (which includes monographs, articles, dissertations, and media sources) is largely concerned with "Biographical and Critical Studies" (by artist). The appendixes include listings of reference works, research centers, artists by nation, and artists by instrument. Author, title, and subject indexes have also been provided.

485.   Harrison, Max, Charles Fox, and Eric Thacker. **The Essential Jazz Records. Volume 1: Ragtime to Swing.** Westport, CT: Greenwood, 1984. 595p. Index, bibl., discog. (Discographies, No. 12.) LC 84-7926. ISBN 0-313-24674-2.

The authors have highlighted 250 recordings deemed most representative of the genre from the first four decades of the twentieth century (most of which are still readily available). The discographical data in each entry is supplemented by extensive annotations that critique solo work and the personnel utilized.

486.   Leder, Jan, comp. **Women in Jazz: A Discography of Instrumentalists, 1913-1968.** Westport, CT: Greenwood, 1985. 305p. Index, discog. (Discographies, No. 19) LC 85-17657. ISBN 0-313-24790-0.

Useful primarily as a means of identifying female jazz performers, the work consists of two main parts: (1) recording sessions arranged alphabetically by performer (subdivided by date), and (2) a chronological listing of sessions employing at least two women.

487.   Rust, Brian. **Jazz Records 1897-1942: Fourth Revised and Enlarged Edition.** 2 Vols. New Rochelle, NY: Arlington House, 1978. Indexes, discog. LC 78-1693. ISBN 0-87000-404-2.

This standard tool covers 30,000 recordings prior to 1943 utilizing standard discographic form: arrangement by artist, with personnel and instrumentation, and then chronologically organized sessions and locations, followed by titles (in order of matrix number), and, finally, label and catalog issue number. Artist and song indexes have also been provided.

488.   Timner, W. E., comp. **Ellingtonia: The Recorded Music of Duke Ellington and His Sidemen.** 3rd ed. Metuchen, NJ: Institute of Jazz Studies/Scarecrow, 1988. 534p. Bibl. (Studies in Jazz, No. 7.) LC 86-21967. ISBN 0-8108-1934-1.

The listing spans 1923 to 1974, with more than 1,000 recordings from the studio, films, concerts, dances, and television and radio broadcasts in chronological order. Supplementary sections include a listing of outside recordings by Ellington's key sideman, an alphabetical compilation of Ellington compositions, and a chronological chart outlining the personnel employed in recording sessions.

Biographies

489. Balliett, Whitney. **American Musicians: Fifty-Six Portraits in Jazz.** New York: Oxford University, 1986. 415p. LC 86-12491. ISBN 0-19-503758-8.

Following an opening essay on two pioneers of jazz writing, Hugues Panassie and Charles Delaunay, forty-nine biographical portraits of seminal musicians are arranged in chronological order. Source material consists of interviews with the artist (or close associates), biographies, and accounts of recordings and live performances.

490. Chilton, John. **Who's Who of Jazz: Storyville to Swing Street.** 4th ed. New York: Da Capo, 1985. 375p. Illus., bibl. LC 84-20062. ISBN 0-306-76271-4; 0-306-80243-0 pap.

Limited to musicians born before 1920 and raised in the United States, the more than 1,000 entries range from a brief paragraph to a couple of pages in length. A listing of jazz periodicals, arranged according to the country in which it is published, is also included.

491. Lyons, Len, and Don Perlo. **Jazz Portraits: The Lives and Music of the Jazz Masters.** New York: William Morrow, 1989. 610p. Illus., index, bibl. LC 88-8929. ISBN 0-688-10002-3.

In attempting to survey jazz history via biographies, more than 200 notable artists are covered. The entries incorporate musical commentary, historical insights, biographical data, and recording notes. An appendix arranges musicians by instrument and a glossary defines important jazz terms. Access is enhanced by a name index.

Dictionaries

492. Clayton, Peter, and Peter Gammond. **Jazz A-Z.** Enfield, U.K.: Guinness Books; distr., Sterling Publishing, 1986. 262p. Illus., index, bibl. ISBN 0-85112-281-7.

The terms included here cover musical jargon, cities, song titles, performing groups, clubs, nicknames of individuals, instruments, journals, and more expansive headings (e.g., blues). The index lists those individuals referred to in the text.

493. Kernfeld, Barry, ed. **The New Grove Dictionary of Jazz.** 2 Vols. New York: Stockton/Grove's Dictionaries of Music, 1988. Bibl., discog. LC 87-25452. ISBN 0-935859-39-X.

The work—based on the highly respected *New Grove Dictionary of Music and Musicians* (Edited by Stanley Sadie. 20 Vols. 6th ed. 1980.)—consists of 4,500 essays (signed by some 250 contributors) touching upon individuals, ensembles, styles, topics and terms, instruments, record companies and labels, and institutions. Biographical entries (over 3,000 in all) represent a particular strength.

Encyclopedias

494. Case, Brian, and Stan Britt. **The Harmony Illustrated Encyclopedia of Jazz.** Revised and updated by Chrissie Murray. New York: Harmony/Crown, 1986. 208p. Illus., index, discog. LC 86-15040. ISBN 0-517-56442-4; 0-517-56443-2 pap.

The main text includes more than 450 biographical entries in addition to a few topics (e.g., Blue Note). An appendix provides terse entries for approximately 100 less important musicians. A name index has also been included.

495. Feather, Leonard. **The Encyclopedia of Jazz.** New York: Da Capo, 1984, c1960. 527p. LC 83-26164. ISBN 0-306-80214-7 pap.

496. Feather, Leonard. **The Encyclopedia of Jazz in the Sixties.** New York: Da Capo, 1986, c1966. 312p. Illus., bibl. LC 85-31125. ISBN 0-306-80263-5 pap.

497. Feather, Leonard, and Ira Gitler. **The Encyclopedia of Jazz in the Seventies.** New York: Da Capo, 1987, c1976. 393p. Illus., bibl. LC 87-517. ISBN 0-306-80290-2 pap.
   Each title consists of about 2,000 biographical essays that focus on professional accomplishments, including lists of compositions, television appearances, and recordings. Coverage is concentrated on musicians active between 1950 and 1975.

Handbooks

498. McRae, Barry. **The Jazz Handbook.** Boston: G. K. Hall, 1989, c1987. 272p. Index, bibl., discog. LC 89-77757. ISBN 0-8161-9096-8.
   The source is organized into chapters that correspond to decades. Each chapter is composed of a decade synopsis and alphabetically arranged entries for key musicians for that period. A final segment includes a survey of record labels, a bibliography, a glossary, and an international directory of jazz festivals and periodicals.

499. Meeker, David. **Jazz in the Movies: A Guide to Jazz Musicians 1917-1977.** New Rochelle, NY: Arlington House, 1977. Unpaged. Illus., index. LC 77-30238. ISBN 0-905983-00-9.
   The tool contains 2,500-odd international theatrical and 16mm non-commercial films utilizing jazz musicians (even where the music is not jazz). The alphabetically arranged title entries include country, year produced, length , director, and a critique of the film from a jazz perspective.

500. Swenson, John, ed. **The Rolling Stone Jazz Record Guide.** New York: Rolling Stone/Random House, 1985. 219p. Bibl. LC 84-42510. ISBN 0-394-72643-X pap.
   A complement to *The New Rolling Stone Record Guide* (which contains jazz), the work covers more than 4,000 "currently available albums." The entries, alphabetically arranged by artist, consist of a one-star ("poor") to five-star ("indispensable") rating and an evaluative commentary.

Rock 'n' Roll/Rock

Bibliographies/Discographies

501. Aeppli, Felix. **Heart of Stone: The Definitive Rolling Stones Discography, 1962-1983.** Ann Arbor, MI: Popular Culture, Ink, 1985. 580p. Illus. ISBN 0-87650-192-7.
   This is a chronological listing of all the musical recordings of the band appearing on either record or film between July 1962 and December 1983. Releases by individual members of the band, as well as bootleg records, are also included. It earns high marks for accuracy and comprehensiveness.

502. Banney, Howard. **Return to Sender: The First Complete Discography of Elvis Tribute and Novelty Records, 1956-1986.** Ann Arbor, MI: Popular Culture, Ink, 1985. 336p. Illus., indexes. ISBN 0-87650-238-9.

The work chronicles more than 1,000 songs—over 600 on singles and 400 on albums—recorded in praise of, containing references to, or sung in imitation of Presley. It effectively documents the extent to which Presley affected other musicians. Performer, song and album title, and record number indexes have also been provided.

503. Bartlette, Reginald J. **Off the Record: Motown By Master Number, 1959-1989; Volume 1: Singles.** Ann Arbor, MI: Popular Culture, Ink, 1991. 512p. Illus., indexes. ISBN 1-56075-003-0.

The main section of the book—encompassing the entire discographical history of the Motown label's singles (some 6,400 songs)—consists of ten master number series. The exhaustive "Introduction" provides invaluable definitions and background information about the major sections of the text, in addition to including several sidebars: (1) Checklist of Motown-Related Labels; (2) Inventory of Motown-Related Labels (along with brief histories); (3) Motorcity Records Discography; and (4) Motorcity Records Artist Roster. The substantial appendixes section covers picture sleeves, colored vinyl, recording oddities (e.g., promotional releases, 10-inch acetates), related Motown labels, Yesteryear reissues, Delta numbers (on singles pressed at L.A.'s Monarch Pressing Plant), two- and three-letter Matrix Codes (used on recordings from the mid-1980s until Motown's sale to MCA/Boston Ventures in June 1988), and other miscellaneous Matrix numbers. Access is enhanced by song and record title, performer, date, and label and catalog number indexes. This is a monumental work deserving of inclusion in all research collections concerned with popular music.

504. Blair, John. **The Illustrated Discography of Surf Music, 1961-1965.** 2d ed., rev. Ann Arbor, MI: Popular Culture, Ink, 1990. 184p. Illus. LC 89-92312. ISBN 0-87650-174-9.

This is the definitive guide to virtually all American surf music recordings issued from 1961 through 1965. Entries, organized under alphabetically arranged artist headings, include song or album title, label and number, and release date.

505. Blair, John, and Stephen McParland, comps. **The Illustrated Discography of Hot Rod Music 1961-1965.** Ann Arbor, MI: Popular Culture, Ink, 1990. 167p. ISBN 1-56075-002-2.

The book lists every known hot rod recording from the 1961-1965 watershed period, as well as notable examples from later years, in two sections: singles and albums. Entries (collected under alphabetically arranged artist headings) include song or album title, label and number, and release date. Capsule bios introduce most singles listings and album entries include pertinent cuts. Valuable appendixes list compilation albums, define racing terms, list U.S. releases of foreign recordings, summarize a number of "notable" hot rod movies, and identify top 100 charting releases.

506. Castleman, Harry, and Walter Podrazik. **The Beatles Again.** Ann Arbor, MI: Popular Culture, Ink, 1977. 280p. Illus., index, discog. (Rock & Roll Reference Series, No. 2) LC 77-9322. ISBN 0-87650-089-0.

The volume supplements and updates *All Together Now* (New York: Ballantine, 1976), bringing coverage up to mid-1977 (from mid-1975). It stands alone, however, in presenting a concise overview of the band's career as well as incorporating subject matter absent in the original tool. Coverage includes tours, club dates, concerts, black-and-white photos of album and singles jackets, a "questions and answers" section, and notations on recordings (even rarities such as deejay promo records). The index (to song-titles, album titles, performers) covers both this volume and *All Together Now. Choice* termed it "the definitive discography and history of the Beatles."

507.   Castleman, Harry, and Walter Podrazik. **The End of the Beatles?** Ann Arbor, MI: Popular Culture, Ink, 1985. 582p. (Rock & Roll Reference Series, No. 10.) Illus., indexes. ISBN 0-87650-162-5.

The work updates the discography and other sections in *All Together Now* (New York: Ballantine, 1976) and *The Beatles Again* (see entry 507) between 1977 and 1983. The text is enhanced by fifteen indexes and a wealth of attractive photographs.

508.   Duxbury, Janell R. **Rockin' the Classics and Classicizin' the Rock: A Selectively Annotated Discography.** Westport, CT: Greenwood, 1985. xix, 188p. Index. (Discographies, No. 14.) LC 84-22419. ISBN 0-313-24605-X.

The source is organized into three main parts: (1) "Rockin' the Classics" illustrates the instances where rock borrowed themes from classical music; (2) "Classicizin' the Rock," identifies classical versions of rock music; and (3) "Other Connections Between Rock and the Classics" (e.g., the impact of rock album packaging on classical releases). The entries (898 in all) are arranged by artist in each section. A name and title index has also been provided.

509.   Elliott, Brad. **Surf's Up! The Beach Boys on Record, 1961-1981.** Ann Arbor, MI: Popular Culture, Ink, 1991. Reprint of 1982 ed. 512p. Illus. (Rock & Roll Series, No. 6.) ISBN 1-56075-022-7.

The wealth of information amassed about each song has been carefully researched; perceptive analysis punctuates the factual material throughout in this definitive survey of the band's recordings up to that point. The major flaw is the dated nature of the book; over a decade of the group's career is absent.

510.   MacPhail, Jessica. **Yesterday's Papers: The Rolling Stones in Print, 1963-1984.** Ann Arbor, MI: Popular Culture, Ink, 1986. 236p. Illus.; indexes. (Rock & Roll Series, No. 19.) ISBN 0-87650-209-5.

The bibliography includes citations to books (and portions of books), fanzines, newspaper articles, magazine articles, periodical theme issues, and reviews (of, for example, books, films, and sound recordings) by or about the band. The compilation is fairly comprehensive with respect to U.S. material; however, entries devoted to European publications are piecemeal, barely scratching the surface of the resources available on this topic. Author, title, subject, date, and publication indexes have also been provided.

511.   Reinhart, Charles. **You Can't Do That! Beatles Bootlegs & Novelty Records, 1963-1980.** Ann Arbor, MI: Popular Culture, Ink, 1989. Reprint of 1981 edition. 450p. Illus. (Rock & Roll Series, No. 5.) ISBN 1-56075-009-X.

This is an extensive listing—with lengthy discographical data—of almost 900 Beatles bootlegs and counterfeit recordings (the former are nonauthorized releases of live concerts, studio outtakes, home recordings, interviews, etc., whereas the latter masquerade as the authorized product). It includes a lengthy discussion of the historical, legal, and copyright aspects of making and selling bootlegs. The absence of CD titles diminishes the book's pretentions to comprehensiveness. Nevertheless, a definitive source containing much information not available elsewhere.

512.   Russell, Jeff. **The Beatles Album File and Complete Discography.** Rev. ed. London: Blandford/Cassell; distr., Quality Books, 1989. 310p. Illus., index, discog. ISBN 0-7137-2065-4 pap.

Covering every official Beatles album released from 1961 through 1988, the volume is broken down into five main parts: British albums, American albums, further British albums, Christmas albums, and appendixes (alternate versions of songs; unreleased tracks;

and a look at songs available only on singles, videos, and interview albums). Each entry includes release dates, catalog number, producer, and length, as well as recording dates and location, composers, musicians, and vocalists for separate songs. Annotations are appended to entries on albums and most songs.

513.   Stannard, Neville. **The Beatles: The Long & Winding Road: A History of the Beatles on Record.** Edited by John Tobler. New York: Avon, 1984, c1982. 240p. Illus., index, bibl., discog. LC 83-45915. ISBN 0-380-85704-9.

Billed as the "most informative and complete Beatles discography ever compiled," the source organizes songs chronologically within two major headings: "British Section" and "American Section." There are also eight appendixes, including "Unreleased Studio Recordings," "The Beatles' Bootlegs," "The Hamburg Recordings," "The Beatles' Christmas Records," and a listing of song recording dates and locations.

514.   Taylor, Paul. **Popular Music Since 1955: A Critical Guide to the Literature.** Boston: G. K. Hall, 1985. 533p. Indexes. LC 85-8732. ISBN 0-8161-8784-3.

The bibliography, featuring critical annotations, covers English-language monographs, journals, and fiction from 1955 to 1982. Strengths include an exhaustive biographical section and informative glossary. Author, title, and subject indexes have also been provided.

515.   Terry, Carol D. **Here, There and Everywhere: The First International Beatles Bibliography, 1962-1982.** Ann Arbor, MI: Popular Culture, Ink, 1985. 304p. Illus., indexes. LC 84-61229. ISBN 0-87650-163-3.

The publisher of the work terms it "the most extensive list of books on the Beatles ever assembled." Its 8,000 citations follow a classified arrangement. Access is enhanced by author, title, and subject indexes.

516.   Walters, David. **The Children of Nuggets: The Definitive Guide to "Psychedelic Sixties" Punk Rock on Compilation Albums.** Ann Arbor, MI: Popular Culture, Ink, 1990. 384p. Illus., index. (Rock & Roll Reference Series, No. 30.) LC 89-92331. ISBN 1-56075-001-4.

The book provides access to nearly 3,800 songs by over 2,600 garage/punk performers of the mid- to late 1960s on 333 compilation albums modeled after the definitive release of this school, "Nuggets." The text divides LP information into three differing arrangements: by album title, by performer name, and by song title. An original release label index has also been provided.

Biographies

517.   Clifford, Mike. **The Harmony Illustrated Encyclopedia of Rock.** 4th ed. New York: Harmony/Crown, 1983. 272p. Illus., index. LC 83-19354. ISBN 0-517-55261-2; 0-517-55262-0 pap.

More than 600 artists are covered by the book's stable of ten authors. The appendix includes 400 lesser figures, such as one-hit wonders, management and promotion executives, record companies, and musical instrument manufacturers. Many of these entries are not available in later editions of the title (see entry 523).

518.   Jakubowski, Maxim, and others, eds. **MTV, Music Television, Who's Who in Rock Video.** New York: Quill/William Morrow, 1984. 190p. Illus., index, discog., videography. LC 84-60325. IBSN 0-688-04042-X pap.

The source offers thumbnail sketches of 100 artists who "have played an important role" in the evolution of MTV and video clips in general. It also provides an introduction that surveys the medium (along with concise bios of the five original MTV VJs) and listings of video directors referring to (1) performers, and (2) videos they created. An artist-director index has also been provided.

519.   York, William, comp. and ed. **Who's Who in Rock Music.** Seattle, WA: Atomic, 1978. 260p. Pap.
The work contains over 6,000 artist entries focusing on career-related facts seemingly derived from album jackets and musical output.

Directories

520.   Muirhead, Bert. **The Record Producers File: A Directory of Rock Album Producers 1962-1984.** Poole, U.K.: Blandford; distr., Sterling Publishing, 1984. 288p. Index. ISBN 0-7137-1429-8; 0-7137-1430-1 pap.
The 1,000-odd producer entries, arranged alphabetically, indicate records produced (along with respective titles, artist, labels, and release dates). This useful directory provides information not readily available in other reference books devoted to popular music. Access is enhanced by an artist index.

Encyclopedias

521.   Bianco, David. **Who's New Wave in Music: An Illustrated Encyclopedia, 1976-1982.** Ann Arbor, MI: Popular Culture, Ink, 1989. Reprint of 1985 ed. 430p. Illus. (Rock & Roll Reference Series, No. 14.) ISBN 1-56075-008-1.
This is an A to Z listing of 854 new wave artists active between 1976 and 1982. Punk rock, ska, mod, power pop, electro- and technopop, the new romantics, and neo-rockabilly represent some of the subgenres included here. The concise entries are both informative and engaging in nature.

522.   Brown, Ashley, ed. **The Marshall Cavendish Illustrated History of Popular Music.** 21 Vols. Freeport, NY: Marshall Cavendish, 1990. Illus., index. ISBN 1-85436-015-3.
An exhaustive chronicle of the popular music scene in the English-speaking world from 1955 up to the late 1980s, the work is built around two-to-six-page articles, written by rock journalists and academics. The biographical entries (which are appended by concise "Recommended Listening" discographies) are complemented by topical features (e.g., "Carnaby Street," "Woodstock") and annual chronologies of milestone events. The indexes have been cumulated in the final volume.

523.   Clifford, Mike, ed. **The Harmony Illustrated Encyclopedia of Rock.** 6th ed. New York: Harmony/Crown, 1988. 208p. Illus., discog. LC 88-21473. ISBN 0-517-57164-1.
This remains a lavishly illustrated, informative source despite the deletion of some of the worthwhile features of the fifth (1986) edition; i.e., appendixes of management and promotion personnel, directories of record firms and musical instruments, and an index to performers. The focus is on 600-odd artist entries, arranged in alphabetical order.

524.   Hardy, Phil, and Dave Laing. **Encyclopedia of Rock.** Rev. by Stephen Bernard and Don Perretta. New York: Schirmer Books/Macmillan, 1988. 480p. Illus. ISBN 0-02-919562-4.

Comparable in look and feel to another British-based pop music encyclopedia, *The Harmony Illustrated Encyclopedia of Rock* (see entry 523) the more than 1,500 entries composing the work offer intelligent observations of key artists, styles, and events.

525.   Jasper, Tony, and others. **The International Encyclopedia of Hard Rock & Heavy Metal.** New York: Facts on File, 1985, c1983. 400p. Discog. LC 84-10236. ISBN 0-8160-1100-1; 0-8160-1133-8 pap.

This represents a particularly useful tool in that the genre generally receives little attention from serious rock journalists. The alphabetically arranged artist entries include home nation, lineup and instrumentation of band members, career highlights, and an assessment of recordings.

526.   Nite, Norm N., with Charles Crespo. **Rock On: The Illustrated Encyclopedia of Rock 'n' Roll. Volume 3: The Video Revolution.** New York: Harper & Row, 1985. 444p. Illus., index, discog. LC 85-42723. ISBN 0-06-181644-2.

The latest installment of this standard source covers about 600 artists, all of whom rose to prominence during the 1979-1984 period. In addition to rock stars, it includes country, pop, and novelty acts reaching the Top 100 charts. Also provided are a song title index and introductions by Nina Blackwood, Mark Goodman, Alan Hunter, J. J. Jackson, and Martha Quinn.

527.   Nite, Norm N., with Ralph M. Newman. **Rock On: The Illustrated Encyclopedia of Rock 'n' Roll. Volume 2: The Years of Change, 1964-1978.** Updated ed. New York: Harper & Row, 1984. 749p. Illus., index, discog. LC 83-48371. ISBN 0-06-181643-4.

This update covers the same 1,000-plus artists from the original 1978 edition, noting career and personnel changes during that time interval. The straightforward entries are prefaced by remarks from deejay Wolfman Jack. Access is enhanced by a song title index.

528.   Stambler, Irwin. **Encyclopedia of Pop, Rock & Soul.** Rev. ed. New York: St. Martin's Press, 1989. 881p. Illus., discog. LC 88-29860. ISBN 0-312-02573-4.

The work updates and supplements the first edition (1975). Focusing on notable artists, the 500-plus entries attempt "to reflect all of the pivotal influences in the evolution of today's popular music spectrum" (p. ix). The lucidly written, substantial entries—averaging 1,000 words in length—represent a notable strength.

Handbooks

529.   Aquila, Richard. **That Old Time Rock & Roll: A Chronicle of an Era, 1954-1963.** New York: Schirmer Books/Macmillan, 1989. 370p. Illus. LC 89-2384. ISBN 0-02-870081-3; 0-02-870082-1 pap.

This intriguing source is organized into three sections: Part 1 "traces the rise of rock & roll, describes the various rock styles, explains the relationship of music to culture, and places the music in historical perspective"; Part 2 is composed of lists of themes, topics, and hit records; and Part 3 offers brief profiles (averaging two or three sentences) of most artists charting between 1954 and 1963.

530.   Bianco, David. **Heat Wave: The Motown Fact Book.** Ann Arbor, MI: Pierian Press, 1988. 542p. Indexes, bibl., discog. LC 86-60558. ISBN 1-56075-011-1.

This definitive sourcebook covers 5,500 recordings released by the Motown label in the United States and U.K. during the 1959-1986 period. The two record lists (arranged by nation, then chronologically) cite label and record number, release date, title and artists, and availability on compact disc or cassette. An appendix notes the releases of five record companies related to Motown. Name, song and record title, date, and record number indexes have also been provided.

531. Campbell, Colin, and Allan Murphy. **Things We Said Today: The Complete Lyrics and a Concordance to The Beatles' Songs, 1962-1970.** Ann Arbor, MI: Popular Culture, Ink, 1980. 430p. Illus. (Rock & Roll Reference Series, No. 4.) LC 80-83203. ISBN 0-87650-104-8.

The work is unparalleled in its encyclopedic exposition of the band's lyrics. The full text of the 189 songs written and recorded by the group has been provided. B. Lee Cooper termed it "an indispensable text for Beatles research. . . . There is no other work that is so clearly organized, so free of errors and inconsistencies, and so pointedly dedicated to promoting 'serious critical analysis' of the lyrics."

532. Cotten, Lee. **The Elvis Catalog.** Garden City, NY: Dolphin, 1987. 255p. Illus. LC 87-9133. ISBN 0-385-23705-7; 0-385-23704-9 pap.

This is an exhaustive survey—with price valuations—of memorabilia associated with Presley, including photos of past homes, cars, clothes, etc., actually belonging to the performer as well as handouts and newspaper headlines. Organized chronologically around a concise biography of Presley's life, the items pictured, both in color and black-and-white, feature concise descriptive captions not directly tied into the main text. The book, which carries the authorization of Elvis Presley Enterprises, includes an alphabetically arranged Directory of Licensed Manufacturers of Presley merchandise. Access is hindered somewhat by the absence of an index. Although not as comprehensive in its listing of some memorabilia as is Cranor's *Elvis Collectibles* (see entry 533), Cotton includes a broader form of coverage, including an entire chapter on collectibles produced since Presley's death.

533. Cranor, Rosalind. **Elvis Collectibles.** Paducah, KY: Collector Books, 1983. 366p. Illus. ISBN 0-89145-205-2.

Cranor has compiled an entertaining pictorial (black-and-white) guide to memorabilia manufactured during Presley's career, 1956 to 1977. The running commentary considers only those more recent materials—with price valuations—that might be confused with the older items. Records have been covered in only a peripheral manner—e.g., photo inserts to albums, front covers—"because of the many books on the market devoted to [them]" The inclusions (divided under the following headings of memorabilia: novelty items, RCA collectibles, postcards, sheet music, photographs, Las Vegas and concert items, publications, movie collectibles) are far from complete. Nevertheless, they offer a rich testament to the depth of the Presley phenomenon. No index has been provided.

534. Fenick, Barbara. **Collecting The Beatles: An Introduction & Price Guide to Fab Four Collectibles, Records & Memorabilia, Volumes 1 & 2.** Ann Arbor, MI: Popular Culture, Ink, 1985. 296p./320p. Illus. (Rock & Roll Reference Series, No. 16.) ISBN 0-87650-147-1; 0-87650-176-5.

Volume 1 is the indispensable portion of the set; in laying the groundwork for the beginning collector, it covers the history of Beatles memorabilia, the Beatles collecting phenomenon, strategies for locating items and obtaining them at the least cost. Volume 2 updates all segments of the first work. Of particular interest are a new chapter on selling Beatles memorabilia, a more thorough analysis of the practice of counterfeiting, and 150 new photographs of the rarer collectibles. This is the only authoritative Beatles collectible price guide on the market.

535.   Fitzpatrick, Jack, and James E. Fogerty. **Collecting Phil Spector: The Man, the Legend, and the Music.** Ann Arbor, MI: Spectacle/Popular Culture, Ink, 1987. 128p. Illus., bibl., discog. ISBN 0-9622446-0-0.

Goldmine has referred to it as "a focused, valuable aid to anyone whose interests extend to the work of rock's most legendary producer." The work includes a career history, complete discography of U.S. and U.K. releases, a selective listing of international recordings, a discography of Spector sound-alikes, an extensive bibliography on both Spector and the major artists he recorded, and reviews of the hallmark Spector collectibles.

536.   Gambaccini, Paul. **The Top 100 Rock 'n' Roll Albums of All Time.** New York: Harmony/Crown, 1987. 96p. Illus. LC 86-25726. ISBN 0-517-56561-7.

This is a compilation of the critical opinions of rock historians, journalists, deejays, and MTV veejays regarding the "greatest" rock music albums (each submitted a list of ten). The entries include basic release data, production information, track listings, a cover portrait, and a commentary. A list of the top thirty albums from the 1977 survey conducted by Gambaccini has also been included.

537.   **Goldmine's Rock 'n' Roll 45 RPM Record Price Guide.** 2nd ed. Iola, WI: Krause, 1992. Illus., pap.

The source covers 45 r.p.m. records, twelve-inch singles, EPs, and seven-inch picture sleeves. Song title entries, arranged alphabetically under artist and subdivided by release date, include label name and catalog number, format designations, and market valuations for the most collectible grades: "very good" and "near mint." Additional materials include 150 photos and complete discographies of the more collectible artists.

538.   Goldstein, Stewart and Alan Jacobson. **Oldies but Goodies: The Rock 'N' Roll Years.** New York: Mason/Charter, 1977. 328p. Illus., index. LC 76-28242. ISBN 0-88405-365-2; 0-88405-431-4 pap.

Covering the period 1953-1965, the volume covers all recordings appearing on *Billboard's* pop Top 40 chart from 1955 to 1963 as well as other songs. Also included are an introduction by Paul Anka, breakdowns of the era's 100 statistical leaders and 100 leading instrumentals, several chapters of trivia, and an oldies trivia quiz.

539.   Hammontree, Patsy Guy. **Elvis Presley: A Bio-Bibliography.** Westport, CT: Greenwood, 1985. 301p. Illus., index, bibl., discog. (Popular Culture Bio-Bibliographies.) LC 84-12773. ISBN 0-313-22867-1.

The source comprises a biography, a bibliography essay and selective bibliography, a chronology, a filmography, a discography, and an index. This is a competent, albeit flawed (e.g., missing data, clumsy writing), effort.

540.   Hendler, Herb. **Year by Year in the Rock Era: Events and Conditions Shaping the Rock Generations That Reshaped America.** Westport, CT: Greenwood, 1983. 350p. Index, bibl. LC 82-11722. ISBN 0-313-32456-6.

This chronological listing is divided between rock artists and events and social, cultural, and political information. Despite the implications of the title, the connection between the rock world and society in general is often tenuous at best.

541.   Henkel, David K. **Official Price Guide to Rock and Roll—Magazines, Posters, and Memorabilia.** North Syracuse, NY: Collectors Clearinghouse, 1992. 560p. Illus., pap.

This is a somewhat diffuse, but nevertheless very useful, collectors guide. Arranged by artist, it reveals a decided predilection for paper items (e.g., periodicals, music scores, advertising placards, and trading cards).

542. Hounsome, Terry. **Rock Record: A Collectors' Directory of Rock Albums and Musicians.** 3rd ed. New York: Facts on File, 1987. 738p. Index. LC 86-29026. ISBN 0-8160-1754-9; 0-8160-1755-7 pap.

Truly monumental in scope, this source encompasses 7,678 major artists, 78,000 performers, and 45,681 albums and EPs up through 1986. Within each artist entry are included album titles (not always in chronological order), year of release, record label and number, and participating musicians along with the instruments played.

543. Jancik, Wayne. **The Billboard Book of One-Hit Wonders.** New York: Billboard Books/Watson-Guptill, 1990. 420p. Illus., indexes. LC 90-884. ISBN 0-8230-7530-3.

Jancik provides background information regarding artists who appeared on the *Billboard* top 20 singles chart only once between January 1, 1955, and November 11, 1984. The chronologically arranged text is supplemented by a foreword that attempts to provide a rationale for one-hit wonders as well as a listing of artists who reached positions 21-40 only once in their respective careers. Artist and song title indexes have also been provided.

544. Jorgensen, Ernst, Erik Rasmussen, and Johnny Mikkelson. **Reconsider Baby: The Definitive Elvis Sessionography, 1954-1977.** Edited by Thomas Schultheiss. Reprint ed., with additions. Ann Arbor, MI: Popular Culture, Ink, 1986. 308p. Illus., index. ISBN 0-87650-220-6.

Based on studio and record company files, the work provides the most detailed and authoritative account of Presley's studio sessions available in any form. Originally published in Denmark as *Elvis Recording Sessions,* the U.S. edition has improved the work with (1) additions and corrections to the sessionography; (2) an updated U.S. discography; (3) an expanded index to song and album titles; and (4) a new index to personal names, group names, corporate names, places, locations, and other topics.

545. Krogsgaard, Michael. **Positively Bob Dylan: A Thirty-Year Discography, Concert & Recording Session Guide, 1960-1961.** Ann Arbor, MI: Popular Culture, Ink, 1991. xiv, 498p. Illus., indexes. ISBN 1-56075-000-6.

This volume must be owned by any serious Dylan researcher or collector. The work—in essence a third edition updating *Twenty Years of Recording: The Bob Dylan Reference Book* (1981) and *Master of the Tracks: The Bob Dylan Reference Book of Recordings* (1988)—attempts to systematically outline Dylan's music, including (1) all officially released sound recordings of songs, interviews, and press conferences; (2) unreleased sound recordings from concerts, studios, home settings, etc., that have been circulated among collectors; (3) unreleased and generally uncirculated material that the author has come across; and (4) video material.

The possibilities for use of the volume are seemingly limitless: to double-check concert itineraries against those of personally owned bootleg recordings, to nostalgically retrieve the past, to analyze some element of songcraft, to better understand the sociological and historical significance of Dylan's place in largely extra-musical movements like civil rights and antiwar protest.

Accessibility to this body of information is assisted by a wide array of indexes—all of which are detailed, accurate, and lucidly described to the reader—including Index to Recorded Songs and Interviews; Index to Songs on Records and in Films; Index to Musicians; Chronological Index to Dylan Singles; Alphabetical Index to Dylan Singles; Index to Dylan Albums (Chronological and Alphabetical); Comprehensive Index to Commercially-Released Recordings; Venue Index to Recorded Concert Performances; Geographic Index to Recorded Concert Performances; Label & Catalog Number Index; Index to Studio Sessions; Index to Recorded Radio & Television Broadcasts; Index to

Recorded Interviews; Index to Recorded Press Conferences; and Index to Dylan-Related Films (Chronological and Alphabetical).

As might be expected in a work of such breadth, gaps—and occasional discrepancies between the information provided and other sources—do arise at various points in the text. Nevertheless, the earlier portions of Dylan's career have been more thoroughly documented with the appearance of each new edition of the book.

546.   Lazell, Barry, ed., with Dafydd Rees and Luke Crampton. **Rock Movers & Shakers.** New York: Billboard, 1989. 560p. Illus. LC 88-19260. ISBN 0-8230-7608-3.

This source lists alphabetically about 1,000 U.S. and U.K. artists and provides chronological listings of notable facts about their lives, careers, and recordings. Despite the absence of indexing and criteria for the inclusion of data, the tool should prove useful to researchers and fans alike.

547.   Machlin, Milt. **The Michael Jackson Catalog: A Comprehensive Guide to Records, Videos, Clothing, Posters, Toys and Millions of Collectible Souvenirs.** New York: Arbor House, 1984. 128p. Illus., bibl., discog., videography. LC 84-72091. ISBN 0-87795-664-2 pap.

This attractive volume includes an introductory survey of Jackson's career, a selective listing of authorized merchandise, and a "Collectibles" section (e.g., programs, posters).

548.   Marsh, Dave, and John Swenson, eds. **The New Rolling Stone Record Guide.** Rev. and updated ed. New York: Random House, 1983. 648p. Index. LC 82-40116. ISBN 0-394-72107-1 pap.

The book reviews 12,000 popular music albums that had been released up through mid-1982 and were readily available at the time of publication. The cross-reference index indicates where an artist's entire corpus has been deleted since the first edition. Jazz releases, which appeared in original volume, were pulled with the aim of producing a separate title.

549.   McCoy, William, and Mitchell McGeary. **Every Little Thing: The Definitive Guide to Beatles Recording Variations, Rare Mixes and Other Musical Oddities, 1958-1986.** Edited by Thomas Schultheiss. Ann Arbor, MI: Popular Culture, Ink, 1990. 380p. Illus., indexes. (Rock & Roll Reference Series, No. 20.) LC 1-56075-004-9. ISBN 1-56075-004-9.

The authors analyze the many technical recording variations of Beatles' songs that are commercially available. The work includes chapters on such topics as the Tony Sheridan/Beat Brothers discs, the Star Club tape, the White Album, the "Rarities" LPs, box sets released worldwide, and "audiophile" half-speed mastered discs. A substantial portion of the book is given over to an alphabetically arranged song listing of known variations of material by the Beatles, both as a group and as solo artists. Song and record title, personal name, and record number indexes have also been included.

550.   Mulvaney, Rebekah Michele. **Rastafari and Reggae: A Dictionary and Sourcebook.** Westport, CT: Greenwood, 1990. 253p. Illus., index, bibl., discog., videography. LC 90-3591. ISBN 0-313-26071-0.

The volume—via a concisely worded dictionary and annotated bibliography, discography, and videography—delineates Rastafari and reggae, as well as the relationship between the two. The biographical entries include all notable Rastafari leaders and reggae practitioners.

551. Robbins, Ira A., ed. **The New Trouser Press Record Guide.** 3rd ed. New York: Collier Books/Macmillan, 1989. 657p. LC 88-25821. ISBN 0-02-036370-2 pap.

The source covers 1,900 new wave, punk, roots music, and esoteric folk artists and 6,200 record albums. Each alphabetically arranged artist entry cites complete LP listings (in addition to some EPs, compact discs, and cassettes) and provides a critique of this output.

552. **The Rolling Stone Rock Almanac: The Chronicles of Rock & Roll.** by the editors of *Rolling Stone.* New York: Collier Books/ Macmillan, 1983. 371p. Illus., indexes. LC 83-16178. ISBN 0-02-081320-1 pap.

This chronicle covers the period 1954-1982, giving a daily rundown of rock-related events. Also included are an introduction surveying the essence and history of rock and roll; essays outlining the developments of each year; and "Milestones," an alphabetical listing of names, birth dates, and (where applicable) death dates. Illustration and personal/group name indexes have also been included.

553. Sauers, Wendy, comp. **Elvis Presley: A Complete Reference.** Jefferson, NC: McFarland, 1984. 194p. Illus., index, bibl. LC 84-789. ISBN 0-89950-110-9.

The tool consists of a biography; "Memories"; a chronology; a concert listing; a movie listing; a list of recordings; "Memorabilia"; assorted documents concerning Presley's life; separate bibliographies for books, the *New York Times,* and other periodicals; and an index.

554. Schwartz, David. **Listening to the Beatles: An Audiophile's Guide to the Sound of the Fab Four. Volume I: Singles.** Ann Arbor, MI: Popular Culture, Ink, 1990. 354p. Illus., index. (Rock & Roll Reference Series, No. 35.) LC 89-92316. ISBN 1-56705-005-7.

This book is similar in concept to McCoy and McGeary's *Every Little Thing* (see entry 549). But whereas they deal with the technical makeup of the recording of a song (e.g., running time, stereo or mono, version used, track substitutions on LPs), Schwartz is concerned with how the recordings of a particular Beatles song "sound" from one record to the next. He evaluates which version is "best sounding" from among the various pressings released around the world. Bootleg recordings are covered along with officially sanctioned releases.

555. Wiener, Allen J., comp. **The Beatles: A Recording History.** Jefferson, NC: McFarland, 1986. 614p. Index. LC 85-43597. I 0-89950-209-1.

Wiener attempts to provide all important factual, biographical, and recording information concerning the Beatles (both as a group and as solo performers), utilizing a series of chronological listings. His failure to cite references undercuts the credibility of some of the data presented here.

556. Worth, Fred L. **Rock Facts.** New York: Facts on File, 1985. 416p. Illus., index. ISBN 0-8160-1099-4; 0-8160-1145-1 pap.

This is a compilation of "facts, anecdotes and lists" relating to rock music. The 3,000-plus alphabetically arranged entries (consisting of songs, albums, artists, topics, and categories) span the period from 1949 to the mid-1980s.

557. Worth, Fred L., and Steve D. Tamerius. **Elvis: His Life from A to Z.** Avenal, NJ: Outlet, 1992. Reprint of 1988 ed. 640p. Illus. I: 0-517-06634-3.

This dictionary offers bite-sized morsels of information about Presley's life and career.

Indexes

558. Gargan, William, and Sue Sharma, eds. **Find That Tune: An Index to Rock, Folk-Rock, Disco & Soul in Collections.** New York: Neal-Schuman, 1984. 303p. Indexes. LC 82-22346. ISBN 0-918212-70-7.

This index to 203 sheet music collections of rock, folk-rock, soul, and disco includes more than 4,000 songs from 1950 to 1981. Five indexes are included: song title, first line, performer, title of collection, and composer/ lyricist. The most comprehensive section, the title index, notes for each song the publisher's name, copyright data, composers, lyricists, and keyed numbers indicating the collections containing the song. The emphasis upon rock-based styles separates this title from the Havlice sourcebooks (see entries 459-462)

559. Sharma, Sue, and William Gargan, eds. **Find That Tune: An Index to Rock, Folk-Rock, Disco & Soul in Collections. [Volume 2].** New York: Neal-Schuman, 1989. 387p. Indexes. LC 82-22346. ISBN 1-55570-019-5.

The second volume follows the same format as its predecessor, indexing more than 4,000 songs during the period 1950-1985. Song title, first line, performer, title of collection, and composer/lyricist indexes have been provided.

Chapter 8

Religion/Psychic Phenomena

(See also: Social Phenomena—Minorities, pp. 133-41, 189-90, 233-34)

General

Bibliographies

560.   Menendez, Albert J. **School Prayer and Other Religious Issues in American Public Education: A Bibliography.** New York: Garland, 1985. x, 168p. Indexes. (Garland Reference Library of Social Science, no. 291.) ISBN 0-8240-8775-5.

This listing includes 1,566 citations (books, articles, theses, dissertations, and newspaper articles) organized under twenty-one subject headings concerned with religion in public education. Access is enhanced by author and subject indexes.

561.   Richardson, Marilyn. **Black Women and Religion: A Bibliography.** Boston: G. K. Hall, 1980. 139p. Illus., index. (A Publication in Black Studies.) LC 80-20457. ISBN 0-8161-8087-3.

The 867 annotated entries are arranged according to such headings as literature, music, art, films, reference materials, and biographies.

Biographies

562.   Melton, J. Gordon. **Religious Leaders of America.** Detroit: Gale Research, 1991. 604p. Indexes, bibl. ISBN 0-8103-4921-3.

The source profiles both living and deceased religious luminaries from a wide variety of backgrounds—Christian, Jewish, Native American faiths, Islam, New Age, Orthodox churches, Asian religion, etc. Each entry gives vital statistics, an encapsulated biography, and that individual's particular faith as well as his or her role within it. Religious affiliation and keyword indexes have also been provided.

Directories

563.   Melton, J. Gordon. **Religious Bodies in the United States: A Directory.** New York: Garland, 1992. 313p. Index, bibl. (Religious Information Systems, Vol. 1.) LC 91-41564. ISBN 0-8153-0806-X.

Organized into sections on interfaith groups, individual denominations, and periodicals, the tool provides names, headquarter addresses, phone numbers, cable and fax numbers (where applicable), and concise sketches of all known U.S. religious bodies. The entries are arranged alphabetically by name; alternative names can be located via cross-references or the index.

Dictionaries

564. Drury, Nevill. **Dictionary of Mysticism and the Occult.** New York: Harper & Row, 1985. 281p. ISBN 0-06-062093-5; 0-06-062094-3 pap.

The tool incorporates nearly 3,000 entries, both concepts and thumbnail portraits of the practitioners and writers of the occult sciences. The only real flaw is the absence of etymologies for the terms included here.

Encyclopedias

565. Hirschfelder, Arlene, and Paulette Molin. **The Encyclopedia of Native American Religions.** New York: Facts on File, 1992. 352p. Illus., maps, index, bibl. ISBN 0-8160-2017-5.

This wide-ranging survey of Native American religions includes major religious sites, specific rites, biographies of spiritual leaders and Christian missionaries, and other relevant topics. Despite its superficiality in covering certain areas, it remains unrivaled as an introduction to this field.

566. Melton, J. Gordon, and others. **New Age Encyclopedia: A Guide to Beliefs, Concepts, Terms, People, and Organizations.** Detroit: Gale Research, 1990. 586p. Index. ISBN 0-8103-7159-6.

The work focuses on the socio-religious aspects of the movement, attempting to provide an objective, comprehensive survey of the New Age world—its people, organizations, and opinions. No attempt has been made to cover the occult-psychic metaphysical movements, territory best covered in Leslie Shepherd's *Encyclopedia of Occultism & Parapsychology* (2 Vols. 3rd ed. Detroit: Gale Research, 1990). Sections include the "Introduction" (which delineates the book's concerns); "Introductory Essay: An Overview of the New Age Movement"; "Chronology of the New Age Movement"; "Descriptive Listings" (the alphabetically-arranged main section); "Educational Institutions Appendix"; and an "Alphabetical and Keyword Index." The latter provides access (by numerical key) to all organizations, people, terms, subjects, and other significant details noted within the text of the descriptive listings section and within the entries from the Educational Institutions Appendix. The entries provide biographical and historical background information, an assessment of the importance of each to the movement, directory data, and a select list of bibliographic citations.

Chapter 9

Social Phenomena

General

Atlases

567.   Kidron, Michael, and Ronald Segal. **The New State of the World Atlas.** 4th ed. New York: Touchstone/S. & S., 1992. 159p. Maps. LC 91-6798. ISBN 0-671-74639-1; 0-671-74556-5 pap.

The work includes 50 two-page world maps devoted to various contemporary topics (e.g., AIDS, the greenhouse effect, the drug trade). Explanations of the maps and source notes are provided in the latter part of the volume. Despite its broad scope, a substantial portion of the material concentrates on the United States.

Bibliographies

568.   Hanna, Archibald. **A Mirror for the Nation: An Annotated Bibliography of American Social Fiction, 1901-1950.** New York: Garland, 1985. 472p. Indexes. (Garland Reference Library of the Humanities, Vol. 595.) LC 85-12868. ISBN 0-8240-8727-5.

This source provides 4,000-odd entries (arranged alphabetically by author), including novels, short story collections, plays, and narrative poems. The annotations concentrate on the principal subject matter and geographical setting. Subject, title, and illustrator indexes have also been provided.

Dictionaries

569.   Jary, David, and Julia Jary, eds. **The HarperCollins Dictionary of Sociology.** New York: HarperPerennial/HarperCollins, 1992. 601p. Bibl. LC 91-55446. ISBN 0-06-46106-5 pap.

Designed to be a study aid rather than the definitive dictionary on the subject, the volume includes over 1,800 terms, topics, and theorists of major importance Each entry is composed of a definition and frequently further analysis and examples.

Encyclopedias

570.   Kohn, George C. **Encyclopedia of American Scandal.** New York: Facts on File, 1989. 368p. Illus., index. LC 88-16294. ISBN 0-8160-1313-6.

The tool's 400-odd entries (arranged alphabetically by name or event) focus on scandals throughout U.S. history. (The introduction defines a scandal as "a grave loss or injury to reputation resulting from actual or apparent breach of morality, ethics, propriety, or law.")

Handbooks

571. McFarlan, Donald, ed. **The Guinness Book of Records.** New York: Facts on File. Annual. 320p. Illus., index. ISBN 0-8160-2643-2

This universally popular sourcebook devoted to natural, human, and scientific oddities has been published in the United States by Facts on File for the past several years. The overall enterprise is divided into a number of similarly formatted editions, each of which emphasizes features of interest to the targeted country; e.g., additional baseball and football material in the American edition.

Automobiles

Handbooks

572. Kimes, Beverly Rae. **Standard Catalog of American Cars, 1805-1942.** 2nd ed. Iola, WI: Krause Publications, 1989. 1568p. Illus., index. LC 85-050390. ISBN 0-87341-111-0.

The entries—covering 5,000-plus car models and ranging in length from a short statement to over twenty pages—provide a historical overview, a description, basic specifications, factory price, and estimated current value. Supplementary segments include listings of (1) alternative power sources, and (2) cyclecars and highwheelers. A geographical index has also been provided.

573. Langworth, Richard M. and Chris Poole. **Great American Automobiles of the 50s.** New York: Beekman House/Crown, 1989. 320p. Illus. LC 88-63609. ISBN 0-517-67556-0.

All makes and models from that era are present in this source; the entries note development, technical features, and production levels.

Awards

Biographies

574. Opfell, Olga S. **The Lady Laureates: Women Who Have Won the Nobel Prize.** 2nd ed. Metuchen, NJ: Scarecrow, 1986. 316p. Bibl. LC 85-19670. ISBN 0-8108-1851-5.

The work profiles the twenty women who have received the Nobel Prize from 1905 (Bertha von Suttner, Peace) to 1983 (Barbara McClintock, Science). These biographies— which include anecdotes and quotations from family and associates, and document the efforts of women to acquire a status comparable to that of men—are prefaced by an essay on Alfred Nobel and the origin of the prize bearing his name. A chronology of events connected with the award (spanning the period 1883-1984) has also been provided.

575. Siegman, Gita, ed. **World of Winners: A Current and Historical Perspective on Awards and Their Winners.** Detroit: Gale Research, 1991. 2nd ed. 1,000p. Indexes. ISBN 0-8103-0665-4.

The source covers almost 2,000 awards of note worldwide (although the majority are based in the United States) organized under twelve headings, including "Arts and Letters," "Design and Architecture," "Lifestyles," "Live Performance," "Mass Media," "Music," "Public Affairs," and "Sports and Hobbies." Award recipients are listed by year (in chronological order), then alphabetically by name. Organization name, winner, and award indexes have also been provided.

Celebrations/Holidays

Handbooks

576. Gregory, Ruth W. **Anniversaries and Holidays.** 4th ed. Chicago: American Library Association, 1983. 262p. Index, bibl. LC 83-3784. ISBN 0-8389-0389-4.

First published in 1928, this source—arranged chronologically—identifies, for each day of the year, holy and feast days, civic and official holidays, and "special events days." A supplementary section includes movable holidays of both a religious and secular nature.

577. MacDonald, Margaret R. **The Folklore of World Holidays.** Detroit: Gale Research, 1992. 739p. Index, bibl. ISBN 0-8103-7577-X.

This chronologically arranged sourcebook delineates the folkways associated with 340 holidays in more than 150 nations worldwide. Access is enhanced by a subject index.

The Columbus Controversy

Encyclopedias

578. Bedini, Silvio A., ed. **The Christopher Columbus Encyclopedia.** 2 Vols. New York: Simon & Schuster, 1991. 809p. ISBN 0-13-142662-1.

Produced to coincide with from the Quincentenary of Columbus's discovery of the New World, this authoritative tool includes 363 articles written by 131 contributors. Not only the Columbus voyages, but the Age of Discovery and early phases of European expansion into the Americas are covered at length.

Crime

Encyclopedias

579. Nash, Jay Robert. **World Encyclopedia of Organized Crime.** Paragon House, 1992. 617p. Illus., index, bibl. LC 91-40697. ISBN 1-55778-508-2.

The tool focuses on American mobsters, particularly Mafia figures. The entries, varying from less than 100 words to several pages in length, feature a sensationalized writing style. Nevertheless, its value as an information source is surpassed only by Nash's *Encyclopedia of World Crime* (6 Vols. CrimeBooks, 1990. 5,500p.).

Handbooks

580. Sifakis, Carl. **Encyclopedia of Assassinations.** New York: Facts on File, 1991. 228p. Illus., index, bibl. LC 90-3435. ISBN 0-8160-1935-5.

The volume is organized around alphabetically arranged biographies of about 350 victims (or near victims). Each entry encapsulates the subject's career, describes the assassination attempt, and reports on what happened to the assassin(s).

The Ecology Movement

Dictionaries

581.   Rodes, Barbara K., and Rice Odell. **The Dictionary of Environmental Quotations.** New York: Simon & Schuster Academic Reference, 1992. 288p. Indexes. ISBN 0-13-210576-4.

This listing includes 3,700 quotations organized under 143 headings (e.g., acid rain, hazardous wastes), then subdivided chronologically. The quotes have been culled from proverbs, slogans, bumper stickers, speeches, magazines, newspapers, monographs, and scientific papers. Author and subject indexes has also been provided.

Directories

582.   **Gale Environmental Sourcebook: A Guide to Organizations, Agencies, and Publications.** Detroit: Gale Research, 1992. 688p. Index. (Environmental Library.) ISBN 0-8103-8403-5.

This is an exhaustive compilation; i.e., some 9,000 entries arranged under six headings: "U.S. and International Organizations," "Government Agencies and Programs," "Publications and Information Services," "Research Facilities and Educational Programs," "Green Consumerism," and "Scholarships and Awards." Supplementary sections include a glossary and appendixes devoted to an endangered wildlife and plants roster, the Environmental Protection Agency National Priorities List, and EPA Superfund sites.

Guides to the Literature

583.   Rudd, Robert L. **Environmental Toxicology: A Guide to Information Sources.** Detroit: Gale Research, 1977. 266p. Indexes. (Man and the Environment Information Guide Series, Vol. 7.) LC 73-17540. ISBN 0-8103-1342-1.

This bibliography—consisting largely of journal articles, monographs, and book chapters—is organized into four sections: "General Sources of Environmental Toxicology," "Consequences of Intentional Environmental Pollution," "Consequences of Unintended Environmental Pollution," and "Special Aspects of Environmental Pollution." These headings (and subsections) are introduced by concise discussions of relevant environmental issues. The appendix list abbreviations and the common and chemical names of frequency cited compounds. Access is enhanced by author and subject indexes.

Handbooks

584.   Darnay, Arsen J., ed. **Statistical Record of the Environment.** Detroit: Gale Research, 1991. 855p. Maps, index, bibl. (Environmental Library, Vol. 1.) LC 91-30214. ISBN 0-8103-8374-8.

The tool is built around more than 800 statistical tables concerned with environmental pollution. Although interpretative analysis would have enhanced the value of these tables, the assembled data is most impressive taken as a whole.

585.   Holum, John R. **Topics and Terms in Environmental Problems.** New York: John Wiley, 1978. 728p. Illus., maps, index. LC 77-12805. ISBN 0-471-01982-8.

This volume defines 239 environmental topics and issues like air pollution and water pollution. The concisely worded entries offer a wealth of information regarding the context of these concepts.

586. Rifkin, Jeremy, and Carol Grunewald Rifkin. **Voting Green: Your Complete Environmental Guide to Making Political Choices in the 1990's.** New York: Doubleday, 1992. 384p. Illus. ISBN 0-385-41917-1 pap.
Looking at 264 bills introduced in the first two Congresses of the 1990s, the authors grade senators and House members on the basis of their respective responses to these issues. The Bush administration is also evaluated according to its record on environmental matters. In short, it articulates a pro-green platform for the 1990s and brings out in strong relief those politicians for and against such a stance.

Indexes

587. **Environment Abstracts.** New York: Environment Information Center. Vol. 1-, 1971-. Monthly. Indexes. ISSN: 0093-3287.
Intended as an introductory guide to the environmental literature, each issue covers more than 1,000 concisely annotated articles and reports culled from scientific and technical journals, government publications, conference proceedings, and popular periodicals. The twenty-one groupings employed include wildlife and food and drugs.

Fame/Heroism

Biographies

588. Browne, Ray B., ed. **Contemporary Heroes and Heroines.** Detroit: Gale Research, 1990. 451p. Illus., bibl. ISBN 0-8103-4860-8.
The 103 subjects included in this biographical compendium were selected for their embodiment of heroic virtue that might inspire youth; e.g., Hank Aaron, Lee Iacocca, John F. Kennedy, C. Everett Koop, Ralph Nader, Margaret Thatcher. The lucidly written three-to four-page profiles summarize their subjects' lives and focus upon their achievement (e.g., calling society's attention to pressing problems). With student research in mind, each entry incorporates a first-person quotation typifying that individual's outlook, a fact box summarizing vital data, a portrait, and a brief bibliography.

589. Stetler, Susan L., ed. **Almanac of Famous People.** 3 Vols. Volume I: A-I; Volume II: J-Z; Volume III: Index. 5th ed. Detroit: Gale Research, 1993. ci, 3083p. ISBN: 0-8103-2784-8.
The source, formerly titled *Biography Almanac,* covers notable figures in the following fields: TV and movies, sports, business, science, and politics. The more than 25,000 entries include name, pseudonym, nickname, group affiliation, nationality, occupation, career or best-known activity, one-line descriptor, dates and places of birth and death, and alphabetically arranged codes for relevant biographical materials. Chronological, geographic, and occupational indexes have been provided.

Fads

(See also: Social Phenomena—Fashion, p. 232)

Encyclopedias

590. Hoffmann, Frank, and William G. Bailey. **Arts and Entertainment Fads.** Binghamton, NY: Haworth, 1990. Illus., index, bibl. ISBN 0-86656-881-6; 0-918393-72-8 pap.

The work is composed of 123 concisely written essays (ranging from one to six pages in length) documenting fads within the fine arts field. Topics—including "Beatlemania," "Charlie Chaplin," "Dime Novels," "Disco," "Mickey Mouse," "The Night Before Christmas," "Mary Pickford," "Ragtime," "The $64,000 Question," "Shirley Temple," "Yankee Doodle," and "The Ziegfield Follies"—span the entire history of the United States.

591. Hoffmann, Frank, and William G. Bailey. **Mind and Society Fads.** Binghamton, NY: Haworth, 1992. Illus., index., bibl. ISBN 1-56024-178-0; 1-56023-010-X pap.

Keeping to the format established in earlier volumes of the series, the work includes such science and society fads as The Bermuda Triangle, Biorhythms, Coueism, Craniometry and Polygeny, Death Education, Forteans, Genius Sperm Bank, Hippie Communes, Marian Socialism, Orgonomy, Phrenology, Sex Surrogates, and UFOs.

592. Hoffmann, Frank, and William G. Bailey. **Sports and Entertainment Fads.** Binghamton, NY: Haworth, 1991. Illus., index, bibl. ISBN 1-56024-056-3; 0-918393-92-2 pap.

A handy guide to the nation's favorite leisure activities of the past 200 years. Entries include "Aristocratic Pastimes," "Arnie's Army," "Bagatelle," "Baseball Card Collecting," "The Dallas Cowboy Cheerleaders," "Dance Marathons," "Bobby Fischer and the Chess Craze," "Flagpole Sitting," "Bo Jackson and 2-Sport Athletes," "Lotteries," "Frank Merriwell," "Miniature Golf," "Monopoly," "Surfing," "The Topless Bathing Suit," "WrestleMania," and "Yo-Yos."

593. Marum, Andrew, and Frank Parise. **Follies and Foibles: A View of 20th Century Fads.** New York: Facts on File, 1984. 220p. Illus., index, bibl. LC 82-2355. ISBN 0-87196-820-7.

The authors survey over 200 fads from 1890 to the early 1980s. The concise entries (one page or less) offer descriptive overviews of more notable manias, such as Davy Crockett, video games, and the Smurfs.

Fashion

594. Stegemeyer, Anne. **Who's Who in Fashion.** 2nd ed. New York: Fairchild, 1988. 243p. Illus., index. LC 87-82511. ISBN 0-87005-574-7.

595. Stegemeyer, Anne. **Who's Who in Fashion: Supplement.** New York: Fairchild, 1991. Illus., index. ISBN 0-87005-746-4.

These alphabetically arranged collections of concisely written profiles of designers are international in scope. The "Names to Know" section appended to main text includes up-and-coming personalities.

Feminism

(See also: Social Phenomena—Homosexuality, pp. 130, 191, 214, 233)

Almanacs

596. Clark, Judith Freeman. **Almanac of American Women in the 20th Century.** New York: Prentice Hall Press, 1987. 274p. Index. LC 86-43172. ISBN 0-13-022658-0.
The entries include short date-and-event entries in addition to longer entries devoted to major movements (e.g., suffrage, labor activism) and biographies of notable professionals. A name index has also been provided.

Atlases

597. Gibson, Anne, and Timothy Fast. **The Women's Atlas of the United States.** New York: Facts on File, 1986. 248p.
The tool chronicles the experiences of women in the United States, encompassing areas of crime, domestic life, demography, education, employment, health, and politics. Despite its presentation of a wealth of information, its reliance upon 1980 census data may pose problems for some researchers.

Bibliographies/Filmographies

598. Barnes, Dorothy L., comp. **Rape: A Bibliography, 1965-1975.** Troy, NY: Whitson, 1977. 154p. Index. LC 77-8964. ISBN 0-87875-120-3.
The compilation covers a wide array of perspectives, including medical, psychological, legal, and sociological. The bibliography proper is divided into three parts: (1) an alphabetically arranged author listing of about 100 monographs; (2) approximately 650 articles culled from more than 300 journals and organized by title; and (3) the journal references arranged under 126 topical headings. Access is enhanced by the author index (to journal articles).

599. Buvinic, Mayra. **Women and World Development: An Annotated Bibliograhy.** Prepared under the auspices of the American Association for the Advancement of Science. Washington, D.C.: Overseas Development Council, 1976. 162p. Index, pap. LC 76-14601.
Culled from an international seminar held in June 1975 by the AAAS, the work focuses on contemporary research on the "effects of socio-economic development and cultural change on women and on women's reactions to these changes." The listing is organized into nine topical sections (e.g., work, education, health), each of which is subdivided geographically. The appendixes cite bibliographies and special periodical issues focusing on this subject. An author index has also been provided.

600. Carson, Anne. **Feminist Spirituality and the Feminine Divine: An Annotated Bibliography.** Trumansburg, NY: Crossing, 1986. 139p. Index. (The Crossing Press Feminist Series.) LC 86-4192. ISBN 0-89594-200-3.

The bibliography—arranged alphabetically by author or editor—incorporates monographs, periodicals, articles, taped lectures, primary sources, and microform collections (739 entries) that provide "new ways of looking at old religions, and...seek to create new myths, new patterns of social and spiritual interaction." Access is enhanced by a subject index.

601. Harrison, Cynthia E., ed. **Women in American History; A Bibliography.** Vols. 1-2. ABC-Clio, 1979; 1985. 375p.; ix, 383p. Indexes. (Clio Bibliographic Series, no. 20.) ISBN 0-87436-450-7.

Volume 1 contains abstracts of 3,395 periodical articles that "touch on the full range of women's experience in the United States and Canada." The material has been taken from the first fourteen volumes of *America: History and Life* (1964-1977). Volume 2 covers the period between 1978 and 1984, with 3,700 descriptive annotations in all, ranging from lengthy signed contributions to one-sentence summaries. The entries are organized under eleven broad topics: "Women's History and Studies and the Historiography of Women"; "Women in North American History"; "Domestic, Social and Personal Roles"; "Women and Religion"; "Women and Education"; "Women and Ethnicity"; "Women in American Culture"; "Women in the Work Force"; "Women and Politics"; "Women and Violence"; and "Women and Biology". The text is then subdivided alphabetically by author. The source provides more focused access via an author index and the "Bibliographic Center Subject Profile Index"; regarding the latter, each entry is composed of a string of descriptors—subjects, geographical or biographical information, and the time span covered by the article—intended to form a profile of the article.

602. Kemmer, Elizabeth Jane. **Rape and Rape-Related Issues: An Annotated Bibliography.** New York: Garland, 1977. 180p. Index, bibl. LC 76-52701. ISBN 0-8240-9873-0.

The listing consists of thirty monographs and more than 300 articles from 174 periodicals (i.e., medical, legal, feminist, and general magazines and newspapers) appearing between 1965 and 1976.

603. Krichmar, Albert. Assisted by Virginia Carlson Smith and Ann E. Wiederrecht. **The Women's Movement in the Seventies: An International English-Language Bibliography.** Metuchen, NJ: Scarecrow, 1977. 875p. Index. LC 77-21416. ISBN 0-8108-1063-8.

The 8,637 geographically arranged entries (the majority of which have terse annotations) cover doctoral dissertations, monographs, research reports, journal articles, and government publications that focus on "change, attempted change, and continuing problems confronting women in the countries in which they live" (Introduction).

604. Loeb, Catherine R., and others. **Women's Studies, 1980-1985: A Recommended Core Bibliography.** Abridged ed. Englewood, CO: Libraries Unlimited, 1987. LC 87-17015. ISBN 0-87287-598-9.

The tool represents an abridgment of *Women's Studies: A Recommended Core Bibliography, 1980-1985* (Libraries Unlimited, 1987) for more general high school and college audiences. The 645 entries (featuring critical annotations) have been organized into broad topics, such as law, sports, occupations, and feminist theory.

605. Mumford, Laura Stempel. **Women's Issues: An Annotated Bibliography.** Pasadena, CA: Salen, 1989. 163p. LC 89-10831. ISBN 0-89356-654-3.

The main text is arranged under broad such headings as history, politics, and education; health issues and sexuality; family, home, and relationships; violence against women; and women and the arts. Selected materials (generally available in libraries) tend to reflect diversified and frequently opposing perspectives.

606.   Myerson, Joel. **Margaret Fuller: An Annotated Secondary Bibliography.** New York: Burt Franklin, 1977. 272p. Index. LC 77-3187. ISBN 0-89102-026-8.

Devoted to one of the nation's earliest crusading feminists, the work includes three parts: (1) a compilation of commentaries on Fuller dating as far back as 1834; (2) a listing of poems, satirical sketches, novels with characters based on Fuller, and other literary tributes to and abuses of Fuller; and (3) a description of the Fuller manuscript collection.

607.   Nordquist, Joan, comp. **Comparable Worth.** Santa Cruz, CA: Reference and Research Services, 1986. 62p. (Contemporary Social Issues: A Bibliographic Series, No. 2.) ISBN 0-937855-03-0 pap.

The 500-odd entries included here—covering monographs, documents, dissertations, and journal articles largely published during the first half of the 1980s—have been organized into eight groupings: introductory information on women in the workforce; general information on comparable worth and pay equity; business and personnel literature and literature about specific industries, occupations, and labor unions; material from the legal literature; information about comparable worth and cities and states; comparable worth and the international community; federal documents on comparable worth; and bibliographies and resource organizations (addresses, publications, etc.). Despite its brevity, this is a useful research tool.

608.   Reese, Lyn, and Jean Wilkinson, comps. and eds. **Women in the World: Annotated History Resources for the Secondary Student.** Metuchen, NJ: Scarecrow, 1987. 220p. LC 87-16436. ISBN 0-8108-2050-1.

This work delineates the historical role of women throughout the world, as well as their contributions to culture and economics. Arranged primarily by continent, the citations are subdivided by such categories as autobiography/biography, first-person accounts, and fiction. Entries include annotations, reading level, time period, place, theme, description, and suggested applications.

609.   Schlechter, Gail Ann, with Donna Belli. **Minorities and Women: A Guide to the Reference Literature in the Social Sciences.** Los Angeles: Reference Service Press, 1977. 349p. Indexes. LC 76-53061. ISBN 0-918276-01-2.

This annotated listing includes more than 800 entries concerned with women, native Americans, Asian Americans, black Americans, and Spanish Americans, particularly regarding such areas as civil rights, education, employment, and legal considerations. The entries are arranged by title within two major groupings: information sources (biographies, documentary sources, directories, statistical materials, etc.) and citation sources (subdivided by ethnic group). Author, title, and subject indexes have also been provided.

610.   Sullivan, Kaye. **Films for, by and About Women. Series II.** Metuchen, NJ: Scarecrow, 1985. x, 780p. Indexes, bibl. ISBN 0-8108-1766-7.

The misleading title notwithstanding, this is an annotated listing (alphabetically arranged by title) of animated work, documentaries, videotapes, film shorts, instructional films, features, etc. The entries include running time, color or black-and-white designation, producer, director, screenwriter, a rental/sales symbol, and a brief descriptive note. The appendixes provide a list of symbols and a directory of film sources and filmmakers. Access is enhanced by women filmmakers and subject indexes.

611.   Sweeney, Patricia E. **Biographies of American Women: An Annotated Bibliography.** Santa Barbara, CA: ABC-Clio, 1990. 290p. Indexes. LC 89-28277. ISBN 0-87436-070-6.
   The source consists of 1,291 biographies of 700 American women, including Amelia Earhart, Mahalia Jackson, Gene Stratton-Porter, and Belle Starr. Name, profession, and vocation indexes have also been provided.

Biographies

(See also: Social Phenomena—Awards, p. 118)

612.   Blain, Virginia, Patricia Clement, and Isabel Grundy. **The Feminist Companion to Literature in English: Women Writers from the Middle Ages to the Present.** New Haven, CT: Yale University, 1990. ISBN 0-300-04854-8.
   Although an expansive time period is covered is this alphabetical listing, American authors are well represented. The entries—including birth and death dates, a discussion of the times in which each wrote, and a bibliography of writings—range from 250 to 500 words in length.

613.   Congress. House. Office of the Historian. **Women in Congress, 1917-1990.** Washington, D.C.: GPO-SuDocs, 1991. v, 266p. (House Document No. 101-238. SL 91-293-P. Item 556-C. S/N 052-071-00919-1; 052-071-00918-3 pap.) Y 1.1/7:101-238.
   This is a listing of 115 representatives and sixteen senators (representing forty states) elected or appointed to Congress since 1917.

614.   Herman, Kali. **Women in Particular: An Index to American Women.** Phoenix, AZ: Oryx, 1984. xviii, 740p. Index. ISBN 0-89774-088-2.
   The tool is organized into four parts: field and career, religious affiliation, ethnic or racial identity, and geographical area. The subjects are listed chronologically by birthdate and often appear in more than one sequence; brief biographical data is provided in each instance. The fifty-four collective biographical sources selected here are limited to the English language. Access is enhanced by a name index.

615.   James, E. T., J. W. James, and P. S. Boyer, eds. **Notable American Women, 1607-1905: A Biographical Dictionary.** 3 Vols. Cambridge: Belknap/Harvard University, 1971. LC 76-152274. ISBN 0-674-62734-2.

616.   Sicherman, Barbara, and Carol H. Green, eds. **Notable American Women: The Modern Period.** Cambridge: Belknap/Harvard University, 1980. 773p. LC 80-18402. ISBN 0-674-62732-6; 0-674-62733-4 pap.
   The set is modeled after the *Dictionary of American Biography,* which included only 700 women among 17,000 entries. The James volumes consist of 1,359 articles and are supplemented by another 442 (women born between 1857 and 1943 and deceased by 1975) in the Sicherman work. With the exception of wives of U.S. presidents, all women here were selected on the basis of influence in their respective fields or innovative contributions to society.

617.   Kulkin, Mary-Ellen. **Her Way: A Guide to Biographies of Women for Young People.** 2nd ed. Chicago: American Library Association, 1984. 415p. Indexes. LC 83-22375. ISBN 0-8389-0396-9.
   The work is composed of 1,000 concise sketches of notable women in history, appended by a graded and annotated list of biographies geared to school students. It also

includes lists of nationalities besides American organized by ethnic groups and by vocation or avocation. Author-title and subject indexes have also been provided.

618.   Petteys, Chris. **Dictionary of Women Artists: An International Dictionary of Women Artists Born Before 1900.** Boston: G. K. Hall, 1985. xviii, 851p. Bibl. LC 84-22511. ISBN 0-8161-8456-9.
       Profiling over 21,000 women painters, sculptors, printmakers, and illustrators born before 1900, the tool's expressed aim is "to provide essential biographical information about the thousands of women artists who played a part . . . in women's art heritage."

619.   Entry number not used.

620.   Uglow, Jennifer, ed. **The Continuum Dictionary of Women's Biography.** Rev. ed. New York: Continuum; distr., Harper & Row, 1989. 621p. Index, bibl. LC 88-28224. ISBN 0-8264-0417-0.
       The thumbnail bios (generally a paragraph or two in length) include prominent women—rulers, reformers, entertainers, artists, etc.—throughout history. Access is enhanced by a subject index.

Catalogs/Union Lists

621.   Library of Congress. Photoduplication Service. **Women's Studies.** Washington, D.C.: IA, 1991. 16p. Illus. (Special Resources for Research No. 1. SL 91-793-P. Item 815-C. LC 30.31:1.)
       The catalog describes research collections—including the papers of Margaret Sanger, Clara Barton, and Elizabeth Cody Stanton—on women's studies microfilmed by LC's Photoduplication Service and available for sale.

Dictionaries

622.   Mills, Jane. **Womanwords: A Dictionary of Words About Women.** Free Press, 1992. 300p. Bibl. ISBN 0-02-921495-5.
       This thoroughly researched dictionary traces how, when, and why selected words dealing exclusively with women have evolved in meaning over time.

623.   Kramarae, Chris, and Paula A. Treichler, with Ann Russo. **A Feminist Dictionary.** New York: Pandora/Routledge & Kegan Paul/Methuen, 1985. 587p. Bibl. LC 85-9278. ISBN 0-86358-060-2; 0-86358-015-7 pap.
       Employing the standard dictionary format, this tool assumes a more focused stance in (1) defining terms coined by the feminist movement (e.g., displaced homemaker); (2) taking a revisionist look at traditional words (e.g., divorce); (3) revealing the double standard characterizing some terms; (4) awakening the social conscience with respect to such social issues as sexual preference; (5) analyzing lexicographical terms from a feminist perspective; and (6) providing background on notable feminist events, organizations, texts, etc.

Directories

624.   Doss, Martha Merrill, ed. **Women's Organizations: A National Directory.** Garrett Park, MD: Garrett Park, 1986. 302p. Illus., index. LC 86-081710. ISBN 0-912048-42-5.

The organizations, arranged alphabetically by name, include journals and presses headed by women in addition to activist, professional, technical, religious, and union groups. An economical alternative to more expensive, comprehensive directories, the more than 2,000 entries include address, telephone number, key personnel, and a concise statement of objectives. A subject index has also been included.

Encyclopedias

625.   Tierney, Helen, ed. **Women's Studies Encyclopedia.** Westport, CT: Greenwood, 1989-1991. Index, bibl. LC 88-32806. ISBN 0-313-27358-8.

The articles, ranging from 750 to 1,500 words in length and arranged alphabetically by topic, compose three volumes: *Volume 1: Views from the Sciences* (natural, behavioral, and social sciences; health and medicine; politics; law; economics; and linguistics); *Volume 2: Literature, Arts and Learning* (literature, the arts, and education); and *Volume 3: History, Philosophy, and Religion.* Written from a feminist perspective, they define terms and examine the role of women in a wide variety of fronts. Access is enhanced by a subject index.

626.   Tuttle, Lisa. **Encyclopedia of Feminism.** New York: Facts on File, 1986. 399p. Bibl. LC 85-31212. ISBN 0-8160-1424-8.

The tool consists of titles, figures, slogans, terms, and events relevant to the women's movement. A particular strength is its inclusion of many early feminists omitted from mainstream historical works.

Handbooks

627.   Tinling, Marion. **Women Remembered: A Guide to Landmarks of Women's History in the United States.** Westport, CT: Greenwood, 1986. 796p. Index, bibl. LC 85-17639. ISBN 0-313-23984-3.

Arranged by geographic region (subdivided by state, city or town, and personal name), the work encompasses homes, monuments, memorials, workplaces, markers, and plaques. The entries include travel directions, hours the sites are open, sites included in historic registers, etc. Supplementary material includes introductions to each geographic region, notes on sources, classified lists of women, and a chronology of significant dates in women's history.

628.   Adelman, Clifford. See: **Women at Thirtysomething: Paradoxes of Attainment.**

629.   Bureau of Labor Statistics. **Working Women: A Chartbook.** Washington, D.C.: IA-SuDocs, 1991. vii, 53p. Illus., charts, tables. (Bulletin 2385. SL 91-714-P. Item 768-A-1. S/N 029-001-03081-9. L 2.3:2385.) ISBN 0-1603-5841-8.

A cornucopia of occupational data regarding U.S. women, including earnings, employment patterns, demographic breakdowns, and domestic relationships.

630.   Department of Defense. **Military Women in the Department of Defense. Vol. VIII.** Washington, D.C.: IA, 1990. viii, 122p. Charts. (MC 91-4498. SL 90-675-P. Item 306-A. D 1.90:990.) LC 88-640585.

This chartbook contains contemporary (circa 1990) statistics regarding officer and enlisted women in the armed forces; e.g., grade and years of service, military occupation group, civilian education, retention and reenlistment rates, time in service at promotion.

631.   Office of Educational Research and Improvement. **Women at Thirtysomething: Paradoxes of Attainment.** by Clifford Adelman. Washington, D.C.: IA-SuDocs, 1991.

vi, 70p. Tables. (OR 91-530. MC 91-21500. OCLC 24039587. SL 91-418-P. Item 461-D-5. S/N 065-000-00451-8. ED 1.302:W 84.)

The study focuses on women who participated in the National Longitudinal Study of the High School Class of 1972 up through thirty-two years old. Despite having educational achievements superior to those of men, women's earnings were less by comparison.

632. Partnow, Elaine. **The New Quotable Woman: From Eve to the Present.** New York: Facts on File, 1992. 720p. Indexes. LC 91-25960. ISBN 0-8160-2134-1.

A combined edition of Partnow's *The Quotable Woman, 1800-1981* (see entry 633) and *The Quotable Woman: Eve to 1799* (see entry 634), the source incorporates 15,000 quotations culled from approximately 2,500 women. The thematic text can be efficiently accessed by means of subject, biographical, occupation, and nationality/ethnicity indexes.

633. Partnow, Elaine, comp. and ed. **The Quotable Woman: 1800-1981.** Rev. ed. New York: Facts on File, 1984. 608p. Indexes. ISBN 0-8160-2134-1.

634. Partnow, Elaine, with Claudia B. Alexander, comps. and eds. **The Quotable Woman from Eve to 1799.** New York: Facts on File, 1985. 533p. Indexes. LC 82-15511. ISBN 0-87196-307-8.

No other reference tool offers the depth and number of quotations (20,000 in the 1984 volume alone) attributed solely to women. The subject and biographical-fact indexes provide access via dates, nationality, profession, family relations, and honors.

635. Taeuber, Cynthia, comp. and ed. **Statistical Handbook on Women in America.** Phoenix: Oryx, 1991. 385p. Index, tables. LC 90-41624. ISBN 0-89774-609-0.

The book's tables (437 in all) delineate various aspects of the lifestyles of women since World War II; for example, crime, demographics, economic status, education, employment, health, political behavior. Each topical section is prefaced by a survey essay.

636. Zophy, Angela Howard, ed. **Handbook of American Women's History.** Hamden, CT: Garland, 1990. 763p. Bibl. (Garland Reference Library of the Humanities, v.696.) LC 89-17120. ISBN 0-8240-8744-5.

The concise essays (generally ranging from 250 to 350 words) span women's movements, historical events, literary and art works, and notable figures. An informative source, despite the relatively skimpy coverage of colonial times and minority women.

Indexes

637. Ireland, Norma O., ed. **Index to Women of the World from Ancient to Modern Times: Biographies and Portraits.** Metuchen, NJ: Scarecrow, 1970. 573p. LC 75-120841. ISBN 0-8108-2012-9.

638. Ireland, Norma O., ed. **Index to Women of the World from Ancient to Modern Times: A Supplement.** Metuchen, NJ: Scarecrow, 1988. 774p. LC 87-35934. ISBN 0-8108-2092-7.

The entries, arranged alphabetically by name, provide birth and death dates, field of activity, and references to sources. The 1970 volume cites approximately 2,500 women appearing in almost 1,000 collective biographies, several magazines, and various compilations. The supplement accesses almost 400 sources from the 1970s and early 1980s, broadening the original listing as well as inserting many new women.

639. Manning, Beverley. **We Shall Be Heard: An Index to Speeches by American Women, 1978 to 1985.** Metuchen, NJ: Scarecrow, 1988. 620p. Indexes. LC 88-6644. ISBN 0-8160-2122-2.

The main text (i.e., author index) cites 2,500 women, noting the monographs, serials, and government publications where each speech can be located. The speeches—concerned with a wide variety of topics—are by entertainers, feminists, politicians, and historical personages. Title and subject indexes have also been included.

640. **The New York Times Cumulative Subject & Personal Name Index: Women, 1965-1975.** New York: Microfilming Corp. of America, 1978. 1,150p. Illus.; indexes, bibl.

Utilizing the same format as the *New York Times Index,* the material is organized under nine main headings (each of which has an introduction summarizing relevant trends and listing prominent women) such as "Personal Concerns and Interests" and "Labor Market, Business and Finance." These sections are broken down into thirty-eight chapters; these are each further subdivided by more specific subjects. The information included here has been selected with the aim of reflecting the evolution of female roles during this period. Access is enhanced by geographic, name, organization, and subject indexes.

641. Jay, Susan, ed. **Women's Studies Index.** Annual. Boston: G. K. Hall, 1989- .

The 100-odd titles now indexed include popular women's magazines, feminist publications in a wide array subject fields, and periodicals focusing on lesbians, racially-diverse populations, and foreign countries. Author, title, and subject headings (along with cross-references) are integrated into one listing. The subject terms are based on Library of Congress headings.

Homosexuality

(See also: Social Phenomena—Feminism, pp. 123, 190, 214, 232)

Bibliographies

642. Grier, Barbara. **The Lesbian in Literature.** 3rd ed. Tallahassee, FL: Naiad, 1981. 168p. Illus. LC 81-82859. ISBN 0-930044-23-1.

The 7,000 entries (arranged alphabetically by author) focus on novels, short stories, poetry, plays, fictionalized biography, and—to a lesser extent, nonfiction material—"concerned with Lesbianism or having Lesbian characters." Grier employs a coding system that uses letters (i.e., A, B, C) to denote degree of lesbian content and asterisks (1-3) to indicate quality.

Indexes

643. Grier, Barbara. **Lesbiana: Book Reviews from the Ladder, 1966-1972.** Reno, NV: Naiad, 1976. 309p. Index. LC 76-45683 pap.

Originally appearing as the "Lesbiana" column of the lesbian journal *The Ladder,* the material covers the literature of lesbianism, including books, magazines, newspapers, and films. Arranged chronologically, the source supplements *The Lesbian in Literature: A Bibliography* (2nd ed., Naiad: 1975), by Gene Damon (Grier), Jan Watson, and Robin Jordan. An author index has also been provided.

644. Potter, Clare, comp. and ed. **The Lesbian Periodicals Index.** Tallahassee, FL: Naiad, 1986. 413p. LC 85-21798. ISBN 0-930044-74-6.

The tool represents an author and subject guide to forty-two lesbian periodicals. The book organizes these periodicals—many of which are no longer published—alphabetically and includes complete publishing data for them. Four sections compose the index: (1) "Authors and Subjects," (2) "Lesbian Writings," (3) "Book Reviews," and (4) "Visual Arts."

Immigration

(See also: Social Phenomena—Minorities, pp. 133-41, 189-90, 233-34)

Dictionaries

645. Cordasco, Francesco, ed. **Dictionary of American Immigration History.** Metuchen, NJ: Scarecrow, 1990. 784p. Bibl. LC 89-37041. ISBN 0-8108-2241-5.

The entries (over 2,500 in all) consist of comprehensive surveys of ethnic groups, profiles of prominent individuals associated with colonization movements, and concise profiles of organizations.

Handbooks

646. Coldham, Peter Wilson. **The Complete Book of Emigrants. Volume 1: 1607-1660; Volume 2: 1661-1699; Volume 3: 1700-1750.** Baltimore, MD: Genealogical Publishing, 1987; 1990; 1992. 600p.; 900p.; 743p. Indexes. ISBN 0-8063-1192-4; 0-8063-1282-3; 0-8063-1334-X.

These volumes provide extracts from the original records concerning the emigrants to America (over 75,000 extracts thus far, with a fourth volume spanning the period 1751-1776 due for release in 1993). The entries—organized by year and subdivided by date of record—give name, age, occupation, residence, ship, destination, and source citation. Indexes to persons and ships are located in each volume.

Lifestyles

Encyclopedias

647. Wilson, Charles Reagan, and William Ferris, eds. **Encyclopedia of Southern Culture.** Chapel Hill: University of North Carolina, 1989. 1634p. Illus., maps, index. LC 88-17084. ISBN 0-8078-1823-2.

Concerned with the Confederate states or "wherever southern culture is found," this exhaustive source is divided into twenty-four alphabetically arranged parts representing academic fields or cultural themes (e.g., agriculture, music, violence). These units each comprise three segments: an interpretive essay by one of more than 800 contributors; thematic articles, arranged alphabetically; and more focused biographical and topical entries (also arranged in alphabetical order).

Handbooks

648.   Baldrige, Letitia. **Letita Baldrige's Complete Guide to the New Manners for the '90s.** New York: Rawson Associates, 1990. 646p. Index. LC 89-43052. ISBN 0-89256-320-6.

Following the introduction, "Manners from the Heart," the author provides an authoritative update on social behavior for the 1990s, incorporating advice on present day activities and concerns, such as wind surfing, the use of Ms., and telephone answering machines.

Indexes

649.   Ireland, Norma Olin. **Index to America: Life and Customs—Nineteenth Century.** Metuchen, NJ: Scarecrow, 1984. 350p. LC 76-7196. ISBN 0-8108-1661-X.

This "representative sample" (161 popular books) covers works that delineate nineteenth century life; e.g., domestic affairs, amusements, education, public figures, science, politics. It should be noted that the majority of titles covered were published after 1960.

Magic

Bibliographies

650.   Gill, Robert. **Magic as a Performing Art: A Bibliography of Conjuring.** New York: R. R. Bowker, 1976. 252p. Indexes. (College of Librarianship Wales Bibliographies.) ISBN 0-85935-038-X.

This listing of over 1,000 English-language titles is confined largely to the 1935-1975 period. The entries—geared to collectors, librarians, and practicing conjurers—include descriptive and evaluative annotations. Although availability was a prime consideration in the compilation of the bibliography, certain resources may be difficult for users in the 1990s to locate. Subject, title, and name indexes have also been provided.

Encyclopedias

651.   Waters, T. A. **The Encyclopedia of Magic and Magicians.** New York: Facts on File, 1988. x, 372p. Illus. ISBN 0-8160-1349-7.

This engaging source comprehensively covers Western subjects with a particular emphasis on the period from 1800 to the late 1980s. Entries are divided between individuals (with a focus on their respective contributions) and tricks (described in detail with its key exponents noted). Aside from title and author references within the text, no bibliography has been provided.

Minorities—General

(See also: Popular Literature—Minority Writers, pp. 66-68; Social Phenomena—Minorities, pp. 133-41, 189-90, 233-34; Sports, pp. 5-7, 147-70, 192-95, 215-20, 235-38)

Atlases

652.   Allen, James, and Eugene Turner. **We the People: An Atlas of America's Ethnic Diversity.** New York: Macmillan, 1988. 315p. Index. LC 87-28194. ISBN 0-02-901420-4.

Based primarily upon the 1980 census, the tool employs 111 color-coded maps to reveal the distribution and density of sixty-seven ethnic and racial groups for each of the 3,100 U.S. counties, parishes, etc. Down-scaled maps show contrasting data for the 1920 census, and the appendixes include tables of ethnic and racial populations organized by state and county. Access is enhanced by an ethnic group and geographic location index.

Bibliographies

653.   Weinberg, Meyer, comp. **Racism in the United States: A Comprehensive Classified Bibliography.** Westport, CT: Greenwood, 1990. 682p. LC 89-78118. ISBN 0-313-27390-1.

The listing encompasses sexism and anti-Semitism in addition to racism. Organized by eighty-seven subject headings and subdivided alphabetically by author, the entries will be of value to high school students up through graduate level researchers.

Encyclopedias

654.   Thernstrom, Stephan, ed. **Harvard Encyclopedia of American Ethnic Groups.** Cambridge, MA: Harvard University, 1980. 1,102p. Maps. LC 80-17756. ISBN 0-674-37512-2.

The work surveys the historical, cultural, religious, social, and economic features of 106 ethnic minority, religious, and regional groups. In addition, the text includes twenty-nine exhaustive articles on related topics (e.g., migration) and statistical tables.

Handbooks

655.   Buenker, John D., and Lorman Ratner, eds. **Multiculturalism in the United States: A Comparative Guide to Acculturation and Ethnicity.** Westport, CT: Greenwood, 1992. 280p. Index, bibl. ISBN 0-313-25374-9.

Featuring a wide array of scholars who cover ethnic groups at various points in American history, each section focuses on the institutions that have held these groups together. The role such institutions have played in the groups' assimilation into mainstream society is also emphasized.

Minorities—African Americans

Almanacs

656.   Ploski, Harry A,. and James Williams, comps. and eds. **The Negro Almanac: A Reference Work on African Americans.** 5th ed. Detroit: Gale Research, 1989. 1622p. bibl. LC 86-72654. ISBN 0-8103-7706-3.

This classic tool, which first appeared in 1967, is organized into thirty-three chapters. They include statistical data of both a historical and contemporary bent, biographies, an extensive chronology of black history through 1989, and essays on broad topics (with an emphasis on black culture in the present day).

Bibliographies

657.   **The Black Experience in Children's Books, 1989,** by the Black Experience in Children's Books Committee, New York Public Library. New York: New York Public Library, 1989. 64p.

The work annotates 450 books devoted to black culture. Arranged geographically (i.e., the United States, Africa, Latin America, the Caribbean, and England), entries include picture books, fiction, folktales, and biographies.

658.   Consortium for Research on Black Adolescence, with Velma McBride Murry and Georgie Winter. **Black Adolescence: Current Issues and Annotated Bibliography.** Boston: G. K. Hall, 1990. LC 89-26995. ISBN 0-8161-9080-1.

The source is divided into topical sections covering developmental issues, psychological and physical health, academic performance, educational and occupational choice, employment, family relationships, sexuality, teen parenting and other topics. Each section includes overviews, applicable statistics, documentation, and a discussion of contemporary implications.

Biographies

659.   Altman, Susan. **Extraordinary Black Americans from Colonial to Contemporary Times.** Chicago: Children's Press, 1989. 240p. Illus., bibl. LC 89-11977. ISBN 0-516-00581.

Among the eighty-five individuals profiled here are both famous black Americans, such as Martin Luther King, Jr., and Jesse Jackson, as well as more obscure historical figures who have left their mark on U.S. history. The work also includes fifteen concise essays focusing on notable historical events.

660.   Cloyd, Iris, ed. **Who's Who Among Black Americans.** Detroit: Gale Research, 1985/86-. Biennial. Indexes.

The tool covers contemporary African Americans from a wide range of fields, including corporate executives, government officials, physicians, lawyers, athletes, artists, mass media professionals, scientists, and educators—approximately 17,000 entries in each issue. An obituary section covers the biographees who had died since the publication of the immediately prior edition. Biographical and occupational indexes have also been provided.

661.   Congress. House. Office of the Historian. **Black Americans in Congress, 1870-1989.** by Bruce A. Ragsdale and Joel D. Treese. Washington, D.C.: GPO-SuDocs, 1990. xii, 164p. Illus. LC 89-600409. (House Document No. 101-117. MC 90-15419. OCLC 20935421. SL 90-163-P. Item 1008-E. S/N 052-070-00892-6; 052-071-00891-8 pap.)

Arranged alphabetically by surname, the directory is composed of concise bios of the sixty-five African Americans serving in the U.S. Congress from 1870 (when Hiram Revels of Mississippi, the first black congressman, occupied his Senate seat on February 25, 1870) through 1989.

662.   Gaymon. Gloria Leaks. **215 African American Women You Should Know About: Trivia Facts.** Philadelphia: Nationtime Publications, 1992. 90p. Indexes. ISBN 0-9633393-2-X pap.

Despite the omission of some notable women (e.g., Nikki Giovanni) and the absence of cross-references, the source is a useful compendium of information regarding African American women. Century, profession, and name indexes have also been provided.

663.   Hawkins, Walter L. **African American Biographies: Profiles of 558 Current Men and Women.** Jefferson, NC: McFarland, 1992. 490p. Illus., index. LC 91-50938. ISBN 0-89950-664-X.

The source includes 558 individuals, one-third of whom are not profiled elsewhere. The information relates primarily to careers rather than the biographees personal lives.

664.   LaBlanc, Michael L. **Contemporary Black Biography: Profiles from the International Black Community.** Vol. 1-, Detroit: Gale Research, 1992-. Illus., index, bibl. 1992 ed.: 261p. LC 91-821. ISBN 0-8103-5546-9.

Defining "contemporary" as individual born as far back as the nineteenth century, the work provides seventy-one biographies—two- to four-pages in length—covering people from a variety of areas, including the arts and the entertainment world, law, politics, the civil rights movement, and business. Some of the entries are not listed in other sources, particularly a number of personalities fairly new to the public arena.

665.   Lee, George L. **Interesting People: Black American History Makers.** Jefferson, NC: McFarland, 1989. 210p. Illus. LC 88-43542. ISBN 0-89950-403-5.

Lee covers more than 200 African Americans; the profiles are arranged in chronological order and are accompanied by his pen-and-ink drawings of each subject. The entries include political leaders, artists, athletes, scientists, writers, and soldiers, from such notables as James Baldwin and George Washington Carver to more obscure individuals like Sadie Tanner Alexander (the first black woman to receive a Ph.D).

666.   Litwack, Leon, and August Meier, eds. **Black Leaders of the Nineteenth Century.** Champaign: University of Illinois, 1988. 344p. Illus. LC 87-19439. ISBN 0-252-01506-1.

The work is divided into sixteen chapters, each of which profiles a significant African American leader from the nineteenth century.

667.   Logan, Rayford W., and Michael R. Winston, eds. **Dictionary of American Negro Biography.** New York: W. W. Norton, 1983. 680p. Bibl. ISBN 0-393-01513-0.

The entries are devoted to approximately 800 historically significant African Americans who died prior to 1970. The source complements *Dictionary of American Biography* (Reprint Services Corporation, 1992) and *Notable American Women* (see entries 615, 616).

668.   **Profiles of Black Mayors in America.** Compiled and edited by the Joint Center for Political Studies. Jeanne J. Fox, associate director of research. Chicago: Johnson, 1977. 247p. Illus., index. LC 76-40949.

The book is divided into three main portions: (1) "The Black Mayor," which provides a historical survey of both black political involvement and black mayors; (2) "Profiles of Black Mayors," which is composed of individual biographies arranged by state and then subdivided by last name of mayor (a separate listing notes twenty-eight mayors for whom not enough information could be found to construct a profile); and (3) "Appendices and Statistical References," which includes several tables and charts (e.g., "Cities with Black Mayors Ranked by Population," "Majority White Communities with Black Mayors and Method of Election").

669.   Smith, Jessie Carney, ed. **Notable Black American Women.** Detroit: Gale Research, 1992. 1334p. Illus., bibl. ISBN 1-8103-4749-0.

Although not a truly comprehensive volume, the text includes essays on 500 African American women born between 1730 and 1958. The entries are generally very well written and cover achievement in all areas of human endeavor.

Dictionaries

670.   Miller, Randall M., and John David Smith. **Dictionary of Afro-American Slavery.** Westport, CT: Greenwood, 1988. 866p. Maps, index, bibl. LC 87-37543. ISBN 0-313-23814-6.

This tool covers a wide variety of topics relating to the overriding theme, including historical figures, religion, geographic entities, economics, and legal developments. Among the supplementary material is a chronological outline and encapsulated notes about the more than 230 contributors.

Directories

671.   **The Black Resource Guide.** 1990-91 ed. Washington, D.C.: Black Resource Guide, 1990. Annual. 316p. LC 85-91077. ISBN 0-9608374-7-7.

The directory-type entries include various businesses, associations, organizations, book publishers, bookstores and other media, adoption services, institutions of higher education, churches, and other entities of value to blacks. Statistical information on black economic and social concerns is also provided.

672.   Smith, Darren, ed. **Black Americans Information Directory, 1990-91.** Detroit: Gale Research, 1990. 424p. Index. LC 90-648616. ISBN: 0-8103-7443-9.

The tool's seventeen chapters cover nonprofit, private, public, religious, educational, and governmental organizations; notable library collections, resource centers, awards, and educational programs; and the mass media. An organization/publication name and key word index has also been provided.

Encyclopedias

673.   Low, W. Augustus, ed. **Encyclopedia of Black America.** New York: McGraw-Hill, 1981. 921p. Index, bibl. ISBN 0-07-038834-2; 0-306-80221-X pap.

This exhaustive volume incorporates 325 articles and over 1,000 biographies, signed and arranged alphabetically with numerous cross-references. Major coverage has been given to such topics as African American literature, dance, athletics, religion, and science.

674. Lowery, Charles D., and John F. Marzalek. **Encyclopedia of African-American Civil Rights: From Emancipation to the Present.** Greenwood, 1992. 672p. Illus., index, bibl. LC 91-27814. ISBN 0-313-25011-1.

The work's more than 800 entries encompass "grass-roots" participants in addition to significant laws, court cases, events, and publications.

Handbooks

675. Bureau of the Census. **The Black Population in the United States: March 1990 and 1989.** by Claudette E. Bennett. Washington, D.C.: IA-SuDocs, 1991. v, 141p. Charts, tables. (Current Population Reports, Series P-20, No. 448. MC 92-1284. SL 91-700-P. Item 142-C-1. S/N 803-005-00047-8) ISBN 0-1602-9359-6.

Drawn largely from the Current Population Surveys conducted in March 1989 and 1990, the report offers a statisitical delineation of the demographic, social, and economic features of African Americans.

676. Cantor, George. **Historic Landmarks of Black America.** Detroit: Gale Research, 1991. Illus. ISBN 0-8103-7809-4.

Cantor, a former *Detroit Free Press* travel editor, cites more than 300 African American landmarks (e.g., churches, battlefields, parks, museums, grave sites, schools) covering forty-six states, the District of Columbia, and Ontario. It is divided into six geographical regions, with entries arranged alphabetically by state and then by city. Each entry includes a description, location, hours, admission fee, facilities (food, lodging), special programs, telephone number, and notation (when needed) of permanent exhibits, displays, and additional attractions.

The guide is further enhanced by a regional outline map with numbered sites preceding each regional listing; "A Brief History of Black America," an essay by Cornell University professor Robert L. Harris; and a timeline of key dates in African American history between 1539 and 1989.

677. Department of Defense. **Black Americans in Defense of Our Nation: A Pictorial Documentary of the Black American Male and Female Participation and Involvement in the Military Affairs of the United States.** Washington, D.C.: IA-SuDocs, 1991. 300p. Illus. (MC 91-21295. OCLC 24145850. SL 91-499-P. Item 306. S/N 008-000-00585-1.) ISBN 0-1603-3825-5.

With coverage dating back to 1775, the tool provides profiles of notable African American four-star generals and admirals; lists of African American graduates of the U.S. military service academies; and photographs of African American executives in the Defense Department, recipients of the Medal of Honor, and generals and flag officers past and present.

678. **Ebony Pictorial History of Black Americans.** 4 Vols. Chicago: Johnson Publishing, 1971-1973. Illus. ISBN 0-87485-073-8.

Focusing on the contribution of African Americans to American life, the work is chronologically arranged as follows: Volume 1—African roots through the Civil War; Volume 2—Reconstruction through the Supreme Court decision of Brown vs. Topeka, Kansas, Board of Education (1954); Volume 3—Civil Rights Movement to the end of the 1960s; Volume 4—Developments between 1970 and 1972.

679.   Horton, Carrell P., and Jessie Carney Smith, eds. **Statistical Record of Black America.** Detroit: Gale Research, 1990. Biennial (projected). 1,000p. ISBN 0-8103-7724-1.
The source provides approximately 1,000 graphs, tables, and charts of statistics arranged by topic (e.g., the arts, professions, military affairs, population, and religion).

680.   Smith, Jessie Carney, ed. **Images of Blacks in American Culture: A Reference Guide to Information Sources.** New York: Greenwood, 1988. xvii, 390p. Bibl. LC 87-24964. ISBN 0-313-24844-3.
Following Smith's survey of the stereotypical views of blacks in American culture in the preface, an array of experts provide chapters depicting the roles of blacks in American art, 1700-1900; the musical stage; film and TV; instrumental music and song; literary criticism; children's books; popular perceptions of females; popular perceptions of males; and toys, games, and dolls. The concluding chapter lists resources and collections in Black Americana, arranged by state.

Minorities—Asian Americans

Bibliographies

681.   Jenkins, Esther C., and Mary C. Austin. **Literature for Children about Asians and Asian Americans: Analysis and Annotated Bibliography, with Additional Readings for Adults.** Westport, CT: Greenwood, 1987. 303p. Indexes, bibl. LC 87-23627. ISBN 0-313-25970-4.
The book's main groupings—Chinese, Japanese, Koreans, and Southeast Asians—are subdivided by a survey of the literature, an annotated bibliography organized by grade level, and a reading list for adults. Author, title, and subject indexes have also been provided.

Dictionaries

682.   Hyung-Chan, Kim, ed. **Dictionary of Asian American History.** Westport, CT: Greenwood, 1986. 627p. ISBN 0-313-23760-3.
The work incorporates approximately 800 alphabetically arranged entries concerned with people, places, events, and concepts related to the Asian American lifestyle, in addition to fifteen essays providing broader brushstrokes (e.g., notable subgroups in the United States).

Directories

683.   Haseltine, Patricia. **East and Southeast Asia Material Culture in North America: Collections, Historical Sites, and Festivals.** Westport, CT: Greenwood, 1989. 163p. ISBN 0-313-25343-9.
Arranged by state (and Canadian province), the tool delineates notable library and archival collections, historical sites, and Asian festivals.

Handbooks

684.   Li, Marjorie H, and Peter Li, comps. and eds. **Understanding Asian Americans: A Curriculum Resource Guide.** New York: Neal-Schuman, 1990. 186p. Bibl. ISBN 1-55570-047-0.

The tool is divided into three sections: Part 1 reproduces a survey on the perception of Asian Americans by non-Asians and by Asian Americans, Part 2 sets forth twenty-five classroom programs concerned with promoting interracial and intercultural understanding, and Part 3 provides insights regarding the implementation of these activities within the school curricula.

Minorities—Hispanic Americans

Bibliographies

685.   Schon, Isabel. **A Hispanic Heritage: A Guide to Juvenile Books about People and Cultures.** Metuchen, NJ: Scarecrow, 1980. 178p. LC 80-10935. ISBN 0-8108-1290-8.

686.   Schon, Isabel. **A Hispanic Heritage: A Guide to Juvenile Books about Hispanic People and Cultures. Series II.** Metuchen, NJ: Scarecrow, 1985. 164p. LC 84-13964. ISBN 0-8108-1727-6.

687.   Schon, Isabel. **A Hispanic Heritage: A Guide to Juvenile Books about Hispanic People and Cultures. Series III.** Metuchen, NJ: 1988. 158p. LC 88-18094. ISBN 0-8108-2133-8.
      These nonfiction, drama, poetry, folklore, etc., sources (in the English language) concerned with Latin Americans, Spaniards, and Hispanics in the United States are supplemented by critical annotations that both recommend and provide warnings as to their educational value.

Dictionaries

688.   Meier, Matt S. **Mexican American Biographies: A Historical Dictionary, 1836-1987.** Westport, CT: Greenwood, 1988. 300p. Index. LC 87-12025. ISBN 0-313-24521-5.
      The concisely worded entries focus on the activities for which each person is best known. The appendix organizes the biographees according to area of activity and subdivides them by state. A subject index has also been provided.

689.   Meier, Matt S., and Feliciano Rivera. **Dictionary of Mexican American History.** Westport, CT: Greenwood, 1981. 498p. Bibl. LC 80-24750. ISBN 0-313-21203-1.
      The 1,000-odd entries cover individuals and events since the Texas Revolution (1835-1836). The appendix includes a chronology of Mexican American history, texts of notable documents (e.g., the Treaty of Guadalupe Hidalgo), a glossary, and statistics on areas such as population trends.

Directories

690.   Graham, Joe S., comp. **Hispanic-American Material Culture: An Annotated Directory of Collections, Sites, Archives, and Festivals in the United States.** Westport, CT: Greenwood, 1989. 257p. (Material Culture Directories, no. 2.) ISBN 0-313-24789-7.
      Confined to institutions in the United States and Puerto Rico, the entries provide key personnel, hours of service, usage rules, and descriptive information.

691.   Schorr, Alan Edward. **Hispanic Resource Directory, 1992-1994.** Juneau, AK: Denali, 1992. 380p. Indexes. ISBN 0-938737-26-0.

The 6,200 entries are organized along the following lines: federal, state, and local programs; organizations and associations; research centers; libraries and museums; state and local Hispanic commissions; Hispanic studies programs; educational institutions with a significant Hispanic enrollment; migrant and bilingual education; migrant health; human rights agencies; Hispanic chambers of commerce; minority and small business programs; Hispanic employment programs; Hispanic print and electronic media; and Latin American and Spanish diplomatic offices.

692.   Smith, Darren L., and Donna L. Weyd, eds. **Hispanic Americans Information Directory, 1990-91.** Detroit: Gale Research, 1990. 395p. Index. ISBN 0-8103-7444-7.

Included among the work's 4,500 entries are publications; national, state, and local Hispanic associations; print and broadcast media; bilingual education programs and Hispanic studies; and governmental agencies of interest to Hispanic Americans.

Handbooks

693.   Department of Defense. **Hispanics in America's Defense.** Washington, D.C.: GPO-SuDocs, 1990. iv, 237p. Illus. (MC 90-14239. OCLC 21889022. SL 90-343-P. Item 306. S/N 008-046000133-2.)

In documenting the contributions of Hispanic Americans to the American armed forces from the Hispanic exploration of North America (1492-1541) to current times, the volume incorporates a listing of Hispanic American recipients of the Medal of Honor, biographies of Hispanic American generals and flag officers, a roll call of Hispanic American graduates of the U.S. service academies between 1966-1989, and photos of Department of Defense civilian employees affiliated with the senior executive service.

694.   Schick, Frank, and Renee Schick, eds. **Statistical Handbook of U.S. Hispanics.** Phoenix, AZ: Oryx, 1991. 272p. Index. LC 90-48167. ISBN 0-89774-554-X.

The work's reprints of statistical charts, tables, and graphs (largely drawn from sources published in the second half of the 1980s) are arranged under the following topical headings: demographics, immigration, education, politics, employment, economic status, health, and social characteristics. The text is arranged thematically with a subject index permitting access to specific aspects of the data.

Minorities—Jewish Americans

Biographies

695.   Wigoder, Geoffrey. **Dictionary of Jewish Biography.** New York: Simon & Schuster, 1991. 567p. Illus., bibl. LC 90-29276. ISBN 0-13-210105-X.

The tool profiles almost 1,000 Jews throughout recorded history "who have left an indelible mark on Humankind." The entries include many contemporary figures, many of which are Americans. It is notable not only for first-rate writing, but for the inclusion of boxed inserts giving quotations or anecdotes about many of the biographees.

Encyclopedias

696. Fischel, Jack, and Sanford Pinsker. **Jewish-American History and Culture: An Encyclopedia.** Garland, 1992. 710p. Index. (Reference Library of Social Sciences, Vol. 429.) LC 91-14188. ISBN 0-8240-6622-7.

The source combines concise entries with broad essays in covering individuals, locations, institutions, events, and concepts relevant to American Jews. Despite some omissions, the substantiative approach characterizing most of the entries renders it a worthwhile volume for all types of users.

Minorities—Native Americans

Atlases

697. Prucha, Francis Paul. **Atlas of American Indian Affairs.** Lincoln: University of Nebraska, 1990. LC 90-675000. ISBN 0-8032-3689-1.

A valuable complement to Carl Waldman's definitive *Atlas of the North American Indians* (see entry 698), its maps portray native American populations by counties, urban areas, local cessions, reservations, agencies, schools, and hospitals (based upon U.S. census data). A "Notes and References" section provides statistics and sources relating to the maps.

698. Waldman, Carl. **Atlas of the North American Indians.** New York: Facts on File, 1985. 288p. Illus., index, bibl. LC 83-9020. ISBN 0-87196-850-9; 0-8160-2136-8 pap.

The text is supplemented by seventy-five photos and 120 two-color maps depicting themes, such as migration movements and military battles. The appendixes provide a chronology of historical developments, Indian place names, current tribal reservations and locations, and a directory of museums and historical societies.

Bibliographies

699. Kuipers, Barbara J. **American Indian Reference Books for Children and Young Adults.** Englewood, CO: Libraries Unlimited, 1991. 176p. (Libraries Unlimited Data Book.) Indexes. LC 91-6880. ISBN 0-87287-745-0.

The tool's two major sections include (1) an analysis of reference materials for native American youth (appended by an evaluative checklist for educators and librarians), and (2) an annotated bibliography of 200 or so works composing a core reference collection. The listing is arranged by Dewey classification fields and subdivided alphabetically by author. Author-title and subject indexes have also been provided.

Biographies

700. Waldman, Carl. **Who Was Who in Native American History: Indians and Non-Indians from Early Contacts through 1900.** New York: Facts on File, 1990. 416p. Illus. ISBN 0-8160-1797-2.

The 1,000-odd biographees include tribal leaders, warriors, soldiers, explorers, army scouts, traders, artists, government officials, reformers, and scholars. Each entry includes tribal affiliation, key dates, his or her legacy, and other notable biographical data.

Dictionaries

701. Leitch, Barbara A. **A Concise Dictionary of Indian Tribes of North America.**
Algonac, MI: Reference Publications, 1979. 646p. Index, bibl. ISBN 0-917256-48-4.

The entries cover 281 native American tribes, noting the history, location, culture, religion, and current status of each. The work is supplemented by maps and a glossary.

702. Wolfson, Evleyn. **From Abenaki to Zuni: A Dictionary of Native America Tribes.** New York: Walker, 1988. 215p. Illus. ISBN 0-8027-6790-7.

Geared to school-aged children, the tool covers sixty-eight native American tribes. The two-to four-page entries provide tribal name, pronunciation, and meaning; cultural area; geographical location; dwelling type; clothing material; mode of transportation; and staple food.

Directories

703. La Potin, Armand S., ed. **Native American Voluntary Organizations.** Westport, CT: Greenwood, 1987. 204p. (Ethnic American Voluntary Organizations Series.) Index. LC 86-25764. ISBN 0-313-23633-X.

The source surveys 121 of the more historically significant voluntary American Indian organizations of the nineteenth and twentieth centuries. The appendix lists organizations in chronological order as well as under one of four headings: political-reformist, cultural-educational, social-fraternal, or professional.

704. Library of Congress. American Folklife Center. **The Federal Cylinder Project: A Guide to Field Cylinder Collections in Federal Agencies. Vol. 5: California Indian Catalog, Middle and South American Indian Catalog, Southwestern Indian Catalog—I.** Ed. by Judith A. Gray and Edwin J. Schupman. Washington, D.C.: IA-SuDocs, 1990. ix, 528p. Maps, bibl. (Studies in American Folklife, No. 3, Vol. 5.) (MC 91-5399. OCLC 08785183. SL 90-724-P. Item 818-G-4. S/N 030-000-00218-1) LC 82-600289. ISBN 0-8444-0677-5.

Fifth in a six-volume set (the others don't fit the geographic parameters of this listing), which includes catalogs of American Indian collections in the Federal Cylinder Project series, it contains three catalogs encompassing tribes from California, Mexico, and South America, and the Southwestern United States. The entries—grouped by collections—include cylinder number, Archive of Folk Culture number, original number, recording time, quality, description of recording, identification of performer, location and site of recording, and notes.

Encyclopedias

705. Klein, Barry T. **Reference Encyclopedia of the American Indian.** 5th ed. West Nyack, NY: Todd; distr., ABC-Clio, 1990. 1078p. LC 90-070527. ISBN 0-915-34416-5.

This cornucopia of information on native Americans is divided into four sections: (1) Reservations, tribal councils, government agencies, associations, crafts centers, health facilities, Indian schools, colleges offering courses in native American history and culture, and information centers arranged alphabetically by state with directory-type data; (2) a similar listing for Canada; (3) a bibliography (approximately 3,500 books) arranged alphabetically by title with a subject index; and (4) a biographical listing of 2,400 contemporary Indians and others presently involved in Indian activities.

706. Waldman, Carl. **Encyclopedia of Native American Tribes.** New York: Facts on File, 1988. 293p. LC 86-29066. ISBN 0-8160-1421-3.

The work provides historical background, major conflicts, and cultural information for approximately 150 North American Indian tribes (arranged alphabetically by tribal name with entries under cultural names and language families).

Handbooks

707. **The Chelsea House Series on Indians of North America.** New York: Chelsea House, 1987-1988. 53 Vols. Illus., maps, bibl. ISBN 1-55546-685-0.

Each volume provides historical background, contemporary problems (e.g., poverty), and cultural 'issues of a particular tribe; the tribes range from well-known ones to obscure entities such as the Quapaw.

708. Indian Health Service. **Trends in Indian Health, 1991.** Rockville, MD: IA, 1991. vi, 93p. Charts, tables. (MC 92-4635. OCLC 20789041. SL 91-730-P. Item 486-I-3) LC 90-641173.

The source delineates the Indian Health Service program and the general health of native Americans under the following headings: Indian Health Service structure, population statistics, natality and infant/maternal mortality statistics, general mortality statistics, patient care statistics, and community health statistics.

709. Moss, Joyce, and George Wilson. **Peoples of the World: North Americans: The Culture, Geographical Setting, and Historical Background of 37 North American Peoples.** Detroit: Gale Research, 1991. 441p. Illus. ISBN 0-8103-7768-3.

The tool focuses on the history, population, location, language, and culture of thirty-seven (three of which have since disappeared) different groups of native Americans.

710. Stuart, Paul. **Nations within a Nation: Historical Statistics of American Indians.** Westport, CT: Greenwood, 1987. 251p. Index. ISBN 0-313-23813-8.

Stuart deploys text and statistical tables to gauge the past and present status of native Americans with regard to land and climate, population, relocation and urbanization, vital statistics and health, government activities, health care and education, employment and earnings, and economic development.

711. Smithsonian Institution. **Handbook of North American Indians. Vol. 7. Northwest Coast.** Edited by Wayne Suttles. Series edited by William C. Sturtevant. 20 Vols. Washington, D.C.: GPO-SuDocs. Illus., index, maps, tables, bibl.

This twenty-volume set attempts to provide a historical and cultural overview of native American societies. Series titles applicable to this compilation include *Volume 4: History of Indian-White Relations; Volume 7: Northwest Coast; Volumes 9-10: Southwest; Volume 11: Great Basin;* and *Volume 15: Northeast.*

Space Exploration

Dictionaries

712. Reithmaier, Larry. **The Aviation/Space Dictionary.** 7th ed. Blue Ridge Summit, PA: Aero/TAB Books, 1990. 461p. Illus. LC 89-17948. ISBN 0-8306-8092-6.

Containing more than 8,000 terms (many updated from the 6th edition, published in 1980), the source encompasses air traffic control, meteorology, space flight, aviation, and related topics. The appendixes (sixteen in all) survey new trends in the field.

Handbooks

713. **Astronauts and Cosmonauts: Biographical and Statistical Data.** Washington, D.C.: GPO, 1989. 447p. Illus., pap. (S/N 052-070-06065-4.)

Concise biographies of all U.S. astronauts and most Soviet cosmonauts (215 in all), as of June 30, 1989, are provided. Also included are crew rosters for 121 different missions and a chronology of key travel events.

UFOs

Atlases

714. Spencer, John. **World Atlas of UFO's.** New York: Smithmark. 1992. 192p. Illus. ISBN 0-8317-9498-4.

This is a compendium of abductions, sightings, and close encounters with extraterrestrials, etc. It compiles cases from around the world in concise eyewitness reports, complemented by an abundance of photographs and artists' recreations.

War

Almanacs

715. Summers, Harry G. **Korean War Almanac.** New York: Facts on File, 1990. 288p. Illus., maps. LC 89-33560. ISBN 0-8160-1737-9; 0-8160-2463-4 pap.

716. Summers, Harry G. **Vietnam War Almanac.** New York: Facts on File, 1987. 288p. Illus., maps. LC 83-14054. ISBN 0-8160-1017-X; 0-8160-1813-8 pap.

These works are both organized in the following manner: a survey of the war's origin; a chronology of events; and the main text (arranged alphabetically), with concise entries for notable leaders and officers, skirmishes, strategies and tactics, weapons, political forces, and the impact of the war on the participating nations.

Bibliographies

(See also: Mass Media—Films, pp. 174, 198, 224)

717. Hager, Philip E., and Desmond Taylor. **The Novels of World War I: An Annotated Bibliography.** New York: Garland, 1981. 513p. Indexes, bibl. (Garland Reference Library of the Humanities, Vol. 232) LC 80-8496. ISBN 0-8240-9491-3.

The listing encompasses 884 adult and 370 juvenile novels concerning World War I followed in most cases by an annotation summarizing the plot or evaluating the work or both. The entries are arranged by reading level, then chronologically, and within each year alphabetically by author. Author and title indexes have also been provided.

718. Newman, John, with Ann Hilfinger. **Vietnam War Literature: An Annotated Bibliography of Imaginative Works about Americans Fighting in Vietnam.** 2nd ed. Metuchen, NJ: Scarecrow, 1988. 285p. Indexes, bibl. LC 88-15747. ISBN 0-8108-2155-9.

The work is organized into chapters devoted to various categories of "imaginative" work: novels, short stories, poetry, drama, and miscellaneous (e.g., comics). Entries are arranged chronologically within each chapter and are appended by descriptive annotations that occasionally include critiques. Access is enhanced by author and title indexes.

Dictionaries

719. Olson, James, ed. **Dictionary of the Vietnam War.** Westport, CT: Greenwood, 1988. 585p. Index, bibl. LC 87-12023. ISBN 0-313-24943-1; 0-87226-238-3 pap.

The source covers all facets of the war—the causes, the antiwar movement at home, chief strategies and battles, its legacy. etc. The appendix greatly enhances the work, including a topical bibliography, a chronology, census table for South Vietnam, a glossary of slang terms and acronyms, and maps of military regions.

World's Fairs

Dictionaries

720. Findling, John E., and Kimberly D. Pelle, eds. **Historical Dictionary of World's Fairs and Expositions, 1851-1988.** Westport, CT: Greenwood, 1990. 443p. Illus., index, bibl. LC 89-17217. ISBN 0-313-26023-0.

The volume consists of ninety-five chronologically arranged essays that each focus on a particular fair, exhibition, or exposition. Six appendixes complement the text: an explanation of the Bureau of International Expositions (the governing body with respect to fairs), fair statistics, fair officials, fairs not included, fairs that never existed, and fairs yet to come (1990-2000).

Chapter 10

Sports and Recreation

(See also: General References—Collecting, pp. 5-8)

General

Almanacs

721.   Meserole, Mike, ed. **The Information Please Sports Almanac.** Boston: Houghton Mifflin. Annual. 700-800p. Illus., index, bibl. pap.

In recounting a given sports year (November-October), the tool includes an article summarizing highs and lows; essays on individual sports; tables documenting final standings, championship series, award winners, coaching changes, team rankings, etc.; a necrology; rolls of the Halls of Fame; a directory of professional teams and governing organizations; and a chronological listing of stadiums and arenas used by professional teams.

Bibliographies

722.   Redekop, Paul. **Sociology of Sport: An Annotated Bibliography.** New York: Garland, 1988. 153p. Index. ISBN 0-8240-8464-0.

The work incorporates both journal literature and books from the late 1960s to 1985 devoted to the sociological analysis of sports. The majority of entries, arranged in classified order, include descriptive annotations. An author index has also been provided.

723.   Thomas, Jerry R., and Raymond A. Weiss, eds. **Completed Research in Health, Physical Education, and Recreation Including International Sources.** Annual. Washington, D.C.: Research Council of the American Alliance for Health, Physical Education, and Recreation, 1959-. 235p. Index, bibl., pap.

The document is organized into three sections: (1) an index of the subjects covered in research, (2) a bibliography of journal literature featuring research results, and (3) a listing of theses and dissertation abstracts (arranged alphabetically by university, followed by author).

724.   Wise, Suzanne. **Sports Fiction for Adults: An Annotated Bibliography of Novels, Plays, Short Stories, and Poetry with Sporting Settings.** New York: Garland, 1986. x, 203p. Index. (Garland Reference Library of the Humanities, no. 553.) ISBN 0-8240-8820-4.

Defining sports in the broadest sense of the word (e.g., including bridge), Wise has compiled 1,355 citations (novels, plays, poems, short stories) under fifty-five different sports. Although the lack of qualitative criteria for inclusion and the large quantity of out-of-print titles cited may diminish its value somewhat, the work has staked out a unique cross-section of the sports literature.

Biographies

725.   Condon, Robert J. **The Fifty Finest Athletes of the 20th Century: A Worldwide Reference.** Jefferson, NC: McFarland, 1990. 152p. Illus. LC 89-43643. ISBN 0-89950-374-8.

Condon's selection criteria included domination of a particular sport for one decade or more, achievement of an unsurpassed level of performance, or widespread support as the best ever in a sport. A variety of sports are represented, although baseball players (and U.S. males) dominate. Entries include biographical data, career accomplishments, and comparisons with other performers in the same sport.

726.   Porter, David L., ed. **Biographical Dictionary of American Sports: Basketball and Other Indoor Sports.** Westport, CT: Greenwood, 1989. 801p. Index. ISBN 0-313-26261-6.

The 558 entries cover athletes from basketball (over half of the total), bowling, boxing, diving, figure skating, gymnastics, ice hockey, swimming, weightlifting, wrestling, and miscellaneous other sports. The appendixes list players according to sport, position played, and place of birth; hall of fame members; conferences; women by sport; and ring names and real names of boxers.

727.   Porter, David L., ed. **Biographical Dictionary of American Sports: Outdoor Sports.** Westport, CT: Greenwood, 1988. 728p. Index. ISBN 0-313-26260-8.

The subjects have been culled from auto racing, golf, horse racing, lacrosse, skiing, speed skating, tennis, track and field, and miscellaneous other sports. The appendixes include an alphabetical list of biographees with references to their respective sports, lists of entries categorized by sport (with a separate section for women) and state of birth, halls of fame, sports associations, and sites of Olympic Games.

728.   Woolum, Janet. **Outstanding Women Athletes: Who They Are and How They Influenced Sports in America.** Phoenix, AZ: Oryx, 1992. 276p. Illus., bibl. ISBN 0-89774-713-5.

The work analyzes the lives and careers of sixty notable female athletes. It includes forewords by Billie Jean King, Anita DeFrantz (an International Olympic Committee official), Deborah Slaner Anderson (Executive Director of the Women's Sports Foundation).

Dictionaries

729.   Palmatier, Robert A., and Harold L. Ray. **Sports Talk: A Dictionary of Sports Metaphors.** New York: Greenwood, 1989. 227p. Index (arranged by sport). ISBN 0-313-26426-0.

The book has collected over 1,700 metaphors; each entry gives the full, popular form of the expression; an illustration of proper grammatical usage; a definition; an etymology; a coded source of other works recognizing the source of the metaphor; and comparative and contrastive cross-references to other entries.

730.   **Webster's Sports Dictionary.** Springfield, MA: Merriam-Webster, 1976. 512p. Illus. LC 72-42076. ISBN 0-87779-067-1.

Despite its datedness, the tool provides useful definitions of approximately 7,000 terms from more than 100 sports. The entries (arranged alphabetically) delineate rules, playing areas specifications, signals, equipment, language, etc. The appendixes note abbreviations, referee signals in football and basketball, and scorekeeping in baseball and bowling.

Directories

731. Bast, Carol J., and others, eds. **Masters Guide to Sports Camps.** Grand Rapids, MI: Masters Press, 1987. (various paging). LC 87-10994. ISBN 0-940279-00-2.

A compilation of approximately 4,000 summer sports camps in North America available to children up to age eighteen, the work is arranged by geographical section (northwest, midwest, south, and west)and subdivided by sport (forty-eight in all) and camp name. The entries include information about staffing, facilities, dates, cost, address, and phone number.

732. Kobak, Edward T., **The 1991 Sports Address Bible: The Comprehensive Directory of Sports Addresses.** 5th ed. Santa Monica, CA: Global Sports Productions, 1991. 336p. ISBN 0-9619181-2-8 pap.

The book is geared to sports collectors, sports executives, media representatives, college students looking for a career-oriented position in sports, librarians, educators, administrators in school athletics, and general fans. It is organized by topical headings, including major sports, miscellaneous minor sports, museums, international sports, publications, sports for the disabled and handicapped, the media, Intercollegiate Athletics, the sports business industry, state high school athletic federations, and sports collecting. Subheadings for each topic include all relevant amateur and professional teams and league offices, related institutions and events (e.g., bowl games), etc.

Encyclopedias

733. Frost, Reuben B., ed. **Encyclopedia of Physical Education, Fitness, and Sports: Sports, Dance, and Related Activities.** Reading, MA: Addison-Wesley, 1977. 973p. Illus., index. LC 76-46608. ISBN 0-201-01077-1.

The work provides historical background and information on playing, teaching, and coaching seventy-one sports and recreational activities. Despite a decided lack of depth, it functions as a useful introduction to these subjects.

734. Hickok, Ralph. **The Encyclopedia of North American Sports History.** New York: Facts on File, 1992. 352p. Illus., index, bibl. LC 91-6667. ISBN 0-8160-2096-5.

The alphabetically arranged entries cover the history, biography, governance, achievement awards, cities, playing arenas, and other aspects of North American sports.

735. Hickok, Ralph. **New Encyclopedia of Sports.** New York: McGraw-Hill, 1977. 543p. Illus. LC 76-45633. ISBN 0-07-028705-8.

The coverage ranges from individual sports to related concepts such as "Black Athletes" and the "Pan American Games." Minor topics are limited to as little space as one paragraph (e.g. "Codeball"), whereas major sports span many pages (e.g., forty-two for baseball), touching upon historical background, a delineation of rules, a glossary of terms, and selected statistical breakdowns.

736. Remy, Bob. **Louisiana Sports Encyclopedia.** Gretna, LA: Pelican, 1977. 358p. ISBN 0-88289-120-0 pap.

Every state should be covered by a source such as this! A compilation of individual and team records in eighteen sports between 1892-1976, it extends beyond state boundaries to provide information about intercollegiate and professional athletic conferences including Louisiana teams. There are also sections documenting the involvement of Louisianians in the Olympics and professional sports, the Louisiana Sports Hall of Fame, the Corbett-Sullivan heavyweight championship bout in 1892, the New Orleans Athletic Club Turkey Day Race, etc.

737.   White, Jess R. **Sports Rules Encyclopedia.** 2nd ed. Champaign, IL: Leisure Press/Human Kinetics, 1990. 732p. Illus. LC 89-2280. ISBN 0-88011-363-4.

The definitive source for accessing the rules of a given sport as set forth by that sport's ruling body in the United States. Although not all agencies may utilize these regulations (e.g., high school and college teams do not fall under the jurisdiction of the U.S. Soccer Federation), the presence of directory information pertaining to governing bodies and their respective publications should help offset this flaw.

738.   Windhausen, John D., ed. **Sports Encyclopedia North America.** Gulf Breeze, FL: Academic International, 1987. Volume 1. Bibl. ISBN 0-87569-094-7.

The projected fifty-volume set will, in the words of the editor, be the "most complete reference guide to American and Canadian sports, present and past . . . both in the breadth of its subject entries and its insistence upon depth of coverage, including statistical information and reference aids." At present, however, its promise remains unfulfilled.

Handbooks

739.   Boehm, David A., Jim Benagh, and Cyd Smith, eds. **Guinness Sports Record Book 1990-91.** New York: Sterling; distr., Quality Books, 1990. 252p. Illus. LC 82-64236. ISBN 0-8069-7304-8; 0-8069-7305-6 pap.

Encompassing ninety-three different sports and recreational pursuits (e.g., bridge, Twister), the alphabetically arranged entries provide information regarding the sport's origins, followed by notable, representative, or attention-getting records. It should be particularly valuable in tracking data pertaining to more obscure pastimes.

740.   Carruth, Gorton, and Eugene Ehrlich. **Facts and Dates of American Sports.** New York: Perennial Library/Harper & Row, 1988. 373p. Index. LC 87-46126. ISBN 0-06-055124-0; 0-06-096271-2 pap.

Devoted to a wide variety of sports, the chronologically arranged entries begin with the date 1540 (the horse is imported to North America) and continue through January 31, 1988 (the Washington Redskins win the 22nd Super Bowl). The text is punctuated throughout by accounts of ten legendary sporting events, thirty-eight tables of records and statistics, and 222 thumbnail biographies of notable performers.

741.   Emery, David, and Stan Greenberg. **The World Sports Record Atlas.** New York: Facts on File, 1986. 192p. Illus. ISBN 0-8160-1378-0; 0-8160-1579-1 pap.

Statistics and text are intermingled in the book's coverage of ballooning, baseball, boxing, channel swimming, fencing, football, golf, horse racing, long distance walking and running, mountaineering, parachuting, racing, soccer, squash, tennis, track and field, water sports, weightlifting, and winter sports.

742.   **Guinness Book of Sports Records.** New York: Facts on File, 1991. 256p. Illus., index. ISBN 0-8160-2649-1; 0-8160-2650-5 pap.

More than seventy-five sports are arranged alphabetically; each entry includes historical background and world, U.S., and Olympic records.

743. Killpatrick, Frances, and James Killpatrick. **The Winning Edge: A Complete Guide to Intercollegiate Athletic Programs.** Alexandria, VA: Octameron; distr., Longman Trade, 1989. 290p. ISBN 0-945981-27-9 pap.

This book is geared to helping high school athletes sift through the options in college athletics and select a suitable college program. Despite the absence of many notable colleges and universities, the volume's straightforward treatment of recruiting rules, guidelines for the prospective recruit, and surveys of each sport, data on more than 200 colleges and universities offering athletic scholarships (including a breakdown, by sport, of competition level, scholarship details, budgets, coaching staffs, facilities, and degree of athletic success) render it a valuable guide.

744. Lessiter, Mike. **The College Names of the Games: The Stories Behind 293 College Sports Teams.** Chicago: Contemporary Books, 1989. 342p. LC 88-39124. ISBN 0-8092-4476-4 pap.

745. Lessiter, Mike. **The Names of the Games: The Stories Behind the Nicknames of 102 Pro Football, Basketball, Baseball, and Hockey Teams.** Chicago: Contemporary Books, 1988. 126p. LC 88-17699. ISBN 0-8092-4477-2 pap.

The definitive source for those requiring information on the mascots and nicknames of college and professional athletic teams. Additional background data on these teams (e.g., name and seating capacity of arena or stadium) is also provided.

746. Liddle, Barry, comp. **Dictionary of Sports Quotations.** London; New York: Routledge & K. Paul, 1987. 210p. Index. ISBN 0-7102-0785-9.

This is a comprehensive listing, arranged by sport. The sources of quotations are noted. An author index has also been provided.

747. Lipsey, Richard A., ed. **Sports Market Place, 1985.** Grey House Publishing, 1985. 509p. Index. ISBN 0-939300-50-8.

The purpose of this tool is to assist users in making marketing contacts within the sports world. To this end it includes data on U.S., Canadian, and international sports organizations; radio and television broadcasting, publications, marketing and promotion services, market data services, and equipment suppliers. Access is enhanced by a master index (by key word) to organizations, publications, and businesses.

748. Luschen, Gunther R. F., and George H. Sage, with the assistance of Leila Sfeir. **Handbook of Social Science of Sport; with an International Classified Bibliography.** Champaign, IL: Stipes Publishing Company, 1981. 720p. Indexes, bibl. ISBN 0-87563-191-6.

Following an introductory survey of the field, six subject areas (e.g., cross-cultural and cross-national analysis of sport and games, social problems and deviance in sport) are explored in greater detail. The appendix lists sport and sport science agencies. Author and subject indexes have also been included.

749. Maikovich, Andrew J. **Sports Quotations: Maxims, Quips and Pronouncements for Writers and Fans.** Jefferson, NC: McFarland, 1984. 168p. Indexes. LC 83-20005. ISBN 0-89950-100-1.

The compendium is arranged alphabetically by author within seventeen respective sport categories. The profession is provided for the author of each of the 1,782 entries. Access is enhanced by name and subject indexes.

750. Markel, Robert, Nancy Brooks, and Susan Markel. **For the Record: Women in Sports.** New York: World Almanac Publications; distr., Ballantine Books, 1985. 195p. Illus., index. ISBN 0-345-32192-8 pap.

The source devotes a section to each of the following: badminton, basketball, bowling, canoeing and kayaking, cycling, equestrian sports, fencing, field hockey, golf, gymnastics, ice skating, luge, rowing, skiing, softball, water sports, table tennis, tennis, track and field, triathlon, volleyball, and Women's Sports Foundation award winners. These units each include an introduction, concise thumbnail sketches of the key personalities, and statistical breakdowns. A name index has also been provided.

751. Paciorek, Michael J., and Jeffrey A. Jones. **Sports and Recreation for the Disabled: A Resource Handbook.** Indianapolis, IN: Benchmark, 1989. 396p. Illus., bibl. LC 88-42866. ISBN 0-936157-31-3.

The work is organized alphabetically into fifty-three chapters (each representing a different sport or recreational pursuit). These sections note rule modifications, organizations sponsoring competitive events, the reasons for offering the given activity to disabled persons, adapted equipment, suppliers, additional resources, etc. The five appendixes cite equipment sources, lightweight wheelchair manufacturers, sports organizations, national handicapped sports and recreation chapters, and Special Olympics international chapters and directors.

752. **Racing on the Tour de France: And Other Stories of Sports.** Columbus, OH: Zaner-Bloser, 1989. 63p. ISBN 0-88309-546-7 pap.

This anthology features eighteen articles published in *Highlights for Children* magazine during the 1970s and 1980s. These well-written, three-page essays provide a history of the sport in question as well as the rules, equipment, and skills necessary to excel in it.

753. **Rules of the Game.** by the Diagram Group. Rev. ed. New York: St. Martin's Press, 1990. 320p. Illus., indexes. ISBN 0-312-04574-3.

The tool organizes 150 sports under thirteen headings (e.g., water, court). The entries incorporate strategy, playing area, equipment, rules, timing, scoring, participants, and officials. Relevant national and international governing agencies in the U.S., Canada, and Great Britain are combined in a chart listing. Access is enhanced by general and sports indexes.

754. Soderberg, Paul, Helen Washington, and Jaques Cattell Press, comps. and eds. **The Big Book of Halls of Fame in the United States and Canada: Sports.** New York: R. R. Bowker, 1977. 1,042p. Index. LC 77-82734. ISBN 0-0800-0990-3.

In providing background information regarding 171 halls of fame in the U.S. and Canada (organized under thirty-one sports headings), this exhaustive volume includes biographical profiles of every inductee (human and animal) of forty-one museum-type institutions and lists—by date of attaining membership—all members of 130 award- and association-type halls.

755. Sparhawk, Ruth M., et al., comps. **American Women in Sport, 1887-1987: A 100-Year Chronology.** Metuchen, NJ: Scarecrow, 1989. 149p. Illus., indexes, bibl. LC 89-6150. ISBN 0-8108-2205-9.

A terse historical survey of female athletes is followed by a four-part chronology: "The Preorganizational Era, 1887-1916"; "The Organizational Years, 1917-1956"; "The Competitive Period, 1957-1971"; and "The Title IX Era, 1972-1987." These sections are further divided by year, and then by a listing of names and feats. Sports (type) and name indexes have also been provided.

756. **Thrill Sports Catalog.** by the eds. of Consumer Guide. New York: E. P. Dutton, 1977. Illus. (A Dutton Paperback.) LC 77-77942. ISBN 0-525-47470-X pap.

Separate chapters cover twenty-three different thrill sports (e.g., rafting, sky diving). Each section provides a participant's description of the sport, safety tips, training guidelines, the selection and use of equipment, and a listing of relevant organizations and publications ("Sources").

757. Tomlinson, Gerald. **Speaker's Treasury of Sports Anecdotes, Stories, and Humor.** Englewood Cliffs, NJ: Prentice-Hall, 1990. 395p. Index, bibl. LC 89-38752. ISBN 0-13-826942-4 pap.

A compilation of anecdotes, tales, and quips organized alphabetically under fifty-four categories of activities (ability to versatility), the tool provides two chronological approaches to locating information: by date and by speakers' birth dates. Access is enhanced by a proper name index.

758. Trager, Oliver, ed. **Sports in America: Paradise Lost?** New York: Facts on File, 1990. 224p. LC 89-49285. ISBN 0-8160-2412-X.

This collection of editorials and cartoons from U.S. and Canadian newspapers focuses on the controversies in sports during the last half of the 1980s (e.g., the Pete Rose gambling scandal, drug abuse, player strikes). Arranged under five chapters, each topic features a summary of the issues involved followed by several editorials providing commentary on it.

Indexes

759. **Sport & Leisure.** Waterloo, Ontario: University of Waterloo, Spring 1989-. v. 1, n. 1-. 3/year. ISSN: 0838-4061.

This indexing service has pulled together the resources on sports and recreation with a sociological bent, including journal articles, monographs, conference papers, dissertations, and other unpublished documents. Despite the lack of a subject arrangement or cumulated issues, the comprehensive coverage and well-written abstracts render it a valuable tool.

760. **Sports Periodicals Index.** Edited by Grant Elderidge. Ann Arbor, MI: National Information Systems, 1985-. Monthly with annual cumulations.

The tool provides access by subject and name to approximately 100 popular sports magazines covering virtually all sports.

Baseball

Bibliographies

761. Smith, Myron J. **Baseball: A Comprehensive Bibliography.** Jefferson, NC: McFarland, 1986. 915p. Illus., indexes. ISBN 0-89950-222-9.

The compilation includes monographs, government publications, theses and dissertations, fiction and poetry in anthologies, and articles from 365 journals. It is organized into the following sections: reference works, general works, history, special studies; professional leagues and teams; youth leagues, college, and amateur/ semiprofessional play; rules and techniques; a collective bibliography; and individual biographies. Author and subject indexes have also been provided.

Biographies

762. Carter, Craig, ed. **Daguerreotypes.** 8th ed. St. Louis, MO: Sporting News, 1990. 320p. Illus. LC 89-63683. ISBN 0-89204-332-0.

Originally published in 1934, the work's 397 biographees (arranged in alphabetical order) include all hall of fame members and players who have had a significant impact upon the game. Entries for players include a photograph, a listing of records held, notable awards and background information, and comprehensive season-by-season statistics at all professional levels of play. The non-player entries consist of a concise biographical survey. An appendix noting the selection criteria has been included.

763. Porter, David L., ed. **Biographical Dictionary of American Sports: Baseball.** New York: Greenwood, 1987. 713p. Indexes. ISBN 0-313-23771-9.

The source provides biographical essays of 423 players, twenty-seven managers, six umpires, and sixty-one executives. The appendixes list professional leagues, Negro Leagues, Hall of Fame members, and contributors to the volume. Access is enhanced by job category, player position, birthplace (by state), and Negro League indexes.

764. Shatzkin, Mike, ed. **The Ballplayers: Baseball's Ultimate Biographical Reference.** New York: Arbor House/William Morrow, 1990. 1230p. Illus. LC 89-77086. ISBN 0-87795-984-6.

Some readers might take issue with the fact that short careers receive little attention (length of career represents the primary consideration for inclusion, followed by fan interest). Created under the auspices of the Society for American Baseball Research, the book's utility is enhanced by the inclusion of fans, managers, executives, minor leaguers, and notable Japanese, Mexican, and Negro League players. Flaws include editing errors and the lack of cross-references regarding the entries. The wealth of statistical data combined with well-written character portrayals, however, render this an interesting read as well as a useful research source.

Dictionaries

765. Dickson, Paul. **The Dickson Baseball Dictionary.** New York: Facts on File, 1989. 438p. Illus., bibl. LC 88-23583. ISBN 0-8160-1741-7.

The work includes almost 5,000 words, phrases, and terms relating to baseball. For each entry, the definition is followed by a note delineating its etymology and first appearance. Usages outside baseball and cross-references are included where applicable.

766. Scholl, Richard. **Running Press Glossary of Baseball Language.** Philadelphia: Running Press, 1977. 94p. Illus. LC 77-410. ISBN 0-914292-79-2; 0-914294-80-6 pap.

The approximately 700 alphabetically arranged terms included here, although far from complete, will prove useful for lay users. The appendix contains illustrations of the strike zone; measurements of the baseball diamond and batter's box; and the layout of the infield, coaches' boxes, and dugouts.

Encyclopedias

767. Neft, David S., and Richard M. Cohen. **The Sports Encyclopedia: Baseball.** 9th ed. New York: St. Martin's Press, 1989. 629p. LC 88-29854. ISBN 0-312-026447 pap.

This densely packed compendium of data includes statistics for teams as well as for players (i.e., batters and pitchers). Information has also been provided regarding the league playoffs and World Series, in addition to annual and lifetime batting and pitching leaders.

768. Reichler, Joseph L., ed. **The Baseball Encyclopedia: The Complete and Official Record of Major League Baseball.** 7th ed., rev., updated, and expanded. New York: Macmillan; London: Collier Macmillan, 1988. 2,875p. LC 87-34581. ISBN 0-02-579030-7.

In addition to the Player Register (hitting statistics) and Pitcher Register, the work includes team and managerial figures and data regarding the World Series, championship playoffs, All-Star Games, and All-Time Leaders. The appendixes delineate sources, the decision of special records committees, and major modifications of professional rules.

Handbooks

769. Benson, Michael. **Ballparks of North America: A Comprehensive Historical Reference to Baseball Grounds, Yards, and Stadiums, 1845 to Present.** Jefferson, NC: McFarland, 1989. 475p. Illus., index, bibl. ISBN 0-89950-367-5.

The entries—arranged alphabetically by city and subdivided chronologically—designate league, the first team to play there, location, dimensions, seating capacity, and attendance records. A name index has also been provided.

770. **The Complete Baseball Record Book.** St. Louis, MO: Sporting News. Annual. Pap.

The tool contains complete records for players, managers, umpires, and clubs in the major leagues. In addition to regular statistics, the records of All-Star games, the Championship series, and the World Series are included.

771. James, Bill. **The Bill James Historical Baseball Abstract.** Rev. ed. New York: Villard, 1988. c1985. 723p. Illus., index, bibl. LC 87-40570. ISBN 0-394-75805-6 pap.

The parent volume for the annual editions of *The Baseball Abstract,* this work frequently debunks traditional wisdom with new perspectives emanating from James' pioneering statistical research. The book is divided into three major sections: I. "The Game," a decade-by-decade (the 1870s through the 1980s) exposition of the game, focusing on (a) the "how, where, and by whom" via an introductory essay; (b) the decade in a box (i.e., small questions with short answers); and (c) headlined articles, featuring notable sidelights in each era, such as nicknames, uniform styles, etc.; II. "The Players," self-described by James as the "Who-Was-Better-Than-Whom section," consisting mainly of information and arguments about the relative merits of the few hundred all-time best players on a position-by-position basis; and III. "The Records," containing the most complete data ever published for the 200 or so greatest players. An integrated subject and proper name index has also been provided.

772. Jarrett, William S. **Timetables of Sports History: Baseball.** New York: Facts on File, 1989. 90p. Illus., index. ISBN 0-8160-1918-5.

Limited to the major leagues, the tool offers a year-by-year chronology of the key events from 1903 to 1988. Each season includes final team standings, performance leaders, awards, etc.

773. Lowry, Philip J. **Green Cathedrals.** Cooperstown, NY: Society for American Baseball Research, 1986. 157p. Illus. ISBN 0-09-103721-8 pap.

A guide to baseball stadiums, it covers the major and minor leagues, the Negro League, and neutral parks. Each entry provides the stadium name (and nickname or alternate name), style, occupants (in chronological order), location, surface, dimensions, fences, former and current use, and phenomena of historical importance. This source is not quite as comprehensive as Benson's *Ballparks of North America* (see entry 769).

774.   Mote, James. **Everything Baseball.** New York: Prentice-Hall, 1989. 429p. Illus. LC 88-28816. ISBN 0-13-292889-2 pap.

Attempting to note every reference to baseball in the arts from an eighteenth-century poem about "Base Ball" to the late 1980s film, *Bull Durham,* the volume is organized by medium: books, movies, sheet music, recordings, poetry, radio, television, theater, and the fine arts. The text is frequently punctuated by essays enlarging upon various sources.

775.   Nathan, David H., comp. **Baseball Quotations: The Wisdom and Wisecracks of Players, Managers, Owners, Umpires, Announcers, Writers and Fans on the Great American Pastime.** Jefferson, NC: McFarland, 1991. 231p. Indexes. ISBN 0-89950-562-7.

This is a selective collection of more than 2,000 quotes divided into twenty-nine categories, including hitters and pitchers, winning and losing, fundamentals and money, etc. Name, subject, and keyword indexes have also been provided.

776.   Reichler, Joseph L. **The Baseball Trade Register.** New Tork: Macmillan; London: Collier Macmillan, 1984. 567p. ISBN 0-02-603110-8.

Divided into the National and American Leagues, the text consists of a player roster, listing date of trade, team acquired from, and for whom exchanged, and a team roll, incorporating sections on managers and owners and best and worst trades.

777.   Reichler, Joseph L., and Ken Samelson. **The Great All-Time Baseball Record Book.** Rev. ed. New York: Macmillan, 1992. 544p. Index. LC 91-38197. ISBN 0-02-603101-9.

This an expansive compilation of Major League individual and team statistics (reaching back to the nineteenth century) that includes far more than the standard hitting, pitching, and fielding categories. The large dollops of offbeat data (e.g., hardest and easiest players to double up) are reminiscent of the series of books compiled by Bill James (without the narrative analysis supplied by the latter).

778.   Schoor, Gene. **The Complete Dodgers Record Book.** New York: Facts on File, 1984. 439p. LC 82-15695. ISBN 0-87196-117-2.

The work is composed of player statistics on Dodger teams from 1890 to 1983, along with team records (including the World Series) and all-time hitting and pitching leaders.

779.   Schoor, Gene. **The History of the World Series.** New York: Morrow, 1990. 431p. ISBN 0-688-07995-4.

Melding text and statistics, Schoor covers every World Series game from 1904 through 1989. Series records are listed in an appendix.

780.   Siwoff, Seymour, Steve Hirdt, Tom Hirdt, and Peter Hirdt. **The Elias Baseball Analyst.** New York: Fireside/Simon & Schuster, 1985-. Annual.

Along with the Bill James series (see entry 771), this is the leading statistical compendium devoted to outlining the contemporary scene in major league baseball. It is used by fans and baseball insiders (e.g., general managers, managers, players, broadcasters, writers) alike. The classified arrangement includes the "Team Section," "Batter Section" (alphabetical by players within each league), "Pitcher Section" (same arrangement as the prior section), "Rookies and Prospects Section" (alphabetical by "batters" and "pitchers"), and "Ballpark" (with rankings by such factors as effect on batting average, effect on slugging percentage, etc.).

The depth of information contained within each entry is most impressive. For example, each batter includes the following subcategories: team, season stats, as well as breakdowns of the players performance versus left-handers and right-handers, versus ground-ballers, versus fly-ballers, at home games, at road games, on grass fields, on artificial turf, each month of the season, leading off an inning, with runners on, with bases empty, with runners in scoring position, with runners on and two out, with runners in scoring position and two out, with late-inning pressure, and such categories as RBIs from each base, loves to face, loves to hate, miscellaneous statistics, and comments (the latter a free-form text of observations about the player).

781. Skipper, James K. **Baseball Nicknames: A Dictionary of Origins and Meanings.** Jefferson, NC: McFarland, 1992. 384p. Index, bibl. ISBN 0-89950-684-4.

The book provides nicknames for baseball personalities in five separate categories: "I. Players, Nonplayer Managers, Officials, Sportswriters, Broadcasters, Owners, Fans;" "II. All American Girls Baseball League Players;" "III. Negro League Players;" "IV. Umpires;" and "V. Influential Nonplaying Baseball Personalities." Each entry includes the given name of the individual (arranged alphabetically by last name), followed by nickname, position, years played (or associated with the game), and origin of the nickname. Despite ten years of painstaking research, the origins of many nicknames couldn't be determined; this constitutes the greatest weakness of an otherwise well-focused work. The work is further enhanced by the introduction (entitled "The Sociological Significance of Nicknames: The Case of Baseball Players"), which analyzes the place of nicknames in American culture as well as the frequency of their appearance in professional baseball.

782. Spink, C. C. Johnson, ed. **Official Baseball Register.** St. Louis, MO: Sporting News. Annual. Pap.

The work provides lifetime personal and statistical data for every active player and manager in the major leagues.

783. Spink, C. C. Johnson, ed. **Official Baseball Dope Book.** St. Louis, MO: Sporting News, 1977. 256p. Illus. ISBN 0-89204-021-1 pap.

A cornucopia of names, facts, and figures appearing in various annuals published by the *Sporting News,* it will be appreciated most by trivia buffs.

784. Spink, C. C. Johnson, ed. **Official Baseball Guide.** St. Louis, MO: Sporting News, 1977-. Annual. 500-600p./issue. Illus., index., pap.

Focusing on the performances of players and teams for the preceding season (including a substantial section on the Minor Leagues), the *Guide* also includes leaders in a variety of categories (e.g., total hits, slugging percentage) for earlier seasons.

785. Sugar, Bert Randolph, ed. **Baseballistics: The Absolutely, Positively, Greatest Book of Baseball Facts, Figures, and Astonishing Lists Ever Compiled.** New York: St. Martin's Press, 1990. 400p. LC 89-27091. ISBN 0-312-03789-9.

The tool is divided into seven sections: batting, pitching, Hall of Fame, awards, All-Star games, miscellany, and team-by-team leaders. It includes many features not present in comparable titles, such as the *Baseball Encyclopedia* (see entry 768).

786. Thorn, John, and Bob Carroll, with David Reuther, eds. **The Whole Baseball Catalogue.** New York: Simon & Schuster, 1990. 369p. Illus., index. LC 89-49090. ISBN 0-671-68347-0 pap.

The work mixes solid practical advice and humor. Organized into nine sections ("innings") containing one to four articles contributed by guest writers, it covers a wide-ranging array of subjects (e.g., game equipment, executives).

787.   Thorn, John, and Pete Palmer, with David Reuther. **Total Baseball.** New York: Warner Books, 1989. 2,294p. Bibl. ISBN 0-446-51389-X.

This comprehensive source is composed of essays (thirty-eight in all), biographical sketches, and a wealth of statistical breakdowns. Topics covered include historical profiles of the game and major league teams, defunct clubs and leagues, post-season play, a chronology of key events, foreign-born players, Japanese baseball, mascots, scandals, umpires, awards and honors, armed services baseball, and professional rules.

788.   Weiner, Eric. **The Kids' Complete Baseball Catalog.** New York: Julian Messner, 1991. 254p. Illus., indexes. LC 90-45155. ISBN 0-671-70196-7; 0-671-70197-5 pap.

This guide is organized into thirteen chapters covering material of practical value for younger fans, including baseball camps, Halls of Fame and museums, television and radio stations of each major league team, baseball card collecting, fan clubs, magazines and newsletters, videos and software, uniform suppliers, and sources of free items. The text is punctuated by sidebars devoted to crossword puzzles, personal anecdotes, quizzes, etc. Personal name and subject indexes have also been provided.

789.   Wolff, Rick, ed. **The Baseball Encyclopedia: The Complete and Official Record of Major League Baseball.** 8th rev. ed. New York: Macmillan, 1990. 2,781p. LC 89-29902. ISBN 0-02-579040-4.

Long considered a definitive tool, it includes a historical survey of the sport; player and pitcher registers; special achievements and awards; a chronological listing of team standings, team rosters, player records, playoffs, and World Series games; rules; and sidelights, such as an essay on the origins of the Negro League.

Basketball

Bibliographies

790.   Krause, Jerry V., and Stephen J. Brennan. **Basketball Resource Guide.** 2nd ed. Champaign, IL: Leisure Press/Human Kinetics, 1990. 238p. Index. LC 89-12507. ISBN 0-88011-369-3.

The tool is organized into six sections: books, periodical articles (all culled from the *Athletic Journal* and *Scholastic Coach*), theses and dissertations, pamphlets, and resource-oriented visuals (two chapters).

Encyclopedias

791.   Hollander, Zander, and Alex Sachare, eds. **The Official NBA Basketball Encyclopedia: The Complete History and Statistics of Professional Basketball.** New York: Villiard/Random House, 1989. 766p. Illus., index. LC 89-40201. ISBN 0-394-58039-7.

'   This comprehensive source includes the following: a history of basketball's developmental years; a history of the NBA though the 1988-1989 season, punctuated by seasonal statistics; coaches; players selected in the ABA and NBA drafts; members of the Hall of Fame; official NBA rules; and the "All-Time Player Directory."

792.   Neft, David S., and Richard M. Cohen. **The Sports Encyclopedia: Pro Basketball.**
3rd ed. New York: St. Martin's Press, 1990. 589p. ISBN 0-312-05162-X.

Covering professional basketball from its first game in Trenton, New Jersey, in
1896, the work is divided into six units, each spanning roughly a decade and including
year-by-year overviews, chronologies, statistical breakdowns, and a listing of the top
players. Player rosters offer statistical data for each season and entire career. Although not
as visually attractive or informative as *The Official NBA Basketball Encyclopedia* (see
entry 791), it provides insights not always available in that source.

793.   Savage, Jim. **The Encyclopedia of the NCAA Basketball Tournament.** New
York: Dell. 745p. Illus., index. ISBN 0-440-50362-0.

The volume surveys the first fifty-two years of the tournament, including accounts
of notable games, analysis of the most outstanding coaches and players (ten apiece),
seedings and diagrams of the draw, the won-lost records of all participating schools, and
box scores and other statistics.

Handbooks

794.   Bollig, Laura E., ed. **NCAA Basketball's Finest: All-Time Great Players and
Coaches.** Chicago: Triumph Books, 1992. 240p. Illus., index. ISBN 1-880141-04-3.

The work provides the collegiate achievements of 301 leading Division I stars since
1948 (the date the NCAA began keeping official statistics), based on their attainment of
national honors or statistical records. Other sections include the won-lost records of the
ninety-seven Division I coaches winning over 500 games or a national championship and
a roster of players who've been honored as All-Americans (arranged by college).

795.   Earle, Michael V., ed. **Final Four Records, 1939-1991.** Chicago: Triumph Books,
1992. 240p. ISBN 1-880141-02-7.

An exhaustive guide to the NCAA Division I Men's Basketball Tournament, the
statistical breakdowns even include attendance figures and the dates when particular
categories of data first began to be compiled.

796.   Heeren, Dave. **The Basketball Abstract.** Englewood Cliffs, NJ: Prentice-Hall.
Annual. Pap. 1991/1992 ed.: ISBN 0-13-202995-2.

The author employs data analysis to compare the performances of players, teams,
and coaches in the NBA for the season covered. Typical topics include the greatest team,
sixth men, and the players of the year. The formula on which he has based his insights is
referred to as "TENDEX," which analyzes ten statistical departments: points, rebounds,
assists, turnovers, steals, blocked shots, missed field goal and free throw attempts, minutes
played, and game pace. Despite the immense amount of data presented here, Heeren's
reliance upon formulas weighs down the flow of his narrative.

797.   Jarrett, William S. **Timetables of Sports History: Basketball.** New York: Facts
on File, 1990. 77p. ISBN 0-8160-1920-7.

Jarrett chronicles the sport from 1891 through the 1989 season, spanning both the
collegiate and professional realms.

798.   **Official NBA Guide.** edited by the Sporting News Staff. St. Louis, MO: The
Sporting News. Annual. ISSN 0078-3862 pap.

799. **Official NBA Register.** edited by the Sporting News Staff. St. Louis, MO: The Sporting News. Annual. ISSN 0739-3067 pap.

The *Guide* gives current rosters and schedules, statistical data for the season immediately past, NBA records and award winners, and season-by-season team and individual records going back to 1946-1947. On the other hand, the *Register* provides career statistics for all active players as well as information regarding current coaches.

800. Savage, Jim. **The Encyclopedia of the NCAA Basketball Tournament: Complete Independent Guide to College Basketball's Championship Event.** New York: Dell, 1992. 745p. Pap. ISBN 0-440-50511-9.

The book covers the entire history of the tournament (which began in 1939), including box scores, seedings, statistics, accounts of key games, players and teams, how winning players became legends in the Final Four, analysis of the noteworthy coaches, etc.

Card Games

Encyclopedias

801. Frey, Richard L., ed.-in-chief. **The Official Encyclopedia of Bridge.** 3rd ed., rev. and expanded. Authorized by the American Contract Bridge League and prepared with the assistance of its staff. New York: Crown, 1976. 858p. Illus., bibl. LC 76-17053. ISBN 0-517-52724-3.

Considered the definitive guide to contract bridge, it can also be used as an instructional manual and player's handbook. Features include definitions for relevant terms; comprehensive essays on the history of the game (as well as playing cards in general); bridge etiquette and ethics, tournaments; bridge clubs; and illustrated descriptions of every standard bid, established convention, and type of play.

Handbooks

802. Arnold, Peter. **The Book of Card Games.** London: Christopher Helm; distr., Hippocrene Books, 1988. 279p. Illus., index. ISBN 0-87052-730-4 pap.

Written by a recognized authority in this field, the book consists of alphabetically arranged game entries, each including background information, the number of competitors, card pack, preliminaries of play, dealing, the action, and strategies. A glossary introduces the games and provides brief definitions of card terms.

803. Markey, Kay, comp. **The Neal-Schuman Index to Card Games.** New York: Neal-Schuman, 1990. 153p. Bibl. (Neal-Schuman Indexes Series, 1.) LC 90-30508. ISBN 1-55570-052-7.

The source is divided into two alphabetically arranged sections: by game and by game category. Each game is not only identified, but defined in a broad historical context along with its variants.

Chess

Encyclopedias

804. Sunnucks, Anne, comp. **The Encyclopedia of Chess.** London: Robert Hale; distr., St. Martin's Press, 1976. 619p. Illus., index. LC 76-21149. ISBN 0-7091-4697-3.

The work is comprehensive in approach, including biographical information on current International Masters and Grandmasters, results of major tournaments, data on chess organizations, a discussion of chess games and sample problems, and essays devoted to the relationship of the game to other fields, such as drama and philately.

Fishing

Handbooks

805. Henkin, Harmon. **The Complete Fisherman's Catalog.** Philadelphia: Lippincott, 1977. 463p. Illus., index, bibl. LC 76-56200. ISBN 0-397-01186-5 pap.

A cornucopia of fishing lore intermingling facts and humor, the tool's wide-ranging approach encompasses specifications and recommendations regarding equipment; advice on tying flies; directory information on manufacturers; a listing of organization involved with the sport; articles on the habitat, distribution, feeding habits, and suggested tackle for game-fish; and a fishing mystery authored by Henkin.

Football

Bibliographies

806. Smith, Myron J., **The Pro Football Bio-Bibliography.** West Cornwall, CT: Locust Hill, 1989. 288p. Bibl. LC 88-37741. ISBN 0-933951-23-X pap.

The work lists biographical materials on approximately 1,400 individuals (players, coaches, and executives) involved with the National Football League since its inception in 1920. The alphabetically arranged entries include terse biographical data followed by citations for books, articles, league publications, and annuals. The work has been updated, in part, by the author's *Professional Football: The Official Pro Football Hall of Fame Bibliography* (Greenwood, 1993).

Biographies

807. Porter, David L., ed. **Biographical Dictionary of American Sports: Football.** New York: Greenwood, 1987. 763p. Index, bibl. ISBN 0-313-25771-X.

The 520 biographies, arranged alphabetically, include players, coaches, executives, league administrators, rule developers, and promoters. The appendixes arrange biographees by category, position players, state of birth, collegiate and Professional Hall of Fame members, and conferences and leagues.

Encyclopedias

808.   Bennett, Tom, and others, ed., writer, and comp. **The NFL's Official Encyclopedic History of Professional Football.** NFL, 1977. 512p. Illus. (A National Football League Book.) LC 76-30547. ISBN 0-02-589010-7.

The definitive source of its type, the historical survey is accented by many engaging sidelights, such as "A Diagram History of Football," "Pro Football Language," "Extinct Teams, Extinct Leagues," and "A History of Football Equipment."

809.   Treat, Roger. **The Encyclopedia of Football.** 15th rev. ed. New York: Doubleday, 1977. 702p. Illus. (A Doubleday/Dolphin Book.) ISBN 0-385-12264-0 pap.

The seven chapters composing the text include comprehensive National Football League, American Football League, and All American Football Conference records; team rolls; information on all pro players; draft data, a year-by-year analysis of pro football from 1919 onward; Hall of Fame members, and listings of individual and team champions.

Handbooks

810.   Baldwin, Robert. **College Football Records: Division I-A and the Ivy League, 1869-1984.** Jefferson, NC: McFarland, 1987. 198p. Index. ISBN 0-89950-246-6.

This covers the currently active 111 Division I-A teams. Arranged by conference (independents have their own section), the entries include won-lost records, nickname, colors, location, stadium capacity, first year of competition, date entered conference, and number of conference championships. The appendixes look at various team performances in conferences and bowls.

811.   **Football Register.** St. Louis, MO: The Sporting News. Annual. ISSN: 0071-7258 pap.

The tool is divided into alphabetically arranged player and coaching sections. The entries in the former cover age, weight, birthplace, education, awards, honors, records, and pro stats by season, whereas biographical data and career highlights are provided for coaches.

812.   Jarrett, William S. **Timetables of Sports History: Football.** New York: Facts on File, 1989. 82p. Illus., index. LC 89-30418. ISBN 0-8160-1919-3.

Arranged chronologically (i.e., college: 1865-1890, 1890-1905, 1905-1915, 1915-1920; professional: 1890-1920; annual breakdown, 1920 on for college, professional, and postseasonal football), the book provides hard facts ideal for ready reference needs.

813.   **NCAA Football's Finest: All-Time Great Collegiate Players and Coaches.** Chicago: Triumph Books, 1991. 232p. Illus. LC 91-065984. ISBN 1-880141-03-5.

Rather than biographical data, the tool provides statistical information on the leading players and coaches of the Division I-A game.

814.   **Official NFL Record & Fact Book,** by the NFL Staff. New York: Workman. Annual. Pap.

This is a useful compendium of pro football game schedules; key dates, such as when clubs can sign free agents; rules; awards; performance leaders; key historical events (in chronological order); Hall of Fame members; etc.

815. **Official NCAA Football.** Shawnee Mission, KA: National Collegiate Athletic Association. Annual. 564p. Illus.

The NCAA-sponsored statistical guide is notable for its inclusion of all levels of plays; in addition to the highly visible I-A, I-AA, II, and III are also covered. Schedules, attendance figures, records, awards, and a wealth of performance data are included in the text.

816. **Pro Football Guide.** St. Louis, MO: The Sporting News. Annual. Pap.

The source focuses on the NFL scene—the previous year's statistics, all-time records, the upcoming season's schedule, and team data.

817. Spink, C. C. Johnson, publisher. **The Sporting News' National Football Guide: Including All-Time Pro Records—NFL, AFL, AAFC.** St. Louis, MO: The Sporting News, Annual. 400-500p. Illus. pap.

This volume ranks with the *Sporting News* and Workman annuals as a vital compilation of pro football data.

Gambling

(See also: Sports and Recreation—Card Games, p. 160)

Dictionaries

818. Clark, Thomas L. **The Dictionary of Gambling & Gaming.** Lexik House, 1988. xxi, 263p. LC 87-82866. ISBN 0-936368-06-3.

This comprehensive tool spans all major forms of gambling, including casinos, racing, and sports betting. The alphabetically arranged entries include grammatical labels, multiple definitions, pronunciation, etymological notes, usage notes, and a citation to an oral or written source.

Encyclopedias

819. Sifakis, Carl. **Encyclopedia of Gambling.** New York: Facts on File, 1990. 340p. Illus., index, bibl. LC 89-33107. ISBN 0-8160-1638-0.

The book's recency constitutes its prime advantage over comparable titles (e.g., Peter Arnold's *Encyclopedia of Gambling,* New York: Chartwell, 1977; Clement McQuaid's *Gambler's Digest,* DBI Books, 1971; E. Silberstang's *New American Guide to Gambling and Games*, New York: New American Library, 1987). The alphabetized entries feature succinct writing with a distinct bias against professional gambling establishments.

Gliding

Handbooks

820. **Soaring Directory, 1976.** Santa Monica, CA: Soaring Society of America, 1976. 389p. pap. bibl.

In addition to listing SSA officers and members, the tool covers virtually all aspects of the sport, including directory listings of soaring schools and clubs, world and state soaring records, SSA and other soaring awards, the international sporting code for gliders, FAA regulations pertaining to gliders, etc.

Golf

Almanacs

821.   **The Golf Digest Almanac.** New York: Times Books/ Random House. Annual. Illus.
The volume blends historical and contemporary data, and notes amateur as well as professional statistics. It provides tournament schedules, golf course descriptions, biographies, USGA rules, and a section on the historical evolution of the sport.

Encyclopedias

822.   Morrison, Ian. **The Hamlyn Encyclopedia of Golf.** Topsfield, MA: Salem House, 1986. 175p. Illus. ISBN 0-600-50218-X.
The volume incorporates biographies, golf terms, slang, records, rules, famous courses, histories of major tournaments, and a variety of statistical data.

Handbooks

823.   Hogan, Bill. **Golf Gadgets.** New York: Macmillan, 1989. 278p. Illus., index. LC 86-15863. ISBN 0-02-043601-7 pap.
A catalog of golf equipment and accessories, Hogan's descriptive commentaries—often complemented by black-and-white photos—should assist users in their selection process. Manufacturers are listed in a special section of the book. A source and product index has also been provided.

824.   Stravinsky, John. **The Complete Golfer's Catalog: The Famous, Best and Most Unusual.** Los Angeles: Price Stern Sloan, 1989. 191p. Illus. LC 88-31945. ISBN 0-89586-743-5.
This factual compendium to the sport is organized into four sections: equipment; courses, resorts, and clubs; instruction; and a miscellany of golf's lighter moments.

Hockey

Handbooks

825.   **Hockey Register.** St. Louis, MO: The Sporting News. Annual. pap. ISSN: 0090-2292.
The tool focuses on the career data of still-active professional and amateur hockey players. It is arranged in two alphabetical parts, one for forwards and defensemen, the other for goaltenders.

826.   **The National Hockey League Official Guide & Record Book.** Philadelphia: Running Press. Annual. Illus. LC 88-42749. ISBN 0-89471-737-5.
The NHL-sanctioned bible includes an analysis of each team (e.g., the prognosis for the upcoming season, draft data, historical background), team and individual statistics

for the prior season, the "NHL Record Book," the "Stanley Cup Guide & Record Book," the player and goaltending registers, etc.

Horsemanship

Handbooks

827.   Rodenas, Paula. **The Random House Book of Horses and Horsemanship.** New York: Random House, 1991. 180p. Illus. LC 86-42934. ISBN 0-394-88705-0.

The work provides a historical and scientific survey of horses as well as a delineation of the fundamentals of horsemanship. It includes insights culled from professionals in such areas as stunt rising and veterinary medicine and directory information on associations and protection agencies. The text moves smoothly from general to specific topics with the assistance of a detailed table of contents.

Martial Arts

Bibliographies

828.   Nelson, Randy F., with Katherine C. Whitaker. **The Martial Arts: An Annotated Bibliography.** New York: Garland, 1988. 436p. Illus. by Forrest Williams and Jerry Lilly. ISBN 0-8240-4435-5.

Limited to monograph and journal articles, the source is organized by the following headings: general topics, specific forms of martial arts, other arts, weapons, and works prior to 1920.

Encyclopedias

829.   Winderbaum, Larry. **The Martial Arts Encyclopedia.** Washington, D.C.: Inscape; distr., Gale Research, 1977. 215p. Illus., bibl. LC 76-43250. ISBN 0-87953-6004.

This groundbreaking work encompasses virtually all aspects of the field (in an alphabetically arranged text). The appendixes list camps and training centers and cover the following topics: "Selecting a Commercial School," "The Martial Arts in the Colleges," and "Women in the Martial Arts."

Motorcycling

Encyclopedias

830.   Carrick, Peter, comp. **Encyclopedia of Motor-Cycle Sport.** New York: St. Martin's Press, 1977. 224p. Illus. LC 76-62754. ISBN 0-312-24867-9.

The 500-odd entries span the entire history of motorcycle racing as far back as the turn of the century. Despite a European bias, America is also strongly represented.

Mountaineering

Bibliographies

831. Krawczyk, Chess, comp. **Mountaineering: A Bibliography of Books in English to 1974.** Metuchen, NJ: Scarecrow, 1977. 180p. Indexes. LC 76-45415. ISBN 0-8108-0979-6.

The 1,141 entries, arranged alphabetically by author, cover "rock, snow and ice climbing" as well as few minor topics of related interest. It has long been the most comprehensive listing of its kind. Title and subject indexes have also been provided.

The Olympic Games

Bibliographies

832. Mallon, Bill. **The Olympics: A Bibliography.** New York: Garland, 1984. 258p. (Garland Reference Library of Social Science, Vol. 246.) LC 84-4072. ISBN 0-8240-8926-X.

This is a selective listing of the books and journals on the Olympics Games from around the world. The work's efficient organization represents a major plus; publications by official bodies are followed by those of private authors (within sections, entries are arranged by date of publication).

Biographies

833. Davis, Michael D. **Black American Women in Olympic Track and Field: A Complete Illustrated Reference.** Jefferson, NC: McFarland, 1992. 170p. Illus., index. LC 91-50946. ISBN 0-89950-692-2.

The source consists of concise biographical profiles of more than seventy African American women in the Olympics (1932-1988).

Encyclopedias

834. Mallon, Bill and Ian Buchanan, with Jeffrey Tishman. **Quest for Gold: The Encyclopedia of American Olympians.** New York: Leisure; distr., Scribner's, 1984. 495p. Illus. LC 84-966. ISBN 0-88011-217-4.

The biographical entries, which range considerably in length (from one line to the several pages allotted Jim Thorpe), are limited to medal winners from 1896 to 1980.

Handbooks

835. Greenberg, Stan. **Olympic Games: The Records.** New York: Guinness Superlatives; distr., Sterling Publishing, 1987. 176p. Illus., index. ISBN 0-85112-896-3.

In addition to documenting all medal winners in the Olympics from 776 B.C. to 1988, the work provides highlights of each of the summer and winter games and profiles some of the more prominent heroes.

836. Hugman, Barry J., and Peter Arnold. **The Olympic Games: Complete Track and Field Results, 1896-1988**. New York: Facts on File, 1988. [385]p. Illus., bibl. ISBN 0-8160-2120-1.

Arranged chronologically by Olympic Game (and subdivided alphabetically by nation), each section includes a narrative summary followed by statistical records for all competitors in these events.

837. Jarrett, William S. **Timetables of Sports History: The Olympic Games.** New York: Facts on File, 1990. Illus., index. LC 89-48159. ISBN 0-8160-1921-5.

Primarily a listing of medal winners for the Olympic Games since 1896, the book also includes anecdotal comments and a number of topical essays throughout the text (e.g., Asian athletes, black medalists). A name index has also been included.

838. Mallon, Bill. **The Olympic Record Book.** New York: Garland, 1988. 522p. LC 87-22511. ISBN 0-8240-2948-8.

The source lists overall Olympic records up through the twenty-fourth Olympiad (1988) as well as related data (e.g., torch bearers, number of nations and athletes competing in the game).

839. Page, James A. **Black Olympian Medalists.** Englewood, CO: Libraries Unlimited, 1991. 190p. Index. LC 90-46660. ISBN 0-87287-618-7.

The 471 biographical sketches include data on the subject's country, birthplace, dates of their competitions, medals won and information about the competition. The appendixes cite athletes by event and nation.

840. Wallechinsky, David. **The Complete Book of the Olympics.** rev. ed. New York: Viking, 1988. 680p. Illus. (54p. of plates.) ISBN 0-670-82110-1; 0-14-010771-1 (Penguin pap.)

First published in 1984, the coverage—largely statistical in nature—is provided up through the Los Angeles games of that year. The exhaustive statistical data is complemented by many anecdotes culled from Olympic lore.

Rodeos

Handbooks

841. Fleming, Steve, ed. **Official Professional Rodeo Media Guide, 1990.** Colorado Springs, CO: Professional Rodeo Cowboy Association, 1990. 287p. Illus., pap.

The premier publication of its kind, it provides historical background, statistics, and biographical profiles of clowns, bullfighters, etc., as well as rodeo competitors.

842. **Professional Rodeo Official Handbook, 1987.** Boulder, CO: Johnson Books, 1987. 254p. Illus. ISBN 1-55566-015-0 pap.

Produced by the Professional Rodeo Cowboys Association, the book covers notable performers (as well as others associated with the sport), historical background, the National Finals Rodeo, and the circuit system.

Skateboarding

Handbooks

843. Cassorla, Albert. **The Skateboarder's Bible: Technique, Equipment, Stunts, Terms, etc.** Philadelphia: Running Press, 1976. 204p. Illus. LC 76-28511. ISBN 0-914294-59-8 pap.
   The volume scopes out the entire field, providing a historical survey of the sport, suggestions on locating a good place to ride, descriptions of performing techniques, safety and maintenance requirements, a list of relevant associations, a directory of manufacturers and distributors equipment, lists of films and sound recordings, and a glossary of terms.

Soccer

Handbooks

844. Rollin, Jack. **The World Cup, 1930-1990: Sixty Glorious Years of Soccer's Premier Event.** New York: Facts on File, 1990. 191p. Illus., index. ISBN 0-8160-2523-1.
   The volume is divided into three parts: coverage of the competitive events, concise biographies of twenty-one well-known players, and an analysis of the teams reaching the 1990 finals. The appendixes include World Cup records, World Cup trivia, FIFA-affiliated nations, and a look at the 1994 event (scheduled to take place in the United States). A personal name index has also been provided.

Surfing

Handbooks

845. Filosa, Gary Fairmont R. **The Surfer's Almanac: An International Surfing Guiding.** New York: E. P. Dutton, 1977. 208p. Illus., index, bibl. (A Sunrise Book.) LC 77-2233. ISBN 0-87690-252-2.
   Although the bulk of the source describes surfing locales around the world, it also includes a historical survey and discussions on water conditions, techniques of surfing, select equipment, and safety. A lengthy glossary, entitled the "Surfer's International Lexicon," is also provided.

Swimming

Encyclopedias

846. Besford, Pat, comp. **Encyclopedia of Swimming.** 2nd ed. London: Robert Hale; distr., St. Martin's Press, 1976. 302p. Illus., index. LC 76-16687. ISBN 0-7091-5063-6.
   The work combines biographies, relevant topics, and lists of many champions and records relating to competitive swimming.

Tennis

Handbooks

847.   Lumpkin, Angela. **A Guide to the Literature of Tennis.** Westport, CT: Greenwood, 1985. 235p. Indexes. ISBN 0-313-24492-8.

The work consists of bibliographic essays on the following topics: history of the sport; history of championship players and performance; rules and administration; equipment, facilities, and travel; technique; players and teaching professionals; health and fitness; psychology; biography; children's books, humor, and films; general works; periodicals; and promotional organizations. The appendixes note organizations, halls of fame, and various champions. Author and subject indexes have also been provided.

Treasure Hunting

Handbooks

848.   Perrin, Rosemarie D. **Explorers Ltd. Guide to Lost Treasure in the United States and Canada.** Harrisburg, PA: Cameron House; distr., Two Continents Publishing Group, 1977. 204p. Illus., index, bibl. LC 77-5595. ISBN 0-8117-2074-8 pap.

Arranged alphabetically by state and province, the book consists of 300 instances of lost treasure lore. The inclusions met the criterion that enough substantive information be present to permit further research (e.g., type of lost treasure is identified, either topographical map or nautical chart be available). A highly informative appendix includes a bibliography of treasure site references, an analysis of maps and charts, an essay on the law of treasure hunting, a delineation of metal detectors, and a list of state and provincial archives and historical societies available for further study.

Video Games

Handbooks

849.   **Video Games Quest: The Complete Guide to Home Video Game Systems, Video Games and Accessories.** Northridge, CA: VMS, 1990. Illus. LC 90-080079. I: 0-9625057-2-2 pap.

Geared to the video game fan, the work provides a history of the genre, a market analysis, suggestions to parents for regulating game play, and—in the main section—a survey of the different types of games divided into seven categories: arcade action, action adventure, quest adventure, educational, family, shooting, sports, and strategy. The entries include the title, manufacturer, number of players, description (off the package), and (in most cases) a trademark picture. Supplementary material consists of a listing of game accessories and a personal checklist for the user to record games owned or loaned.

Wrestling

Encyclopedias

850.   Chapman, Mike. **Encyclopedia of American Wrestling.** Champaign, IL: Leisure Press/Human Kinetics, 1990. 533p. Illus., bibl. LC 89-2701. ISBN 0-88011-342-1.

The work is devoted to amateur (Greco-Roman) wrestling rather than the show business variant available in arenas and on television. Areas covered include the American champions in the Olympics, the World Championships and other international meets, the AAU National Freestyle Championships, the U.S. Freestyle Senior Open, the Greco-Roman Nationals, the Collegiate Nationals, the Midland Championships, the Junior Nationals, the Junior World Tournaments, special honors and awards, Halls of Fame, and other issues relevant to the sport.

Chapter 11

Special Collections

Collectibles—Americana

851. **Hake's Americana and Collectibles.** c/o Theodore L. Hake, P.O. Box 1444, York, PA 17405. 717-848-1333. Accessibility: Monday-Friday, 10-5. Scholars only. Fees: Sometimes applied to photographs.

The collection, which emphasizes character and personality items, has been in existence for more than 20 years. Specialties include comic characters, Disneyana, western heroes, space heroes, and radio/television/film. A negative file with over 100,000 items is complemented by a large amount of physical artifacts.

Collectibles—Dolls

852. **McCurdy Historical Doll Museum.** c/o Shirley B. Paxman, Director, 246 North 100 East Provo, UT 84601. 801-377-9935. Accessibility: Tuesday-Saturday, 12-6. Scholars, public. Fees: Adults, $2; children under 12, $1.

The collection includes reference books devoted to dolls and toys, in addition to over 4,000 objects, most notably story book dolls, international dolls, women of the Bible, wives of U.S. presidents, American Indian dolls, black dolls, Shirley Temple dolls, American folk dolls, and Russian nesting dolls. It also includes antique teddy bears; wooden toys, games, and miniatures; paper dolls dating from 1810; and Noah's Arks.

Collectibles—Toys

853. **Perelman Antique Toy Museum.** c/o Leon J. Perelman, Director, 270 S. 2nd Street Philadelphia, PA 19106. 215-922-1070. Accessibility: Daily, 9:30-5 (except Thanksgiving and Christmas Day). Scholars, public.

The museum encompasses over 4,000 early American tin and cast-iron toys, the largest known collection of mechanical and still banks in the United States, and a library of several hundred books about toys.

Mass Media—General

854. **Burbank Public Library.** c/o Mary Ann Grasso and Barbara Stones, Coordinators, Media Project, Warner Research Collection, 110 N. Glenoaks Blvd., Burbank, CA 91502. Accessibility: Available by appointment only. Fees: Based on the nature of services rendered.

The WRC is a full-service division serving the production needs of the motion picture, television, theatrical, and creative arts communities. The collection spans 32,000 cataloged volumes and vertical files housing pictures and clippings. Subject specialties include costumes, the U.S. military, crime and criminals, transportation, license plates, and Sears catalogs.

855. **University of California, Los Angeles.** c/o Audree Malkin, Head, Theater Arts Library, Los Angeles, CA 90024. Accessibility: Limited photocopying.

This is a leading research collection covering the historical, critical, aesthetic, biographical, and technical aspects of film, radio, and television. In addition to 12,500 cataloged books, the collection encompasses photographs, microforms, sound recordings, 166,000 pamphlets, over 4,000,000 moving picture stills, over 33,000 screenplays, scripts from American and British films, approximately 2,000 radio scripts, 3,000 television scripts, 100,000 manuscripts, over 7,000 posters (from 1915 to date), and a host of supplementary materials (e.g., portraits; clippings files; film festival programs; motion picture programs; lobby cards; original sketches and production materials; records and correspondence of actors, directors, producers, art directors, and screen and television writers).

856. **University of Georgia.** c/o Vesta Lee Gordon, Assistant Director for Special Collections, Libraries Special Collections Division, Athens, GA 30602.

The archive of over 26,300 bound volumes is supplemented by the Arbitron Collection of television and radio program ratings, 1949-present, which includes in-depth statistical analyses of the listening public by age, sex, county, some ethnic groups, farm population, listening preferences, etc.

857. **University of Iowa.** c/o Robert A. McCown, Manuscript Librarian, University Libraries, Iowa City, Iowa 52242.

The institution includes five special collections: (1) The Robert Blees Collection includes stories, still production photos, and film and television scripts of a script writer. It covers the period 1925-1965. (2) The David Swift Collection includes scripts, posters, photos, drawings, and blueprints for final set construction of a motion picture. It spans the 1951-1965 period. (3) The Albert Jay Cohen Collection, 1948-1958, includes correspondence, film scripts, stories, photos, financial and production papers, and censorship records. (4) The Arthur A. Ross Collection includes correspondence, scripts, photos, production records, and artists' sketches of a motion picture and television script writer. It covers the period 1943-1965. (5) The Norman Felton Papers, 1937-1978, includes notes, correspondence, notebooks, subject files, budgets, other financial records, photographs, and scripts relating to such television series as "The Man From U.N.C.L.E.," "Jericho," and "Dr. Kildare," produced by Felton.

858. **Library of Congress.** Motion Picture, Broadcasting & Recorded Sound Division, Jefferson Building, Washington, D.C. 20540. Accessibility: General public; some collections only available to scholars by special permission. Duplication requests must be accompanied by the written authorization of those holding copyright and proprietary rights.

The collection includes over seven million titles (more than two million being music and speech recordings) dating from the late nineteenth century. Noncommerical material (e.g., field recordings, off-the-air broadcast tapes) compose a significant portion of the archive. Formats include wax cylinders, instantaneous discs, pressed discs, magnetic wire, magnetic tape in various configurations, film stock, videotape, etc. Also included are specialized inventories, indexes, and catalogs prepared for access to portions of the collection. Specialized holdings include, for films and videotapes, the American Film Institute Collection, the Edison Laboratory Collection, the Mary Pickford Collection, the Theodore Roosevelt Association Collection, and United Artists Collection; for sound recordings, the Arthur Godfrey Time Collection, the George and Ira Gershwin Collection, the Oscar Hammerstein II Collection, the Jim Walsh Collection, the NBC Radio Collection, the National Public Radio Collection, and the Voice of America Collection.

859. **Los Angeles Public Library.** c/o Sally Dumaux, Librarian, Frances Howard Gold-wyn Hollywood Regional Library, 1623 Ivar Avenue, Los Angeles, CA 90028. Accessibility: General public.

The archive covers films, radio broadcasting, and television. Materials include over 2,000 motion picture and television scripts, biographical data, credits for over 1,500 films from the 1920s to the present, posters, lobby cards, souvenir programs, scrapbooks, vertical files, and more than 3,000 publicity stills. Notable special collections include the Fred Archer Collection (photographs and information devoted to personalities of the stage and screen, 1907-1930), Gilbert A. Adrian Collection (designer sketches and photos), and Hazel Flynn Collection (photographs and publicist correspondence).

860. **Museum of Broadcasting.** c/o Douglas Gibbons, Directo,r Library 1 E. 53rd Street, New York, NY 10022.

The museum, which is dedicated to the study and preservation of the history of broadcasting, includes a collection of significant radio and television programs from the 1920s to the present (i.e., recordings of 10,000 radio and 10,000 television programs, 2,550 original scripts, 2,000 reference tools).

861. **National Film, Television and Sound Archives.** c/o Jana Vosikovska, Chief, Documentation & Public Service, 395 Wellington Street, Ottawa K1A 0N3, Canada.

The institution embraces several collections documenting the mass media. Resources include 1,060 periodical titles (450 current; some on microfilm), 265,000 picture stills, 6,000 film posters, 33,000 cataloged microfiche, and index cards (Film Title Index: 250,000 cards; Personalities Index: 84,000 cards).

Mass Media—Comic Books/Comic Strips/ Cartooning

862. **Bowling Green State University.** c/o Popular Culture Archive, Jerome Library, Bowling Green, OH 43403. Accessibility: Regular library hours. Scholars, public.

The collection includes 50,000 comic books and extensive holdings of other graphic arts media, such as newspaper strips, Big-Little books, fanzines, picture postcards, posters, etc.

863. **California State University, Fullerton.** c/o Kathy Morris, Archivist, Library, Box 4150, Fullerton, CA 92634. Accessibility: Regular library hours. Scholars, public.

The holdings include several thousand comic books (both commercial releases and underground titles) and fanzines.

864. **Comic Research Library.** c/o Doug Kendig, Librarian, Cassidy V0R 1HO, Canada. Accessibility: Open to the public by appointment.

This private archive contains almost 200,000 newspaper strips and over 1,000 volumes of related material in book form. The strips are clipped, organized, and mounted in books, covering the 1920s through the 1950s.

865. **Iowa State University.** c/o Stanley Yates, Librarian, Department of Special Collections, Ames, Iowa 50011. Accessibility: Regular library hours. Scholars, public.

The collection features over 1,000 underground comics and a substantial number of EC titles.

866. **Library of Congress.** c/o Government Publications Division, Washington, D.C. 20540. Accessibility: Restricted to scholarly research.

The collection includes more than 2,300 titles in approximately 50,000 pieces (growing by 200-odd issues per month). Although most comprehensive from 1950 to the present, it possesses fairly complete collections of such long-running series as *Action Comics, Archie, Detective Comics, Tarzan,* and *Wonder Woman.*

867. **Michigan State University.** c/o Jannette Fiore, Librarian, Special Collections Division, Libraries, East Lansing, MI 48824. Accessibility: Regular library hours. Scholars, public.

The Comic Art archive, part of the Russel B Nye Popular Culture Collection, includes approximately 100,000 comic books and extensive holdings of books, magazines, and fanzines about comics. The superhero comics of the 1960s are a prime emphasis; however, other genres (e.g., war comics, funny animal comics, underground comics) are also available in large quantities. The James Haynes Collection of "Golden Age" comics includes 21,000 items. The titles are cataloged, with author-title and subject access and a checklist of holdings. A quarterly newsletter about the archive and the comic book genre in general, edited by Peter Berg and Randall Scott, is available free upon request.

868. **Museum of Cartoon Art Library.** Comly Avenue, Rye Brook, NY 10573.

Devoted to original comics and cartoon art, the holdings include over 60,000 pieces with 800 animated cartoons and an extensive Disney archive. The original art collection includes Hal Foster, Walt Kelly, Gene Byrns, Ted Dorgan, Chester Gould. Big-Little books, foreign comics, fanzines, cartoon-related games, posters, pulps, and undergrounds are also represented here.

869. **Ohio State University.** c/o Lucy Caswell, Curator, Library for Communication and Graphic Arts, 242 W. 18th Street, Columbus, OH 43210.

The archive includes extensive original cartoon art. Its notable holdings include the original comic art of Caniff, Foster, Dunn, and Dudley T. Fisher. The comic book collection, especially those featuring Katy Keene, is rapidly attaining world-class status. Movie posters and stills, numbering well over 110,000 items, represent another focal point of the collection.

870. **San Francisco Academy of Comic Art.** Library, 1850 Ulloa, San Francisco, CA 94116. 415-681-1737. Accessibility: Use by appointment only. Photocopies and interlibrary loan available.

The academy possesses the largest collection of pulp magazines in the United States. It also has extensive holdings of all major American newspapers (in the paper format with an emphasis upon the Hearst Syndicate); Sherlockiana; early motion picture tapes, books, magazines, and posters; comic strips (more than one million); comic books (approximately 25,000); hard cover mystery books (12,500); and hard cover science fiction books (8,000).

Mass Media—Films

871. **American Film Institute.** c/o Anne G. Schlosser, Library Directo,r Louis B. Mayer Library, P.O. Box 27999, 2021 N. Western Avenue, Los Angeles, CA 90027. 213-856-7655. Accessibility: Open to the public.

The Script Collection includes thousands of film and television scripts, many of which were working copies for directors, writers, editors, and script supervisors. The MGM Script Collection encompasses 400 scripts from the silent period up to the mid-1950s. The Columbia

Pictures Stills Collection covers the period 1930-1950. The Oral History Program Collection has interviews with pioneers of the industry as well as transcripts of AFI seminars. A film production and file index provides documentation on nearly all U.S. films from 1930 to 1969; each title is tracked from the first trade announcement regarding film production to its final release.

872. **Sherman Grinberg Film Libraries, Inc.** c/o Bill Brewington, 1040 N. McCadden Place, Hollywood, CA 90038-3787. 213-464-7491. New York Office: Nancy Casey, 630 Ninth Avenue, New York, NY 10036-3787. 212-765-5170. Accessibility: Monday-Friday, 9:30-5:30. Scholars, public. Fees: $25 per hour, $50 minimum; includes viewing, research, and computer printouts.

This is the largest known news and stock footage film and tape library covering the twentieth century. Its resources include footage from ABC News (1963-present), Pathe News (1989-1957), Paramount News (1926-1957), MGM features and television stock footage, *Nova* and *Odyssey* television stock footage, selected BBC programming, Fitzpatrick Short Subjects, etc.

873. **Walt Disney Archives.** c/o David R. Smith, Archivist, 500 S. Buena Vista Street, Burbank, CA 91521. 818-840-5424. Accessibility: Monday-Friday, 8-5. Scholars, public. Advance appointment and specific research projects required.

The definitive Disney archive, including the founder's office correspondence files (1930-1966) and assorted earlier files, in addition to personal memorabilia, recordings and transcripts of speeches, awards, 8,000 photographs of Disney, a Disney family history, and a collection of miniatures. Also present are about 1,000 Disney books published in the United States, a representative collection of Disney books published in thirty-five languages, a complete run of domestic Disney comic books and most foreign comics (1932-present), a nearly complete collection of phonograph records issued by the Walt Disney Music Company, several hundred singles and albums of Disney songs issued by other recording companies, tape recordings, sheet music of Disney titles, a vast clippings file dating from 1924, over 500,000 negatives of photographs related to Disney and his enterprises, thousands of Disney toys and memorabilia, copies of Disney films (along with scripts, cutting continuities, and other production information), a large collection of movie props and artifacts, data covering the history of Disney theme parks and Audio-Animatronics, most of Disney's original artwork, and oral histories of Disney conducted with his key employees. All resources are organized, with key materials fully indexed.

Mass Media—Journalism

874. **Alternative Press Center.** c/o Peggy D'Adamo, P.O. Box 33109, 1443 Gorsuch Avenue, Baltimore, MD 21218. 301-243-2471. Accessibility: Photocopying available upon request.

The center collects materials of an alternative, progressive, and radical nature dating from 1969. Prime topics include gay and lesbian liberation, racism, animal rights, and the environmental movement.

875. **American Newspaper Publishers Association.** Library, 11600 Sunrise Valley Drive, Reston, VA. (Mailing address: c/o Yvonne Egertson, Librarian, P.O. Box 17407, Dulles International Airport, Washington, D.C. 20041.)

The collection—including books, serials, and cataloged microforms—focuses on newspaper publishing and the history of newspapers.

876. **University of Illinois, Urbana/Champaign.** c/o Nancy Allen, Librarian, Communications Library, 122 Gregory Hall, Urbana, IL 61801.

Journalism history, as well as theoretical foundations and practitioner skills associated with the profession, form the core of the collection. It also includes studies of individual journalists, newspapers, and other news media.

877. **Library of Congress.** c/o John C. Broderick, Chief Manuscript Division, Washington, D.C. 20540.

The papers of Roy W. Howard (1883-1964), past president and chairman of the board of Scripps-Howard Newspapers, form the centerpiece of the collection. Included are some 85,000 items for the years 1923-1964, including correspondence, with separate files in each year for the various chain newspapers, especially for the New York *World Telegram.* Other notable acquisitions have included the papers of Joseph Wood Krutch, Joseph Alsop, and Stewart Hensley.

Mass Media—Photography

878. **Library of Congress.** Prints & Photographs Division, Washington, D.C. 20540.

The most notable materials are the complete photographic files of *Look* magazine, spanning more than thirty-five years, with 17.5 million black-and-white negatives, 1.5 million color transparencies, 450,000 contact sheets, and 25,000 movie stills.

Mass Media—Radio

879. **Broadcast Pioneers Library.** c/o Catharine Heinz, Director, 1771 N Street, NW, Washington, D.C. 20036.

The resources include over 20,000 pictures, 1,450 phono-records, and 1,200 audio-tapes. Among the special collections are Oral History, the Havrilla Collection (photos, soundtracks featuring radio performers), the William S. Hedges Collection, the Elmo Neale Pickerill Collection, the Joseph E. Baudino Collection, and the Archive of Federal Communications Bar Association.

880. **George Mason University.** c/o Ruth Kerns, Public Services Librarian, Special Collections Dept., Fenwick Library, 4400 University Drive, Fairfax, VA 22030.

The materials of prime interest belong to the Federal Theatre Project Collection, which includes 5,000 play scripts, 2,500 radio scripts, 25,000 photographs, musical scores, etc.

881. **University of Illinois, Urbana/Champaign.** (See: Mass Media—Journalism)

882. **New York Public Library.** (See: Mass Media—Television)

883. **North American Radio Archives.** Janis DeMoss, Executive Officer. 134 Vincewood Dr., Nicholasville, KY 40356. (606) 885-1031. Accessibility: Available to NARA members only.

The collection includes print resources as well as audio tapes of original radio shows.

884. **Temple University Libraries.** c/o Thomas M. Whitehead, Curator, Special Collections Department, Rare Books & Manuscript Section, Philadelphia, PA 19122.

The archive possesses a substantial number of American and British radio and television rehearsal and camera scripts, including *Lux Radio Theatre* (1934-1955), *One Man's Family,* and *I Love a Mystery.*

Mass Media—Telecommunications

885. **Museum of Independent Telephony.** c/o Peg Chronister, 412 S. Campbell, Abilene, KS 67410. 913-263-2681.

The museum includes books, periodicals, over 1,000 manuscripts, over 100 oral history cassettes, and about 4,000 artifacts devoted to the telephone and its role in society.

Mass Media—Television

886. **National Broadcasting Company.** c/o Vera Mayer, Vice President, Information and Archives Reference Library, 30 Rockefeller Plaza, Room 1426, New York, NY 10020.

The collection—comprising monographs, periodicals, clippings, microforms, and other formats—documents the entire history of the medium as well as related topics, such as business, politics, and social issues.

887. **New York Public Library.** c/o Dorothy L. Swerdlove, Curator, Billy Rose Theatre Collection, Performing Arts Research Center, 111 Amsterdam Avenue, New York, NY 10023.

Since 1941, it has been the official repository of the American Television Society. The holdings include clipping files on radio and television programs and their respective personnel; photographs of these individuals, of radio and television studios, equipment, etc.; television production scripts (most notably, most of the *Hallmark Hall of Fame* specials and *Studio One* scripts); radio scripts; and monographs devoted to the history of broadcasting and telecasting and the techniques of the industry.

Oral History

888. **Columbia University Oral History Research Office.** c/o Ronald J. Grele, Director, Butler Library, Box 20, New York, NY 10027. 212-280-4012. Accessibility: Monday-Friday, 9-5. Scholars, public. Some materials are restricted.

The archive includes the following resources: the Popular Arts Project, Radio Pioneers Project, Hollywood Film Industry Project, Children's Television Workshop Project, American Cultural Leaders Project, Book-of-the-Month-Club Project, Mercury Theater/Theater Union Project, and New York's Art World Project.

Performing Arts—The Circus

889. **Circus Historical Society.** c/o Fred D. Pfening, Jr., 2515 Dorset Road, Columbus, OH 43221. 614-294-5461. Accessibility: Available by appointment only.

Limited to authors of circus books. The collections are particularly strong with respect to photographs and the various types of printed material used by American circuses.

890. **Circus World Museum Library and Research Center.** c/o Robert L. Parkinson, Director, 415 Lynn Street, Baraboo, WI 53913. 608-356-8341. Accessibility: Monday-Friday, 8-12; 1-5. Scholars, public. Advance notification by letter or telephone recommended.

This world class collection includes 8,000 original circus lithographs, 400 circus route books, 1,800 circus books, 1,600 circus heralds and couriers, 1,200 circus programs, 50,000 photo prints, 20,000 photo negatives, 12,000 circus newspaper ads, and other materials. It also houses a Ringling Brothers and Barnum & Bailey Circus Archive, statistical records, circus movies, a circus music library, materials relating to Wild West Shows, and show business periodicals, such as *Billboard, New York Clipper, White Tops,* and *Bandwagon.*

891. **Illinois State University.** c/o Robert Sokan, Librarian, Department of Special Collections, Milner Library, Normal, IL 61761.

The archive is built around 6,200 books (dating back to the sixteenth century, many of which are limited editions, presentation copies, or autographed copies) and approximately 250,000 nonbook items. Topics covered include the circus past and present, vaudeville, music halls and variety theaters, theatrical and animal history, biographies, autobiographies and memoirs, novels, poetry, drama, juvenilia, etc. One notable inclusion is the Dobritch International Circus collection.

892. **Memphis State University.** c/o John Terreo, Special Collections Librarian, John Willard Brister Library, Memphis, TN 38152. Accessibility: Regular library hours.

The Brister Library's reputation is based upon the Dyer Marion "Ichabod" Reynolds Circus Collection, which spans the 1878-1980 period. It includes negatives and prints, letters, newspaper and periodical clippings, scrapbooks, albums, handbills, posters, route cards, couriers, lithographs, and small artifacts documenting the former preeminence of the American Circus within the show business sector.

893. **New York Public Library.** (For address, see entry 941.)

The focal point is the Townsend Walsh Collection, a rare assemblage of nineteenth- and early twentieth-century circus material—route books, programs, posters, etc.—primarily concerned with the circus in the United States and Great Britain.

Performing Arts—Theatrical Arts

894. **Free Library of Philadelphia.** Geraldine Duclow, Librarian-in-Charge, Theatre Collection, Logan Square, Philadelphia, PA 19103. Accessibility: Regular library hours. In-house use only.

The archive contains books, magazines, playbills, broadsides, posters, photographs, and other memorabilia covering theater, motion pictures, minstrels, vaudeville, circus, radio, and television. The Philadelphia Theatre Index lists the major productions in that city beginning in 1855 and partially indexes the collection of local playbills dating back to 1803. Various files contain autographs, photographs, and newspaper articles and reviews in all pertinent subject areas.

Popular Art

895. Number not used.

896. **California Institute of the Arts.** c/o James Elrod, Director, Library, 24700 McBean Parkway, Valencia, CA 91355.

This wide-ranging collection includes slides and print materials devoted to the following genres: abstract art, conceptual art, concrete art, environment art, minimal art, pop art, Dadaism, surrealism, happenings, caricatures, and cartoons.

897. **Museum of Norman Rockwell Art.** c/o Joyce E. Devore, 227 S. Park Street, Reedsburg, WI 53959. 608-524-2123. Accessibility: Daily, April 1-October 31, 9:30-5; by appointment during remainder of the year. Scholars, public.

Housed in a small brick church, the collection includes over 3,000 original covers, illustrations, advertisements, postcards, catalogs, posters, and other items spanning Rockwell's sixty-five-year career.

898. **Norman Rockwell Museum.** c/o Fred Brinckerhoff, RR 3, Box 7209, Rt. 4, East Rutland, VT 05701. 802-773-6095.

The institution owns some of the artist's personal artifacts and other resources documenting his career.

Popular History—The Old West

899. **National Cowboy Hall of Fame and Western Heritage Center.** c/o A. J. "Ace" Tytgat, 1700 NE 63rd Street, Oklahoma City, OK 73111. 405-478-2250. Accessibility: Daily, 9-5; Summer hours (Memorial Day-Labor Day): Monday-Friday, 8:30-6. Scholars, public. Advance notice required.

The archive includes more than 7000 books, covering art, artists, folklore, early western development, Indian and cowboy data, etc.

900. **University of Oklahoma.** c/o Nathan E. Bender, Librarian, Western History Collections, 630 Parrington, Oval Monnet Hall, Room 452, Norman, OK 73019. 405-325-2904. Accessibility: Monday-Friday, 8-5; during fall and spring semesters, also Saturday, 9-1. Scholars, public.

The WHC encompasses the Mr. and Mrs. Robert Fay Collection (St. Louis World's Fair memorabilia) and the Frank Phillips Collection. The latter includes approximately 50,000 volumes on the western frontier and native American history. Notable topics represented are cowboy songs and humor, western women, and western fiction (e.g., Buffalo Bill dime novels) represented are cowboy songs and humor, western women, and western fiction (e.g., Buffalo Bill dime novels).

Popular History—War

901. **Confederate States of America Collection**. Rare Book & Special Collections Division, Library of Congress, Washington, D.C. 20540. Accessibility: Scholars, public.

The collection is composed largely of publications issued in the South by the individual states as well as the Congress, departments, and offices of the Confederacy.

902. **Civil War Library and Museum.** c/o Russ A. Pritchard, Directo,r 1805 Pine Street, Philadelphia, PA 19103. 215-735-8196. Accessibility: Monday-Friday, 10-4. Scholars, public.

All aspects of the Civil War are covered. Although the institution's artifacts and print resources emphasize the Union army, Confederate materials are also available in ample quantities.

903. **Civil War Photograph Collection**. Prints & Photographs Division, Library of Congress, Washington, D.C. 20540.

The archive is built around the Civil War photos by Mathew Brady's staff and others. The holdings consist primarily of 10,000 original and copy glass plate negatives acquired in 1943.

Popular Literature—Best Sellers

904. **California State University at Domingue**. Special Collections, Hills Library, 800 E. Victoria Street, Carson, CA 90749. 213-516-3700. Accessibility: Regular library hours. Available to the public. In-house use only.

The University Library houses the Claudia Buck Collection of American Best Sellers, which spans the entire history of the country.

905. **University of Wisconsin-Superior**. c/o Bob Carmack, Librarian (also, Leo J. Hertzel, Curator) Jim Dan Hill Library, Superior, WI 54880. 715-394-8465 and 715-394-8346. Accessibility: Daily, 9-5. Scholars, public. Prior consultation with one of the above contact persons required.

The institution's Literary Guild Collection contains the papers of John W. R. Beecroft, editor of the Literary Guild from the middle 1930s through the early 1960s. The collection also includes a full run of *Wings,* the monthly magazine mailed to all Guild members, and copies of every Guild title (and book dividend) selected during this period.

Popular Literature—Dime Novels

906. **Athenaeum of Philadelphia**. c/o Keith A. Kamm, 219 S. 6th Street, Philadelphia, PA 19106. 215-925-2688. Accessibility: Monday-Friday, 9-5. Available to scholars only through appointment.

The Athenaeum houses the Sawyer Dime Novel Collection; its more than 1,600 titles heavily represent the output of publishers Beadle and Adams.

Popular Literature—Genre Fiction

907. **Michigan State University**. c/o Jannette Flore, Librarian, Special Collections Division, Libraries, East Lansing, MI 48824.

The popular fiction category of the Russel B Nye Popular Culture Collection is spread over the following genres: juvenile, detective-mystery, science, western, and women's fiction. In addition, the archive includes many dime novels, story papers, and pulp magazines that fall into none of the clearly delineated genre headings noted above. One of the finest archives of its type.

Popular Literature—Science Fiction

General

908. **Bowling Green State University**. Popular Culture Library, Jerome Library, Bowling Green, OH 43403. 419-372-2450. Accessibility: Regular library hours. Scholars, public. In-house use only.

The archive includes over 10,000 volumes of fiction in addition to a comparable number of periodicals. American magazines (1926-1960), pulps, and fanzines represent a particular strength; especially notable are the Michael L. Cook Collection of fanzines (e.g., rare issues of *Flying Saucers, Twilight Zone,* and *Spacecraft Digest*) and the H. James Horvitz Collection of pulp magazines (e.g., runs of *Amazing Stories, Tales of Magic and Mystery,* and *Weird Tales*). The Ray Bradbury Collection spans approximately 1,000 books and more than fifteen linear feet of nonbook materials, including manuscripts, rare pamphlets, comic book adaptations, original art by Bradbury, tapes, phonodiscs, cassettes, broadsides, maps, photographs, galley proofs, scripts, programs, screenplays, diary notes, posters, promotional material, interviews, speeches, and periodicals. Approximately 1,000 items are being added per annum.

909. **University of California at Los Angeles.** Special Collections A1713 University Research Library, Los Angeles, CA 90024 213-825-4988 Accessibility: Regular library hours. Scholars, public.

The institution houses more than 11,000 volumes of fiction and approximately 5,000 periodical issues. The Nitka Collection of Fantastic Fiction possesses extensive English-language magazine holdings as well as over 3,000 paperbacks. It also includes 400 early editions of the works of H. Rider Haggard and oral histories of Ray Bradbury and A. E. van Vogt.

910. **University of California, Riverside.** J. Lloyd Eaton Collection, University Library, 4045 Canyon Crest Drive, Box 5900, Riverside, CA 92517.

The collection covers science fiction/fantasy literature from the sixteenth century to the present. It includes strong individual author collections of Jules Verne, H. Rider Haggard, H. G. Wells, Edgar Rice Burroughs, and Philip K. Dick. It also incorporates about 6,000 pulp magazines. Allied genres and formats include horror, supernatural, and Gothic mystery fiction; boys' books; utopian and dystopian fiction, imaginary voyages, future war, and lost race fiction; French language science fiction and fantasy; critical and scholarly works pertaining to these genres; videotapes of science fiction/fantasy films; and shooting scripts. The institution adds several thousand items annually to the base holdings of over 50,000 volumes.

911. **California State University, Fullerton.** c/o Linda Herman, Special Collections Librarian, University Library, Box 4150, Fullerton, CA 92634. Accessibility: Regular library hours.

The library is a Science Fiction Writers of America regional depository. In addition, it includes several hundred document boxes of manuscripts from over thirty authors and a major collection of science fiction magazines dating from the 1920s (including a complete run of *Amazing,* the first important science fiction magazine).

912. **Dallas Public Library.** Science Fiction and Fantasy Collection, 1954 Commerce Street, Dallas, TX 75201. 214-749-4261. Accessibility: Regular library hours. Researchers only.

The archive incorporates a wide variety of the media, most notably approximately 15,000 volumes of fiction. The Brian Aldiss Collection consists of 2,350 fantasy titles, 187 fantasy and science fiction serial runs, personal correspondence, photographs, speeches, illustrations, introductions, posters and cover art, book and film reviews, radio plays, and notes and typescripts for short stories, novels, and poetry.

913. **Eastern New Mexico University.** c/o Mary Jo Walker, Special Collections Librarian, Golden Library Portales, NM 88130. Accessibility: Regular library hours. Scholars, public.

The collection originated with gifts from author Jack Williamson and now consists of about 25,000 items. Strengths include the pulp magazine acquisitions, old editions of classic novels, and the manuscript holdings (representing such authors as Williamson, Leigh Brackett, Edmond Hamilton, Forrest J. Ackerman, Piers Anthony, James Blish, Marcia Howl, and Woody Wolfe and *Analog* and other publications). It is an SFWA and Science Fiction Oral History Association depository.

914.   **University of Kansas.** c/o Alexandra Mason, Librarian, Special Collections Dept., Kenneth Spencer Research Library, Lawrence, KS 66045. Accessibility: Regular library hours. In-house use only.
    The archive spans monographs, periodicals, and fan literature (uncataloged). It is the North American repository for the World Science Fiction Association, and houses the manuscripts of notable authors and the Science Fiction Research Association.

915.   **Louisiana State University.** The Clarence J. Laughton Library of the Arts, Middleton Library, Baton Rouge, LA 70803. 504-388-6572. Accessibility: Much of the collection is presently boxed.
    The primary focus of the Laughton archive is science fiction, fantasy, and mystery fiction. The extensive fiction holdings, the runs of many pulps, and the presence of specialty presses, such as Gnome Press and Arkham House, render this a major collection.

916.   **University of Louisville.** Patterson Room, Library, Louisville, KY 40208. 502-588-6762.
    In addition to the more than 10,000 pulp magazines and other assorted media, the centerpiece of the collection is 20,000 items by and related to Edgar Rice Burroughs. Included here are English- and foreign-language first editions (most in dust wrappers), personal memorabilia, scrapbooks, Burroughs's school textbooks, comics, posters, photos, manuscripts, fanzines, toys, movies (all but a couple of the Tarzan films, some with scripts), correspondence, and a complete file of all syndicated Sunday and daily comic strips of Tarzan (1928-present).

917.   **MIT Science Fiction Society Library.** MIT Student Center, Room 420-421, Cambridge, MA 02139. 617-253-1000, ext. 5-9144. Accessibility: Members, scholars; inquire regarding hours and restrictions. Fees: A copy of the catalog is available at the requester's cost.
    The collection, numbering about 40,000 items (roughly 2,000 items added per annum), includes a nearly complete file of American and British science fiction magazines. Another strength is the substantial run of foreign-language magazines. Many foreign translations are held.

918.   **University of Maryland, Baltimore County.** c/o Ann Copeland, Special Collections Librarian, Azriel Rosenfeld Science Fiction Research Collection, Albin O. Kuhn Library and Gallery, 5401 Wilkens Avenue, Catonsville, MD 21228. 301-455-2353.
    The archive includes over 25,000 items; its major strength consists of the Walter Coslet fanzine collection (mostly pre-1960) and pulp holdings, numbering about 12,000 and 5,000 items, respectively.

919.   **Michigan State University.** (See: Popular Literature—Genre Fiction)

920. **Ohio State University.** Special Collections Libraries, 1858 Neil Avenue, Columbus, OH 43210. 614-422-5938.

The institution possesses substantial holdings of American and British science
fiction magazines from 1926 to the present, as well as two major special collections: the
Lovecraft Collection, which contains more than 700 items by and about H. P. Lovecraft
supplementing more than 5,000 of his manuscripts (essays, letters, poems, stories, etc.),
and over 3,000 items by 200 of his correspondents; and the Smith Collection, which
contains more than 5,000 manuscripts (1893-1972) of essays, fiction, poetry, and miscellaneous material by Clark Ashton Smith and over 5,000 letters written to him.

921. **San Francisco Academy of Comic Art.** (See entry 870.)

922. **Temple University.** Special Collections Libraries, Philadelphia, PA 19122. 215-
787-8230.

The David C. Paskow Collection, established in 1972, receives many publications
on standing order. Manuscript holdings are a particular strength, including the archives of
Fantasy Press and Prime Press, in addition to such authors as Ben Bova, Gardner Dozois,
Jack Dann, Tom Purdom, Pamela Sargent, George Zebrowski, Michael Bishop, Felix
Gotschalk, John Varley, Miriam DeFord, and Richard Peck.

923. **Texas A&M University.** Science Fiction Research Collection, Sterling Library,
College Station, TX 77843. 409-845-1951. Accessibility: Regular library hours. Photocopies available upon request. Instituted in 1970, the archive houses over 30,000 items.

The pulp magazine holdings compose its core; 95 percent of the American and British
science fiction magazines from 1923 to the present are represented, as are a growing number
of foreign-language titles. The library attempts to acquire all historical, critical, and reference
materials in all languages, including master's theses and doctoral dissertations.

Private Collections

924. **Forrest J. Ackerman.** 2495 Glendower Avenue, Los Angeles, CA 90027. Accessibility: Scholars, public. Available by appointment.

Believed to be the largest collection of a private nature, it contains some 300,000
items, including 36,000 books, complete runs of all science fiction and fantasy magazines
(as well as other pulps, most notably the Munsey publications), most fanzines dating from
1930, much original fantasy illustration, extensive correspondence and clipping files, a
large number of original manuscripts, and strong holdings of film memorabilia (125,000
stills, 18,000 lobby cards, posters, props, etc.). Ackerman—a long-time fan, editor, and
agent—has been reportedly seeking a buyer since the late 1980s.

925. **Darrell C. Richardson.** 899 Stonewall, Memphis, TN 38107.

The collection's strengths include all science fiction/fantasy and early pulps; 29,000
books (many first editions and fine copies; more than 100 authors covered completely,
with a heavy E. R. Burroughs concentration); 7,500 fanzine issues, 1930-1950; and
roughly 7,000 comics, mostly Tarzan, Flash Gordon, and Buck Rogers.

926. **Oswald Train.** 1129 W. Wingohocking Street, Philadelphia, PA 19140.

The archive includes over 10,000 books, extensive magazine runs, artwork (old
photographs, slides, etc.), and allegedly the finest collection of H. Rider Haggard in the
United States.

Popular Music—Phonographs

Private Collections

All Great Collections Series VHS tapes are available from *The Vestal Press Resource Catalogue*, 1993. ISBN 1-87511-11-8.

927. **Howard Hazelcorn.**
Hazelcorn, who has authored *A Collector's Guide to the Columbia Spring-Wound Cylinder Graphophone*, has concentrated on very early, prototypical machines. These include a coin-operated Bell-Tainter Gramophone with a four-spring Amet motor, a Polyphone Eagle, and a Metaphone/Echtophone (the first $5 phonograph, which revolutionized the industry). They are profiled in U.S.S.'s "Great Collections Series" (VHS tape, #GC1).

928. **Charley Hummel.**
Hummel is a trustee to the Edison National Historical Site and a noted lecturer and collector of phonographs and Edisonia. The collection includes a gold-plated Polyphone Edison Soncert set in an oak cylinder cabinet, a coin-operated Rosenfeld with glass slide changing mechanism, and an Edison pantagraphic cylinder duplicator. It is surveyed in U.S.S.'s "Great Collections Series" (VHS tape, #GC2).

929. **Allen Koenigsberg.**
Publisher of the *Antique Phonograph Monthly* and author of *Edison Cylinder Records 1889-1912*, Koenigsberg possesses an eclectic array of rare machines, including an 1896 Chicago Ediphone with Amet motor, a Lionet talking clock, and an Edison talking doll. In U.S.S.'s "Great Collection Series" (VHS tape, #GC3), he spices a tour of his holdings with patent-related anecdotes and an overview of phonograph patent history.

930. **Fran Merancy.**
Merancy's inventory includes early Berliner phonographs and the complete 1901 Victor product line, as well as many other rare and special pieces. It has been profiled in U.S.S.'s "Great Collections Series" (VHS tape, #GC4).

931. **Ray Philips.**
Philips began collecting in 1936 as a teenager, acquiring a Bergman tin foil phonograph. He has since traveled worldwide in search of phonograph rarities. In U.S.S.'s "Great Collection Series" (VHS tape, #GC5), he walks the viewer through his collection, highlighting the only known Edison treadle machine, the Edison waterpower phonograph, the Edison goldplated class M phonograph, and many others.

932. **John Woodward.**
Woodward is presently serving his fourth term as president of the California Antique Phonograph Society. A collector since 1973, his treasures include the only known Edison Clockwork Home, a metal-cased ratchet-wind Berliner (#97, the oldest surviving example of a spring-driven disc phonograph), a weight-driven Stroh tin foil modified for wax recording (with a recording in the grooves from the mid-1800s), and a Multiphone. They are profiled in U.S.S.'s "Great Collections Series" (VHS tape, #GC7).

Popular Music—Recordings

933. Archives of Contemporary Music. c/o David Wheeler and Zach Snow, 110 Chambers Street, New York, NY 10017. 212-964-2296 or 212-619-3505. Accessibility: Scholars. Available by appointment only. Material can be obtained on-line.

The collection contains more than 150,000 records, press kits, interviews, literature, and other materials relating to the recording industry.

934. Chicago Public Library. (See: Popular Music—Sheet Music)

935. Country Music Foundation. c/o Charlie Seemann, Director, Library & Media Center, 4 Music Square East, Nashville, TN 37203.

Billed as the largest collection worldwide devoted to American country music, its wide array of resources (phono-records, audiotapes, videotapes, 16mm films, microforms, slides, manuscripts, pictures, books, periodicals, etc.) also incorporate related subject areas, such as Anglo-American folksong, popular music in general, recorded sound technology, music law, etc.

936. Fitz Hugh Ludlow Memorial Library. c/o Michael R. Aldrich, Executive Curator, P.O. Box 99346, San Francisco, CA 94109. Accessibility: Interlibrary lending and telephone inquiries are discouraged. Important mail requests are considered.

The archive emphasizes books, songbooks, discographies, and phonograph records relating to psychoactive drug-using musicians and their art.

937. University of Illinois, Urbana/Champaign. (See: Popular Music—Sheet Music)

938. Institute of the American Musical. c/o Miles Kreuger, President & Curator, 121 N. Detroit Street, Los Angeles, CA 90036. 213-934-1221. Accessibility: Open to qualified scholars by appointment.

The institute maintains the world's largest collection of reference resources on the American theater and film musical, including over 100,000 phonograph records; tapes; cylinders dating back to the 1890s; record catalogs; thousands of theater and film playbills and programs; periodicals; sheet music and vocal scores as early as 1836; motion picture press books; over 200,000 film stills from 1914 to the present; every musical comedy script published in America; 16mm silent film excerpts from Broadway musicals taken during actual performances from 1931 to 1973; original or photocopied materials from movie palaces, and film and recording companies, including discographies of major Broadway and Hollywood stars; and thousands of books on these and other areas of showmanship.

939. Louisiana State Museum. c/o Edward F. Haas, Chief Curator, Louisiana Historical Center, 400 Esplanade Avenue, New Orleans, LA 70016. (Mailing address: 751 Chartres St., New Orleans, LA 70016.)

The institution houses the New Orleans Jazz Museum and Archives Collection, which includes 12,000 phono-records, 15,000 pictures, 8,000 pieces of sheet music, 1,000 slides, and 1,000 audiotapes concerned with New Orleans jazz.

940. Milwaukee Public Library. c/o Donald J. Sager, City Librarian, 814 W. Wisconsin Avenue, Milwaukee, WI 53233.

In addition to a circulating collection of 40,000 albums, the archive holds recordings of all types from 1900 to the present, including 66,350 seventy-eight r.p.m. discs, 6,800

LPs, and 850 transcription discs from the 1940s and 1950s of local and international events and speeches.

941. **New York Public Library.** c/o Frank C. Campbell, Chief, Music Division, 111 Amsterdam Avenue, New York, NY 10023.

In addition to world class holdings of sheet music (almost 400,000 items), clippings and programs (over two million), broadsides (roughly 2,000), songsters, pictures, and manuscripts, the Rodgers & Hammerstein Archives of Record Sound includes more than 400,000 sound recordings on disc, tape, wire, and cylinder. They span classical and popular music, jazz, and the spoken word. c/o Catherine J. Lenix Hooker Interim Administrator Schomburg Center for Research in Black Culture, 515 Lenox Avenue New York, NY 10037. The center functions as a repository for over 10,000 phonodiscs and 2,000 tapes covering African and West Indian folk music, early blues, and jazz.

942. **Rutgers, The State University of New Jersey.** c/o Dan Morgenstern, Director, Edward Berger, Curator, and Maxie Griffin, Librarian, Institute of Jazz Studies, 135 Bradley Hall, Newark, NJ 07102.

The institute includes 50,000 phono-records, books, manuscripts, pictures, and an oral history project.

943. **Towson State University.** Edwin L. Gerhardt, Curator, Gerhardt Library of Musical Information, Fine Arts Building, Room 457, Towson, MD 21204. 301-242-0328. Accessibility: Available by appointment. A detailed outline will be supplied upon request.

The collection embraces music literature, phonograph and tape recordings, pictures, and artifacts. There are special sections on Thomas Alva Edison and the phonograph, John Philip Suosa and bands, old popular songs, and percussion.

944. **Tulane University.** c/o Richard B. Allen, Acting Curator, William Ransom Hogan Jazz Archive, Special Collections Division, Howard-Tilton Memorial Library, 7001 Freret, New Orleans, LA 70118.

The archive focuses on jazz music history and musicians, encompassing phono-records, audiotapes, videotapes, slides, 16mm films, microforms, pictures, manuscripts, music scores, books, serials, catalogs, and other archival material.

945. **University of Virginia.** c/o Edmund Berkeley, Jr., Curator, Manuscripts Department, Alderman Library, Charlottesville, VA 22901.

The Virginia Folklore Collection includes one particularly notable resource, the Virginia WPA Folklore Files, compiled during the period 1936-1943 under the U.S. Works Project Administration. It features black and white folklore and folk music collected by field workers from informants throughout Virginia. Formats represented include phono-records, manuscripts, and reports.

Popular Music—Sheet Music

946. **Barnard A. & Morris N. Young Library of Early American Popular Music.** c/o Morris N. Young, Curator, 270 Riverside Drive, New York, NY 10025.

The holdings, numbering over 50,000 items, document American popular music, largely from 1790 to 1910. Materials include books, serials, sheet music, broadsides, anthologies, air checks, broadcasting and music business memorabilia, and correspondence.

947. **Brown University.** c/o Mark N. Brown, Curator, John May Library, 20 Prospect Street, Providence, RI 02912.

The Sheet Music Collection, composed largely of American imprints, numbers over 350,000 pieces. Its major strengths are nineteenth-century music (especially prior to 1830), Civil War music, lithographic covers, World War I songs, political campaign songs, and band music.

948. **Chicago Public Library.** c/o Richard C. Schwegel, Head, Music Section, Fine Arts Division, 78 East Washington Street, Chicago, IL 60602. Accessibility: In storage at the Record Center Corporation, the library's storage facility for little-used materials.

The Sheet Music Archive (1,700 cubic feet) of the Plitt Theatre Corporation contains thousands of pieces of music played during intermissions in the Plitt Theatre palaces in Chicago from the 1920s to the 1940s.

949. **Harmony Foundation, Inc., Old Songs Library.** c/o Ruth Marks, 6315 3rd Avenue, Kenosha, WI 53140-5199. 414-654-9111. Accessibility: Monday-Friday, 8-12; 1-5. Scholars, public.

The holdings consist primarily of over 600,000 titles of sheet music spanning the late 1700s to the present.

950. **University of Illinois, Urbana/Champaign.** c/o William M. McClellan, Librarian, Music Library, Urbana, IL 61801.

The vast holdings include 30,000 titles of American vocal sheet music covering the period 1790-1970; the Rafael Joseffy Collection of about 2,000 pieces of nineteenth-century piano music; 500,000 items from the stock of Hunleth Music Store (St. Louis), consisting mainly of early twentieth-century imprints of songs, sets of theater orchestra parts, dance band orchestrations, etc.; and music publishers' catalogs from the 1860s to the 1950s (126 cubic feet).

951. **Indianapolis-Marion County Public Library.** c/o Daniel H. Gann, Head, Arts Division, P.O. Box 211, Indianapolis, IN 46202. 317-269-1705. Accessibility: Monday-Friday, 9-9; Saturday, 9-5; Sunday, 1-5. Scholars, public. In-house use only.

The Old Song Collection is composed of 7,000 sheet music titles of American popular songs spanning the period 1850-1980.

952. **Los Angeles Public Library.** c/o Melvin H. Rosenberg, Mgr. & Principal Librarian, Art, Music & Recreation Dept., 630 W. Fifth Street, Los Angeles, CA 90071.

The institution includes 44,000 music scores, 3,000 manuscripts, 100,000 song sheets, and newspaper clippings.

953. **New Orleans Public Library.** c/o Marilyn Wilkins, Head, Art & Music Division, 219 Loyola Avenue, New Orleans, LA 70140.

The holdings consist of over 700 pieces of early New Orleans and early southern sheet music.

954. **Saint Paul Public Library.** c/o Delores Sundbye, Supervising Librarian, Arts & Audiovisual Services, 90 West Fourth Street, Saint Paul, MN 55102.

The Field Collection comprises 15,000 pieces of sheet music of nineteenth- and twentieth-century popular songs.

Religion

955.   **Graduate Theological Union Library.** c/o Diane Choquette, Head, New Religious Movements Research Collection, Public Services and Special Collections Dept., 2400 Ridge Road, Berkeley, CA 94709.

The collection focuses on religious movements new to America since 1960, as well as unorthodox religious movements resurgent since 1960. American forms of Hinduism, Buddhism, Sikhism, and Sufism are included, along with occultism, Neo-Paganism, esoteric and alternative forms of Christianity, feminist spirituality, and human potential movements having a spiritual aspect. It functions as a depository for publications of the Unification Church in America, the Church of Scientology, and the International Society for Krishna Consciousness. Also included are the responses of mainstream religions and concerned citizens groups and information about such issues as deprogramming and relations between church and state.

956.   **Museum of Church History and Art.** c/o Curator, 45 N. West Temple, Salt Lake City, UT 84150. 801-531-3310. Accessibility: Monday-Saturday. Scholars, public.

The institution possesses hundreds of Mormon journals describing early congregation members' experiences as pioneers, outcasts, and members of early Salt Lake society, 1830s-1900s. It also has a children's museum devoted to early frontier toys.

Social Phenomena—Assassinations

957.   **University of Wisconsin-Stevens Point.** c/o John S. Walters, Special Collections Library, Stevens Point, WI 54481. Accessibility: Monday & Wednesday, 9-8:30; Tuesday, Thursday, & Friday, 9-4:30. Scholars, public. In-house use only.

The Assassination Collection includes more than 400 hours of audiotapes (radio and television talk shows) and 30 hours of videotapes (culled from a national symposium held at UWSP in 1976) devoted to the assassinations of John F. Kennedy, Robert F. Kennedy, and Martin Luther King, Jr.

Social Phenomena—Automobiles

958.   **Henry Ford Museum & Greenfield Village.** c/o Research Center, P.O. Box 1970, Dearborn, MI 48121. 313-271-1620 ext. 650. Accessibility: Monday-Friday, 8:30-5. Scholars, public. Advance appointments recommended.

The artifacts relate to such areas as transportation, communication, agriculture, industry, and domestic life. The archive includes over 5,000 trade catalogs and brochures, with a special emphasis on agricultural machinery, industrial equipment, decorative arts, and women's clothing (eighteenth to twentieth century); 2,000 trade cards; 600 greeting cards, covering most major holidays; 5,500 items of sheet music concerning social and political events and popular tunes (1776-1960); paper doll sets, both commercial and handmade (1850-1959); 100 broadsides (eighteenth and nineteenth centuries); 1,250 almanacs (eighteenth to twentieth centuries); 600 children's books; 250 *McGuffey Readers* (numerous editions); travel literature, including tour books, maps, brochures, souvenirs, booklets, and excursion tickets (1835-1975); World's Fairs and Exhibitions materials; 1,500 historical and decorative prints; 20,000 scenic postcards (including 15,000 Detroit Publishing Co. cards, 1890-1980); 1,000 posters (most notably, circus and World War I); 30,000 photographic images, including daguerreotypes, tintypes, cabinet cards, cartes de visite, stereographs, and 25,000 photoprints from the Detroit Publishing Co. (1890-1915);

and over 350,000 graphics, including architectural drawings and advertising graphics related to Henry Ford's personal and company interests (1863-1947) and Ford Motor Co. products and activities from 1903 to 1950.

Social Phenomena—Ethnic and Racial Minorities

959. **Balch Institute for Ethnic Studies.** c/o Joseph Anderson, Library Director, 18 S. 7th Street, Philadelphia, PA 19106. 215-925-8090. Accessibility: Monday-Saturday, 9-5. Scholars, public.

The Ethnic Images in Advertising Collection consists of 300 popular advertisements depicting stereotypical images of twenty-five ethnic groups in America from 1913 to the present. Another collection, Advertising Ephemera and Trade Cards, is composed of postcards showing stereotypes of various ethnic groups in the United States.

Social Phenomena—Minorities— African Americans

960. **African American Museum.** c/o Dr. Eleanor Engram, Director, 1765 Crawford Road, Cleveland, OH 44106. 216-791-1700.

The artifacts, and the volumes within the affiliated library, are primarily concerned with documenting African American and minority race achievements and contributions.

961. **Museum of African American History.** c/o Dr. Marian J. Moore, Executive Director, 301 Frederick Douglass Street, Detroit, MI 48202. 313-833-9800; (Fax) 313-832-7933.

The museum is dedicated to preserving, documenting, interpreting, and exhibiting the cultural heritage of African Americans and their ancestors. It incorporates a reference library containing books, films, and audiotapes of African world history, art, and culture. An oral history project is involved in taping interviews with and stories by elderly blacks.

962. **Museum of Afro-American History.** c/o Monica Fairbairn, President, 46 Joy Street, Boston, MA 02114. 617-742-1854.

This charitable nonprofit institution was established to locate, collect, conserve, preserve, and secure for exhibition and research, historical material pertaining to the life, thought, material culture, and heritage of Afro-Americans in New England. It maintains a library of films, filmstrips, and print materials documenting the history and literature of black Americans.

963. **Providence Public Library.** c/o Lance J. Bauer, Special Collections Librarian, 150 Empire Street, Providence, RI 02903. Accessibility: In-house use only. Photocopying permitted when condition of material allows.

The Harris Collection on the American Civil War and Slavery includes eighteenth- and nineteenth-century books, rare pamphlets, periodicals, sheet music, broadside ballads, and over eighty-five editions of *Uncle Tom's Cabin* in fourteen languages.

Social Phenomena—Minorities—Irish Americans

964. **American Irish Historical Society.** c/o Damian Doyle, 991 5th Avenue, New York, NY 10028. 212-288-2263. Accessibility: Monday-Friday, 10-5. Scholars, public.

The extensive primary-source documents include the personal papers of the Reverend Donald M. O'Callahan and Daniel F. Cohalan, as well as the records of the American Irish Historical Society, the Society of the Friendly Sons of St. Patrick, the Friends of Irish Freedom, the Catholic Club, and the Guild of Catholic Lawyers.

Social Phenomena—Feminism

(See also: Social Phenomena—Sexuality, pp. 191, 214)

965. **Business & Professional Women's Foundation.** c/o Cheryl A. Sloan, Librarian, Marguerite Rawalt Resource Center, 2012 Massachusetts Avenue NW, Washington, D.C. 20036.

The holdings emphasize the working woman and encompass such issues as education for women, working mothers, sex roles, women executives, counseling for women, and work-force entry by mature women. Media represented include over 200 oral history tape recordings, over 500 microfilms (mainly doctoral theses), and about 13,000 vertical file items (studies, periodical articles, newspaper clippings, documents, etc.).

966. **University of California, Los Angeles.** c/o Oscar L. Sims, Social Sciences Bibliographer, Social Science Collection, Research Library, 405 Hilgard Avenue, Los Angeles, CA 90024.

The archive includes a comprehensive microfilm collection of literature by and about women on about 1,300 reels. It is arranged chronologically through the year 1920, and is divided into five sections: monographs, pamphlets, periodicals, manuscripts, and selected photographs.

967. **University of Colorado.** Western Historical Collections Libraries, Boulder, CO 80309.

The collection contains minutes of the Boulder Chapter of the Colorado WCTU (1881-1950) plus those of other local chapters for shorter periods of time. It also includes state convention proceedings (1882-1969), state officers' minutes and reports, and many other pamphlets and publications.

968. **Library of Congress.** c/o John C. Broderick, Chief, Manuscript Division, Washington, D.C. 20540.

The division houses the papers of both Maud Wood Park (1871-1955), first president of the League of Women Voters, and Carrie Chapman Catt (pertaining to her efforts to secure voting rights for women). There are also many materials concerned with Susan B. Anthony.

969. **Susan B. Anthony.** c/o William Matheson, Chief Rare Book & Special Collections Division, Washington, D.C. 20540.

The division possesses the Susan B. Anthony Collection, books from the personal libraries of many other feminist reformers, and materials presented by the National American Woman Suffrage Association. It also contains the official reports of the National

Suffrage Conventions, addresses made at Congressional hearings, scrapbooks containing clippings from newspapers and periodicals, handbills, and other memorabilia.

970. **Los Angeles Public Library.** c/o Marilyn C. Wherley, Principal Librarian, Social Sciences Department, 630 West Fifth Street, Los Angeles, CA 90071.

The department's holdings include clippings, pamphlets, periodicals, government publications, bibliographies, and popular and scholarly monographs on women and their role and place in society, with particular emphasis on the suffrage and liberation movements.

971. **Radcliffe College.** c/o Patricia Miller King, Director, Elizabeth Schlesinger Library on the History of Women in America, 3 James Street, Cambridge, MA 02138.

The collection focuses on women's rights, suffrage, feminism, and the women's movement; the family; women in government and politics, social welfare and reform, and the trade unions; and women's education, employment, and health. Substantial numbers of manuscripts have been donated by the Blackwell family, the Beecher-Stowe family, Betty Friedan, Charlotte Perkins Gilman, Emma Goldman, Dr. Alice Hamilton, the National Abortion Rights Action League, the National Organization for Women, Leonora O'Reilly, and the Women's Equity Action League; in all, there are 463 personal and family collections and 103 organizational collections as well as 40,000 pictures, 10,000 microforms, and oral history tapes and transcripts.

972. **State Historical Society of Wisconsin.** c/o James P. Danky, Librarian, Newspaper and Periodicals Section, Library, 816 State Street, Madison, WI 53706.

The institution is alleged to possess the largest collection of women's periodicals and newspapers in the United States.

973. **Women's History Research Center.** c/o Librarian, Microfilm Library, 2325 Oak Street, Berkeley, CA 94708.

The center includes an extensive collection of women's periodicals, 1956-1974, on microfilm. The original resource material is housed at the Northwestern University Library, Special Collections Department, Evanston, IL 60201. The material is available for purchase (with reel guides) from the center.

974. **Women's Resources & Research Center.** c/o Joy Fergoda, University of California at Davis, Davis, CA 95616. 916-752-3372. Accessibility: Public.

The archive includes books of fiction and nonfiction; about 130 periodicals relevant to women's studies; over 6,000 pamphlets, papers, etc.; over 500 audiotapes documenting the center's programs; and hundreds of commercial and oral history tapes.

Social Phenomena—Sexuality

975. **Homosexual Information Center.** c/o Don Slater, 6758 Hollywood Blvd. #28, Hollywood, CA 90028. 213-464-8431. Accessibility: Open to the public at large.

The center, which began in the 1950s, is now considered a major research facility.

976. **Lesbian Herstory Educational Foundation Inc.** c/o Deborah Edel, Treasurer, Lesbian Herstory Archives, P.O. Box 1258, New York, NY 10116.

The collection includes books and periodicals on all aspects of lesbian—and, to a lesser extent, gay—culture; photographs and slides of lesbians and lesbian art; records and tapes; graphics; crafts; and unpublished materials, such as first drafts, term papers from lesbian and Gay studies courses, diaries, letters, poetry, and conference notes.

Sports and Recreation

977. **First Interstate Bank.** c/o W. R. Schroeder, Managing Director, Athletic Foundation, 2141 West Adams, Los Angeles, CA 90018. Accessibility: In-house use only.

Billed as one of the most extensive library and museum collections relating to sports, it includes bound volumes of the sports sections from several newspapers; a large file of college and university annuals and yearbooks; souvenir publications from amateur, college, and professional events; sports memorabilia; and a ledger of halls of fame with thousands of names of athletes who have excelled in a wide variety of sports (the Athletic Foundation is a repository for the Association of Sports Museums and Halls of Fame).

978. **University of Notre Dame.** University Libraries, South Bend, IN 46556.

Alleged to be the largest collection of sporting materials in the world, over 500 sports and games are covered in some 500,000 documents.

979. **Smithsonian Institution Libraries.** c/o Rhoda S. Ratner, Branch Librarian, National Museum of American History Branch, Washington, D.C. 20560.

The branch emphasizes the history of American sports and recreation, including about 2,000 baseball cards from cigarette and chewing gum packets, 103 scrapbooks and other memorabilia relating to Joe Louis, and extensive resources on bicycling and skating.

980. **Society for the North American Cultural Survey.** c/o John Rooney, Director, Department of Geography, Oklahoma State University, Stillwater, OK 74078.

The society has access to a wealth of research data related to its work mapping the continent-wide distributions and participation patterns for the major and minor professional, college, and high school sports.

Sports and Recreation—Automobile Racing

981. **Indianapolis Motor Speedway Hall of Fame Museum.** c/o Jack L. Martin, Director, 4790 West 16th Street, Indianapolis, IN 46222. 317-248-6747. Accessibility: Daily, 9-5 (except Christmas Day). Scholars, public.

The collection—including many of the original cars—is devoted to the history of the Speedway and to auto racing in general.

Sports and Recreation—Baseball

982. **Detroit Public Library.** c/o Alice Dalligan, Chief, Burton Historical Collection, 5201 Woodward Avenue, Detroit, MI 48202.

The institution houses the extensive Ernie Harwell Collection on sports, with a particular emphasis on baseball in general and, specifically, the Detroit Tigers.

983. **Little League Baseball Museum.** c/o Jim Campbell, Director, and Marc G. Pompeo, Curator, P.O. Box 3485, Williamsport, PA 17701. 717-326-3607. Accessibility: Monday-Saturday, 10-5; Sunday, 1-5. Memorial Day through Labor Day: Monday-Saturday, 10-8; Sunday, 1-5. Scholars, public.

Files and records available upon permission from the director or curator. The museum includes over 500,000 rosters of Little League Baseball teams dating back to 1954; a full run of *Little Leaguer* magazine and *This Is Little League;* all Little League

World Series programs from 1947 to the present; numerous monographs, pamphlets, booklets, rule books, literary articles, and assorted records tracing the growth and development of Little League; films and videocassettes providing full-length treatments and highlights of Little League World Series Games (1947-present); and training films and other films dealing with Little League in some manner.

984.   National Baseball Hall of Fame and Museum. c/o Thomas R. Heitz, Librarian, National Baseball Library, Cooperstown, NY 13326.

Special collections include Literature, a comprehensive collection of biographies, general histories, team and league histories, encyclopedias, directories, dictionaries, fiction, poetry, and children's books; complete runs of *Baseball Digest, Baseball Magazine, Sports Magazine, Sports Illustrated,* team publications, and many other journals of interest to baseball researchers; public official documents of the major and minor leagues; biographical files containing an estimated 2.5 million documents, questionnaires, and news clippings; and extensive phonograph and tape recordings of baseball music, interviews, season highlights, and game play-by-play descriptions.

Sports and Recreation—Basketball

985.   Naismith Memorial Basketball Hall of Fame. c/o June Harrison Steitz, Librarian, Edward J. & Gena G. Hickox Library, 460 Alden Street, Box 175, Springfield, MA 01109.

The archive includes forty-eight vertical file drawers of reports, documents, programs, pressbooks, etc.; twenty vertical file drawers of pictures and photographs; a complete set of basketball rule books; NBA and ABA guides; Converse Baseketball Yearbooks; minutes of NABC conventions; phono-records, 16mm films; and substantial book holdings.

986.   Springfield College Library. c/o Henry Dutcher, Reference Librarian, Babson Library, Springfield, MA 01109.

Springfield College, the birthplace of basketball, offers extensive holdings relating to various aspects of the sport.

Sports and Recreation—Football

987.   College Football Hall of Fame. c/o Don Schumacher, Curator, Library, P.O. Box 300, Kings Mills, OH 45034. Accessibility: Library available for research only.

In addition to football memorabilia, the collection features documents and publications relating to college football.

988.   Pro Football Hall of Fame. c/o Anne Mangus, Librarian, and Joe Horrigan, Curator, Library, 2121 Harrison Avenue NW, Canton, OH 44708.

The library, primarily intended for research, includes 17,000 pictures, 1,500 slides, 50 audiotapes, 1,300 16mm films, 3,000 game programs, and 500 team media guides. Although all aspects of professional football are covered, NFL Hall of Famers receive a special emphasis.

Sports and Recreation—Fishing

989. **American Museum of Fly Fishing.** c/o John H. Merwin, Executive Director, P.O. Box 42, Manchester, VT 05254. 802-375-9256. Accessibility: May 1-October 31: Daily, 10-4; November 1-April 30: Monday-Friday, 10-4 (weekends by appointment only). Scholars, public.

The collection includes more than 1,000 rods, 400 reels, thousands of flies, and other items and memorabilia related to the history of fly fishing.

990. **Gladding International Sport Fishing Museum.** Octagon House, South Otselic, NY 13155.

The museum includes substantial resources concerned with angling and associated subjects.

Sports and Recreation—Golf

991. **James River Golf Museum and Library.** c/o Weymouth Crumbler, Librarian, James River Country Club, 1500 Country Club Road, Newport News, VA 23606.

The library's resources cover the history of the sport; highlights of the artifacts include 450 gold clubs (1780 to the present) and 150 golf balls (primarily from the 1820-1830 period).

992. **U.S. Golf Association.** c/o Janet Seagle, Librarian, Golf House, Route 512, P.O. Box 708, Golf Far Hills, NJ 07936.

With over 7,000 volumes devoted to golfers and golfing, this is alleged to be one of the largest collections of its type.

Sports and Recreation—Horse Racing/ Horsemanship

993. **Kentucky Derby Museum.** c/o Leslie A. Bush, P.O. Box 3513, Louisville, KY 40201. 502-637-1111. Accessibility: Sunday-Saturday, 9-5. Scholars, public. Research by advance appointment only.

The museum includes an unparalleled assemblage of artifacts and library resources concerned with the premiere American horse race.

994. **National Museum of Racing.** c/o Elaine E. Mann, Director, The Thoroughbred Racing Hall of Fame, Union Avenue, Saratoga Springs, NY 12866.

Since its inception in 1950, the institution has been collecting materials relating to the origin, history, and development of breeding and racing thoroughbred horses.

995. **National Sporting Library.** c/o Judith Ozment, Librarian, Chronicle of the Horse Bldg., Publishing Offices, P.O. Box 1335, Middleburg, VA 22117.

The library acquires materials (over 11,000 volumes at present) concerned with horse sports.

996. **Salem College.** c/o Myron J. Smith, Librarian, Library, Salem, WV 26426.
The collection supports what is reputed to be the most complete equestrian studies
program available anywhere.

Sports and Recreation—Lacrosse

997. **Lacrosse Foundation Hall of Fame and Library.** c/o Ann Gwyn, Librarian,
Newton H. White, Jr., Athletic Center, Homeswood, Baltimore, MD 21218.
The institution contains a large collection of books, microforms, and memorabilia
devoted to lacrosse.

Sports and Recreation—Tennis

998. **International Tennis Hall of Fame and Tennis Museum.** c/o Jan Armstrong, Curator
194 Bellevue Avenue, Newport, RI 02840. 401-849-6378. Accessibility: May-October: Daily,
10-5; November-April: Daily, 11-4. Scholars, public. Research by advance appointment only.
The varied resources all relate to tennis and its history.

999. **Racquet & Tennis Club.** c/o Gerald Belliveau, Jr., Librarian, Library, 370 Park
Avenue, New York, NY 10022.
The holdings, numbering around 18,000 titles, focus on court tennis and lawn tennis.

Sports and Recreation—Track and Field

1000. **National Track and Field Hall of Fame.** c/o Gisela Terrell, Historical Research
Library, Irwin Library, Butler University, 4600 Sunset Avenue, Indianapolis, IN 46208.
317-283-9265. Accessibility: Monday-Friday, 9-5. Scholars, public.
The collection includes monographs, periodicals, films, tapes, documents, and
memorabilia covering the history of track and field in the United States.

Sports and Recreation—Wrestling

1001. **National Wrestling Hall of Fame.** 405 West Hall of Fame Avenue, Stillwater,
OK 74075.
The archive resources and memorabilia focus on collegiate and amateur (Greco-Roman)
wrestling, including Olympic competition, from the late 1890s to the present day.

Women's Studies *(See: Social Phenomena—Feminism, pp. 190, 214, 232)*

Chapter 12

Societies and Associations

General

1002. **American Culture Association.** c/o Ray B. Browne, Secretary-Treasurer, William T. Jerome Library, Bowling Green State University, Bowling Green, OH 43403. (Fax) 419-372-8095.

The ACA provides a forum for college students, faculty, and scholars interested in the multi- and interdisciplinary study of past and present popular culture in North and South America. Founded in 1978, it includes seven regional groups and 1,300 members. It sponsors workshops and an annual conference (in conjunction with the Popular Culture Association) and publishes the *Journal of American Culture* (quarterly).

1003. **Popular Culture Association.** c/o Ray B. Browne, Secretary-Treasurer, William T. Jerome Library, Bowling Green State University, Bowling Green, OH 43403. (Fax) 419-372-8095.

Instituted in 1969 as an adjunct to the Popular Culture Center at BGSU, it provides a focus for the academic study of the mass media, folklore, the popular arts, ethnic culture, and various social phenomena ranging from large-scale movements, such as feminism, civil rights, and gay liberation, to more temporary preoccupations, such as fads. The organization administers a placement service and a hall of fame, compiles statistics of interest to the field at large, and holds an annual conference in large cities throughout North America. Its numerous publications include the *Journal of Popular Culture* (quarterly), *Clues; A Journal of Detection* (semi-annual), *Journal of Cultural Geography* (semiannual), *Popular Culture and Society* (quarterly), the *PCA Newsletter,* and books concerned with popular culture. With more than 2,500 members, it is the premier association concerned with all aspects of popular culture.

Collecting

(See also: Collecting—Sports and Recreation, pp. 5-8)

1004. **American Numismatic Association.** Robert J. Leuver, Executive Director, 818 N. Cascade Avenue, Colorado Springs, CO 80903-3279. 719-632-2646; (Fax) 719-634-4085.

Geared to collectors of coins, medals, tokens, and paper money, the ANA promotes the study, research, and publication of articles and books on coins, coinage, and the history of money. Founded in 1891, the organization boasts 31,000 members in addition to 13 regional and 670 local groups. Its staff of thirty sponsors correspondence courses, National Coin Week, and semiannual national meetings; operates a speakers' bureau and the American Numismatic Association Authentication Bureau; and maintains a museum, an archive, a library of more than 35,000 volumes, and a hall of fame. Its ambitious publishing program includes the *ANA Communique* (quarterly), *First Strike Supplement: Emerging Collectors* (quarterly), the *ANA Resource Directory* (periodic), *The Numismatist: For*

Collectors of Coins, Medals, Tokens and Paper Money (monthly), *The ABC's of Money—A Numismatic Primer, Consumer Alert—Investing in Rare Coins, ANA Grading Guide,* and *ANA Numismatic Correspondence Course.*

1005. **Smurf Collectors' Club International.** c/o Suzanne Lipschitz (founder), 24 Cabot Rd., W., Dept. E, Massapequa, NY 11758. 516-799-3221.

Founded in 1986, its members include collectors and dealers of Smurf cartoon character collectibles as well as anyone interested in the phenomenon. The club facilitates information exchange regarding the history of Smurf merchandise, which dates from 1957. Publications include the *Smurfs Collectors' Club Newsletter* (quarterly), *The Smurfs: A Legend in Their Own Time* (periodic), the *SCCI News Bulletin* (semiannual), and a character identification brochure and related reprint materials.

1006. **Souvenirs Card Collectors Society.** c/o Dana M. Marr, Secretary, P.O. Box 4155, Tulsa, OK 74159-0155. 918-747-6724.

The membership is composed of four regional groups and approximately 1,000 dealers and collectors of souvenir cards; i.e., 8 1/2" by 11" cards with steel-engraved reproductions of philatelic or numismatic designs from the original plates of the Bureau of Engraving and the American Bank Note Co. as well as stories about the designs. The SCCS, formed in 1981, promotes the hobby, conducts research, sponsors periodic meetings, and publishes a quarterly directory and *The Souvenir Card Journal* (quarterly).

1007. **Sport of Kings Society.** c/o Charlotte Mower, Secretary-Treasurer, 1406 Annen Lane, Madison, WI 53711. 608-274-6340.

The group, founded in 1968, promotes an appreciation of horse racing and correspondence among members (approximately 650) to exchange information and enhance collections of memorabilia, such as totes, postcards, programs, and admission tokens. It holds periodic regional meetings and publishes *Castaways* five times per year.

1008. **World's Fair Collectors Society.** c/o Michael R. Pender, Executive Director, P.O. Box 20806, Sarasota, FL 34276-3806. 813-923-2590.

The WFCS consists of approximately 450 enthusiasts from five countries committed to preserving the history of world expositions by collecting and researching World's Fair memorabilia. Formed in 1968, it promotes information dissemination through the maintenance of a museum and library of statistical books, guide books, maps, photo albums, and newspaper supplements. In addition to sponsoring periodic exhibitions, the society publishes an annual *Directory* and the bimonthly magazine, *Fair News.*

Mass Media—Films

1009. **Academy of Science Fiction, Fantasy, and Horror Films.** c/o Dr. Donald A. Reed, President. 334 W. 54th St., Los Angeles, CA 90037. (213) 752-5811.

Instituted in 1972, the ASFFHF is composed of twelve state groups and 3,000 members— actors, writers, producers, directors, special effects personnel, and others connected with the film industry, as well as educators and researchers. The academy is primarily concerned with recognizing outstanding work in the science fiction, fantasy, and horror film genres relating to the fields of acting, music, direction, writing, cinematography, special effects, makeup, film criticism, set decoration and design, stop motion animation, publicity, and advertising. This goal is accomplished in part through the presentation of the Saturn Awards, the Scroll Awards, and the Science Fiction Film Awards. It also conducts lectures and seminars, maintains a hall of fame, and publishes a quarterly newsletter.

1010. **Count Dracula Society.** c/o Dr. Donald A. Reed, President. 334 W. 54th St., Los Angeles, CA 90037. (213) 752-5811.

Named for the character in Bram Stoker's novel, the society's approximately 1,000 members include academicians, teachers, writers, librarians, movie producers, and others devoted to the serious study of horror films and gothic literature. It presents the Ann Radcliffe Awards in literature, movies, and television; the International Cinema Achievement Award; the Horace Walpole Gold Medal; and the Rev. Dr. Montague Summers Memorial Award. Affiliated with the Academy of Science Fiction, Fantasy, and Horror Films, the CDS maintains the Horror Hall of Fame and publishes *The Count Dracula Quarterly.* It was founded in 1962.

1011. **Hollywood Studio Collectors Club.** c/o Ralph E. Benner, Executive Officer. 3960 Laurel Canyon Blvd., Ste. 450, Studio City, CA 91614. (818) 990-5450.

The HSCC promotes interest in collecting movie memorabilia and related artifacts; conducts research on motion picture history; encourages trading, buying, and selling among members; exchanges relevant information with its 9,000-odd constituency and with film museums and halls of fame. Established in 1957, it oversees a biographical archive on the cinema and publishes *Hollywood Studio Magazine.*

Mass Media—Journalism *(See: Social Phenomena—Feminism,*

pp. 190, 214, 232)

Mass Media—Radio

(See also: Mass Media—Television, pp. 44, 177, 200, 226)

1012. **Antique Radio Club of America.** c/o Barbara Rankin, Secretary. 300 Washington Trails, Washington, DC 15301. (412) 746-0942.

Formed in 1972, the club has approximately 900 members interested in the history and preservation of early radio equipment. Affiliated with the Antique Wireless Association, ARCA sponsors semiannual conferences (held in the spring and fall) and publishes the quarterly *Antique Radio Gazette.*

1013. **Antique Wireless Association.** Bruce L. Kelley, Dir. Main St., Bloomfield, NY 14469. (716) 657-7489.

AWA bills itself as "the largest group of radio historians and collectors in the world." For $12 per year, members receive four issues of the journal, *The Old Timer's Bulletin,* as well as notification of meetings and conventions worldwide. An information packet is available upon request.

1014. **Friends of Old-Time Radio.** c/o Jay Hickerson, President. P.O. Box 4321, Hamden, CT 06514. (203) 248-2887.

FOTR, founded in 1976, is a loosely organized group of individuals (about 500) who trade and collect recordings of radio shows dating back to its Golden Age. It sponsors an annual October convention, publishes *Hello Again* (bimonthly), and bestows awards to people active in radio between 1930 and 1960.

1015. **International Radio Club of America.** c/o Donald E. Erickson, Secretary-Treasurer. 6059 Essex St., Riverside, CA 92504. (714) 687-5910.

Composed of radio enthusiasts interested in receiving distant radio stations on the standard AM broadcast band, IRCA provides members with information on radio listening, the Federal Communications Commission, and the industry at large. Affiliated with the Association of North American Radio Clubs, it sponsors annual DX contests in addition to the Ted Vasilopoulos Award for substantial contributions to the hobby. Established in 1964, its publications include the *DX Monitor,* the annual *Condition of Frequencies List,* and irregulars, such as an abbreviations list, a technical manual, and an almanac.

1016. Radio/Video Yesteryear. c/o Craig Gallichotte, Box C, Sandy Hook, CT 06482. 800-243-0987; (Fax) 203-797-0819.

Carries a large variety of classic radio and video recordings; catalogs provide much data about these two genres. Offers a custom research service for hard-to-find titles.

1017. Revival of Creative Radio. c/o Timothy J. Coco, P.O. Box 1585, Haverhill, MA 10830. 508-373-5420; (Fax) 508-521-4636.

A national old-time radio club, RCR publishes a newsletter and maintains a library. It provides classic radio shows on cassette via mail order.

1018. Southern California Antique Radio Society. c/o Dan Mason, 1325 N. Lima Street, Burbank, CA 91505.

Publishes quarterly gazette and sponsors quarterly and annual conventions in the Los Angeles area.

Mass Media—Television

1019. Academy of Television Arts and Sciences. c/o James L. Loper, Executive Director. 5220 Lankershim Blvd., North Hollywood, CA 91601. (818) 754-2800.

Established in 1948, ATAS is composed of more than 6,500 professionals in the television and film industry. Its service goals include advancing the arts and sciences of television through the delivery of education to the industry, the preservation of programming, the enhancement of community relations, and the nurturing of creative leadership in the industry. The Academy presents the Primetime Emmy Awards, the Los Angeles Area Emmy Awards, and Student Video Awards, all on an annual basis. It sponsors the Television Academy Hall of Fame and maintains the Television Academy Archives and a collection of over 35,000 programs at UCLA. Internships are offered to students; educational offerings include symposia, luncheon speakers series, faculty seminars, workshops, and meetings devoted to resolving the problems of various crafts. Publications include *Debut,* a semiannual newsletter focusing on the educational programs of the Academy; *Emmy Directory* (annual); and *Emmy Magazine* (bimonthly), a general interest magazine of the TV industry.

1020. Hollywood Radio and Television Society. c/o Oliver Crawford, Executive Director. 5315 Laurel Canyon Blvd., Ste. 202, North Hollywood, CA 91607. (818) 769-4313.

Founded in 1947, this group of approximately 1,000 members includes those involved in radio, television, broadcasting, and advertising. HARTS sponsors seminars on the business and creative aspects of broadcasting, competitions, and monthly luncheons featuring top industry and government speakers. It bestows annual International Broadcasting Awards for the best radio and television commercials and maintains a film and audio library of outstanding radio and television commercials. Publications include the quarterly *Spike,* and two annuals, the *Hollywood Radio and Television Society Roster* and *International Broadcasting Awards Book.*

1021. **Star Trek: The Official Fan Club.** c/o Daniel H. Madsen, President, P.O. Box 111000, Aurora, CO 80042. 303-341-1813.

The club, formed in 1980, is composed of more than 50,000 fans of *Star Trek* (which originally aired on NBC from 1966 to 1969) and *Star Trek: The Next Generation*. Its primary role is to keep members informed about the program, cast members, and film spin-offs. Activities include the operation of pen pal and actor forwarding services, the maintenance of a library and biographical archives, sponsorship of competitions, and the compilation of statistics. It publishes *The Official Star Trek Magazine* (bimonthly, also available on-line) and *The Star Trek Fan Club Merchandise Catalog* (bimonthly).

1022. **Star Trek WelCommittee.** c/o Shirley S. Maiewski, Chairperson, P.O. Drawer 12, Saranac, MI 48881. 413-247-5339.

The STW functions as a central information center whose sixty-five-odd volunteer workers answer fans' questions about *Star Trek*. Founded in 1972, its departments include College and Library Programming, Convention Listing, Costume, Editors and Contributors Exchange, Foreign, Library Computer/General, Library Computer/Science and Technology, Military Fan Liaison, Newsclipping Service, Penpal Listing Service, Personal Computer, Sight Loss Services, Star Trek Educational Programs, Zine Acquisition, Zine Publishing Information. Sponsors a quarterly mail auction of Star Trek merchandise and memorabilia and publishes the following: *Directory of Star Trek Organizations* (semiannual), *The Fan's Little Golden Guide to Throwing Your Own Con, How to Start a Club, History of the STW, The Neofan's Guide to Star Trek Fandom, Protocols: A Guide to Fanzines,* and *So You Want Publicity.*

1023. **Starfleet.** c/o Jeannette Maddox, Vice President, P.O. Box 430, Burnsville, NC 28714. 704-682-4338.

Composed of 12 regional groups, 140 local groups, and 4,200 members, it is open to anyone interested in science fiction films and television programs, particularly the television and motion picture series *Star Trek*. The organization conducts service activities, bestows awards, and produces the bimonthly *Starfleet Communique*. It was established in 1974.

1024. **Starfleet Command.** c/o Donald H. Dailey, Chief of Staff, P.O. Box 26076, Indianapolis, IN 46226. 317-897-5454.

For space and science fiction enthusiasts, the SFC upholds the Star Trek philosophy of Infinite Diversity through Infinite Combinations and its application to everyday living. Formed in 1974, the 2,500 members, twelve regional groups, one state group, and 100 local groups attempt to help individuals realize their full potential; promote the peaceful exploration and use of space; support the development of a permanent working space station or moon base; and encourage the support of environmental, conservation, and resource management programs. Programs include charitable activities, bestowing awards, maintaining a library, serving as a forum for the exchange of ideas and information, and sponsoring an annual convention. The SFC publishes *Starfleet Communications* (quarterly) and a newsletter covering organization news and activities, science and space-related issues, and Star Trek updates.

Minorities—African Americans

1025. **African American Historical and Cultural Society.** Fort Mason Center, Bldg. C, Rm. 165, San Francisco, CA 94123. 415-441-0640.

The society's primary aim is the preservation of the history and culture of African and African American people. It administers a museum, gallery, and archives in addition to publishing the semiannual newsletter, *Praisesinger.*

1026. **Afro-American Historical and Genealogical Society.** c/o Sylvia Cooke Martin, President, P.O. Box 73086, Washington, D.C. 20056. 202-234-5350.

Founded in 1977, the 1,000-odd members include individuals, libraries, and archives. Programs include the encouragement of scholarly research in Afro-American history and genealogy as it relates to American history and culture; the acquisition, maintenance, and preservation of relevant material; and the conducting of seminars and workshops. The society plans to oversee a library on Afro-American family and church history, as well as to hold competitions and award sixty-day internships in the archive or library.

1027. **Association for the Study of Afro-American Life and History.** c/o Gail Hansberry, Executive Director, 1407 14th St., NW, Washington, D.C. 20005. 202-667-2822.

The 2,200 members, thirty state groups, and five local groups include historians, scholars, and students interested in the research and study of black people as a contributing force in civilization. Formed in 1915, its agenda consists of promoting historical research and writings, collecting historical manuscripts and materials relating to black people throughout the world, and encouraging harmony among the races. The ASALH maintains the Carter G. Woodson home in Washington, D.C., sponsors an essay contest for under-graduate and graduate students and Afro-American History Month, and publishes two quarterlies (*Journal of Negro History* and *Negro History Bulletin*) in addition to brochures, textbooks, and other materials through the Associated Publishers division.

1028. **Black Resources Information Coordinating Services.** c/o Emily A. Copeland, President, 614 Howard Avenue, Tallahassee, FL 32304. 904-576-7522.

Instituted in 1972, BRICS has been designed to solidify the various sources of information and research by and about minority groups in America (particularly African Americans) and convert them into a coordinated information system by using biblio-graphic control, storage, retrieval, transfer, and dissemination. Operations include admin-istering a referral and consulting service; assisting in genealogical research and archival management and organization; providing bibliographic services and lecture demonstra-tions on African American culture; sponsoring seminars, workshops, and institutes; conducting a national exhibit program (which serves as a source of exposure for new books, publications, and other media forms); maintaining a library of over 8,000 items, including nonprint resources; and providing abstracting, indexing, and advisory services to black studies programs and collections. The group publishes the quarterly journal *Brics Bracs,* the bimonthly *Newsletter, Media Showcase* (annual), the *Minority Information Trade Annual,* and *Guide to Afro-American Resources.* An annual conference is held every November.

1029. **Black World Foundation.** c/o Robert Chrisman, President, P.O. Box 2869, Oakland, CA 94609. 415-547-6633.

The BWF, formed in 1969, consists of over 10,000 subscribers united to develop and distribute black educational materials and to develop black cultural and political thought. It administers the Prisoner Fund to supply free copies of foundation publications to incarcerated populations. Publications include *The Black Scholar* (bimonthly), the annual *Listing of Black Books in Print,* and books of poetry and books on black sociology.

1030. **Foundation for Research in the Afro-American Creative Arts.** c/o Joseph Southern, President, P.O. Drawer I, Cambria Heights, NY 11411.

Founded in 1971, the foundation promotes research into the Afro-American creative arts, including music, theater, and dance. It maintains a library on black music and history, including taped oral histories of black musicians. FRACA also publishes the journal, *The Black Perspective in Music.*

Popular Literature—Dime Novels

1031. **Happy Hours Brotherhood.** c/o Edward T. LeBlanc, President. 87 School St., Fall River, MA 02720. (508) 672-2082.

The HHB, established in 1925, consists of approximately 400 collectors and readers of dime novels, story papers, and popular literature for the young published during the nineteenth and early twentieth centuries. It seeks to preserve and promote the collection of these novels and related material, maintains a library, and publishes a magazine, *Dime Novel Round-Up.*

Popular Literature—Mystery and Detective Fiction

1032. **Baker Street Irregulars.** c/o Thomas L. Stix, Jr., 34 Pierson Avenue, Norwood, NJ 07648. 201-768-2241.

The premier Sherlock Holmes group in the United States, it was formed in 1934 and includes 275 members (by invitation only) and 300 local groups. The BSI studies Holmes and his world, sponsors the Silver Blaze Handicap (a horse race), awards Irregular Shillings to members who have shown serious interest over time, hosts an annual dinner, and publishes the *Baker Street Journal: An Irregular Quarterly of Sherlockiana.*

1033. **Mystery Writers of America.** c/o Priscilla Ridgway, Executive Secretary. 17 E. 47th St., 6th Fl., New York, NY 10017. (212) 888-8171.

Founded in 1945, the MWA consists of 2,400 members (professional and unpublished writers in the field; publishers and agents are associate members) eight regional groups, and one local group. It sponsors an annual mystery symposium, the Edgar Allan Poe awards, and an annual (late April or early May) convention. Publications include the *MWA Directory,* the annual *Anthology,* a newsletter, and the *Mystery Writers Annual.*

1034. **Sherlock Holmes Societies.** Limited to U.S. groups; addresses, phone numbers, and contact persons are included in the *World Bibliography of Sherlock Holmes and Dr. Watson,* compiled by Ronald Burt De Waal (Bramhall House).

The Adventuresses of Sherlock Holmes
The Afghanistan Perceivers
Altamont's Agents
The Amateur Mendicant Society of
    Detroit
The Andaman Islanders
The Anderson Murderers
The Arcadia Mixture
The Arkansas Valley Investors, Ltd.
The Arnsworth Castle
The Avenging Angels
The Bagatelle Card Club of Milwaukee
The Baker Street Chroniclers
The Baker Street Students
The Baker Street Underground
The Bee-Keepers

The Beekeepers of Sussex
The Bering Straits Irregulars
The Birdy Edwards Society
The Blustering Gales From the
    South-West
The Board-School Beacons
Boss McGinty's Bird Watchers
The Brothers Three of Moriarty
The Bruce-Partington Planners
The Bruce-Partington Planners of the
    Baker Street Irregulars in the Mili-
    tary Industrial Complex
The Carlton Club
The Cavendish Squares, Ltd.
The Conan Doyle Society

The Conductors of Aldersgate Street
Station
The Confederates of Wisteria Lodge
The Consulting Detectives
The Cornish Horrors
The Council of Four
The Country of the Saints
Cox and Company of New England
The Creeping Men of Cleveland
The Crew of the Barque Gloria Scott
The Crew of the Barque Lone Star
The Criterion Bar Association
The Dame Adelaide Mathilda, Cock-
Bullington Memorial Chapter of
the Dartmoor Kennel Club
The Darlington Substitutes
The Delaware Valley of Fear
The Diogenes Club of New York
Doctor Watson's Colleagues
Doctor Watson's Neglected Patients
The Dogs in the Night-Time
The Double-Barrelled Tiger Clubs
The Drops of Water—The Sherlock
Holmes Society of Niagara
The Elmstalker
The Eyford Engineers
F.G.G.M. (Friends of the Great Grimpen
Mire)
Felonius Commuters
The Fifth Morthumberland Fusiliers
The 1st Bangalore Pioneers
The Five Orange Pips of Westchester
County
The Forensic Faces of Sherlock
The Fortescue Scholarship Examiners
The Friends of Baron Gruner
The Friends of Irene Adler
The Friends of Sahara King
The Game is Afoot
The Gamekeepers of Northern Minnesota
The Giant Rats of Sumatra
The Goose Club of the Alpha Inn
The Great Alkali Plainsmen of Greater
Kansas City
The Greek Interpreters of East
Lansing
The H.W.
The Hansom Wheels
The Hansoms of John Clayton

The High Tors
The Hollywood Hounds
The Hounds of the Baskerville
The Hudson Valley Sciontists
Hugo's Companions
The Illustrious Clients
The Illustrious Clients of Indianapolis
The Inspectors of Scotland Yard
The Inverness Capers
An Irish Secret Society at Buffalo
The Islanders of UffaThe Islanders of
UffaThe Isle of Uffa Chowder and
Marching Society
The Jefferson Hopes of St. Louis
The John Openshaw Society
Knights of the Gnomon
The Lascars of Upper Swandam Lane
The Legends of the West Country
The Long Island Cave Sleuths
The Lying Corn-Chandlers
The Maiwand Jezails
The Master's Class of Philadelphia
The Men on the Tor
The Merripit House Guests
The Mexborough Lodgers
The Mini-Tonga Society
Mrs. Hudson's Cliff Dwellers
Mrs. Hudson's Lodgers
Moulton's Prospectors
The Musgrave Ritualists
The Mycroft Holmes Society
Mycroft's Isolated Companions
The Napoleons of Crime
The Nashville Scholars of the Three Pipe
Problem
The Noble Bachelors and Concubines
The Noble Bachelors of St. Louis
The Noble and Most Singular Order of
the Blue Carbuncle
The Non-Canonical Calabashes of Los
Angeles
The Nonpareil Club
The Norwegian Explorers
The Norwood Builders of Burlington
The Notorious Canary-Trainers
The Occupants of the Empty House
The Old Soldiers of Baker Street of the
Two Saults
The Old Soldiers of Praed Street

The Old Soldiers of Quaker Street—A Scion Society of the Quaker Street Ounce of Shag

The Outpatients, A Department of Doctor Watson's Neglected Patients

The Pawky Humorists

The Pennsylvania Small Arms Company

The Pick of A Bad Lot

The Pin-Point Pupils

Pips of Organge County

The Pleasant Places of Florida

The Practical, But Limited, Geologists

The (Printer's) Devil's Feet

The Priory Scholars

The Priority Scholars of Fenwick High School

The Priory Scholars of New York

The Quaker Street Irregulars

The Rascally Lascars of Beverly Hills

The Red Circle of Washington, D.C.

The Red-Headed League

The Red-Headed League of Jersey

The Red Lamp League

The Reigate Squires

The Resident Patients of Baker Street

The Retired Colourmen of Dayton

S.H.E.R.L.O.C.K. (Sherlock Holmes Enthusiastic Readers League of Criminal Knowledge)

The Saxe-Coburg Squares of Mecklenburg County

The Scandalous Bohemians of New Jersey

The Scion of the Four

The Scowrers and Molly Maguires

The Seventeen Steps of Columbus

The Sherlock Holmes Cipher Society

The Sherlock Holmes Wireless Society

The Sherlockian Fiddlers

The Sherlockian Youth Society

The Silver Blazers

The Sir James Saunders Society

The Six Napoleons of Baltimore

The Society for the Prevention of Cruelty to Canonical Criminals

The Society of Railwaymen and Platelayer

The Society of Solitary Cyclists

The Solitary Cyclists of South Bend

Some Freaks of Atavism

The Something Hunt Club

The Sons of the Copper Beeches

The Sound of the Baskervilles

The Speckled Band of Boston

The Stapletons of Merripit House

The Stormy Petrels of Maumee Bay

The Strange Old Book Collectors

Strollers on the Strand of Galveston, Texas

The Students in Scarlet of Clark University

The Sub-Librarians Scion of the Baker Street Irregulars in the American Library Association

The Sussex Vampires

The Tankerville Club

The Three Garridebs

The Three Students Plus The Three Students of Scarsdale

The Tidewaiters of San Francisco Bay

The Tigers of San Pedro

The Trained Cormorants of Gifu

The Trained Cormorants of Long Beach, California

The Travellers for Nevada

The Trichinopoly Society of Long Island

The Trifling Monographers

The Tropical Deerstalkers

The Unanswered Correspondents

Unravellers of the Scarlet Thread

The Unslippered Persians

The Veiled Lodgers

The Victorian Gentlemen

"VR"

The Wastrels of Watson

Watsonian Society of St. Louis

Watson's Erroneous Deductions

The William Gillette Memorial Luncheon

The Women's Auxiliary to the Baker Street Irregulars

The Yale Sherlock Holmes Society

The Young Sherlockian Corresponding Society

Popular Literature—Science Fiction

1035. **Fan Tek.** c/o Bruce Evry, Executive Officer, 1607 Thomas Road, Ft. Washington, MD 20744. 301-292-5231; (Fax) 301-203-9582.

Founded in 1982, the 3,000-odd members share an interest in science fiction, fantasy, and gaming. The organization seeks to promote creativity and enjoyment in space science, computers, writing and editing, drawing, historical reenactment, costuming, and laser and special effects technology. Fan Tek operates an electronic bulletin board, FANTEK BBES, and publishes two quarterly periodicals, *The Castle* and *The Castle— Past, Present, Sideways.*

1036. **First Fandom.** c/o Ray E. Beam, Executive Officer, 2209 S. Webster Street, Kokomo, IN 46901. 317-455-1958.

Membership is limited to readers, writers, and collectors of science fiction/fantasy publications who can prove a knowledge of the genre's pre-1938 era. Established 1958, the group seeks to promote and pay homage to the early writers of science fiction and to stimulate and revive interest among older fans. It maintains a hall of fame, bestows awards for contributions to the genre, sponsors an annual convention (always beginning the Saturday before Labor Day), and publishes *First Fandom Magazine, First Fandom Newsletter, First Fandom Secretary's Report* (quarterly), and the semiannual *Roster.*

1037. **Gaylactic Network.** c/o Franklin Hummel, Director, P.O. Box 1051, Back Bay Annex, Boston, MA 02117-1051.

Open to gay men, lesbians, and others interested in science fiction and fantasy, the organization (including eight regional groups) promotes the genre in all media, specially material dealing with homosexuality. It provides a network for information dissemination, maintains a speakers' bureau, and publishes an annual directory and the quarterly newsletter, *Gaylactic Gayzette.* It was founded in 1987.

1038. **International Association for the Fantastic in the Arts.** c/o Dr. Donald Palumbo, President, Shippensburg University, Shippensburg, PA 17257. 717-532-1495.

IAFA, formed in 1979, is composed of scholars, educators, writers, critics, and artists sharing an interest in the fantastic, science fiction, horror, and fantasy and their impact on literature, the visual and performing arts, cinema, and other art forms. It provides a forum for the dissemination of scholarship and ideas in addition to encouraging work in the field through publications, financial awards, professional support service, and graduate student scholarships. Publications include the *IAFA Membership Directory* (annual), the quarterly *IAFA Newsletter,* and *Journal of the Fantastic in the Arts* (3 per year). IAFA's International Conference on the Fantastic in the Arts is held every spring in Dania, Florida.

1039. **National Fantasy Fan Federation.** c/o William Center, President, 1920 Division Street, Murphysboro, IL 62966-2320. 618-684-6090.

Founded in 1941, N3F is a correspondence club of persons interested in reading, writing, and collecting science fiction and fantasy books, magazines, articles, and other materials. It sponsors an annual story contest and issues two bimonthly publications, *The National Fantasy Fan* and *Tightbeam.*

1040. **Science Fiction Poetry Association.** c/o Elissa Malcohn, Editor, P.O. Box 1764, Cambridge, MA 02238.

SFPA, formed in 1978, includes professional writers, "poetic dabblers," general readers, and others interested in science fiction poetry and libraries. It operates a placement service and shares marketing news; reviews current science fiction publications; sponsors seminars, panel discussion, and readings at World Science Fiction Society conventions; bestows the annual Rhysling Awards for best long and short poems; and maintains a library of reviewed poetry material. Publications include the *SFPA Directory, Star Line* (bimonthly newsletter), an annual anthology, the *Beginning Poet's Handbook,* bulletins, articles, and a poetry cassette compilation.

1041. **Science Fiction Research Association.** c/o Peter Lowentrout, President, 1250 Bellflower Blvd., Long Beach, CA 90840. 213-431-4483.

Teachers, librarians, students, futurologists, authors, editors, publishers, booksellers, and others interested in science fiction compose the membership of SFRA. Established in 1970, the association attempts to promote the study and teaching of science fiction and modern fantasy and their related fields; to improve access to published and unpublished materials; and to assist libraries in the acquisition of papers and records needed for present and future study. It presents the annual Pilgrim Award to a distinguished scholar in the field and publishes *Extrapolation* and *Science Fiction Studies,* the *Science Fiction Research Association Newsletter,* an annual directory, and *Science Fiction Research Association Anthology of Science Fiction.* An annual conference is held each June.

1042. **Science Fiction Writers of American.** c/o Peter Dennis Pautz, Executive Secretary. 5 Winding Brook Dr., No. 1B, Guilderland, NY 10208-9719.

Founded in 1965, the 1,100 members include professional writers of science fiction stories, novels, radio plays, teleplays, and screenplays. The SFWA encourages general interest in science fiction literature through the use of school and public library facilities; produces and disseminates science fiction literature of high quality; conducts conferences, discussions, lectures, and seminars; presents the Nebula Awards of the best science fiction novel, novella, novelette, and short story of the year, as determined by a poll of the active membership; and maintains a speakers' bureau and library. Publications include a quarterly bulletin, an annual directory, the *Forum* (bimonthly), a handbook, and various brochures.

Performing Arts—Magic

1043. **Magic Collectors' Association.** c/o Walter J. Gydesen, Executive Secretary, 19 Logan Street, New Britain, CT 06051. 203-224-1583.

The MCA, formed in 1950, includes persons interested in the historical aspects of magic, including conjuring books, playbills, magazines, lithographs, and props. It publishes *Magicol* (quarterly), bestows awards, and sponsors an annual convention (usually in April).

Popular Music—General

1044. **Broadcast Music, Inc.** Francis W. Preston, CEO and President, 320 W. 57th Street, New York, NY 10019. 212-586-2000; (Fax) 212-582-5972; (Telex) 12-7823 (BMI); (Toll-free number) 800-USA-BMI1.

A nonprofit music licensing organization, whose staff of 300 and twelve regional groups serves more than 60,000 writer and 35,000 publisher affiliates. In its stewardship role, BMI collects license fees from music users and makes payments to the music creators; to this end, it maintains reciprocal agreements with thirty-nine sister licensing organizations worldwide. Programs include conducting music business seminars; sponsoring competitions, the BMI/Lehman Engel Musical Theater Workshop, and film, television, and jazz composers workshops; presenting awards to student composers; and overseeing a speakers' bureau and computerized music compositions listing. *BMI Music World,* with a circulation of over 100,000, includes profiles of songwriters and coverage of music events; the organization also publishes brochures on concert music affiliates and a variety of booklets and pamphlets.

1045. Nashville Songwriters Association, International. c/o Pat Huber, Executive Director, 1025 16th Avenue, S., Ste. 200, Nashville, TN 37212-1328. 615-321-5004.

Formed in 1967, the membership, numbering over 3,000, includes professional and amateur songwriters as well as other individuals in the songwriting industry. NSAI works to advance the art of musical composition and promote the growth of creative leadership for artistic, cultural, and educational progress in the field; helps songwriters gain recognition for their work; works to participate in legislative work for songwriter benefits; conducts weekly workshops in Nashville with guest speakers including publishers, recording artists, studio personnel, and other songwriters; holds area workshops for songwriters who are unable to travel to major music publishing and recording centers; bestows Song of the Year, Songwriter/Artist of the Year, and Songwriter of the Year awards annually; maintains a hall of fame; sponsors a semiannual convention (March and July); and publishes two bimonthly newsletters, *The Leadsheet* and *Proposition.*

1046. National Academy of Popular Music. c/o Christina Malone, Managing Director, 875 3rd Avenue, 8th Floor, New York, NY 10022. 212-319-1444; (Fax) 212-888-2175.

NAPM's 1,000 members consist of songwriters, record producers, publishers, performers, and other industry professionals. Formed in 1969, the academy honors artists, composers, and entertainers for their contributions to the entertainment field; sponsors songwriting seminars, workshops, and showcases; administers a museum, a multimedia library, and a Songwriters' Hall of Fame; and publishes a quarterly newsletter, *Words About Music.*

1047. National Academy of Songwriters. c/o Daniel A. Kirkpatrick, Managing Director, 6381 Hollywood Blvd., Ste. 780, Hollywood, CA 90028. 213-463-7178; (Fax) 213-463-2146; (Toll-free number) 800-826-7287.

NAS membership, presently numbering approximately 3,000, is open to amateur and professional songwriters as well as others interested in the art, craft, and business of songwriting. Formed in 1974, the academy's aims consist of providing education, protection, and other services to songwriters, in addition to encouraging expansion of social awareness through music. It conducts a weekly song evaluation workshop and three semesters of workshops per year; provides group legal services; operates a bookstore (which offers discounts to members) and Songbank, a registry that provides evidence of original authorship of songs and acts as an interim alternative until federal copyright is secured; lobbies and testifies on legislative matters; researches music-related questions for members; sponsors the Songwriters Network, which matches people who seek some type of collaboration; and maintains the Marilyn and Alan Bergman Library and a lead sheet service for songwriters who cannot write down the music they create. Publications include *Open Ears* (a bimonthly tip sheet listing artists looking for songs), *Songtalk* (quarterly), a bimonthly newsletter, educational cassettes, pamphlets, booklets, and educational fliers.

Popular Music—Blues/Rhythm and Blues

1048. The Blues Foundation. Jay Sheffield, Executive Director, 174 Beale Street, Memphis, TN 38103. 901-527-BLUE.

TBF, instituted in 1980, includes musicians, writers, music promoters, record producers, and blues fans. Serving as an umbrella organization for the National Blues Connection Association, its primary aim is to develop a blues awareness program to educate Americans and people worldwide regarding the historical and musical value of blues music. Programs include conducting a national Blues Amateur Talent Contest; sponsoring a National Blues Music Awards Show; presenting the annual Handy Award for outstanding contribution to the perpetuation, preservation, and promotion of blues music; holding the International Blues Conference every October in Memphis; and publishing a bulletin, *The Blues ExPress.* It also plans to create Blues Hall, a multipurpose facility incorporating a museum, archives, library, hall of fame, and Blues Cabaret.

1049. **Blues Heaven Foundation.** Willie Dixon, President, c/o The Cameron Orgn., Inc., P.O. Box 6926, Burbank, CA 91506. 818-566-8880.
Established in 1982, the foundation is open to anyone interested in the documentation, performance, and preservation of blues music. Currently in the fundraising and organizational stages, planned programs include the Muddy Waters Scholarship Fund for students in music education; assistance to elementary and secondary schools in obtaining musical instruments; copyright and publication protection; and maintaining an audiovisual archive. It publishes a periodic newsletter.

1050. **International Rhythm and Blues Association.** c/o William C. Tyson, President, P.O. Box 288571, Chicago, IL 60628. 312-326-5270.
IRBA consists of musicians, record companies, songwriters, and individuals interested in preserving and promoting rhythm and blues music. Formed in 1966, it operates a library and is currently raising funds for scholarships to award students pursuing careers in rhythm and blues music.

1051. **Rhythm and Blues Rock and Roll Society.** c/o William J. Nolan, Director, P.O. Box 1949, New Haven, CT 06510. 203-924-1079.
Founded in 1974, its 50,000 members and thirteen regional groups include record collectors, disc jockeys, record dealers, performing artists, and others dedicated to the preservation and promotion of rhythm and blues music and related genres (blues, gospel, and jazz) as a part of the U.S. cultural heritage. Programs include sponsoring benefit concerts for prisoners, fundraising events for amateur talent, and music concerts and festivals; conducting workshops on R&B culture; encouraging the employment of minorities in jobs related to blues music; offering training opportunities in the production of educational television shows and films; overseeing "Antique Blues," a radio show presenting live gospel, blues, and R&B performing groups; giving awards to artists, authors, and writers; maintaining an international record review panel; compiling statistics and conducting research; administering a record and tape-book library and archive; and publishing a newsletter, *Big Beat,* and a bulletin.

Popular Music—Country

1052. **Country Music Association.** c/o Edwin Benson, Executive Director, 1 Music Circle S., Nashville, TN 37203-4312. 615-244-2840.
Founded in 1958, the more than 7,000 members include artists, musicians, artist managers or agents, advertising representatives, talent buyers or promoters, disc jockeys, publishers, radio-television personnel, record company staff, record merchandisers, composers, and authors. The CMA has established the Country Music Hall of Fame and affiliated library, and the Country Music Foundation. It also presents annual awards in eleven categories of achievement for country music entertainers; conducts surveys in North America to determine the number of radio stations broadcasting country music; holds the International Country Music Fan Fair (each June), the annual Talent Buyers seminar, and an October convention; and publishes *Close-Up* (monthly).

1053. **Country Music Foundation.** c/o William Ivey, Director, 4 Music Square E., Nashville, TN 37203. 615-256-1639; (Fax) 615-255-2245.

The CMF, formed in 1964 as an arm of the Country Music Association, is dedicated to preserving the history of country music and encouraging scholarly research in that genre and related areas. It operates the Country Music Hall of Fame and Museum, RCA's Studio B, and Hatch Show Print (a historical show poster printer), a library including over a quarter of a million recordings, CMF Records (a re-issue label of historically important recordings), and the Country Music Foundation Press (which focuses on scholarly reprints and books on Anglo-American music). The foundation also sponsors educational programs on songwriting, the history of the phonograph, and the evolution of the genre; conducts special programs for the disabled; and publishes the *Journal of Country Music* (3 per year).

1054. **Country Music Showcase International.** c/o Harold L. Luick, President, P.O. Box 368, Carlisle, IA 50047. 515-989-3748.

Formed in 1984, CMSI is composed of professional and amateur performers, agents, fan club presidents, journalists, and songwriters working together to preserve and foster interest in country music and its various forms, in addition to setting high standards for performers. It sponsors festivals and competitions; owns a stage show, Country Classic's U.S.A.; maintains a hall of fame, museum, library, and biographical archives; gives awards; and operates educational programs, a speakers' bureau, and a placement service. Publications include the *Action Gram News Letter* (monthly) and the *Country Music Showcase International Entertainment News* (quarterly).

1055. **Independent Record Charts.** c/o Wayne Hodge, President, 43 Music Square E., Nashville, TN 37203. 615-244-1027.

Established in 1982, members include independent country-format radio stations, independent record labels, country singers, writers, and publishers. The IRC's primary goal is to achieve recognition and reward for the efforts and contributions of independent recording artists to the country music industry. It offers promotional and marketing programs to artists whose work has been approved by the group's quality board after evaluation of production, sound mixing, pressing, and artistic performance; provides the independent and progressive radio station with a connection in Nashville that may help them attain their respective goals in country music; negotiates distribution arrangements for products approved by the IRC; informs independents of markets in which they have a popular record; monitors radio play lists and tracking sheets to provide artists, labels, publishers, and writers with proof of air play; and provides radio stations with a biweekly listing of the top thirty independent records being played nationwide.

Popular Music—Jazz/Big Band

1056. **Big Band Academy of America.** c/o Milton Gerald Bernhart, President and Managing Director, Kelly Travel Service, 6565 W. Sunset Blvd., Ste. 516, Los Angeles, CA 90028. 213-463-4825.

Founded in 1983, the BBAA is dedicated to perpetuating the memory and sound of the big band as well as introducing the genre to younger generations. It maintains a library of more than 20,000 volumes, operates a speakers' bureau and placement service, sponsors free big band concerts, presents awards, and publishes a newsletter, *The Bandstand,* and annual, *That Was This, Then Is Now.* Plans are also in place to establish a big band museum and to offer scholarships to high school seniors pursuing advanced degrees in big-band-related fields.

1057. **International Association of Jazz Appreciation.** c/o William J. Coffey, President. (Fax) 213-673-0757.

The IAJA, formed in 1982, works to preserve and perpetuate jazz through such educational programs as the Jazz Goes to School program; sponsors the Los Angeles International Jazz Festival and related events; offers consultation on education, presentation, and performance; maintains a speakers' bureau; oversees a biennial International Jazz Conference; and publishes the bimonthly newsletter, *Jazz-Imbat.*

1058. **International Association of Jazz Record Collectors.** c/o Shirley L. Klett, Secretary, 127 Briarcliff Lane, Bel Air, MD 21014. 301-838-7542; (Fax) 301-638-0497.

Formed in 1964, the association aims consist of creating more recognition for accomplished jazz musicians and stimulating increased public acceptance of jazz as a great American art form; promoting communication among collectors, dealers, and musicians; issuing publications (e.g., *IAJRC Journal, IAJRC Membership Directory,* guidebooks, and discographies) and recordings; and encouraging the formation of local jazz clubs. It maintains a research lending library and sponsors an annual summer convention.

1059. **International Federation of Ragtime.** c/o Nick Taylor, 5095 Picket Drive, Colorado Springs, CO 80918-3617, 719-528-1547.

Open to those interested in the preservation, encouragement, and promotion of ragtime music, the federation, founded in 1991, assists in educational programs and the formation of clubs and societies; encourages continued research and publication on ragtime topics; and collects and disseminates information on ragtime music, composers, performers, events, historians, and collectors. Holds semiannual conferences and maintains a library with archives.

1060. **Jazz World Society.** c/o Jan A. Byrczek, Executive Director. P.O. Box 777, Times Square Station, New York, NY 10108. (212) 581-7188.

Established in 1969, the society promotes the development of jazz music and fosters communication among jazz participants. The membership (numbering 3,500) encompasses musicians, composers, record producers, distributors, collectors, journalists, and others actively supporting jazz music. Its programs include operating a multimedia library; organizing competitions and presenting awards; offering specialized education packages; administering a placement service; maintaining a hall of fame and biographical archives; and holding a semiannual general assembly. Publications include *Jazz Festivals International Directory, Jazz World* (bimonthly), and various jazz reference books.

1061. **National Academy of Jazz.**

Established in 1985, NAJ includes musicians, vocalists, composers, arrangers, lyricists, conductors, jazz educators, writers, disc jockeys, students, corporations, educational institutions, and other persons interested in the advancement and artistry of jazz. Its stated goals are to foster cultural, educational, and artistic excellence and to give formal recognition to those who have pursued and achieved excellence in the field of jazz. NAJ sponsors jazz events and workshops, administers the Buddy Rich Scholarship and the Woody Herman Foundation funds, and publishes *Jazz: The National Academy of Jazz Newsletter* (bimonthly).

1062. **National Jazz Service Organization.** c/o Willard Jenkins, Executive Director. 409 7th, NW, Lower Level, Washington, DC 20004-0061. (Fax) 202-347-2604.

The NJSO, formed in 1984, consists of jazz artists, ensembles, orchestras, performing groups and organizations, record companies and retailers, and other individuals and groups dedicated to the creation, instruction, performance, presentation, and preservation of jazz music. It maintains the National Jazz Network, holds periodic conferences, and publishes the quarterly *NJSO Journal, New Perspectives on Jazz,* and *Insights on Jazz* (curriculum series).

1063. **New Orleans Jazz Club.** c/o Marshall Ryals, President. 828 Royal St., Ste. 265, New Orleans, LA 70116. (504) 455-6847.

The NOJC originated in 1948 and numbers over 2,000 individuals interested in jazz, especially the Dixieland or New Orleans style. Club activities include sponsoring jam sessions, concerts, a radio show, lectures and other educational programs, charitable programs, a speakers' bureau; maintaining biographical archives; presenting awards; holding annual meetings; and publishing the quarterly, *Second Line*.

1064. **Oversees Jazz Club.** c/o Wilma Dobie, President. 15 Autenreith Rd., Scarsdale, NY 10583. (914) 725-3145.

Founded in 1970, the OJC attempts to draw attention to jazz as an original art form and to honor jazz artists. It presents a series of jazz programs in New York City, offers an educational program on the heritage of jazz, maintains a library, holds periodic meetings, and publishes the bimonthly journal *Offbeat Jazz*.

1065. **Scott Joplin Foundation of Sedalia.** c/o John Moore, Festival Coordinator, 113 E. 4th Street, Sedalia, MO 65301. 816-826-2271.

The foundation was created in 1974 by fans of Joplin and the ragtime genre. Programs include sponsoring ragtime concerts; holding an annual educational symposium and panel discussions; conducting research trips to other festivals; presenting awards; and maintaining a speakers' bureau, biographical archives, museum, and library of subject biographies, videocassettes of performances, and research materials. Publications include *The Cradle of Ragtime* (brochure) and a newsletter, *Sedalia Rag*.

Popular Music—Rock 'n' Roll

1066. **International Rock 'N' Roll Music Association.** c/o Bernard G. Walters, President, P.O. Box 158946, Nashville, TN 37215. 615-297-9072.

Founded in 1980, members include musicians, composers, managers, promoters, booking agents, disc jockeys, publishers, merchandisers, record companies, and enthusiasts interested in promoting rock 'n' roll music. The association's aims include protecting the interests of persons involved in rock 'n' roll creation, production, and promotion, and establishing a museum and hall of fame to document and preserve the genre. IRMA maintains a multimedia library and publishes the biennial *International Rock 'n' Roll Music Association Communique*.

1067. **Rock and Roll Hall of Fame Foundation.** c/o Suzan Evans, Executive Director, Atlantic Records, 75 Rockefeller Plaza, 2nd Floor, New York, NY 10019.

Although the foundation has been inducting artists and other pioneers of the genre for close to a decade, the construction of the hall of fame, library, archive, and museum at a Cleveland site proceeds at a snail's pace. There are plans for an educational program, legal aid services, and a regularly published newsletter.

Social Phenomena—Civil Rights—Drugs

1068. **Drug Policy Foundation.** c/o Arnold S. Trebach, President, 4801 Massachusetts Avenue, NW, Ste. 400, Washington, D.C. 20016. 202-895-1634; (Fax) 202-537-3007.

Formed in 1987, the DPF promotes alternative methods (such as legalization, decriminalization, and medicalization of currently illegal substances, including marijuana and heroin) to curb drug abuse while protecting the rights of the individual. To these ends, the foundation sponsors debates, conferences, and seminars on drug policy issues; compiles data; maintains a library and speakers' bureau; presents awards; and publishes two bimonthlies (*Drug Policy Action* and *Drug Policy Letter*) and various monographs (e.g., *Drug Policy 1989-90: A Reformer's Catalogue, The Great Drug War*).

Social Phenomena—Civil Rights—Intellectual Freedom

1069. **American Civil Liberties Union.** c/o Ira Glasser, Executive Director, 132 W. 43rd Street, New York, NY 10036. 212-944-9800; (Fax) 212-354-5290.

The ACLU, founded in 1920, comprises 375,000 members, fifty state groups, and 200 local groups. It acts as an advocate for the rights set forth in the Bill of Rights of the U.S. Constitution, as well as equality before the law regardless of race, color, sexual orientation, national origin, political opinion, or religious belief. Sponsors litigation projects; public speaking; maintains a library; and publishes journals (e.g., the quarterly *Civil Liberties* and monthly *Civil Liberties Alert*), policy statements, handbooks, reprints, and pamphlets.

1070. **Center for Constitutional Rights.** c/o Miriam Thompson, Executive Director, 666 Broadway, 7th Floor, New York, NY 10012. 212-614-6464; (Fax) 212-614-6499.

The CCR works in such areas as abuse of the grand jury process, women's rights, civil rights, freedom of the press, racism, electronic surveillance, criminal trials, and affirmative action in order to "halt and reverse the steady erosion of civil liberties in the U.S." To this end, it conducts the Ella Baker Student Program, the Movement Support Network, and, in Mississippi, The Voting Rights Project; sponsors training for law student interns; maintains a speakers' bureau; distributes legal briefs; and publishes an *Annual Report,* the *Docket Report,* the *MSN News,* and various pamphlets. The center was founded in 1966.

1071. **Freedom Information Service.** c/o Jan Hillegas, Treasurer, P.O. Box 3568, Jackson, MS 39207. 601-352-3398.

The FIS, formed in 1965, researches the activities of workers, blacks, and grass roots organizations through its Deep South People's History Project. Projects also include maintaining an extensive Mississippi-centered library and archives, distributing press releases on current Southern news, reprinting items on women's liberation and political education, and publishing the *FIS Mississippi Newsletter* and monographs relevant to the civil rights movement and black candidates.

1072. **Freedom of Expression Foundation.** c/o Dr. Craig R. Smith, 5220 S. Marina Pacifica, Long Beach, CA 90803. 213-985-4301.

Founded in 1983, the membership includes corporations, foundations, broadcasters, and publishers. Its primary aim is to provide information to Congress and the public concerning freedom of speech as guaranteed by the First Amendment. Activities include maintaining the Education and Research Fund; operating the Center for First Amendment Studies at California State University, Long Beach; designating members to testify before Senate and House committees; and distributing videotapes of forty-minute lectures. Publications include periodicals (*Filings with FCC* and a quarterly newsletter) and monographs such as *Fight for Freedom of Expression: Three Case Studies, The 1850 Compromise, Substance and Shadows, All Speech Is Created Equal, The First Amendment in the Information Age, Instructor's Handbook for Courses in Freedom of Expression,* and *The Road to the Bill of Rights.*

Social Phenomena—Civil Rights—Sexuality

1073. **Association for the Sexually Harassed.** c/o Cheryl Gomez-Tumpkins-Preston, Board Chairman, P.O. Box 27235, Philadelphia, PA 19118. 215-952-8037.

Composed of employers, organizations, victims of sexual harassment, and other interested individuals, ASH is concerned with eliminating sexual harassment, which the organization defines as the "unwelcomed exposure to physical contact, pornography, sexual jokes, requests for dates, and demeaning comments, made by male or female, which causes an individual's environment or work place to become intimidating, hostile, or offensive." Programs include conducting professional training on dealing with and preventing sexual harassment in the work environment; carrying out research and statistical studies on posttraumatic stress disorder and the relationship of sexual harassment to homelessness, crime, unemployment, and workmen's compensation injuries; operating a support group for sexual harassment victims, a speakers' bureau, and children's services; and maintaining a newsclip collection on sexual harassment cases. It was instituted in 1988.

1074. **Gay and Lesbian Advocates and Defenders.** c/o Kevin M. Cathcart, Executive Officer, P.O. Box 218, Boston, MA 02112. 617-426-1350; (Fax) 617-426-3594.

GLAD consists of attorneys volunteering time to defend the civil rights of homosexual individuals. Formed in 1978, it operates the AIDS Law Project and speakers' bureau, conducts educational programs, provides an information and referral service that is nationwide in scope, and publishes an annual report and a periodic newsletter, *Glad Briefs.*

Social Phenomena—Feminism

1075. **Center for Women's Studies and Services.** c/o Carol Council, Director. 2467 E St., San Diego, CA 92102. (619) 233-8984.

The CWSS was formed in 1969 to meet the needs of women via feminist services and programs and to advance the cause of women's rights. It provides personal, family, and legal counseling; a crisis hotline and shelter for victims of sexual assault and family violence; information and referral to other women's programs and organizations and to human service agencies; special workshops (e.g., Sexual Assault Prevention, Family Violence, Assertiveness Training); projects, such as a Dissolution Clinic (for uncontested divorces), Rape Crisis Center, and Temporary Restraining Order Legal Clinic; and a speakers' bureau. Publications include the quarterly *CWSS Newsletter, Bylines by Women, The Year of the Fires, Double Jeopardy, Young and Female in America,* and *Rainbow Snake.*

1076. **The Feminist Press at the City University of New York.** c/o Florence Howe, President. 311 E. 94th St., New York, NY 10128. (212) 360-5790.

Founded in 1970, this nonprofit educational and publishing organization is working to eliminate sex-role and social stereotypes in education at all levels, further the rediscovery of the history of women, and provide literature "with a broad vision of human potential." To this end, it researches the status of women's studies at academic institutions across the nation and analyzes the teaching methods and curricula by which stereotypical attitudes can be changed; provides texts for college courses and has created syllabi in which women's history and literature by women are introduced into traditional college courses; reprints lost or neglected literature by women writers; maintains Women's Studies International; and publishes *Women's Studies Quarterly, The Feminist Press* (annual) and reprints of works by women authors.

1077. **National Women's Studies Association.** c/o Deborah Louis, Director. University of Maryland, College Park, MD 20742-1325. (301) 405-5573.

The NWSA, instituted in 1977, includes 4,000 members (teachers, students, community activists, academic- and community-based programs, groups interested in feminist education) and regional groups united in furthering the social, political, and professional development of women's studies programs. Its activities include lobbying for women's studies at the elementary, secondary, and college level; encouraging the development of a network for distributing information on women's studies; cooperating with women's projects in communities; administering graduate scholarships in women's studies; compiling statistics; conducting conferences to address topics, such as new developments and controversies in feminism and theory, curricular development; political and legal issues, the intersection of race and gender; and sponsoring an annual conference. Publications include the *Biennial Women's Studies Program Directory,* the *NWSA Journal* (quarterly), the newsletter *NWSAction,* the *Women's Studies Major: A Report to the Profession* and *Guide to Graduate Studies and Liberal Learning.*

Sports and Recreation—General

1078. **International Association of Sports Museums and Hall of Fame.** c/o Al Cartwright, Executive Director, 101 W. Sutton Place, Wilmington, DE 19810-4115. 302-475-7068.

Founded in 1971, the IASMHF is committed to improving and maintaining standards of sports museums and halls of fame; enhancing their operations; facilitating the exchange of information; and starting projects that may be helpful to all members. It maintains a hall of fame, museum, and biographical archives. Publications include a bimonthly newsletter, a membership directory, and the pamphlet, *How to Start a Hall of Fame.*

1079. **National Collegiate Athletic Association.** c/o Richard D. Schultz, Executive Director, 6201 College Blvd., Overland Park, KS 66211. (913) 339-1906.

Founded in 1906, the NCAA's 1,053 members include institutions of higher education and allied educational athletics associations devoted to the administration of intercollegiate athletics. It operates a statistics service for various collegiate sports as well as publishing and film production services. It also maintains forty-two sports committees and over forty other committees and subcommittees (e.g., Academic Requirements, Competitive Safeguards and Medical Aspects of Sports, Postgraduate Scholarship, Professional Sports Liaison). Publications include record books, rule compilations, handbooks, various special reports (sports programs, finances, television, etc.), and many business-related documents.

1080. **National Federation of State High School Associations.** c/o Brice B. Durbin, Executive Director, 11724 NW Plaza Circle, P.O. Box 20626, Kansas City, MO 64195-0626. 816-464-5400; (Fax) 816-464-5571.

The NFSHSA consists of the sixty-five high school athletic/activities associations from the fifty U.S. states, the District of Columbia, the Virgin Islands, eleven Canadian provinces, the Philippines, and Guam, representing more than 18,100 high schools. Formed in 1920, it protects and supervises the interstate athletic, musical, and speech and debate interests of high schools and coordinates the activities of state associations. Activities include sponsoring TARGET—Helping Students Cope With Alcohol and Drugs; maintaining a national press service, a high school sports hall of fame, and an official sports film service; administering a testing program for sports equipment; compiling statistics; and organizing various training programs. Publications include the *Interscholastic Athletic Administration* (quarterly), *National Federation News: The National Voice of High School Activities* (newsletter, 9 per year), the *National High School Sports Record Book,* and *On Target,* a periodical providing resource information to students on alcohol and other drugs.

1081. **National Senior Sports Association.** c/o Lloyd Wright, President and Executive Director. (Fax) 703-591-4169.

The 10,000 members consist of individuals fifty years of age or older who are interested in sports and recreational activities. The NSSA, established in 1979, conducts tournaments in golf and bowling; offers travel programs; maintains a Member Exchange File, which enables traveling members to contact other members to enjoy sports together; publishes the *Senior Sports News* (monthly); and is affiliated with the National Golf Foundation.

Sports and Recreation—Baseball

1082. **Society for American Baseball Research.** c/o Morris Eckhouse, Executive Director, P.O. Box 93183, Cleveland, OH 44101. 216-575-0500; (Fax) 216-575-0502.

Founded in 1971, membership (numbering over 6,000) is open to anyone possessing an interest in baseball statistics and history. The society's goals include establishing an accurate historical and statistical account of baseball from its origin; facilitating the dissemination of baseball research information; and fostering the study of baseball as a significant American social and athletic institution. Publications include the *Baseball Research Journal: Annual Historical and Statistical Review of the Society for American Baseball Research, The National Pastime: A Review of Baseball History* (semiannual), *National Pastime Pictorial* (biennial), and the monthly newsletter, *SABR Bulletin.*

Sports and Recreation—Basketball

1083. **Continental Basketball Association.** c/o Terdemal L. Ussery, II, Commissioner, 425 S. Cherry Street, Ste. 230, Denver, CO 80222. 303-331-0404; (Fax) 303-329-8822.

The CBA, instituted in 1946, includes sixteen professional basketball franchises that develop players, coaches, and referees for the National Basketball Association. It sponsors competitions, bestows awards, compiles league statistics, and maintains a videotape library and various computer services (e.g., CBS Information System, electronic bulletin board). Publications include the *CBA Update* (newsletter, 24 per year) and *Continental Basketball Association—Official Guide & Register* (annual).

1084. **Naismith Memorial Basketball Hall of Fame.** c/o Joseph M. O'Brien, Executive Director, 1150 W. Columbus Avenue, P.O. Box 179, Springfield, MA 01101. 413-781-6500; (Fax) 413-781-1939.

Established in 1959, the NMBHF regularly inducts persons who have performed outstanding services to the game and presents the Naismith Awards (to the outstanding senior male basketball player under six feet tall and outstanding senior female player under five feet six inches tall in the United States) and the Bunn Award (an individual making significant contributions to basketball). It maintains a museum and the Edward J. and Gena Hickox Library in addition to sponsoring the NCAA Division II Championship, NBA Day, and the Hall of Fame Tip-Off Classic.

1085. **United States Basketball Writers Association.** c/o Joseph F. Mitch, Executive Director. 100 N. Broadway, Ste. 1135, St. Louis, MO 63102. (314) 421-0339.

The USBWA, founded in 1956, consists of individuals who write about collegiate and professional players for newspapers, magazines, and other communications media. It cooperates with other organizations in promoting the game and bestows awards to encourage and recognize outstanding achievements in sportsmanship, play, coaching, sports writing, and other fields (e.g., All-American team, NCAA Coach of the Year).

Publications include the annual directory and *The Tip-Off* (monthly during the basketball season).

Sports and Recreation—Bicycling

1086. **Bikecentennial: The Bicycle Travel Association.** c/o Gary MacFadden, Executive Director, P.O. Box 8308, Missoula, MT 59807. (406) 721-1776; (Fax) 721-8754.

Originally formed in 1973 to develop the TransAmerica Coast-to-Coast Bicycle Trail, the present focus of the group's 26,000 members is on the research, maintenance, and mapping of over 16,735 miles of bicycle touring routes. Other goals include educating the public in bicycle usage and safety and promoting understanding of America through bicycle travel. The association maintains a reference library and publishes *Bicycle Forum: The Journal of Bicycle Programs and Ideas* (quarterly), *Bike Report* (9 per year), and the annual *Cyclists' Yellow Pages.*

Sports and Recreation—Bowling

1087. **American Bowling Congress.** c/o Darold Dobs, Executive Director, 5301 S. 76th Street, Greendale, WI 53129-1127. 414-421-6400; (Fax) 414-421-1194.

The ABC, founded in 1895, numbers almost three million members; i.e., all organized male tenpin bowlers in the United States, Puerto Rico, Canada, and U.S. military installations worldwide. It sponsors an annual tournament competition and writing contest; provides standard rules and tests; approves equipment and supplies employed in sanctioned competitions; conducts research; maintains the Local Association Educational Program and other activities geared to uniting leagues; presents seminars; operates a hall of fame and museum; gives awards; compiles statistics; oversees an annual conference each March; and publishes the *Annual Tournament Program Yearbook, Bowling Magazine* (6 per year), a periodic newsletter, and the *Official Directory* (annual).

1088. **National Bowling Association.** c/o Margaret S. Lee, Executive Secretary-Treasurer, 377 Park Avenue S., 7th Floor, New York, NY 10016. 212-689-8308.

Established in 1939, the NBA's 26,000 members and 80 local groups attempt to foster good sportsmanship and friendship; optimize the interests and talents of bowlers; and create a national awareness and interest in civic and community programs. It participates in and promotes bowling tournaments; sponsors fundraising programs (e.g., for sickle cell anemia, for the United Negro College Fund); bestows bowling awards as well as national and local scholarship and special service awards; maintains a hall of fame; compiles statistics; holds an annual conference; and publishes *Bowler* (quarterly), the monthly *Newsletter/Bulletin,* and the *Souvenir Yearbook.*

1089. **Women's International Bowling Congress.** c/o Sandra Shirk, Chief Operating Officer, 5301 S. 76th Street, Greendale, WI 53129-1191. 414-421-9000; (Fax) 414-421-4420 and 414-421-3013.

Formed in 1916 as the female equivalent of the ABC, it includes 2.8 million members, fifty-four state groups, 2,784 local groups, and 119,612 leagues. It is responsible for providing uniform qualifications, rules, and regulations to govern WIBC sanctioned teams, leagues, and tournaments; conducting leadership training seminars; sponsoring the annual championship and Queens Pro Am tournaments; bestowing awards; maintaining a hall of fame, museum, and biographical archives; compiling statistics; cosponsoring the Young American Bowling Alliance as well as collegiate and senior league programs and National Senior and National Mixed Tournaments; overseeing an annual conference; and publishing the annual *Tournament and Record Guide,* the *WIBC News* (monthly), *WIBC Playing Rules and Bylaws Book* (annual), *Woman Bowler Magazine* (8 per year), and various brochures, handbooks, pamphlets, reports, and printed forms.

Sports and Recreation—Boxing

1090.   **International Boxing Hall of Fame Museum.** c/o Edward P. Brophy, Executive Director, Hall of Fame Drive, P.O. Box 425, Canastota, NY 13032. 315-697-7095.

The IBHFM, instituted in 1982, emphasizes the importance of sports to American society and the role of sports in the development of individual character. It assists organizations contemplating boxing programs, maintains a library of boxing records and literature, sponsors a Hall of Fame weekend in June, and publishes *The Main Event Newsletter* (quarterly).

Sports and Recreation—Football

1091.   **College Football Association.** c/o Charles M. Neinas, Executive Director. (Fax) 303-530-5371.

Founded in 1977, the CFA includes those institutions committed to a major college football program through scheduling strength, adequate playing facilities, and home game attendance. Presents the Academic Achievement Award (which recognizes the university attaining the highest graduation rate among football athletes) and publishes the monthly newsletter, *Sidelines.*

Sports and Recreation—Games

1092.   **American Games Collectors Association.** c/o Anne D. Willians, Secretary, Dept. E, 4628 Barlow Drive, Bartlesville, OK 74006.

The association includes individuals and institutions interested in the study, preservation, and collection of American games, primarily indoor games manufactured before World War II. It encourages the dissemination of information pertaining to games and game companies; maintains an archive of game instructions, catalogs, and game company histories; sponsors an annual conference (usually in the fall); and publishes *Game Researchers' Notes* and *Game Times* (both 3 per year). It was formed in 1985.

1093.   **Committee for the Advancement of Role-Playing Games.** c/o William A. Flatt, Chair, 8032 Locust Avenue, Miller, IN 46403. 219-938-3382.

The organization advocates the role-playing hobby; defends gamers from slander, libel, and illegal action; and promotes the recreational and educational benefits of role-playing games and their use in psychological and sociological treatment. To these ends, it maintains archives and information service for players, game publishers and retailers, and the media; operates a speakers' bureau; conducts seminars on gaming issues; offers a twenty-four-hour "warm line" service; and publishes the bimonthly newsletter *HQ Event Report,* an annual report, *The Gamer's Survival Kit, Law Enforcer's Guide to Censorship and Hate Literature Groups, Operations Guide, CAR-PGa Cocktail* (information packet), and other brochures and pamphlets. CAR-PGa was established in 1988.

1094.   **Role Playing Games Association Network.** c/o Jean Rabe, President, P.O. Box 515, Lake Geneva, WI 53147. 414-248-3625.

The RPGAN, founded in 1980, numbers 9,000 members and forty-nine local groups. It promotes the fantasy and role-playing game hobby, encourages continued improvement of games, and seeks to facilitate communication between players. Programs include holding competitions, bestowing awards, maintaining a library, and publishing *Polyhedron Newszine* (monthly).

1095. **Strategy Gaming Society.** c/o George Phillies, President, 87-6 Park Avenue, Worcester, MA 01605.

Formed in 1973, the SGS includes private hobbyists, game conventions, gaming clubs, and hobby stores. It disseminates information about the gaming community, holds game tournaments, provides matching and ratings services, maintains biographical archives, compiles statistics, and publishes the following titles: *Jeff Pimper's All the World's Wargames* (quinquennial), *Strategist* (monthly), *Wargamer's Encyclopedia Dictionary,* and *SGS Guide to Running Conventions.* The society also produces boardgames such as Madrid II and Fall of Manjukuo.

Sports and Recreation—Golf

1096. **Professional Golfers' Association of America.** c/o Jim Awtrey, Executive Director and CEO, 100 Avenue of Champions, Palm Beach Gardens, FL 33418. 407-624-8400; (Fax) 407-624-8452.

The PGA, founded in 1916, encompasses 20,000 members (golf professionals and apprentices associated with golf clubs, courses, and tournaments) and forty-one regional groups. It sponsors a wide array of tournaments; maintains the PGA Hall of Fame, library, and biographical archives; conducts a program of golf professional education, business schools, clinics, and seminars; certifies college programs in golf management; presents the Vardon Trophy, Professional of the Year, and Player of the Year awards; administers service clubs; offers employment counsel; compiles statistics; holds an annual convention; and publishes the monthly *PGA Magazine.*

Sports and Recreation—Horse Racing

1097. **United States Trotting Association.** c/o Francis X. Ready, Executive Vice President, 750 Michigan Avenue, Columbus, OH 43215. 614-224-2291; (Fax) 614-224-4575 and 614-228-1385. (Harness Racing Hotline) 614-228-1821.

Instituted in 1938, the USTA's 46,000 members include owners, trainers, and drivers of Standardbred horses, officials of harness racing, track officers, sponsors of fairs, and other track organizations. Its goals consist of improving the breed of trotting and pacing horses, licensing drivers and officials, and registering drivers' colors. Activities include maintaining a hall of fame, library, and biographical archives; compiling statistics; making available an automated data base containing complete registration and past racing performance records of all horses, drivers, trainers, owners, and members; and publishing *Hoof Beats* (monthly), in addition to such annuals as *Sires and Dams Book, Trotting and Pacing Guide,* and the *USTA Year Book.*

Sports and Recreation—Olympic Games

1098. **United States Olympic Committee.** c/o William J. Hybl, President, 1750 E. Boulder Street, Colorado Springs, CO 80909. 719-632-5551; (Fax) 719-578-4677; (Telex) 187258 USOC UT; (Cable) AMOLYMPIC-CSP.

The USOC, formed in 1921, is a federation of sports governing bodies responsible for overseeing U.S. participation in the competitions of the Olympics and Pan American games. It selects and cares for team members; operates two Olympic Training Centers and conducts the U.S. Olympic Festival each summer (except the Olympic year); maintains a library, historical archives, and hall of fame; provides a speakers' bureau; presents awards; offers specialized education; and publishes the *Corporate Sponsor Newsletter* (monthly), *The Olympian* (10 per year), the *USOC Newsletter* (monthly), the *USOC Fact Book* (annual), the *U.S. Olympic Book* (quadrennial), and various press guides.

Sports and Recreation—River Sports

1099. **National Organization for River Sports.** c/o Eric Leaper, Executive Director. 314 N. 20th St., P.O. Box 6847, Colorado Springs, CO 80934. (719) 473-2466.

Founded in 1978, the organization's membership (numbering over 10,000) is open to anyone interested in white water river sports, including kayaking, rafting, and canoeing. It provides information on the conservation of wilderness rivers, government regulations, proper equipment, and safety procedures used in river sports; represents the recreational and conservational concerns of its constituents before government agencies; maintains a speakers' bureau; disseminates relevant books and videotapes; and publishes the quarterly, *NORS Journal.*

Sports and Recreation—Tennis

1100. **United States Tennis Association.** c/o M. Marshall Happer, III, Executive Director, 1212 Avenue of the Americas, New York, NY 10036. 212-302-3322; (Fax) 212-764-1838.

The USTA, established in 1881, is a federation of local tennis clubs, educational institutions, recreational departments, and other groups and individuals (more than 500,000 in all) interested in the promotion of tennis. It sanctions thousands of tournaments throughout the United States each year; presents awards; sponsors a Junior Program (under 18 years of age), the U.S. national tennis team, national championships for various age groups, the National Circuit tournament, the Davis Cup, the Federation Cup, the Wightman Cup, and adult recreational leagues; compiles statistics; maintains a library; works closely with the National Tennis Foundation and Hall of Fame in Newport, Rhode Island; and publishes the *Official USTA Yearbook, Tennis Championships Magazine, Tennis USTA* (monthly), the *Official Encyclopedia of Tennis,* clinic kits, rules manuals, and other educational materials.

Chapter 13

Journals

General

1101. **Journal of American Culture: Studies of a Civilization.** 1978-. Quarterly. Ray B. Browne, ed. American Culture Association, Bowling Green Popular Press, Bowling Green State University, Bowling Green, Ohio 43403. Illus.
   A definitive source for coverage of American folk, popular, and elite culture. Articles tend to be both interdisciplinary and multidisciplinary in nature.

1102. **Journal of Popular Culture.** 1967-. Quarterly. Ray B. Browne, ed. Popular Culture Association, Bowling Green Popular Press, Bowling Green State University, Bowling Green, Ohio 43403. Illus.
   The depth and breadth of the scholarly articles included here is extraordinary, encompassing folklore, the mass media, the popular arts, and social phenomena. Perhaps the single most important popular culture publication available.

1103. **Popular Culture Association Newsletter and Popular Culture Methods.** 1971-. Irregular. Michael Marsden, ed. Bowling Green State University, Popular Culture Center, Bowling Green, Ohio 43403. Adv.
   Available free to all members of the Popular Culture Association, this newsletter provides information updates not deemed appropriate for the *Journal of Popular Culture,* with its emphasis on expansive, scholarly features.

1104. **Popular Culture in Libraries.** 1993-. Quarterly. Frank Hoffmann, ed. Haworth Press, Binghamton, New York 13901. Illus.
   The journal attempts to provide information and act as a forum for the exchange of ideas about the evaluation, acquisition, organization, preservation, and utilization of popular culture concepts and materials in a wide array of print, audiovisual, and three-dimensional formats. Geared primarily to librarians, archivists, educators, and other professionals dealing with these collections, the journal also attempts to combat traditional biases against popular culture held by many academics as well as by library users and students.

1105. **Studies in Popular Culture.** 1977-. Semi-annual. Dennis Hall, ed. University of Louisville, Department of English, Louisville, KY 40292. Rev.
   The articles included here employ a multimedia perspective in covering film, literature, radio, television, music, graphics, the print media, and other popular culture concepts.

Collecting—General

1106. The Antique Trader Price Guide to Antiques and Collectors' Items: Complete Price Of All Antiques. 1970-. 6/yr. Kyle Husfloen, ed. Babka Publishing Company, 100 Bryant Street, Dubuque, IA 52001-1050. Illus.

This is an up-to-date guide to the value of both fine antiques and popular items, such as Coca-Cola and world's fair collectibles.

1107. The Antique Trader Weekly. 1957-. Weekly. Kyle Husfloen, ed. The Antique Trader, P.O. Box 1050, Dubuque, IA 52001. Illus., adv.

Billed as "America's Most Widely Used Publication on Antiques & Collector's Items," the publication is primarily composed of ads for popular antiques and collectibles.

1108. Collectors News & The Antique Reporter. 1960-. Monthly. Linda Kruger, ed. Collectors News Co., Grundy Center, IA 50638. Bk. rev., illus., adv.

The tabloid offers features, news, and calendars on a wide variety of collectibles.

Collecting—Hobbies

1109. The Coin Slot: The Newsletter for Collectors of Antique Mechanical Devices. 1974-. Quarterly. Joseph Jancuska, ed. Hoflin Publishing, 4401 Zephyr Street, Wheat Ridge, CO 80033-3299. Illus., adv.

This well-executed publication provides histories, repair tips, and acquisition information on pinballs, one-armed bandits, juke boxes, and other coin-operated machines.

1110. Goldmine: The Record Collector's Marketplace. 1974-. Fortnightly. Trey Foerster, ed. Krause Publications, Inc., 700 E. State Street, Iola, WI 54990. Illus., adv., discog., rev.

The definitive tool for both record collectors and popular music researchers, it includes features of a journalistic nature, interviews, news briefs, etc. The prime focus, however, is on the advertising of recordings that dealers and private collectors wish to purchase or sell.

1111. Postcard Collector. 1983-. Monthly. Diane Allmen, ed. Postcard Collector, 700 E. State Street, Iola, WI: 54990. Illus., adv.

This is a notable example of the type of magazine that focuses on the valuation and exchange of a particular collectible. The pictures represent a particular strength.

1112. Star Trek: The Official Fan Club Magazine. 1980-. Bi-monthly. Dam Madsen, ed. Box 111000, Aurora, CO 80011. Illus., adv., rev.

With a degree of distribution comparable to many mainstream commercial magazines (105,000), it treats everything related to the Star Trek phenomenon.

Collecting—Social Phenomena

1113. Collector Car News: The Magazine that Covers the Collector Car Hobby. 1961-. Monthly. William L. Finefrock, ed. Collector Car News, P.O. Box 5279, Long Beach, CA 80805. Illus., adv.

Primarily concerned with autos manufactured between the late 1920s and late 1950s, it also covers those of more recent vintage.

1114. **Old Cars Weekly.** 1973-. Weekly. John Gunnell, ed. Krause Publications, 700 E. State Street, Iola, WI 54990. Illus., adv.

The tabloid is devoted to the sale and trade of cars from all periods.

Collecting—Sports and Recreation

1115. **Baseball Card News.** 1981-. Bi-weekly. Allan Kaye, ed. Baseball Card News, 700 E. State Street, Iola, WI 54990. Illus., adv.

The newspaper covers a wide array of sports collectibles, most notably the trading cards of the major sports.

1116. **The Gun Report: Dedicated to the Interests of Gun Enthusiasts Everywhere.** 1955-. Monthly. Kenneth W. Liggett, ed. World-Wide Gun Report, Inc., P.O. Box 111, Aledo, IL 61231. Bk. rev., illus., adv.

Each issue consists of several insightful features on guns and their makers as well as accessories—all from a historical perspective. It also includes news notes, show calendars, etc.

Collecting—Toys

1117. **Doll Reader.** 8/yr. Virginia Ann Heyerdahl, ed. Hobby House Press, 900 Frederick Street, Cumberland, MD 21502. Illus., adv.

This publication comprehensively covers all facets of doll collecting; e.g., museums, designers, clothing patterns, auctions, valuations, and clubs.

Economics and Merchandising

1118. **American Journal of Economics and Sociology.** 1941-. Quarterly. Will Lissner, ed. American Journal of Economics and Sociology, 41 E. 72nd Street, New York, NY 10021. Illus., index.

Highly readable, it attempts a synthesis between politics, economics, sociology, cultural history, and other social sciences.

Folklore/Mythology

1119. **Journal of American Folklore.** 1888-. Quarterly. Bruce Jackson, ed. American Folklore Society, 1701 New Hampshire Avenue NW, Washington, D.C. 20009. Illus., index, adv.

The longest running journal in the field, it continues to employ excellence in scholarship in the exploration of all facets of the field, including the folk arts, folkways, and more contemporary phenomena, such as feminism.

1120. **Journal of Folklore Research.** 1964-. 3/yr. John H. McDowell, ed. Indiana University, Folklore Institute, 504 N. Fess, Bloomington, IN 47405. Index.

This academic journal concentrates on theoretical and methodological articles as well as descriptive studies.

Humor

1121. **Mad.** 1952-. 8/yr. Nick Meglin and John Ficarra, eds. E.C. Publications, 485 Madison Avenue, New York, NY 10022. Illus.

Undoubtedly the most popular humor magazine in the country, *Mad* mixes satire and nonsense in truly inspired fashion without losing its core audience.

1122. **National Lampoon: The Bimonthly Humor Magazine.** 1970-. Bimonthly. Matty Simmons, ed. NL Communications, 155 Avenue of the Americas, New York, NY 10013. Illus., adv.

The magazine offers uneven satirical treatment of a wide variety of societal concerns, particularly within the fields of religion and sexuality.

Language and Linguistics

1123. **Language: Journal of the Linguistic Society of America.** 1925-. Quarterly. Sarah G. Thomson, ed. Linguistic Society of America, 1325 18th Street NW, Suite 211, Washington, D.C. 20036-6501. Illus., index, adv.

Topics of an often popular nature are given scholarly treatment in this definitive publication.

1124. **Language and Communication: An Interdisciplinary Journal.** 1981-. Quarterly. Roy Harris, ed. Pergamon Press, Maxwell House, Fairview Park, Elmsford, NY 10523. Adv.

The articles cover the theory, research, applications, and interrelationship of the fields embraced by language and linguistics, including anthropology, the arts, education, philosophy, psychology, and the social sciences.

Mass Media—General

1125. **Audio-Visual Communications.** 1961-. Monthly. Mike Yuhas, ed. Media Horizons, Inc., 50 W. 23rd St., New York, NY 10010-5292. Illus., adv., rev.

The publication concentrates on the uses of media in business, advertising, and promotion, including product reviews and listings as well as news on corporate developments, awards announcements, and the analysis of general media trends.

1126. **Broadcasting: The Fifth Estate.** 1931-. Weekly. Lawrence B. Taishoff, ed. Broadcasting Publications, 1735 DeSales St. NW, Washington, D.C. 20036. Illus., adv., rev.

A leading industry trade, it encompasses radio, television, cable, satellite, home video, and the allied arts in covering new technological developments, relevant legislation, FCC regulations, and market and personnel news.

Mass Media—Films

1127. **American Film: The Magazine of the Film and Television Arts**. 1975-. 10/yr. Susan Linfield, ed. American Film Institute, M.D. Publications, Inc., 3 E. 54th St., New York, NY 10022. Illus., rev.

The highly readable articles focus on contemporary films and television, with a particular emphasis on the Hollywood scene. Features are complemented by interviews, seminars, editorials, and news notes covering both social and technical features of these media.

1128. **Cinefantastique.** 1970-. 5/yr. Frederick S. Clarke, ed. P.O. Box 270, Oak Park, IL 60303. Illus., adv., film rev.

In its analysis of horror, fantasy, and science fiction films, this lavishly illustrated magazine touches upon thematic, aesthetic, financial, and technical considerations.

1129. **Film History.** 1987-. Quarterly. Richard Koszarski, ed. Taylor & Francis, Inc., 242 Cherry St., Philadelphia, PA 19106. Illus.

The wide-ranging articles cover "the historical development of the motion picture, and [its] social, technological, and economic context." Included are profiles of relevant archives as well as reports of current publications, conferences, and research in progress.

1130. **Film Quarterly.** 1945-. Quarterly. Ernest Callenbach, ed. University of California Press, Berkeley, CA 94720. Illus., index, adv., rev.

The scholarly articles concentrate on the social and cultural elements of the film industry. The straightforward writing employed here should appeal to a lay audience in addition to academics.

Mass Media—Journalism

1131. **JQ. Journalism Quarterly: Devoted to Research in Journalism and Mass Communication.** 1924-. Quarterly. Guido H. Stempel III, ed. Association for Education in Journalism and Mass Communication, University of South Carolina, Columbia, SC 29208. Index, adv., rev., bibl.

The material here focuses on scholarship and long-range studies regarding all facets of the media.

1132. **Journalism History.** 1974-. Quarterly. Susan Henry, ed. Department of Journalism, California State University, Northridge, CA. 91330. Illus., adv., rev.

This scholarly journal analyzes key figures, institutions, and events with a historical context.

Mass Media—Radio

1133. **Journal of Broadcasting and Electronic Media.** 1956-. Quarterly. Alison Alexander, ed. Broadcast Education Association, 1771 N. St. NW, Washington, D.C. 20036. Illus., index, rev.

The journal is primarily composed of scholarly articles on programming, commerce, communication theory, and current trends as they relate to radio, television, cable, and other electronic media. The "Research in Brief" section analyzes ongoing research.

1134. **Radio & Records.** 1973-. Weekly. Ken Barnes, ed. Radio & Racords, Inc., 1930 Century Park W., Los Angeles, CA 90067. Illus., adv., rev.

This trade publication comprehensively documents the radio world, including personnel moves, legislation, commercial considerations, ratings, music, promotions, and other news.

Mass Media—Television

(See also: Mass Media—Radio, pp. 44, 176, 199, 225)

1135. Televison Quarterly: The Journal of the National Academy of Television Arts & Sciences. 1962-. Quarterly. Richard Pack, ed. National Academy of Television Arts & Sciences, 110 W. 57th St., New York, NY 10019. Adv., rev.

The publication's stated goal is to "deal with television's role in our complex society and its relationship to new technology." Major topics covered include programming, history of the medium, profiles of key figures, and contemporary issues.

Mass Media—Video

1136. Video Magazine. 1978-. Monthly. Judith Sawyer, ed. Reese Communications, 460 W. 34th St., New York, NY 10001. Illus., adv., rev.

The feature articles cover all aspects of the video revolution from a popular perspective.

1137. Video Review. 1980-. Monthly. James B. Meigs, ed. Viare Publishing Co., 902 Broadway, New York, NY 10010. Illus., adv., rev.

This mass circulation periodical exceeds the high standard achieved by *Video Magazine.* Product evaluations and software reviews are of particularly noteworthy quality.

Performing Arts—Dance

1138. Country Dance and Song. 1968-. Annual. David Sloane, ed. Country Dance Society, Inc., 17 New South Street, Northampton, MA 01060-4012. Illus.

The periodical surveys the history and execution of country dancing, including notable regional variants.

1139. Dance Chronicle: Studies in Dance and the Related Arts. 1978-. 3/yr. George Dorris and Jack Anderson, eds. Marcel Dekker Journals, 270 Madison Avenue, New York, NY 10016. Illus., index, rev.

The well-written articles are devoted to the history of all periods of dance, all styles of dance, and leading practitioners.

Performing Arts—Theater

1140. American Theatre. 1984-. 11/yr. Jim O'Quinn, ed. Theatre Communications Group, 355 Lexington Avenue, New York, NY 10017. Illus., adv., rev.

Concentrating on nonprofit professional theater in the United States, the periodical manages to keep abreast of the major trends in the field (e.g., playscripts, productions) in addition to profiling playwrights, theater specialists, and theater companies.

1141. Performing Arts. 1975-. Monthly. Newsbank, Inc., 58 Pine Street, New Canaan, CT 06840. Monthly & cumulated indexes.

Part of the *Review of the Arts* series, the compilation of reviews and features on theater, dance, music, and the other performing arts makes available a nationwide array of newspapers on microfiche.

1142. **Variety.** 1905-. Weekly. Roger Watkins, ed. Variety, Inc., 475 Park Avenue S., New York, NY 10016-6999. Illus., adv., rev.

This is a definitive trade publication devoted to all aspects of the entertainment business, including the mass media, vaudeville, concerts, and theater. Included are news items, performance reviews, casting data, financial breakdowns (e.g., tour grosses), and show itineraries.

Politics

1143. **Policy Studies Journal.** 1972-. Quarterly. Mel Dubnick and David Rosenbloom, eds. Policy Studies Organization, University of Illinois, 361 Lincoln Hall, 702 S. Wright Street, Urbana, IL 61801. Index, adv., rev.

The journal provides scholarly analysis of a wide array of fields, such as defense, poverty, labor, education, environment, energy, housing, unemployment, and health.

1144. **Political Science Quarterly.** 1886. Quarterly. Demetrios Caraley, ed. Academy of Political Science, 2852 Broadway, New York, NY 10025. Index, adv., rev.

The publication describes itself as a "nonpartisan journal devoted to the study of contemporary and historical aspects of government, politics, and public affairs." Suited to both academics and lay readers alike.

Popular History

1145. **American Heritage.** 1949-. Bi-monthly. Byron Dobell, ed. American Heritage, Inc., 60 Fifth Avenue, New York, NY 10114-0389. Illus., index, adv.

This highly readable periodical covers topics of both a light (e.g., fast foods) and substantive nature. The first-rate illustrations contribute much to the popularity of the magazine.

1146. **America History Illustrated: The Adventures of the American Past.** 1966-. 10/yr. Ed Holm, ed. Historical Times, Inc., 2245 Kohn Road, P.O. Box 8200, Harrisburg, PA 17105-8200. Illus., index, adv., rev.

Founded on the premise that "this country needed a magazine devoted to the popularization of American history," its contents—which profile spies, inventors, poster art, legendary battles, etc.—reflect the eclecticism of the American experience.

Popular Literature—General

1147. **Genre.** 1968-. Quarterly. Ronald Schleifer, ed. Department of English, University of Oklahoma, Norman, OK 73019. Index, adv.

This scholarly publication specializes in generic criticism and the evolution of genres. Specific issues are frequently centered on one theme (e.g., literary treatment of women's history).

1148. **Journal of Popular Literature.** 1985-. Semi-annual. Ray B. Browne, ed. Bowling Green State University, Bowling Green, Ohio 43403. Illus., adv., rev.

This title offers comprehensive, well-researched articles on a wide array of popular literature genres.

1149. **Re/Search.** 1980-. Annual. Andrea Juno and V. Vale, eds. Re/Search Publications, 20 Romolo Street, Suite B, San Francisco, CA 94133. Illus., index, adv.

The annual (similar in look to an oversized paperback and totaling around 250 pages per issue) focuses on one particular artist, author (e.g., William S. Burroughs), or theme per issue. Utilizing striking art and layouts, the title is unique in its serious coverage of alternative art.

Popular Literature—Horror Fiction

(See also: Science Fiction, pp. 74, 180, 206)

1150. **Best New Horror.** 1990-. Annual. Stephen Jones and Ramsey Campbell, eds. Carroll & Graf Publishers, Inc., 260 Fifth Avenue, New York, NY 10001.

This anthology brings together recent horror stories by well-known writers.

1151. **Bibliographies and Indexes in Science Fiction, Fantasy, and Horror.** 1987-. Irregular. Greenwood Press, Inc., 88 Post Road, W., Box 5007, Westport, CT 06881-5007. Bibl.

An indispensable tool for researchers, this loosely related series includes abstracts, bibliographies, and statistical data not available elsewhere.

Popular Literature—Mystery Fiction

1152. **Alfred Hitchcock's Mystery Magazine.** 1956-. 13/yr. Cathleen Jordan, ed. Dell Magazines, 1540 Broadway, New York, NY 10036. Illus., adv., rev.

The title is primarily a collection of short stories; letters and news notes are also included.

1152a. **Mystery Notebook.** 1984-. Irregular. Stephen Wright, ed. and publisher. Box 1341, F.D.R. Station, New York, NY 10150-1341. Rev.

The publication is primarily composed of essays on specific mysteries and their writers.

Popular Literature—Science and Fantasy Fiction

(See also: Horror Fiction, p. 64)

1153. **Amazing Stories.** 1926-. Monthly. Kim Mohan, ed. T S R, Inc., Lake Geneva, WI 53147. Adv., rev.

This fabled periodical (some genre historians feel its appearance marked the true beginning of science fiction as we know it today) provides a blend of sci-fi, fantasy, and horror short stories, in addition to factual articles and opinion-based essays and columns.

1154. **Analog Science Fiction & Fact.** 1930-. 13/yr. Stanley Schmidt, ed. Dell Magazines, 1540 Broadway, New York, NY 10036. Illus., index, adv., rev.

Although *Amazing Stories* pioneered the format, this publication, with a circulation of roughly 100,000, now outsells it roughly ten to one .

1155. **Asimov's Science Fiction.** 1976-. 13/yr. Gardner Dozois, ed. Dell Magazines, 1540 Broadway, New York, NY 10036. Adv., rev.

The formula here is similar to that of *Amazing Stories* and *Analog;* this publication, however, includes a bit more material of a factual, scientific nature.

1156. **New York Review of Science Fiction.** 1988-. Monthly. Robert Killheffer and Donald G. Keller, eds. Dragon Press, Box 78, Pleasantville, NY 10570. Adv., bibl., rev.

This journal is notable for the high order of its essays and reviews on horror, fantasy, and science fiction.

1157. **Science Fiction Age.** 1992-. Bimonthly. Sovereign Media, 487 Carlisle Drive, Herndon, VA 22070. Illus., adv., rev.

This mass circulation periodical analyzes science fiction and fantasy across the mass media.

Popular Literature—Women Writers

1158. **Legacy: A Journal of Nineteenth-Century American Women Writers.** 1984-. Semi-annual. Department of English, University of Massachusetts, Amherst, MA 01003. Illus., adv., rev.

The periodical includes essays, fiction, and biographical surveys relating to nineteenth-century American women writers. Ideal for women's studies programs.

1159. **Tulsa Studies in Women's Literature.** 1982-. Semi-annual. Mary O'Toole, ed. University of Tulsa, 600 S. College, Tulsa, OK 74104. Illus., index, adv., rev.

Probably the finest title concerned with this area, the contents of each issue include extremely focused articles, a review essay, announcements, notes and queries, and letters from readers.

Popular Music—General

(See also: Collecting, pp. 2-3)

1160. **BAM: The California Music Magazine.** 1976-. Fortnightly. Steve Stolder, ed. Bam Publications, Inc., 3470 Buskirk Avenue, Pleasant Hill, CA 94523. Illus., adv., rev.

The tabloid's goal of covering pop music developments from a California perspective may, at first glance, appear extremely narrow in scope. However, when one considers the first-rate writing and attractive layouts as well as the fact that much of the nation's music is produced in that state, the value of the title is more readily evident.

1161. **Billboard: The International Newsweekly of Music and Home Entertainment.** 1894-. Weekly. Sam Holdsworth, ed. Billboard Publications, Inc., One Astor Plaza, 1515 Broadway, New York, NY 10036. Illus., adv., rev.

The trade weekly comprehensively covers all aspects of the music industry as well as related fields (e.g., video). Articles usually take the form of concise news updates on commercial trends, new technologies, legal issues, concert itineraries, etc. The charts, a major raison d'être for the publication, cover virtually all commercially viable music genre.

1162. **Musician.** 1976-. Monthly. Jock Baird, ed. Amordian Press, Inc., P.O. Box 701, 33 Commercial Street, Gloucester, MA 01930. Illus., adv., rev.

Its perceptive analysis of various popular music forms and hardware is the equal of *Rolling Stone,* without the counterculture posturing and preoccupation with show business and fashion in general.

1163. **Popular Music & Society.** 1972-. Quarterly. R. Serge Denisoff, ed. Bowling Green State University, Bowling Green, Ohio 43403. Index, adv., rev.

The journal employs a scholarly approach in covering virtually all genres and time periods of popular music.

1164. **Rolling Stone.** 1967-. Bi-weekly (except monthly July and December). Jann S. Wenner, ed. Straight Arrow Publications, Inc., 745 Fifth Avenue, New York, NY 10151. Illus., adv., rev.

Although no longer the bible of the pop music subculture, the magazine's first-rate feature writing (spanning social, political, and popular culture topics) and reviews (hardware and software) render it a key acquisition for any individual or library interested in post-World War II popular music and culture.

1165. **Spin.** 1985-. Monthly. Bob Guccione, Jr., ed. Camouflage Publishing, Inc., 6 W. 18th Street, New York, NY: 10011-4608. Illus., adv., rev.

Spin approaches the stylishness and intelligent coverage of society, politics, and the arts—particularly music—characterizing *Rolling Stone.* Although lacking the latter's track record for investigative reporting, its attractive layouts have no equal.

Popular Music—Blues/Rhythm & Blues/Black Contemporary

1166. **Living Blues: A Journal of the Black American Blues Tradition.** 1970-. Bi-monthly. Peter Lee, ed. Center for the Study of Southern Culture, University of Mississippi, University, MS 38677. Illus., index, adv., rev.

The features—including both contemporary profiles and retrospectives of pioneer artists—are complemented by news notes (concerning organizations, festivals, concerts), listings of acquisitions by the Center for the Study of Southern Folklore, and exhaustive record reviews.

Popular Music—Country and Western

1167. **Journal of Country Music.** 1970-. 3/yr. Paul F. Kingsbury, ed. Country Music Foundation, Inc., 4 Music Square East, Nashville, TN 37203. Illus., adv., rev.

The publication utilizes primary source materials and interpretative writing in its efforts to chronicle the genre's past and present. Always informative, it succeeds in treading a fine line between industry hype and the objective dissemination of information.

Popular Music—Folk

1168. **Folk Era Today!** 1981-. Quarterly. Bob Grand, ed. Folk Era Productions, Inc., 17 Middle Dunstable Road, Nashua, NH 03062. Adv., rev.
     With *Sing Out!* having relinquished its long-standing role as tastemaker for folk music, this periodical has enhanced its value by expanding the former's narrow definition of folk music (i.e., music generally evolving out of an oral tradition and interpreted in a traditional manner) to include acoustic sounds produced by singer/songwriters from a variety of stylistic backgrounds.

Popular Music—Jazz

1169. **Down Beat: For Contemporary Musicians.** 1934-. Monthly. John Ephland, ed. Maher Publications, 180 W. Park Avenue, Elmhurst, IL 60126. Illus., index, adv., rev.
     The magazine successfully melds a popular journalistic style with impeccable standards of research. Covering all periods and styles of jazz, the articles presume a basic knowledge of jazz history and musicians.

Popular Music—Rock 'n' Roll

1170. **Circus: The Rock & Roll Magazine.** 1969-. Monthly. Gerald Rothberg, ed. Circus Enterprises Corp., 3 W. 18th Street, New York, NY 10011. Illus., adv., rev.
     Incorporating elements of the fanzine and music trade publication, *Circus* offers a distinctly heavy-metal bias.

Religion

1171. **The Humanist.** 1941-. Bi-monthly. Lloyd L. Morain, ed. American Humanist Association, 7 Harwood Drive, P.O. Box 146, Amherst, NY 14226-0146. Illus., adv., rev.
     Perhaps the most visible humanist periodical in the United States, it includes a strong emphasis on social issues (e.g., criminal justice).

1172. **Journal for the Scientific Study of Religion.** 1961-. Quarterly. Don Capps, ed. Society for the Scientific Study of Religion, Marist Hall, Rm. 108, Catholic University of America, Washington, D.C. 20064. Adv., rev.
     The journal surveys the phenomenon of religious worship, both individuals and institutions, from a psychological and sociological perspective.

Social Phenomena—General

1173. **The Futurist: A Journal of Forecasts, Trends, and Ideas about the Future.** 1967-. Bi-monthly. Edward Cornish, ed. World Future Society, 4916 St. Elmo Avenue, Bethesda, MD 20814. Illus., index, adv.
     The publication offers information regarding trends in a diversified array of cultural sectors (e.g., politics, economics, religion, education, leisure time activities).

1174. **Prospects: The Annual of American Cultural Studies.** 1975-. Annual. Jack Salzman, ed. Cambridge University Press, 32 E. 57th Street, New York, NY 10022. Illus.

This scintillating annual employs a multidisciplinary approach in analyzing various facets of American culture.

Social Phenomena—The Automobile

1175. **Motor Trend.** 1949-. Monthly. Mike Anson, ed. Petersen Publishing Company, 8490 Sunset Blvd., Los Angeles, CA 90069. Illus., adv.

Amidst news and reviews of new car models this mass-market publication looks at industry trends and consumer perceptions of various topics.

Social Phenomena—Crime

1176. **Journal of Research in Crime and Delinquency.** 1964-. Quarterly. Vincent O'Leary, ed. Sage Publications, Inc., 2111 W. .Hillcrest Drive, Newbury Park, CA 91320. Illus., index.

The journal analyzes the etiology and characteristics of crime and society's relationship with it. Concepts covered include the victimization of women, unemployment and the severity of punishment, and corporate crime.

Social Phenomena—The Ecology Movement

1177. **Sierra: The Sierra Club Bulletin.** 1893-. Bi-monthly. John F. King, ed. Sierra Club, 730 Polk Street, San Francisco, CA 94109. Illus., index, adv.

This highly readable periodical provides news—often of an anecdotal nature—about positive steps to protect the environment, as well as profiles of social and political issues having an ecological impact. The approach may be biased, but never dull.

Social Phenomena—Fashion

1178. **M: The Civilized Man.** 1983-. Monthly. Kevin Doyle, ed. Fairchild Publications, 7 E. 12th Street, New York, NY 10003. Illus., adv.

This glossy stock men's magazine focuses on people, places, thoughts, and trends with a strong fashion (particularly clothes) orientation.

1179. **W.** 1971-. Bi-weekly. Michael Coady, ed. Fairchild Publications, Inc., 7 E. 12th Street, New York, NY 10003. Illus., adv.

The women's equivalent of *M,* it covers the cutting edge of the fashion world for the affluent reader, including homes, resorts, furniture, art, socializing, the jet-set crowd, food, and drink.

Social Phenomena—Feminism

1180. **Feminist Studies.** 1972-. 3/yr. Claire G. Moses, ed. Feminist Studies, Inc., c/o Women's Studies Program, University of Maryland, College Park, MD 20742. Adv., rev.

The interdisciplinary journal includes scholarly articles, reports, position papers, poetry, etc., aimed at provoking thought, discussion, and the formulation of new theoretical perspectives.

1181. **Signs: Journal of Women in Culture and Society.** 1975-. Quarterly. Jean F. O'Barr. University of Chicago Press, Journals Division, P.O. Box 37005, Chicago, IL 60637. Adv., rev.

Widely regarded as the pace-setting women's studies periodical, it functions as an interdisciplinary forum for ideas relating to women in society.

Social Phenomena—Homosexuality

1182. **The Advocate: The National Gay Newsmagazine.** 1967-. Biweekly. Robert I. McQueen and Gerry Kroll, eds. Niles Merton, P.O. Box 4371, Los Angeles, CA 90078. Illus., adv., rev.

The most widely read gay male magazine, it is devoted to national and international gay news and cultural interests.

1183. **Lesbian Contradiction: A Journal of Irreverant Feminism.** 1982-. Quarterly. LesCon, 1007 N. 47th, Seattle, WA 98103; 584 Castro Street, No. 263, San Francisco, CA 94114. Illus.

This newspaper covers various perspectives on notable social and political issues impacting lesbians; e.g., parenting, classism, separatism.

Social Phenomena—Immigration

1184. **Journal of American Ethnic History.** 1982-. Semi-annual. Ronald H. Bayor, ed. Transaction Periodicals Consortium, Rutgers University, New Brunswick, NJ 08903. Illus., adv.

Produced by the Immigration History Society, the journal concentrates on the immigrant and ethnic history of North American peoples, including such topics as assimilation and group identity.

Social Phenomena—Minorities

1185. **American Visions: The Magazine of Afro-American Culture.** 1986-. Bimonthly. Gary A. Puckrein, ed. The Vision Foundation, Frederick Douglass House, Capitol Hill, Smithsonian Institution, Washington, D.C. 20560. Illus., adv., bibl., rev.

The publication attempts to chronicle black accomplishments in the past as well as to delineate present-day activities and concerns. Features are complemented by a national calendar of events and ongoing columns featuring archives, cultural centers, and museums in the United States.

Social Phenomena—Minorities— Asian Americans

1186. **Amerasia Journal: The National Interdisciplinary Journal of Scholarship, Criticism, and Literature on Asian and Pacific Americans.** 1971-. Semi-annual. Russell Leong and Glenn Omatsu, eds. Asian American Studies Center, 3232 Campbell Hall, University of California, Los Angeles, CA 90024-1546. Illus., adv., bibl., rev.

This journal is unique in its dedication to research on the varied groups of Americans possessing an Asian heritage.

Social Phenomena—Minorities— Hispanic Americans

1187. **Aztlan: International Journal of Chicano Studies Research.** 1970-. Semi-annual. Reymund Paredes, ed. Chicano Studies Research Center, University of California-Los Angeles, 405 Hilgard Avenue, Los Angeles, CA 90024. Rev.

The leading scholarly title of its kind, *Aztlan* covers a wide array of topics within the Mexican American experience; e.g., the arts, economics, education, history, law, politics, and sociology.

1188. **Hispanic: The Magazine of the Contemporary Hispanic.** 1988-. Monthly. Maria Elena Alvarez Sharpe, ed. Hispanic Publishing Corp., 111 Massachusetts Avenue NW, Suite 200, Washington, D.C. 20001. Illus., adv., rev.

The publication is geared to English-speaking Latinos in the United States, including features on key issues of the day (e.g., the immigration amnesty program), biographical sketches, news capsules, and columns, such as the one depicting the activities of Hispanic organizations.

Social Phenomena—Minorities— Jewish Americans

1189. **Moment.** 1975-. Monthly. Hershel Shanks, ed. Moment Magazine, 3000 Connecticut Avenue NW, Suite 300, Washington, D.C. 20008. Illus., adv., rev.

Concerned with American Jewish issues, the magazine delves into the arts, the domestic scene, history, politics, religion, society, and the implications of Israel for American Jews.

Social Phenomena—Minorities— Native Americans

1190. **American Indian Culture & Research Journal.** 1971-. Quarterly. Duane Champagne, ed. American Indian Studies Center, University of California, 405 Hilgard Avenue, Los Angeles, CA 90024-1548. Index, adv., rev.

The articles included here are interdisciplinary in nature, touching upon anthropology, history, culture, and the arts.

1191. **American Indian Quarterly.** 1974-. Quarterly. Robert A. Black and Terry P. Wilson, eds. Native American Studies Program, University of California, 3415 Dwinelle Hall, Berkeley, CA 94720. Illus., index, adv., rev.

Roughly comparable to *American Indian Culture & Research Journal,* it possesses a slightly wider range of coverage.

Social Phenomena—Space Exploration

1192. **Final Frontier: The Magazine of Space Exploration.** 1988-. Bi-monthly. Tony Reichhardt, ed. Final Frontier Publishing Company, 339 Union Plaza, 333 N. Washington Avenue, Minneapolis, MN 55401. Illus., adv., rev.

Featuring a broader editorial range than its rival, *Space World,* it includes news and editorials on space science, research, legislation, and space exploration, in addition to analysis of space fiction.

1193. **Space World.** 1963-. 12/yr. John Rhea, ed. Palmer Publications, Inc., Amherst, WI 54406. Illus., index, adv., rev.

Published in cooperation with the National Space Society, *Space World* will appeal to general readers who are aware of the impact space research is having on their lives.

Social Phenomena—War

1194. **Military Affairs.** 1937-. Quarterly. Robin Higham, ed. Military Affairs, Department of History, Eisenhower Hall, University of Kansas, Manhattan, KS 66506-7186. Illus., index, adv., bibl., rev.

The contents include approximately a half-dozen features; book reviews and bibliographies; and announcements of academic grants and awards, publications, seminars, and conferences. Considered by many to be the leading military history magazine.

1195. **Soldier of Fortune: The Journal of Professional Adventurers.** 1975-. Monthly. Robert K. Brown, ed. P.O. Box 693, Boulder, CO 80306. Illus., index, rev.

In recent years, this publication has reached something approaching legendary status. The articles cover both real-life adventures and pointers for engaging in military adventures. The ads represent a prime source of controversy, not only documenting the availability of weapons and related equipment, but assisting in the location of professional bodyguards and mercenaries.

Sports and Recreation—General

1196. **Inside Sports.** 1979-. Monthly. Michael K. Herbert, ed. Century Publishing Company, 990 Grove Street, Evanston, IL 60201. Illus., adv.

The archetypal publication aimed at general sports fans, it blends features, interviews, profiles, columns, and departments with appealing photographs and layouts.

1197. **Sport.** 1946-. Monthly. Neil Cohen, ed. Sport Magazine Associations, 119 W. 40th Street, New York, NY 10018. Illus., adv.

Best known for its treatment of the behind-the-scenes and motivational facets of sports, the magazine is roughly comparable to *Inside Sport* and *Sports Illustrated* in combining first-rate investigative reporting and spectacular photography.

1198. **Sports Illustrated.** 1954-. 54/yr. Mark Mulvoy, ed. Time, Inc., Time & Life Building, New York, NY 10020. Illus., index, adv., rev.

The most popular sports magazine in the United States by far, it combines lucid, intelligent writing, courageous editorializing, and masterful photography. Minor sports, albeit to a degree that reflects their overall impact on society, are given space along with primary pastimes.

Sports and Recreation—Automobile Racing

1199. **Auto Racing Digest.** 1973-. Bi-monthly. Michael Herbert, ed. Century Publishing Company, 990 Grove Street, Evanston, IL 60201. Illus., adv.

The periodical offers thorough reporting on all major races as well as features on drivers, the various types of vehicles, and track considerations. Illustrations and statistics are a first-rate supplement to the text. It is superior to *Autoweek,* its major competitor, in that coverage is exclusively devoted to racing.

Sports and Recreation—Baseball

1200. **Baseball Digest: Baseball's Only Monthly Magazine.** 1941-. Monthly. John Kuenster, ed. Century Publishing Company, 990 Grove Street, Evanston, IL 60201. Illus., adv.

This highly readable magazine focuses on career profiles and selected topics (e.g., managerial philosophies).

1201. **Baseball History.** 1986-. Quarterly. Peter Levine, ed. Mekler Publishing Company, 11 Ferry Lane W., Westport, CT 06880. Illus., adv., rev.

The periodical melds popular writing and scholarly analysis in its coverage of the history of baseball in the United States.

Sports and Recreation—Basketball

1202. **Basketball Digest.** 1973-. 8/yr. Michael K. Herbert, ed. Century Publishing Company, 990 Grove Street, Evanston, IL 60201. Illus., adv.

Basketball Digest offers the same appealing blend of features, interviews, departments, and statistics typifying the other titles in the Century Publications series.

Sports and Recreation—Body Building

1203. **Muscle & Fitness.** 1938-. Monthly. Joe Weider, ed. Brute Enterprises, 21100 Erwin Street, Woodland Hills, CA 91367. Illus., adv.

Although dedicated to helping would-be body builders at all levels (including women), the features, departments, and ads also provide a fascinating inside look at this sport. The figurehead of the publication, Joe Weider, has evolved from shameless pitchman to legendary status over the course of several generations.

Sports and Recreation—Boxing

1204. **The Ring.** 1922. Monthly. Nigel Collins, ed. Ring Publishing Corp., 130 W. 37th Street, New York, NY 10018. Illus., adv.

Long referred to as the "bible of boxing," *The Ring* includes sectional and national rankings, features authored by experts in the field, and biographical surveys of boxers past and present.

Sports and Recreation—Chess

1205. **Chess Life.** 1933-. Monthly. Don Maddox, ed. U.S. Chess Federation, 186 Rte. 9W, New Windsor, NY 12550. Illus., rev.

The leading periodical devoted to chess, it offers news about the sport, articles on how to improve one's games, and interviews with notable personalities.

Sports and Recreation—Football

1206. **Football Digest: Pro Football's Monthly Magazine.** 1971-. 10/yr. Michael K. Herbert, ed. Century Publishing Company, 990 Grove Street, Evanston, IL 60201. Illus., adv.

Another of the Century Publications titles, it offers more substantial coverage of the professional arm of the sport than is available via *Football News.*

Sports and Recreation—Golf

1207. **Golf Digest.** 1971-. Monthly. Jerry Tarde, ed. Golf Digest/Tennis, Inc., 5520 Park Avenue, Trumbull, CT 06611. Illus., adv., rev.

Despite the heavy emphasis upon instruction, major tournament previews, equipment reviews, fashion, rules analyses, etc., the profiles of leading golfers and historical features offer insight into the societal underpinnings of the sport.

Sports and Recreation—Gambling

1208. **Journal of Gambling Behavior.** 1985-. Quarterly. Henry R. Lesieur, ed. Human Sciences Press, Inc., 72 Fifth Avenue, New York, NY 10011. Adv., rev.

The publication employs a scholarly, interdisciplinary approach in attempting to discern the nature of gambling behavior.

Sports and Recreation—Hockey

1209. **Hockey Digest: Pro Hockey's Monthly Magazine.** 1972-. 8/yr. Michael K. Herbert, ed. Century Publishing Company, 990 Grove Street, Evanston, IL 60201. Illus., adv.

This Century Publications title covers hockey players past and present, teams, and issues of relevance to the professional leagues (most notably the National Hockey League).

Sports and Recreation—The Olympic Games

1210. **The Olympian.** 1975-. 10/yr. Bob Condron, ed. U.S. Olympic Committee, 1750 E. Boulder Street, Colorado Springs, CO 80909. Illus.

The reader is provided an insider's view of the long road to the Olympic Games via profiles, analyses, statistics, and other data emanating from the U.S. Olympic Committee.

Sports and Recreation—Rodeos

1211.   **Prorodeo Sports News.** 1953-. Bi-weekly. Bill Crawford, ed. Professional Rodeo Cowboys Association, 101 Prorodeo Drive, Colorado Springs, CO 80919. Illus., adv.
      This well-executed publication covers not only the major competitive events, but offers much on horses and the lore of riding and cowboys.

Sports and Recreation—Soccer

1212.   **Soccer America.** 1971-. 50/yr. Lynn Berling-Manuel, ed. Berling Communications, Inc., P.O. Box 23704, Oakland, CA 94623. Illus., adv.
      The tabloid includes profiles of key personnel and game records for American professional and college soccer, as well as for the international scene.

Sports and Recreation—Surfing

1213.   **Surfing.** 1964-. Monthly. David Gilovich, ed. Western Empire Publishing, Inc., 950 Calle Amanecer, P.O. Box 3010, San Clemente, CA 92672. Illus., adv.
      The title covers travel, equipment, events, techniques, and personalities relating to all forms of surfing. The emphasis, however, is on the beach or surfer's lifestyle.

Sports and Recreation—Tennis

1214.   **Tennis.** 1965-. Monthly. Alexander McNab, ed. Golf Digest/Tennis, Inc. 5520 Park Avenue, P.O. Box 395, Trumbell, CT 06611. Illus., adv.
      The leading publication for this sport, its articles cover tennis personalities, nutrition and performance, psychology, fitness, clothing, travel, tournaments, player rankings, and various key issues.

Sports and Recreation—Track & Field

1215.   **Track & Field News.** 1948-. Monthly. Bert Nelson, ed. Track & Field News, Inc., P.O. Box 296, Los Altos, CA 94023. Illus., adv.
      Another periodical considered to be the bible of its particular sport. The appellation is well deserved here as coverage includes high school, college, the professional circuits, all meets of note, and the Olympics. Features, interviews, profiles, news notes, opinion essays, and statistical reports are all employed.

Author/Title Index

Numbers cited refer to entry numbers.

Subject Index

Numbers cited refer to entry numbers.